PATRICK KEDDIE is a journalist and essayist based in Istanbul. His writing has appeared in *Al Jazeera*, *Delayed Gratification*, the *Guardian*, the *Huffington Post*, the *LA Review of Books*, *Middle East Eye*, and the *Sunday Herald*, among others.

'I found *The Passion* a captivating account of modern Turkey, its passions and frustrations; perhaps it won't make you fall in love with Turkish football, but it will help you see why it is so central in understanding Turkey's soul.'

KAYA GENC
author of *Under the Shadow: Rage and Revolution in Modern Turkey*

'Patrick Keddie takes us inside the unceasing Turkish football conversation. The game turns out to be a great device to explain this little understood, football-mad country and its football-mad ruler (who recently banned the foreign word "arena", forcing many Turkish stadiums to be renamed). *The Passion* is an energetically researched history of Turkey through football.'

SIMON KUPER
author of *Football Against the Enemy*

PATRICK KEDDIE

Football and the Story
of Modern Turkey

I.B. TAURIS

LONDON · NEW YORK

To my parents

Published in 2018 by
I.B.Tauris & Co. Ltd
London • New York
www.ibtauris.com

References to websites were correct at the time of writing.

ISBN: 978 1 78453 802 6
eISBN: 978 1 78672 333 8
ePDF: 978 1 78673 333 7

A full CIP record for this book is available from the British Library
A full CIP record is available from the Library of Congress

Library of Congress Catalog Card Number: available

Typeset by Tetragon, London
Printed and bound in Sweden by ScandBook AB

MIX
Paper from
responsible sources
FSC
www.fsc.org   FSC® C007584

CONTENTS

LIST OF ABBREVIATIONS

AKP (Justice and Development Party) – a conservative party with its roots in Islamism, co-founded by Recep Tayyip Erdogan in 2001

ANAP (Motherland Party) – a centre-right, neoliberal political party founded by Turgut Ozal

CAS (Court of Arbitration for Sport) – an international body established to settle sports-related disputes

CHP (Republican People's Party) – a Kemalist and social-democratic political party

CUP (Committee of Union and Progress) – an umbrella party for the 'Young Turks' during the Ottoman Empire

DP (Democrat Party) – a centre-right party led by Adnan Menderes

FETO (Fethullahist Terror Organisation) – the Turkish government's name for an alleged Gulenist terrorist group

FIFA (Fédération Internationale de Football Association) – world football's governing body

FSA (Free Syrian Army) – a Syrian opposition group

FSE (Football Supporters Europe) – a European fan network

HDP (Peoples' Democratic Party) – a left-wing and pro-Kurdish political party

ISIS (Islamic State of Iraq and the Levant) – a jihadist terrorist organisation

MHP (Nationalist Movement Party) – a far-right, ultranationalist political party

MUSIAD (Independent Industrialists and Businessmen Association) – a non-governmental organisation of largely conservative small and medium businesses

OHAL (Governorship of Region in State of Emergency) – a state of emergency region in southeast Turkey from 1987 to 2002, during the height of the Turkish state's war with the PKK

PKK (Kurdistan Workers' Party) – a Kurdish militant group

TAK (Kurdistan Freedom Hawks) – a Kurdish militant group, likely linked to the PKK

TOKI (Public Housing Development Administration) – a Turkish government-backed housing agency

TUSIAD (Turkish Industry and Business Association) – a non-governmental organisation of mostly Kemalist businesses

UEFA (Union of European Football Associations) – European football's administrative body

YDG-H (Patriotic Revolutionary Youth Movement) – the urban youth wing of the PKK

INTRODUCTION

In Turkey's political turmoil of the late 1970s, having the wrong kind of facial hair could get you killed.[1]

Left-wing and right-wing groups were murdering each other in street clashes that approached civil war. The Grey Wolves – a militia of the ultra-nationalist MHP – wore horseshoe moustaches; for some it represented 'M' for *milliyetci* (nationalist), or was crescent shaped, like the Islamic symbol on Turkey's flag. Leftists typically favoured thick walrus moustaches that covered the upper lip. Beards tended to be associated with Islamists, scourge of the so-called 'secular' Kemalists.

The violence ended with the 1980 military coup, and Recep Tayyip Erdogan's football career came to an abrupt, supposedly bearded, halt shortly after.

In 1981 Turkey's 27-year-old future leader was captain of the semi-professional team of Istanbul's tram and funicular company. His nickname was apparently 'Imam Beckenbauer',[2] a reference both to his piety and to his supposed skills; like the German libero Franz Beckenbauer, Erdogan was tall and rangy – hagiographers have painted him as a similarly elegant, talented and dominant leader on the pitch. The myth goes that Erdogan was twice made offers to sign for Fenerbahce, the club he has supported since childhood. His detractors tend to portray him more in the vein of a Vinnie Jones-type figure, a blunt and unrefined hardman.

Erdogan has said that a military figure took over the football club in the repressive aftermath of the coup, and ordered all the bearded players to shave. Erdogan claims to have been wearing a beard, and that, while others complied, he refused to shave – resigning from the team in protest in June 1981. This sounds like typical self-mythologising: most photos at the time show him wearing a moustache.

Like many religiously conservative Turks, Erdogan now sports a 'badem': a short, clipped 'almond' moustache. As a politician, Erdogan has long portrayed himself as an underdog and taps into a sense of grievance among the broad swathes of pious, conservative Turks, many of whom were marginalised and repressed by the Kemalist elites who previously dominated the state. But although some Islamists were jailed and persecuted in the brutal post-coup period, they were not the primary victims of the repression. Erdogan was associated with Islamist movements as they were generally growing in strength and were increasingly often supported by the state.

Erdogan has now been the dominant force in Turkish politics for more than a decade and a half: first as mayor of Istanbul, then as Turkey's prime minister, finally as president. He is surely the most powerful and charismatic Turkish leader since the country's founder and first president, Mustafa Kemal Ataturk.

Football became part of Erdogan's mythology as both man of the people and natural-born leader: a shortcut to people's hearts and an easily under-stood language in a football-mad country, where fans are among the most passionate in the world. Football talk is constant in Turkey, whether through the vast, fevered football media, or in everyday speech. Historical myths are used for fan identities in the stands, and battles are restaged in the media, making Turkish football powerful and fascinating, but politically loaded, and potentially dangerous. Football is a lens through which it is possible to make sense of this vital, enthralling, maddeningly complex and contra-dictory country.

While Russia's Vladimir Putin opts to project an image of himself as a strongman, riding around topless on horseback, Turks are now often obliged to watch Erdogan kicking a ball around.[3] Erdogan played in the ceremonial match opening Istanbul Basaksehir's new stadium in July 2014 involving various politicians, footballers and celebrities, wearing a Basaksehir shirt and the number 12 – the match took place just before the elections in which Erdogan became Turkey's 12th president.

In a barnstorming, fairy-tale first half, Erdogan dragged his team from 3–0 down to a 4–3 half-time lead by scoring a hat-trick. One chipped finish led the pro-government newspaper *Daily Sabah* to liken Erdogan to Lionel Messi and Gheorghe Hagi.[4] In fairness, that goal was brilliant – but for the first and third, let's just say that the opposing goalkeeper, Basaksehir's Volkan Babacan, was not quite his usual, agile self that day, and where the bloody hell was the marking? Erdogan was substituted at half-time and Basaksehir have officially retired the number 12 jersey in homage.

Attendees at the match were strictly vetted, because Erdogan had learned from an ego-bruising affair at Galatasaray a few years before, which had revealed an inkling of revolt. Galatasaray opened their new stadium with a match against Ajax in January 2011. Erdogan must have seen the opening ceremony as an opportunity to bask in acclaim for helping to construct the gleaming new arena. But when his presence was announced on the big screen, he was serenaded by boos and whistling from the fans. Erdogan left the stadium in a rage before kick-off.

He later lambasted the fans as 'ungrateful', noting that the state had footed the construction bill and owned the stadium – implying that it could be withheld from the club, as if confiscating the toys of a naughty child.[5] It was a revealing, brittle response to criticism from the supposed strongman.

Turkish passion for football has meant that the authorities have long both feared and favoured the sport. But football in Turkey has never been more important or more politicised than in the twenty-first century, under the ambitious rule of the Justice and Development Party (AKP) – a conservative party with its roots in Islamism, co-founded by Erdogan, that came to power in 2002.

The AKP lavished unprecedented sums of money and attention on the sport, using football as a way to build and shore up domestic popularity and support, as football has become one of the most important networks of power in Turkey. Meanwhile, opposition supporters have challenged the government or pursued activism through football. When the anti-government Gezi protests broke out in 2013, many rival football fans set aside their mutual loathing to unite on the streets and play a significant role at the forefront of the protests.

The 'beautiful game' has become a battleground of identity and politics in Turkey: a site of control and rebellion. The Beckenbauer/Jones polarity of Erdogan is instructive. The divide grew over time, and has many nuances, but to many of his supporters, Erdogan is often a heroic, strongman figure – a pious champion of the poor and the marginalised. To many of his detractors, Erdogan is an increasingly brutal, megalomaniac – albeit elected – dictator.

Erdogan has promised to create a 'New Turkey'. A few years ago, Turkey was gaining widespread admiration for its booming economy and blossoming liberal credentials under the AKP. Erdogan pledged that Turkey would become a regional and global powerhouse and would take its place among the world's top ten economies by 2023, the centenary of the republic. Some began speaking of a 'Turkish model' for other Muslim-majority countries to emulate.

Turkey is among the world's most important Muslim-majority countries – with a young population of almost 80 million. It is in a pivotal locale, divided by continents: a member of the OECD and the Council of Europe, and a candidate for European Union membership. It is a key NATO member in a region of huge significance, bordering Iran, Iraq, Syria, Greece, Bulgaria, Georgia and Armenia – and with a history of tension and conflict with nearby Russia. It hosts the world's highest number of Syrian refugees, right on Europe's doorstep. In our hyper-connected world, what happens in Turkey inevitably impacts far beyond its borders.

Yet the country is now starkly divided as it passes through a troubled, critical point in its history, and the dreams of 'New Turkey' have soured. Turkey is in an increasingly fraught condition in which the economy is faltering, the Kurdish peace process has broken down, terrorism is increasing, regional pressures are mounting – including fallout from the war in neighbouring Syria – and the government is becoming increasingly autocratic. Following a failed coup in the summer of 2016, Erdogan embarked on a huge purge of dissent and of key opposition figures, and held a vote on constitutional changes to vastly extend his executive powers. He is increasingly placed within a perceived wider turn towards populist, authoritarian politics.

The energy and tensions shaping Turkish politics, identity and society are manifest in football. While football can highlight underlying trends, some believe it can be a driver of change, and others try to read it as a kind of bellwether, indicating a likely future. As Turkey changes at an often bewildering pace, football helps us understand its history, its present and where it is going. Football reflects life in all its romance and drudgery, beauty and pain.

There are so many beautiful, addictive, thrilling things about Turkish football – fevered drama, carnivalesque passion, adrenaline-firing spectacles, charismatic characters, a rich history that is alive in the present. It is the only 'Asian' country to have a European trophy winner. The Turkish Super League has Europe's sixth-largest revenues. Turkey's huge, young population make it a (sleeping) football giant. Football is also a dynamic site of activism.

Yet there is also a sense of deep malaise in Turkish football, which is struggling with ballooning debt, corruption, political interference, violence and depleted attendances. Many have suggested that Turkish football could collapse. Some even believe that might not be such a bad thing.

Football has been ignored, trivialised or disdained by many intellectuals and writers, often out of snobbishness or ignorance. It has been derided as silly, dangerous or trivial. While football is certainly silly and dangerous at times, it is far from trivial. Football is now a global phenomenon: undoubtedly Turkey's – and the world's – most significant shared cultural practice.

Football conquered the world partly because it is fundamentally simple. A form of football can be played almost anywhere, with a small amount of space and some vaguely round object. There is also endless scope to talk about football, with its myriad dramas on and off the pitch, cinematic characters, absurdities and tragedies. It is collective and individual, art and war, us and them. It ties people to places and communities, while embodying the kinetics of globalisation. It is a sport of upsets, a rare field in which genuine shocks are possible, where small teams can overturn giants. No other sport is so widely played, watched or talked about, or is so awash with money.

Culture and daily life in Turkey have been sorely neglected in English-language literature – perhaps that's one of the reasons why the country is so frequently misunderstood by outsiders, and so freighted with clichés.

This is the first full-length book in English to tell a story of Turkey through football, tracking the rapid changes in Turkey's politics, economics, culture and society, by travelling the country, and telling the stories of a dizzying cast of colourful characters and clubs, including: ultras in revolt; power-hungry mayors; Kurdish nationalists fighting through football; women asserting their right to wear shorts and play sports; Islamists battling over control of the state; football icons fallen from grace; ultranationalists; refugees trying to make a life; great clubs in crisis and unlikely clubs ascending; gay referees and LGBT teams; and Turkey's charismatic and controversial ruler, Recep Tayyip Erdogan.

The many stories in the book together form a greater narrative about modern Turkey, which asks: how does football explain the profound changes in Turkish society? What will happen to a beautiful, crisis-ridden sport? Where is Turkey heading? What does it mean to be Turkish in the early twenty-first century?

PROLOGUE
Ultra

The colossal Ataturk Olympic Stadium loomed into view. It sat on top of a wind-scoured plateau, at a distant frontier of Istanbul: stark and isolated, looking from a distance like a science-fiction citadel. It was late September 2015 and Besiktas were playing Fenerbahce; both Istanbul sides were early title front-runners, but only Besiktas were playing in exile. After their rickety, beaten-down Inonu Stadium was demolished in 2013, Besiktas were forced to play most of their 'home' matches in this remote stadium, named after the founder and first president of the Turkish republic.

The Ataturk Stadium is a monument to twenty-first-century Turkey's ambition, built to host an Olympics that went to Beijing instead. The venue has seen one of the most thrilling nights in European football, as Liverpool came back from 3–0 down against AC Milan to win on penalties in the 2005 Champions League final. But the stadium is designed for athletics rather than football: a running track keeps the pitch at a little remove. Giant stands fall away to diminutive ends, providing passages for the wind to whip through and play havoc with the flight of the ball and the players' expensive haircuts. While the wind was usually a hindrance, it was sometimes a help. At least one Besiktas cross had been helped into the net already that season by a timely blast of air.

As we navigated the security lines and turnstiles to enter the stadium, the good cheer of the Besiktas fans gave way to a more fraught mood and my companions fretted over whether I might bring good or bad luck. Besiktas had a terrible recent record against their biggest rivals.

The pitch opened up before us and we were struck by guttural, shifting edifices of noise, as the fans threw chants from one stand to another. The spectacle usually requires conductors. Chant-leaders usually spend the whole match up on specially constructed podiums with their backs to the pitch, often aided by a thundering drum. It is a complex feat – to marshal unruly masses and lead them in song, to listen out and coordinate with other stands who want to share a chant. It can be exasperating, and often they become as wild as orchestral maestros. Sometimes they shout abuse back into the stands or scream: 'Go home to your TV if you want to watch the match so much!' This noise stokes fevers in the players. They grapple and lash out and square up, as the fans drive the spectacle on.

Besiktas is a gentrified, formerly working-class, 'secular' central neighbourhood on the Bosphorus, not far from Taksim Square. All kinds of people support the team and in the stadium they are united in love and loathing, but Besiktas's biggest fan group, Carsi, is associated with left-leaning politics. Carsi and many other football fans played a major role in the 2013 anti-government protests, which started in Gezi Park and spread throughout the country. As protests spread to stadiums, the authorities clamped down hard on rebellious football fans, banning political chanting at matches, introducing a controversial Passolig e-ticketing identity-card system, and even charging a group of 35 football fans – most of whom were Carsi members – with trying to mount a *coup d'état*.[1] Feeling the pressure of the government, and in protest at the Passolig system and the remote stadium, Carsi were no longer attending the matches as a group. At this derby, there were swathes of vacant grey seats in the bluffs of the stadium, and – like many derby games – the football federation had banned away fans, fearing trouble.

As the match was about to start, the players and officials lined up, the crowd stood and sang the national anthem and, when it had finished, large groups broke into a nationalist chant, prevalent during times, such as this, of heightened violence between the Turkish state and Kurdish militants: 'Martyrs never die, the homeland will never be divided!'

The match kicked off, the entire stadium chanted down from three and then pogoed en masse, roiling and breaking as human waves. When Fenerbahce had the ball, a searing racket of whistles broke out, like the sudden descent of a plague of locusts, but they were dominating – carving out and squandering a couple of early chances.

Even after Besiktas weathered the storm and pilfered a couple of goals, the Besiktas fans only seemed to grow tenser. 'We never win derby matches, two isn't enough,' my friend explained.

The anxiety was well founded. A Besiktas own goal made it 2–1 at half-time, and when Robin van Persie equalised for Fenerbache in the second half, the Besiktas fans began swearing in bravura, anatomical compounds.

Attacks seesawed between the two sides as each probed for a winning goal. When a Besiktas player scampered down the left wing and whipped a perfectly judged cross into the box, Mario Gomez – Besiktas's star striker – became airborne, smashing a flying header into the net. Everything in the stands became a berserk blur of colour and pumping limbs; one fan found the strength to lift two of his friends, and at the bottom of the stands, a rush of hands rattled the fences. With the score 3–2 at the final whistle, the victory sent Besiktas to the top of the league. 'Sex on the beach! Sex on the beach!' crowed the fans in victory. 'I dunno why… it's a famous song,' said my ecstatic friend by way of explanation.

Unlike Galatasaray, and various other clubs under the AKP government's mind-boggling stadium construction boom, Besiktas avoided being permanently shunted out to the margins of the city. Their new stadium was rebuilt on the same site as the old – perched opposite the grandiose Ottoman-era Dolmabahce Palace, which still hosts offices of the Turkish government. Many Besiktas fans have a match-day tradition: they gather in bars and *meyhanes* across the district, get well lubricated on raki or beer, chant, light flares, and then walk the half a mile or so to the stadium, past the palace.

On 11 May 2013, Besiktas played their last match at the old Inonu Stadium before its demolition. Tension lingered from clashes on 1 May between police and some fans who had attended May Day protests. On the day of the final match, the prime minister (later president) Recep Tayyip Erdogan had been holding a meeting in the Dolmabahce Palace and relations between supporters and the police were even testier than usual. The police attempted to restrict fans on the road leading to the stadium and, as tensions rose, a police motorcyclist enraged them by firing his gun into the air. All hell broke loose.

Pitched battles broke out in Besiktas and around the stadium as the police fired round upon round of tear gas and water cannon, while Besiktas fans pelted them with rocks, bottles and debris. Some sought refuge from the conflict inside the glass booths normally reserved for ceremonial soldiers outside the palace. The match went ahead but the enmity between the authorities and many Besiktas fans had hardened, and a couple of weeks later there would be other opportunities to clash, with the outbreak of the Gezi protests.

The construction of Besiktas's new stadium was repeatedly delayed, often technically ascribed to minor infringements of planning permission and laws never normally applied in Turkey. Many believed the real reason to be political: that the government was in no hurry to have a new stadium in such a sensitive spot until the 'Gezi spirit' of protest and anti-Erdogan sentiment could be quelled.

Football mania

I became a Tottenham Hotspur fan at the age of seven, when my heroes were Gary Lineker and Gazza. My Edinburgh-born dad was a Hearts fan and had followed the Scottish national team. I loved his football stories: 100,000 packed into Hampden Park, whole sets of supporters switching sides at half-time on the open terraces, the time he swung on the crossbar at Wembley Stadium, the vagaries of following a frustrating side (something I could soon relate to). I began playing football every day and irritating people with unsolicited quizzes on arcane football trivia.

I was around ten years old when I first heard of Galatasaray, when they knocked Manchester United out of the Champions League. I later discovered Fenerbahce, Besiktas, Trabzonspor and Bursaspor as they played in Europe. I didn't know much about Turkish football, only that Turkish fans were crazy for their teams, and that the derbies – particularly between Fenerbahce and Galatasaray – were among the most intense and violent in the world.

In 2013 I was living in Egypt. Fans of the two great Cairo clubs, Al Ahly and Zamalek, had united and played a significant role in the 2011 protests that had toppled Egypt's dictator Hosni Mubarak. Even so, while following the Gezi Park protests from afar, I was still surprised to see Turkish fans putting aside their significant mutual loathing to unite in protest.

When I first went to Istanbul for a couple of weeks in 2014, I asked the hotel receptionist how I could get a ticket for a football match. 'Offf, you should have come a few weeks earlier,' he replied. 'Now it's impossible. There is a stupid new system that means you have to get an electronic ticket, it takes weeks.' I returned again for a few weeks in early 2015 and wrote a couple of articles on Turkish football. The more I learned, the more I discovered that Turkish football was full of drama, struggles and insights that went way beyond sport. I realised I could tell a story about modern Turkey through football. I moved full-time to Turkey at the beginning of the 2015/16 season.

It was not uncommon for Turkish shopkeepers, on discovering that I was from the UK, to react by gleefully shouting things like: 'Nottingham Forest!' Few people outside the UK have heard of Reading, the home-counties town where I mostly grew up – except in Turkey. 'Ah, Reading,' people would say knowingly, and then something like: 'Steve Clarke'.[2]

Turkish fans love their clubs with an intensity that often transcends all other loyalties, even in this deeply nationalistic, widely religious society. You don't bother to ask whether someone likes football, you just ask which team they support. According to some estimates, more than three quarters of Turkish people are 'active' football fans[3] and 97.5 per cent support a team.[4]

The popularity of football has meant that the Turkish authorities have always sought to use or control the sport: Turkish football has always been political. Association football was first brought to the Ottoman Empire in the 1870s by British merchants, travellers and expatriates, who played the game in port cities such as Istanbul, Izmir and Salonika. It was soon taken up by Ottoman minorities such as Armenians, Greeks, Italians and Jews.

Muslims, however, were effectively banned from playing the sport under the autocratic Sultan Abdul Hamid II. Some Muslims believed that shorts violated Islamic morals, and some associated the sport with the killing of Husayn Ibn Ali, the grandson of the Prophet Muhammad, whose decapitated head was kicked around like a football. Others simply found running around after an inflated object to be preposterous and worthy of contempt.

But there was also an explicitly political fear among the Ottoman authorities during a time of repression: that football enabled people to come together, that it could be difficult to control. In 1901, after Fuat Husnu Kayacan formed the 'Black Stockings' – the first Turkish-Muslim football team – he was charged in a military court with 'setting up goal posts, wearing the same uniforms as Greeks, and kicking balls around'.[5]

Yet the growing Turkish passion for football could not be repressed for long. Many great Turkish clubs were formed in the following few years, including the *uc buyukler* – the Istanbul 'Big Three' – of Besiktas, Fenerbahce and Galatasaray. The vast majority of Turkish fans support one of these sides.

Muslims became freer to play the sport with the weakening of the sultan's power after the 1908 Young Turk Revolution, and football clubs blossomed in a more liberal environment. Football was used to bolster nascent Turkish nationalism. After the Ottoman Empire was defeated in World War I, football played a role in boosting Turkish pride and prestige during the postwar years as Turkish teams played, and frequently defeated, teams made up of Allied occupation forces. Football clubs later helped smuggle arms to the Turkish National Movement, led by Mustafa Kemal, whose forces drove out occupying troops to win the War of Independence, establishing the Republic of Turkey in 1923. Kemal later took the surname 'Ataturk': 'Father Turk'.

Football helped cement international recognition of the new Turkish republic, although the early republican authorities often distrusted domestic football, fearing that it could foster division and rivalry.[6] But football's appeal continued to grow.

Football was professionalised in 1951. The first National League was formed in 1959 and a Second Division was added in 1963. A burgeoning football press, the expansion of radio broadcasting, a rise in football betting and urbanisation all stoked the popularity of the sport across Turkey.

The authorities recognised football's ability to reach, distract or galvanise the masses. Politicians declared club allegiances and became club presidents, retired players became politicians, and businessmen invested in the sport in order to gain prestige and political influence.

By the late 1970s, Turkey was beset by political violence between right-wing and left-wing militias, which was ended when the military staged a *coup d'état* in 1980. Many see 1980 as a 'Year Zero' in Turkey in terms of politics and economics – and, accordingly, football.

There was a political and economic divergence: while hundreds of thousands were arrested and tortured as civil society and many political parties were repressed by the state, Turkey began opening up to the global market. Economically speaking, Turkey's Margaret Thatcher was Turgut Ozal, a squat man with a moustache, from Malatya. His Motherland Party won the first post-coup elections in 1983 and Turkey embarked on a process of neoliberal reform,[7] which brought Turkey into the global economy, and decisively into the age of industrial football. Economic reforms provided manna for the big clubs, as Turkish banks, swollen with cash borrowed on international markets, lent them money.[8]

The state's monopoly on football television broadcasting was broken illegally in 1991 by Magic Box, a satellite TV channel based in Germany and owned by Turgut Ozal's son.[9] The pirate channel was retransmitted by many Motherland Party municipalities, and Magic Box soon reached a deal with the Turkish Football Federation to legally broadcast matches, guaranteeing the big clubs huge revenues, broadly relative to their fan bases, while the smaller clubs shared a comparatively meagre pot.

New tiers were added to Turkish football and professional teams proliferated. New waves of urban migration swelled Turkish cities during the 1980s, further boosting the popularity and importance of football. Municipalities formed clubs, and local politicians tied their political fortunes to football teams.

Wealthy businessmen increasingly took control of the big clubs throughout the 1990s. With the unprecedented popularity of football, and the increased intersection of football and finance, ambitious people saw opportunities to make economic, political and social capital from football clubs.

Football became one of the most important networks of power in Turkey: but never more so than in the twenty-first century under the ruling AKP.

'Come on and shoot!'

As the 2015/16 season unfolded, and it looked like Besiktas might win the league for the first time since 2009, the urgency to open their new stadium before the end of the season became palpable, and a date was set for April.

By the opening, Besiktas were still top of the league, just, ahead of Fenerbahce. Astonishingly, fans would not be able to attend the opening ceremony due to 'security reasons', although they would be able to attend the first match the very next day against Bursaspor, with whom they share a bitter rivalry. There was a heavy police presence on the day of the opening ceremony. The stadium looked like a kind of modernist coliseum, with hints of the Anitkabir, Ataturk's mausoleum. It also looked unfinished – cables dangled into clear air and stacks of bricks lay covered in tarpaulin. Turkey, Besiktas and Ataturk flags were hung on the stadium's northern stanchions, alongside flags of President Erdogan and prime minister Ahmet Davutoglu. There was considerable glee among many fans when Erdogan and Davutoglu's faces were blown backwards over the stand and out of sight by the Bosphorus winds.

Fans were not invited because Erdogan likely feared he would be booed if they attended the ceremony. Various dignitaries and special guests were invited instead. Erdogan and Davutoglu wore Besiktas scarves and kicked a ball around on the pitch. The Besiktas president, Fikret Orman, made a gushing speech in which he thanked the 'esteemed' President Erdogan umpteen times.

Gaggles of ordinary people and journalists – myself included – gathered around the stadium behind police fencing and gawked up at the people in suits and chic dresses on the stadium's concourse, while they gazed over our heads towards the shimmering, busy sea and the city skyline; taking in the first Bosphorus bridge, the Maiden's Tower off the coast of Uskudar, the dome and minarets of the Hagia Sophia in the old city, and the titanic cruise liners that appear from a distance like outsized bath toys towering over a miniature city.

The following day – as the stadium was set to host the opening match – was an occupation of black and white. Throughout the day ferries and buses constantly disgorged bouncing, chanting supporters. Stalls billowed clouds carrying the aroma of frying *kofte* on the road to the stadium. In dank corners or close to the walls there was the tanginess of alcohol-fortified piss. A great pall of smoke rose around the stadium, formed by endless flares. Hours before kick-off, torrents of raucous fans were making their way along Dolmabahce Caddesi. Debris littered the trampled flower beds close to the stadium. When groups of fans cleared, it looked like the aftermath of a battle fought with flares and bottles. I learned not to stand underneath flares – which spit hot magma drips.

Swaggering down the street, the fans looked like gangs from *The Warriors*. They tried to share chants with the traffic police regulating their flow, but all they got back were a few wry smiles. The police held back the fans until they reached a critical mass and were allowed to pass or simply broke through police lines.

The riot police were a different order of being: machine-like and militarised, swaddled in armour, beetle-plating and padding, some wearing Stormtrooper-type helmets. Their vehicles looked souped up as if ready for conflict on the streets of Baghdad.

About an hour and a half before kick-off I was standing by the Dolmabahce clock tower, absent-mindedly chewing a *simit*, when a man a few metres in front of me was drenched by a direct hit from a water cannon. Skirmishes were breaking out as a group of fans had tried to push their way past the gates. Moments later, an elevated roar rose from further up the hill. In the park overlooking the stadium people scattered and ran as tear gas canisters fell amid the greenery in streaming arcs. I hung back, craned my neck, inched forward. A motorcyclist came down the road, his visor open, eyes puffy and streaming from the gas. A pair of tear-gas intoxicated police officers staggered down the hill. Then a white bus passed through amid a flurry of jeers – it was the away team.

Some football fans gain a skill set that most people don't acquire. They learn how to deal with tear gas, how to avoid it and mitigate its effects, how to pick up burning, streaming canisters with bare hands in order to hurl them back at police lines. They know how to evade the water cannon. They learn what to do when the police charge; they come to understand when to withdraw and when they don't have to run, and when they can advance. It is a skill set that makes them dangerous and difficult to control.

The road had become slick and iridescent from the water cannon spray. The fans simmered down and continued crowding to get into the stadium's prison-like entrance, with its metal gates and tight, electronic turnstiles. There was the sweet and sourness of sweat and polyester in the thicket of fans. In the pink and grey dusk, through drifts of flare smoke and tear gas, the stadium looked quite magnificent.

The presence of Carsi, Besiktas's major fan group, had been low-key, but they were there, keeping their heads down, attending the match as a group again. When I met him later, long-standing member Yener Ozturk claimed to be glad that the fans hadn't been invited to the opening ceremony. '[Erdogan] definitely would have been booed, and that would be enough to put a target on the team's back,' he said.[10]

For the first time in nearly three years they had resurrected their traditions and marched to the stadium. 'It was kind of like a very loving feeling, like coming back home,' he said. Inside the stadium people were crying with joy, including Yener. 'You get emotional when you have like 42,000 people singing at the same time, everyone just going crazy. It is awesome and there's nowhere else you'd rather be at that time. And we waited a long time.'

Carsi were on best behaviour. Their banners were simple. They had a rule of no swearing. 'We're kind of at the point where we don't want to give the government anything to complain about. Because they can ruin our shit,' said Yener. 'We're on the verge of being champions for God knows how long, so we don't want to fuck that up.'

I didn't hear many Gezi chants from fans that day, only one that had become popular at the anti-government protests, which I heard as fans encountered the police outside the stadium. It was a throwback to a time that felt both recent and impossibly distant, when football fans and other protesters were in the epicentre of the city and the country, briefly holding the attention of the world, and taunting the police, gleefully, angrily:

> Come on and shoot!
> Come on and shoot!
> Come and shoot your tear gas!
> Take off your helmet, drop your batons
> And we'll see who's the real man.

1

Fathers and Sons

With his mane of hair, bushy beard and owlish spectacles, the artist Ege Berensel looks like an Anatolian rock star from his father's generation. He was born in 1968 and grew up in Bursa, in the north-west of Anatolia – a couple of hours' ferry journey from Istanbul across the Sea of Marmara. During his childhood, areas in Turkish cities were divided along ideological lines: 'Leftist and rightist neighbourhoods, with leftist and rightist football teams'.[1] By the late 1970s Turkey was mired in a near civil war, as armed groups of the left and right battled each other in the streets. Berensel has documented the story of Dinamo Mesken, an amateur football club that was dragged into the era's political violence and military repression.[2]

The Bursa neighbourhood of Mesken was staunchly leftist during the 1970s. In 1975 many Mesken residents crowded into Bursa's stadium to watch Bursaspor take on the Soviet team Dynamo Kiev in the third round of the UEFA Cup Winners' Cup. Fans from Mesken were thrilled by Dynamo Kiev's speed and style, and they openly supported the Soviet side, which defeated Bursaspor and went on to win the competition. In the following weeks, supporters began chanting 'Dinamo Mesken! Dinamo Mesken!' at the matches of Ertugrulgazi, a Mesken-based amateur team. The club became widely known by their new nickname, which implied a risky expression of affinity with the communist Soviet Union. Dinamo Mesken attracted hundreds-strong crowds to their matches. It was inevitable they would draw attention from the authorities and right-wing groups.

On an overcast February Sunday, around 20 former players, coaches, supporters and officials had gathered in a wood-panelled, male-dominated café in Mesken. The men were garrulous and eager to ply me with tea. The arrival of yet another tray would be followed by a fleeting lull in conversation and the tinkling of spoons in tulip-shaped glasses, before the chatter bubbled up again.

Bulent Merey, 66, was the club's coach in the late 1970s. The police approached him one evening as he was locking up the clubhouse, and asked for information on the players. 'I told them: "This is a sports club – it has nothing to do with politics."' The next morning Merey removed leftist posters that had been pasted onto the clubhouse overnight. 'So I also had to say to the leftists: "This is a football club! You shouldn't involve it in politics."'[3]

Dinamo Mesken's matches became increasingly fraught as rival fans accused them of being communists. By the late 1970s, Mesken was a battened-down neighbourhood, practically at war. Dozens of people were dying every day in violence across the country. Dinamo Mesken players helped man armed checkpoints in the area, trying to prevent right-wing groups from attacking people in the neighbourhood. They weren't always successful.

Cemal Karadag was the photographer of the team. He owned a photography shop a few doors down from the café in which we were drinking tea. His photographs capture the innocence and joy in football: a group of young men in flared trousers playing in a sloped park, a lost era in black and white. But they are also freighted with a degree of dread, perceived in retrospect. A 1976 photograph of Dinamo Mesken's Lego-haired young players – posing in tracksuits, the front row holding chequered footballs – is blurring at the edges. It is a team on the verge of a violent demise.

In late July 1980, there was a murder in a neighbouring right-wing area. On 29 July, a young man stepped into Karadag's shop. He asked for the owner, but Karadag wasn't there, and his friend was minding the shop. The young man stood around and fidgeted. Eventually Karadag walked in. The young man drew a gun from his belt, and shot the photographer. As the assailant fled, he tried to force the gun back into his belt, shot himself in the foot and was caught. He was from the neighbouring area, and told police he had been paid to carry out the killing. Karadag was around 30 years old. 'Since Karadag was close to the team and the neighbourhood, they targeted him,' said Berensel. 'His death caused a trauma in the neighbourhood.'

On 12 September 1980, the military staged a *coup d'état* and vowed to end the violence across the country. In 1981 the authorities declared that Dinamo Mesken's nickname was a 'clear attack on national values' and the club was ordered to close. The players lost their licences and were banned from playing for any club. Several of the club's players and administrators were arrested, tortured, tried and convicted of extortion – charges which they say were politically motivated.[4]

It is very personal for Berensel. His cousin played for Dinamo Mesken and he knew some of the players. His left-wing parents were hounded in the aftermath of the coup. His father died on the road while trying to evade arrest. 'This was the most important event in my life, that's why I make stories about it,' he said.

The Mesken team members were eventually released from jail. Some were traumatised by their experiences and some were left permanently disabled. Many people left the area, and some committed suicide. But it was not the end of the club's story.

A Year Zero of sorts, 1980 was a watershed imposed by brute force and written into law and culture. The military regime promoted a conservative synthesis of nationalism and Islam after the coup to promote 'unity'. Opportunities arose for ambitious men on the Islamic right, such as Recep Tayyip Erdogan. This chapter is a story, told through fragments, that traces Turkish nationalism, militarism and patrimony through football.

Many thought that, as prime minister and president, Erdogan had brought the armed forces under control, restricted them to their barracks and ended the pattern of periodic military coups. But on the evening of 15 July 2016, parts of the military began moving. Tanks left their bases to occupy streets, and fighter jets appeared in the skies. Soldiers told people to go home. There was no word from Erdogan.

Photographs of Fuat Husnu Kayacan show him dressed impeccably in an Ottoman tunic and fez, with a sharply waxed moustache. He was a young man of the establishment – he attended a military school and his father was an admiral in the Ottoman navy. But Fuat Husnu was also a subversive, a criminal: an illicit footballer. He managed to acquire a ball through British contacts in Moda, and formed the first Turkish-Muslim team – the Black Stockings – in 1901 'to smoke out those Greeks and Brits in the fields'.[5]

The team was made up entirely of Muslims at a time when they were effectively banned from playing football by the Ottoman authorities. The sultan feared an uprising or a coup: he didn't want people to come together, not even for the strange custom of chasing after an inflated object. The Black Stockings trained in secret and then played their first match, against a local Greek team, on 8 November 1901. The Black Stockings were beaten 5–1 – Fuat Husnu scored their only goal. Detectives ran onto the pitch after the match and detained most of the players. Fuat Husnu was charged in a military court but was given only a minor penalty – his family connections may have helped. The Black Stockings were forced to fold.[6]

His friend and Black Stockings teammate, the diplomat Resad Bey, was not so fortunate. In Turkish the word for 'ball' is '*top*': 'cannonball'. Goal is '*kale*': 'castle'. Resad's correspondence, which mentioned firing a 'cannonball' into the 'castle', was intercepted with great suspicion by the ever more paranoid Ottoman authorities.

Resad was subject to a lengthy investigation; a football, rules of the game, and his jersey and shorts were confiscated by the palace and examined by a special commission, which was eventually satisfied that Resad was not preparing some kind of rebellion. However, they still considered his behaviour somewhat troubling. Resad was promptly dispatched into exile, appointed as vice-consul in Tehran. 'This may appear perfectly incredible,' reported the *Evening Telegraph* on 13 January 1902, 'but it is absolutely true.'[7]

A coup brought Turkish-Muslim football out into the open. Ali Sami Yen was a Muslim student at the prestigious Galatasaray High School who had become passionate about football. He formed a team but didn't give it a name, in order to avoid the fate of the Black Stockings, but they soon acquired a nickname: 'The Gentlemen of Galatasaray'. 'Our objective is to play football like the English, to have a colour and a name, and to overcome the non-Turkish teams,' declared Ali Sami Yen.[8] In 1905 they became the first largely Muslim team to join the Constantinople Football League. In order to evade suspicion, they were initially listed in the press by the – totally unsuspicious – name AN Other.

By 1905 Turkish nationalism had grown among the Ottoman elite, particularly among the 'Young Turks' of the Committee of Union and Progress (CUP), which may have helped Galatasaray survive.[9]

Fenerbahce was formed in 1907, but could not operate freely in the still repressive climate. In 1908 an uprising within the military, mostly of Young Turks, forced the autocratic sultan to cede powers and restore the more liberal 1876 constitution. It ushered in a more pluralistic, multi-party era, and the de facto ban on Turkish Muslims playing football ended.[10]

The presidents of Fenerbahce and Galatasaray reportedly met in 1912 to discuss merging the two clubs in order to form the strongest possible

Turkish-Muslim side that could compete against non-Muslim teams.[11] The idea was to call the merged team 'Turkkulubu' – the Turkish Club. The team would play in a white kit emblazoned with a red star. But the outbreak of the Balkan Wars that year may have scuppered the plans.

The Ottoman Empire had long been in decline. For much of the nineteenth century, rival powers salivated at the prospect of gaining its territory. World War I became an existential conflict for the empire,[12] which allied itself with Germany, the only Great Power that had not shown any ambitions regarding Ottoman land. Although on the losing side, the Ottoman Empire surprised many by surviving the war.

During the period of occupation that followed, Turkish football teams such as Besiktas, Fenerbahce and Galatasaray gained fans and bolstered nationalist pride by beating teams made up of British and French occupation forces – a national resistance through football. Fenerbahce won 41 out of 50 matches against occupation soldiers – more than any other Turkish team.[13]

The Allied powers intended to carve up the remaining Ottoman territory through the Treaty of Sèvres.[14] It seemed likely that any Ottoman or Turkish nation would have to be satisfied with a rump of land within Anatolia's vast rectangle – territory that no one else wanted.

Mustafa Kemal led a Turkish nationalist rebellion. Kemal had visited Fenerbahce's premises in 1918. During the subsequent war, Fenerbahce's players were recruited to smuggle arms from occupied Istanbul to Kemal's forces in Anatolia.[15] The Turkish army forced occupation troops out of Anatolia, and suppressed internal rivals and dissidents. The Ottoman sultan had collaborated with the occupiers and was forced into exile on a British ship as Kemal's troops advanced on Istanbul. The occupation forces agreed to vacate the city. The Treaty of Lausanne, signed in July 1923, brought an end to the war and settled Turkey's borders. The Republic of Turkey was officially proclaimed on 29 October 1923, with Mustafa Kemal becoming its first president.

General Charles Harrington, the British commander-in-chief of the Allied occupation, wanted his forces to salvage some pride from their somewhat ignominious withdrawal. He placed a newspaper advertisement challenging any Turkish football teams to take on his British forces team. Harrington was confident his team could give the Turks a jolly good thrashing. Fenerbahce accepted the challenge the following day.

Harrington had a metre-high trophy made, which he modestly called 'the General Harrington Cup'. On the day of the match, in a crowded Taksim Stadium, the future Chelsea winger Willie Ferguson opened the scoring for the British team. But two second-half goals in quick succession by Zeki Riza turned the game in Fenerbahce's favour and they saw out the victory. Zeki Riza's brother Hasan Kamil[16] lifted the trophy and the British left with their tails between their legs. The General Harrington Cup now sits proudly in Fenerbahce's museum.[17]

Only the faintest wash of noise rose from the surrounding metropolis as the road ascended to a hilltop above Ankara. Two soldiers in ceremonial uniforms, armed with antiquated rifles, stood in glass boxes like museum exhibits, as still as waxworks. The real security guards, dressed in black, prowled around the compound, muttering into walkie-talkies. Sunlight gleamed off a long walkway, lined with statues of lions, that leads to Anitkabir – the mausoleum of Mustafa Kemal Ataturk – a modernist acropolis with clean columns of travertine-clad concrete.

On Anitkabir's plaza, visitors, eager for photos, flocked round a small troop of young soldiers, who were trying to project gravitas whilst goose-stepping. A group of visitors entered the mausoleum's marbled interior and laid a wreath in front of the sarcophagus – an austere block resting on a podium within the hushed vault.

On a wall near the entrance were words from Ataturk's last speech to the army on 29 October 1938, urging vigilant loyalty to the state: 'Our great nation and I are sure that you are always prepared to carry out your duty of defending the honour of our country and our civilization against any danger, from inside or outside.'

Ankara was chosen by Kemal as his base in 1920 during Turkey's War of Independence, as an easily defendable town in the heart of the Anatolian land mass. Ankara became Turkey's capital city and in the last century has been transformed into a major metropolis.

Kemal chose to bind the disparate people[18] of the new republic through an uncompromising conception of Turkish nationalism,[19] a centralised state and a paternalistic cult of personality.

Ankara's location embodied the centralised, authoritarian state of the new republic. Kemal's government embarked on a series of supposedly modernising reforms – changing the Turkish script from Arabic to Latin, purging Ottoman Turkish of many of its Arabic and Persian words, abolishing the sultanate and the Ottoman caliphate, and adopting a French-inspired *laiklik*[20] – a 'secularism' which actually asserted state control over religion. Education was secularised, and greater rights for women were promoted. Some traditional clothing such as the Ottoman fez were forbidden altogether and the hijab was banned from public institutions. Mustafa Kemal's surname became Ataturk – 'Father Turk' – in 1934.

Ataturk appears preoccupied, impatient even, in most paintings or photographs: his gaze is often upwards and away, as if looking into a bright, hazy future, or a sacred light. Kemalism[21] became the official ideology of the Turkish state in 1935, but Ataturk's love of raki took a toll, and he died of liver cirrhosis three years later. His cult of personality endured in death and Ataturk's mausoleum became a place of pilgrimage.

While early republicans were wary of football's ability to foster rivalry and division, they used football to announce the new republic to the international community. Turkey's first ever international football match, against Romania, took place three days before the proclamation of the republic. Turkey's first ever captain was Hasan Kamil and his brother Zeki Riza scored both Turkey's goals in a 2–2 draw.

Zeki Riza scored an absurd number of goals, both for Fenerbahce (470 in 352 appearances) and for Turkey (15 goals in 16 games). Zeki Riza and Hasan Kamil were given the surname 'Sporel' by Ataturk, a kind of play on 'sport'.[22] Zeki Riza would later become a political dissident of sorts, joining the breakaway Democratic Party led by Adnan Menderes, only to have his reputation smeared by the ruling Republican People's Party (CHP), which had been formed by Ataturk.

Football was absorbed into the wider cultural agenda of the early republic – which sought to demonstrate that 'Turkishness' was a superior culture. Kemal's Turkey faced west, seeking to inculcate European tastes and customs, but Kemalists also looked east, behind them, into a mythical Central Asian past. Ideologues such as Ziya Gokalp constructed theories of Turkishness. The 'Turkish History Thesis' claimed that Central Asian proto-Turks were the progenitors of all modern civilisations. The 'Sun Language Theory' posited that all languages were derived from a single language, closest to

Turkic. Mehmet Cevat Abbas Gurer, a military officer and close friend of Ataturk, took up this theory and claimed that words such as 'sports' and 'athlete' were of Turkish origin.

There is a theory, still held by some, that football is a Turkic invention that was stolen by the British, who codified modern, Association football. But varieties of ball-kicking games have been played since antiquity.[23]

The Turkic game 'Tepuk' – 'kick' in ancient Turkish – was some sort of juggling game, using a ball made out of inflated goat or lamb organs, played around 1,000 years ago in Central Asia. It was probably derived from games like Cuju, played over previous centuries in Japan and China, using leather balls and bamboo posts.[24] There is no evidence that it bore much relation to modern Association football or that Turkic tribes brought the game to Anatolia.[25] It is not clear whether Cevat Abbas Gurer managed to establish the etymology of 'foot' or 'ball', but anyway, modern-day Turks call football 'futbol'.

Recently, Erdogan ruminated on the word 'arena', given to a slew of new football stadiums in Turkey. 'What does arena mean? We don't have such a thing in our language,' mused Erdogan, noting that horrible gladiatorial things had taken place in arenas throughout history. In a stroke he deemed the word to be un-Turkish and clubs will have to remove it from their venues. The name change has echoes of Ataturk's reforms and reflects Erdogan's shift to nationalism.[26]

Galatasaray were the first to announce their compliance – they would change the name of their home from 'Turk Telekom Arena' to 'Turk Telekom Stadyumu'. Is 'stadyumu' – 'stadium' – a Turkish word? Not at all – it is derived from the Greek word *stadion*.

'In Turkey, pretty much everything is based on nationalism,' says Daghan Irak, a football academic and writer. 'We are taught nationalism at school, starting from the age of five, we perceive the world according to this philosophy. Turkish football clubs, especially Besiktas, Galatasaray and Fenerbahce, are just modelled after nations, they are like micro-nations. It's an entity larger than itself.'[27]

The Istanbul 'Big Three' have millions of fans across the country and in the diaspora – most fans in Turkey support one of these teams. Widespread support for the 'Big Three' helped forge huge, disparate communities. But it also offered an opportunity to tap into an identity that was not wholly subsumed by the enforced unity of republicanism. Football teams offered stark rivalries – others – to define oneself against.

'How do you define yourself as a fan in Turkey – as a Besiktas, Galatasaray or Fenerbahce fan – is a completely imagined process,' says Irak. 'One Besiktas fan has nothing [else] in common with another Besiktas fan, it's arbitrary, it's like the nation.'

Cevat Abbas Gurer became the president of a new club created by the state in 1933 that broke away from Galatasaray and called itself Ates Gunes – literally 'Fire-Sun' – as per the Sun Language Theory. Ates Gunes – later shortened to 'Gunes' by Ataturk – also played in red and yellow, like Galatasaray, and hoped to supplant Galatasaray with the support of the state. Gunes won a disputed league title in 1937/38 after a retroactive goal-difference rule was applied. But Galatasaray remained popular while Gunes struggled to attract fans, and the club closed down in 1938 shortly before Ataturk's death.[28]

The Istanbul 'Big Three' have all claimed connections at various times to Ataturk. Supporters often attempt to prove that he supported their team. This is an easy argument to settle: Ataturk did not support any team because he did not like football. In his memoir, the legendary Galatasaray player and coach Gunduz Kilic claimed that Ataturk asked him to teach him the rules of football on a trip to the Soviet Union – in 1934! – three decades after the first Turkish football team was formed.[29]

As a young man before World War I, Adnan Menderes had played football for some of the first Turkish nationalist teams in Izmir – as a striker for Karsiyaka and as a goalkeeper for Altay.[30] He went into politics after the war. He became a member of Ataturk's ruling CHP but was always a poor fit. He joined the Turkish Sports Institution but quit in protest after it ruled that all athletes at the 1936 Olympic Games had to be members of the CHP. Menderes established the breakaway Democratic Party (DP) in 1946, to offer a right-leaning Kemalist alternative that was more liberal economically and softer in its stance on religion.

The Fenerbahce legend Zeki Riza Sporel joined the DP in 1946 and became an Istanbul member of parliament. The CHP decided to try to bring him down by suggesting he was a traitor to Kemalism. CHP deputies alleged he had been a member of the Kuva-yi Inzibatiye, a short-lived army established by the sultanate to fight Ataturk's Turkish National Movement, and that he worked for the Istanbul government under occupation. Zeki Riza admitted he had not joined the Turkish National Movement when called up, but claimed that he had to care for his sick sister. He was expelled from parliament, but was able to return in 1950 as the DP won the first free national multi-party elections.[31]

If the CHP represented 'national destiny', the DP represented 'national will'.[32] Multi-party elections marked the first time that politicians started appealing to voters through religion and football – it was the first time they had to win votes. When Erdogan appears in a city on the campaign trail wearing the scarf of the local team, he is attempting a shortcut to the hearts of the people that first emerged in the 1950s.

Nihat Bekdik made more than 250 appearances as a defender for Galatasaray between 1916 and 1936, many as captain. He wore a badge of a lion on the collar of his jersey: his nickname became 'Aslan' – 'Lion' – and the lion later became Galatasaray's symbol. Bekdik went into politics in 1957, becoming a DP member of parliament, at a time when the DP was becoming increasingly authoritarian. The military stepped in and ousted the party in the 1960 coup.[33] The military saw their moves as recalibrating democracy, as they did again in 1971 when they issued an ultimatum to Suleyman Demirel's government amid increasing chaos, and in subsequent interventions. Bekdik was arrested and imprisoned on the island of Yassiada, but was later released. Menderes was found guilty of treason and hanged in 1961.

Footballing successes became legendary events in Turkish history, including Turkey's 3–1 defeat of the fine Hungary team of 1956, which included Ferenc Puskás, and Fenerbahce's European Cup elimination of Manchester City in 1968.

Galatasaray's popularity surged in the 1950s. 'Metin Oktay was the turning point,' says journalist Alp Ulagay. 'He wasn't from the Turkish elite or from the high school, but he was handsome and talented and scored a record number of goals – records that haven't been broken since. He changed Galatasaray's fan base. He was probably the first sporting icon of Turkey.'[34]

Oktay was from Izmir, but he had a thing for Galatasaray since childhood. 'Galatasaray is like a religion, it's a deep-rooted passion and belief, this is why I chose Galatasaray,' he said.[35]

Oktay was the top goalscorer in six seasons in the Turkish league. In his first stint at Galatasaray between 1955 and 1961 he averaged over a goal a game: 174 in 161 appearances. Fenerbahce's vice-president reportedly offered him a blank cheque in 1959 to sign for the club – Oktay turned it down.[36]

After a brief spell at Palermo, he returned to Galatasaray and scored another 137 goals before his retirement in 1969. He became known as 'Metin the King'. Oktay had a ruffled Jack Kerouac look, like he should have had a cigarette dangling from his mouth at all times. He starred in a 1965 film, *Tacsiz Kral* – 'Uncrowned King' – in which he played himself. Alongside footballing exploits, the film featured Oktay romancing various women.[37]

Half a century later many Galatasaray fans still wear Oktay's classic Galatasaray replica. Oktay died in a car crash in 1991. There are many Metins of a certain age: Turkish boys born in the 1950s and 1960s named after the idol.

'Lefter was so important, besides being the best player ever,' said Erden Kosova, a Fenerbahce fanatic and art critic. 'It is about a lost richness. It's like he was one of the last ties to the old Istanbul.'[38]

Lefter Kucukandonyadis was born in 1924 on the island of Buyukada, a short ferry trip from Istanbul. His father was a Greek fisherman, his mother a Turkish tailor. Many of Lefter's family had emigrated from Turkey following the 1941 Wealth Tax, although his father was saved from exile because of his poverty.

Lefter started out at Taksimspor, a team largely made up of Armenian, Greek and Jewish Turks, but soon transferred to Fenerbahce, becoming their number 10 goal machine from the 1940s to the 1960s. Playing 'inside left' in the old 3–2–5 formation, Lefter was renowned for his dribbling as well as his goal scoring. In two spells at Fenerbahce he scored 423 goals. He was one of the first Turkish footballers to play abroad, playing for Fiorentina,

Nice and AEK Athens. Lefter was the Turkish national team's captain and record goalscorer, until Hakan Sukur broke his record four decades later.

Lefter, who had played for Turkey's 1954 World Cup team,[39] was at home on Buyukada with his family in 1955 when a pogrom broke out, targeting the remaining Greek population of Istanbul, alongside Armenians and Jews. Lefter's house was attacked with rocks. He waited at the door with a gun in his hand until morning. Fenerbahce fans who heard about the attack took a boat to the island and went to Lefter's house.[40] They implored him to tell them who had attacked the house, but Lefter demurred. Decades later he said he had recognised the voices of those attacking his house; some were his near neighbours.

While most remaining Greeks emigrated from Turkey following the pogrom, Lefter kept scoring for Fenerbahce and Turkey. When he passed away in 2012, aged 87, there was an outpouring of tributes – including from Galatasaray fans. His coffin was wrapped in the flags of Turkey and Fenerbahce and he was buried in a Greek Orthodox cemetery on Buyukada.

A statue of Lefter has been erected by Yogurtcu Park, next to Fenerbahce's stadium. Many fans gather here before games to drink beer, sing and pose for photos by the statue. In Lefter's heyday he was so prolific that Fenerbahce fans would simply chant:

'Pass it to Lefter / and add one to the ledger'.

Istanbul is the only city divided by continents. Fenerbahce is located on the Asian side of Istanbul, Galatasaray on the European side – their rivalry is known as the 'intercontinental derby'. It evolved into one of world's most intense derbies. In a not-so-friendly friendly match between the two teams in 1934, fights broke out on the pitch after a series of rough tackles. The fighting spread to the stands, and the referee abandoned the match. The vitriol accumulated over decades: a city rivalry from the continental divide,[41] a rivalry between the two most successful Turkish teams, and a rivalry about who can best represent Turkey on the European stage.

'When I see the colours, it's enough for me,' says Gokhan Karakaya, 36, a Galatasaray fanatic who has supported the club from the age of five or six. At that age, Gokhan already knew that he loathed Fenerbahce. He became a hardcore supporter at 13. At Galatasaray's Ali Sami Yen Stadium he graduated from the Yeni Acik stand, behind the goal, to the Kapali stand, the life of the Galatasaray fans. 'If you wanted to prove yourself you had to take part in the fights, generally against Fenerbahce or Besiktas supporters.'[42]

In 2001 he became a member of the newly formed ultrAslan, which is now the biggest, most ferocious Galatasaray supporters' group. 'You know, I have two or three Fenerbahce friends – we talk about football but we never talk about Fenerbahce or Galatasaray – never! – because, maybe it's not a good word, but it's like a religion.'

Gokhan struggled for words and air when he began talking about passing by Fenerbahce's stadium on the Asian side of the city. 'I... I... I'm wanting to kill someone over there, really. I hate. Really there is no other word but hate. I don't want violence, but the nature of the derbies has to be violent, otherwise it's not a derby, it's a normal game.' Gokhan lamented that away fans were often banned from matches between the major clubs: 'I want them to come to our stadium, and I want to go to theirs, really to show myself, to break some place. Because supporting a team is about showing who is more powerful – who can beat the other one. And I want to show that Galatasaray is much better. I don't care sometimes about the football.'

The intercontinental derby can induce mania, not only in Turks, but in foreigners too. Galatasaray faced their arch-rivals in the 1996 Turkish Cup Final. A Fenerbahce vice-president had labelled Galatasaray's Scottish coach, Graeme Souness, a 'cripple' in the press.[43] Galatasaray won the cup in extra time during a second-leg match at Fenerbahce's stadium. The occasion took over. Souness grabbed a giant Galatasaray flag, ran to the centre circle and planted it in Fenerbahce's turf. The Fenerbahce fans were going berserk; some were trying to get on the pitch. Souness wisely fled down the tunnel. He instantly acquired hero status for Galatasaray fans, who nicknamed him 'Ulubatli Souness' after the Ottoman martyr Ulubatli Hasan, who was killed planting the Ottoman flag during the siege of Constantinople.

Fenerbahce craved revenge. A notorious Fenerbahce fan known as 'Rambo' broke into Galatasaray's stadium on the eve of a derby and hid inside an advertising hoarding overnight, armed with a kebab knife and a

Fenerbahce flag. Rambo cut his way out of his hiding place during the match the next day, waved his knife at anyone who got too close, and planted the flag in the centre circle, before eventually allowing himself to be escorted from the pitch.

Mention Souness to any Galatasaray fan 20 years later and they still growl in approval. Don't mention him to any Fenerbahce fan.

Ultimately, Gokhan concluded that love for Galatasaray was more important than hate for Fenerbahce, but in his mind, it didn't seem like one could exist without the other. 'I'm trying to tell the new generation: hate Fenerbahce more. And bring up your children to hate Fenerbahce. By this process you will have a passion for Galatasaray.'

Gokhan has been arrested several times – for fighting and at political protests. 'They call me a hooligan. Thanks! I say the same. Well, not any more.' Gokhan is mellowing over time. In 2014 he left ultrAslan and stopped going to the games. He hates the Passolig identity-card system. He has already been arrested three times. He worries he could get stabbed. After 20 years, his mother was still asking why he was going to the games. He has become more religious: 'I'm praying and on the other days I'm going to beat people and hurt someone? Which one is the true Gokhan? I have to choose one way.' He misses the excitement, the camaraderie, the sense of achievement. 'There are no levels – you are the same: educated, non-educated, nationalist, Kurdish. You all get on the same bus and go to the same destination, and share everything.'

He recently became engaged and wants to start a family. Gokhan's fiancée is also a Galatasaray fan but works for Fenerbahce. Her father is a former Galatasaray basketball player and fan, but he managed Fenerbahce women's basketball team for ten years. 'I hated him, you cannot imagine!' smiled Gokhan.

I asked her how she felt about that. 'He doesn't hate him any more, hopefully,' she replied. Gokhan went uncharacteristically quiet. Gokhan, you're not saying anything? Gokhan?

'Not any more,' he said, eventually, dredging up the words. 'But it's really hard to marry a woman who is [his] daughter.' He let out a flurry of laughs that faded quickly. He will have to live on the Asian side for the first time once he marries.

You'll be seeing a lot of Fenerbahce fans, scarves and flags. Maybe you'll hear the sound of the stadium? Gokhan looked stricken. 'I have to be far away from there. I cannot live there. We will be far, right?'

'Hmmm, not very close, OK,' replied his fiancée.

'We will not hear them?'

'Hmmm. No, it's not possible.'

'Because it will be terrible. I cannot live with it. It makes me mad.'

'But after some time you get used to it.'

'*You* got used to it.'

'I can hear their voice from the stadium, it's so close to my house. I got used to it after a year.'

You're not such a big fan, says Gokhan: 'And your father worked for Fenerbahce!'

'Mmm, I don't care about it.'

'I care!'

She looked at both of us. 'This is the difference between being a woman and a man. That's it.'

Unlike Ataturk, Recep Tayyip Erdogan is a genuine football fan and an ex-semi-professional player. He has constructed a golden footballing legend, says biographer Nicolas Cheviron, 'that he could have been the big star of Turkish football, that he was compared to [Franz] Beckenbauer'.[44]

Erdogan – born in 1954 – is a charismatic orator who talks in a language many understand. He makes a lot of his humble origins. Erdogan grew up in the tough Istanbul neighbourhood of Kasimpasa and sold lemonade and *simit* as a child for extra money. The family was working class but not poor – his father, who was born in Rize on the Black Sea, was a ship captain. As a child, Erdogan had a knack for declaiming poetry and the Qur'an – his religious family thought that he might become a *hafiz*, someone who can recite the Qur'an from memory. Erdogan attended a religious Imam Hatip high school.

Erdogan was also an amateur footballer from his teens onwards and regularly talks up his footballing past. As a politician he has eagerly associated himself with the sport, because football is an easily understood language in Turkey. 'He is the politician who is most aware of the power of football,' says Mustafa Hos,[45] who wrote a critical biography of Erdogan. Football became part of Erdogan's mythology.

Erdogan started training with Erokspor, an amateur club in Kasimpasa, in 1967, when he was 13 years old. In 1969 he joined the amateur Kasimpasa team Camialti Spor. It seems that Erdogan may have begun as a striker, before moving back into midfield, and then even deeper as a libero.

By 16 he was already tall at 185 cm, and Erdogan has always stressed his height. Sycophants in his circle apparently nickname him 'tall man'. 'He used his physical strength on the pitch. He was an aggressive, angry player,' says the journalist Hos, who used the word '*kazma*'[46] – 'spade' – in his biography to describe Erdogan as a footballer, for which Erdogan sued him. In footballing terms, it translates into something like 'butcher', implying a rough, untechnical style, perhaps in the style of Vinnie Jones.

However, Erdogan's hagiographers describe him as preternaturally skilled. Perhaps the truth is somewhere in the middle. Like Vinnie Jones, Erdogan must have been a somewhat reasonable player, even if he was a bit rough and uncultured, because he played at a decent level.

Erdogan has been a Fenerbahce fan since his childhood and has incorporated the club into his self-mythologising. Erdogan has claimed that, while playing for Camialti against Kasimpasaspor in 1973, he was spotted by Fenerbahce's Brazilian coach Didi and the club made him an offer. Erdogan claims that his father did not allow him to make the transfer – he wanted his son to focus on his studies.

Erdogan's father was quite an authoritarian, even brutal, figure by Erdogan's own accounts. When Erdogan insulted his neighbour as a child, his father hung him by his shirt from a hook on the ceiling. Erdogan had to kiss his father's feet and ask forgiveness when he did something wrong.

In the mid-1970s Erdogan joined the National Turkish Student Union (MTTB) – the youth organisation of the National Salvation Party led by the strident Islamist politician Necmettin Erbakan.[47] Erdogan played the lead role in a play called *Mas-Kom-Ya*, written by an Imam Hatip student[48] – Erbakan apparently first noticed him in a production of this play and he became a mentor of sorts to Erdogan, who joined several of his movements, until the two men split a quarter of a century later with the founding of the AKP.

In 1974 Erdogan was hired by Istanbul's electric tram and funicular company (IETT), and played for their football team – IETT Spor – which was pretty successful in the amateur leagues. Erdogan became captain and they won the Istanbul Amateur One league in 1976/77.

According to teammates, Erdogan did not celebrate the title because he did not want to drink alcohol. They remember him as being intense, serious and stern; Serdar Sahin said that he was once told off by Erdogan for not concentrating in a game, and Erdogan didn't speak to him for a year.[49] Others recall going to the mosque with Erdogan – that he sometimes led prayers, but didn't proselytise religiously or politically within the team.

IETT Spor beat Fenerbahce in a friendly match in 1976 and Erdogan has claimed that he was again made an offer by Fenerbahce, but again turned it down because of his father's objections. It seems unlikely that his father would allow him to play football for IETT Spor but not for a great club like Fenerbahce, and by 1976 he was 22, old enough to make his own decisions. It sounds like a myth. 'He has mentioned several times that his dream had been to become a professional football player but that his hopes had always been blocked by his father,' says Cheviron.[50]

In Turkey, many fathers take their sons to their first football match when they are eight, nine, ten years old. It is an early male rite of passage, before the later masculine ritual of military service. Guven Cicek, 47, went to his first Bursaspor[51] match in 1976 with his father, who was also a member of Teksas – Bursaspor's largest, most vociferous, most feared group of fans, considered by many the epitome of Turkish ultranationalism.

Guven remembers his first away game in 1979, when they travelled to Izmir to watch Bursaspor play Goztepe:

> The left side of the bus was politically leftist, and the right side of the bus was rightist. The leftists and rightists were going throat-to-throat in Bursa – fighting and killing each other – but going to Izmir and during the Goztepe game we became as one, and we fought the Goztepe fans. But when they returned to Bursa they were back to fighting each other![52]

While the military authorities were closing amateur clubs like Dinamo Mesken for political reasons, they also took greater control over the football federation and promoted professional football following the 1980 coup. 'In a sense, they promoted hooliganism,' said Guven. 'They didn't want young people to be politically oriented.'

Bursaspor fans love travelling to away matches. Teksas is one of the oldest fan groups in Turkey – it was established in 1967, mainly to coordinate travel to away matches. There is a legend about a time that the Bursaspor fans travelled to Zonguldak and tore up the place – they made it like the 'Wild West' and the name 'Teksas' probably comes from that.

Teksas are 'nationalists' for their city. 'It's not only about football,' said Tarik Capci, 43, a journalist and former member of Teksas. 'It's about city culture and it's a fight between cities. For example, Fenerbahce supporters came here and they chanted aggressively something "below the belt" about Bursa people. So we couldn't tolerate this and we had to fight.'[53]

Football is bound up with the honour and defence of the city, couched in militarised and sexualised terms: a fear of penetration (of borders and body), the shame of being perceived as unmanly or 'weak'. 'I was in Ankara when I was young, at military service,' recalled Guven. 'I read a newspaper article. It was exaggerating, but it wrote that 50,000 Fenerbahce fans were on the way to Bursa. When I read that I just wanted to drop everything and rush to Bursa's defence! It's like a war, like the city is falling!'

The flip side of this is the desire to conquer other cities. At away matches Teksas behaved like an invading army. They would typically fight with knives. Scars were honourable mementoes of battle. Guven recalled one match in Aydin around 1992. The Bursaspor fans arrived in a convoy of buses, like they were going to war. Aydin locals ambushed them and were shooting at the buses, shouting that they'd fought off Greek soldiers in the War of Independence and would fight Teksas off too. Teksas behaved like marauding soldiers, setting fire to cotton fields near Aydin in retaliation.

The – quite possibly apocryphal – story of Erdogan quitting IETT Spor shortly after the 1980 coup while sporting an illicit beard is a neat myth that encapsulates Islam, politics and injustice, with a little spicing of football for good measure.[54]

'This is something constant in Tayyip's attitude – this [self-] victimisation,' says Erdogan biographer Nicolas Cheviron.[55] It's true that certain expressions and symbols of faith and of politicised Islam had long been oppressed in Turkey. But Islam was also seen as a bulwark against the left and communism from the 1950s and, although the National Salvation Party was shut down after the 1980 coup, and Necmettin Erbakan was temporarily banned from politics, Islamists were not the primary victims of the coup's repression. Erdogan was associated with Islamist movements as they were generally growing in strength and were increasingly often supported by the state, because religion (or at least Sunni Islam) and nationalism were seen as a counterweight to the left and an instrument of national unity. '[Erdogan] was most often in the right place at the right time,' says Cheviron.

In 1981 Erdogan took a job as an accountant at a *sucuk*[56] factory. He was just 27 years old, and had supposedly been scouted – twice – by Fenerbahce, but it's not clear that he ever joined another football team. He certainly never played at that level again. This probably says something about his true skill level and his commitment to the sport.

In 1981 he finally got his diploma. The next year, he completed his military service in Istanbul – a simple, logistical posting close to his house. He returned to the *sucuk* factory after military service as politics was beginning to open up again – at least for Islamists and neoliberals. He joined Erbakan's Islamist Welfare Party, becoming its Beyoglu district chairman in 1984 and the Istanbul chair the following year. His political career was gathering pace in the aftermath of direct military rule. He became mayor of Istanbul in 1994 and gained a reputation for competency and pragmatism, improving the city's ailing infrastructure and taking measures to prevent corruption.

AKP member of parliament Ravza Kavakci Kan says she first became a fan of Erdogan when he was mayor. She thinks much of his appeal is down to his 'sincerity' and his connection with ordinary people:

> You can see him going and having tea at this poor house, maybe they don't even have proper chairs, maybe they sit on the floor. That's something we didn't see before. Another thing maybe that's behind his success is that he listens to the people – and then if he makes a promise, he has to keep it. And people know that.[57]

Now, politicians and the people also have to watch him kick a ball around. Mustafa Hos says that football is a part of the greater sum of Erdogan's mythology.

> You create a character with all these little stories in total. After you create the image there is an aura of the image. He has a personality who likes to conquer and give orders, that's why these myths help him – because people start to think he was a great player, a leader on the pitch, now he is a natural leader in the political arena.[58]

In the two decades following the 1980 military coup, national and international football matches became increasingly charged with emotion and nationalist fervour, peaking in the 1980s and 1990s, at the height of the military's fight against the rebellion of the Kurdish militant group the PKK (the Kurdistan Workers' Party).[59] In 1992, playing of the national anthem was introduced before every league match. There was an explosion of nationalist sentiment in stadiums, reflected in the symbols of Turkishness – flags and anti-separatist, nationalist chants. Turkish footballers dedicated national victories to the families of 'martyrs'. Hostility to teams from majority Kurdish cities grew.

I met Erol Cil, 36, another Teksas member, in Bursa's bazaar district. We chatted over tea in the shop of his friend Ali Reza, a big jovial man who was a member of Teksas during his youth in the 1970s. 'You are very lucky to meet me,' boomed Ali with a grin: he said he was one of only five men in Turkey who made alems – the decorative standards that crown the minarets and domes of mosques.

'Bursa was the Ottoman capital, that's why we are quite conservative and nationalistic, and proud of Bursa,' said Erol. '[But] we forget about political opinions on the stands.' Bursaspor fans estimate that the majority of Teksas members are supporters of the far-right, ultranationalist MHP – but there are many other ideologies in the group. While Tarik supports the MHP, Erol votes for the AKP, and Guven describes himself as a socialist – but they all see themselves as Turkish nationalists.

Teksas are eager to deny that their nationalism often verges into anti-Kurdish racism. They have a leading member who is Kurdish and say that they are against the PKK, not Kurds. 'Basically Teksas supporters are not racist,' argued Erol, 'but – there is a breaking point for us: the unity of Turkey, and the Turkish flag and the national anthem.'[60] Turkish nationalism is embodied in symbols that are held to be sacrosanct. There are stories – possibly apocryphal – of people being hit by cars because they stood to attention after hearing the national anthem while crossing the road. '[Kurdish] fans booed the Turkish national anthem before games and that is a big humiliation for Turkish people,' said Guven. 'And the military is something sacred and holy in Turkey. It is not just the military, it's something religious.'[61]

Being a Turkish man has traditionally meant spending time as a soldier in military service. '[The PKK] kill our soldiers,' said Erol. 'And our soldiers are our sons, our brothers, our cousins.'

'Teksas had another dimension,' said Guven, who is from a poor background. 'If you are a weak person – physically, mentally, economically – you join Teksas and you become supported, and nobody can beat you up, and you have friendships – it's like a family.' All of his friendships were still linked to the group. Guven never married because of his intense relationship with Bursaspor and his low income. 'I was married to Teksas,' he said.

Erol, who owns a printing business, wanted to study law but he never made it to university:

> Being a Teksas member and a Bursaspor fan took a lot of my youth. I fought with my family and my father over it. I didn't go to university because I spent a lot of time and energy supporting the team and going to away matches. I lost a lot of opportunities in my life from supporting the team, but I don't regret it. When I go to the stadium I see all my friends – I made some great friends through Teksas. I'll be a member of Teksas until I die.[62]

I also met a sub-group of Teksas members known as 'Radikal'. They were a rough and ready lot in their early thirties and they didn't want to give their real names, because of their various shenanigans. Radikal Teksas had been given permission to speak to me by their leader, Fahri Ozdeger, otherwise known by his nickname of 'Sampiyon'. I ask how he became the leader. 'A leader always protects,' replied one. 'He is like a father to the fans, he always back us up. There are some things that my father doesn't know, but our leader knows all the details of my life.'[63]

Fahri organises logistics – like tickets and away travel – but it's about more than this. 'We have this emotional connection – you fight for your leader. You can get arrested for your leader and commit a crime for them. He is like my father. You should love your father – how is Fahri so different? He treats us like we are his own children.'

'Football is not about 90 minutes, it's our lives,' said another, expanding on the theme. He said that Fahri helps them when they're in trouble. 'When I had a traffic accident, I called him right away. Fahri came here and dealt with the situation.' He said there were certain traits that a leader should have: 'A leader should be honest. He should be a family man, a father – this is very important – married with two kids. He should be a *good* father.'

If Fahri is their father, then the members of Radikal are all brothers. One member gestured to another at the table: 'Anyone who hurts him I will fight them – anyone.' The guy who gestured is a fervent MHP supporter, his friend a self-avowed socialist.

One member had a double scar just above his eye, caused by a rock thrown by a Konyaspor fan a couple of weeks earlier. He said his wife was used to him getting into scrapes, and held up the knuckles of one hand which were chewed up with scar tissue. His wife was forced to plan her own life around Bursaspor matches. He'd even left his honeymoon early to go to a match.

One Radikal member had been telling people that the happiest day of his life was when Bursaspor won the league in 2010 – better than his wedding day. This had got back to his wife, who was less than pleased.

Unusually, Erden Kosova became anti-nationalist because of Fenerbahce. 'In the kindergarten they were teaching us a song: "the sails of the enemy's ships are blue, the sails of our ships are red." Because of my family's associ-ation with Fenerbahce, blue for me is the iconic colour – and I have always had this kind of discomfort with red.'[64] Of course, even then, he knew that blue was Greek, and red was Turkish. 'So this created some kind of small rupture which continued in my political view of the nation.'[65]

Kosova is a member of the left-wing supporters' group Vamos Bien. Their previous name of Fenerbah*che* – the 'che' is a nod to Che Guevara – did not go down well with Genc Fenerbahceliler (GFB), Fenerbahce's largest fan group, many of whom are conservative and nationalist. They came looking for 'Fenerbahche' in the stands, screaming, 'Where are they? They won't change the name of Fenerbahce!' Kosova's group was small, perhaps 100 people. They didn't have banners and GFB couldn't locate them among the huge crowd. Kosova's group decided to change their name to Vamos Bien – a less controversial reference to the Cuban Revolution.

Vamos Bien now overwhelmingly boycott the matches, partly in protest against the widely hated Passolig identity-card system, and partly because of remaining tensions with GFB. 'Before Vamos I always went to the matches with my dad, so it has this kind of symbolical attachment to it. He died in 2010. But I go still to the matches – I'm one of the 5 per cent who go, because of that. Because I feel like I'm bringing my dad.'

Turkish people are usually incredibly hospitable to foreigners: keen to help, eager to ply you with food and drink and anxious to know what you think of their city. Many fans adore their foreign players – Fenerbahce even built a statue of their Brazilian star Alex de Souza. Galatasaray fans immediately warmed to German forward Lukas Podolski after he slapped an opponent in the face during his first match for the club. Teksas love Liverpool because they once beat arch-rivals Besiktas 8–0 in the Champions League.[66]

However, Galatasaray's Ali Sami Yen Stadium gained a reputation for its hostility to visiting teams. In their 1993 Champions League clash, Manchester United were greeted with relatively good-humoured, if unsettling, scenes at the airport – fans held up a banner that welcomed them to hell, and one fan informed United's right back Paul Parker, 'You will die.' When the team arrived at their hotel, the bellboy stared at Gary Pallister, United's centre back, and drew his finger across his throat.

At the stadium the players were hit by a tumult of noise that, in Pallister's words, 'made Anfield look like a tea party'.[67] Galatasaray knocked out United on away goals. After the match the team got into a fight with Turkish police as they left the field, sparking a mass brawl. A police officer punched Eric Cantona; Bryan Robson hit a police officer and needed six stitches in his elbow. Their team bus was stoned as they left the stadium. Alex Ferguson concluded that United were exposed to 'as much hostility and harassment as I have ever known on a football expedition'.[68]

Football highlights Turkey's conflicted relationship with Europe. There are tensions between Europe as something to be aspired to, supposedly modern and prosperous, and something to be resented as a duplicitous cultural, political – even religious – enemy.[69]

The Turkish media became more explicitly anti-European in the 1980s and 1990s as Turkey was excluded from many European political and economic institutions following the 1980 military coup. Europe was also accused of harbouring support for Armenian militants in the 1980s and the PKK in the 1990s.

When Galatasaray knocked Manchester United out of the Champions League in 1993, a headline boasted of how the Turks had 'mounted' the English.[70] Turkish football chants in matches against European teams are often psychologically revealing. They depict Europeans as effete, feminine

or gay – and Turks as fearsome, masculine and dominant – often in sexualised language.

But there is a degree of awe and respect for European football, reflected in
the immense pride when Turkish teams emerge victorious against European
opposition. When Turkish fans chant, 'Europe, Europe, hear our voice,
this is the sound of the marching Turks!' it is both a challenge and a plea
to be heard.[71]

In the year 2000, two Leeds United fans were stabbed to death by Galatasaray
fans in Istanbul before a UEFA Cup semi-final clash. The defendants later
argued they had been provoked by the behaviour of Leeds fans, which
included insulting the Turkish flag by rubbing it against their genitalia.[72]
There was no evidence that the murdered fans had behaved this way. Tensions
had built over the previous decade after a series of feisty encounters between
Turkish and English teams. Throughout the late 1990s, English fans often
behaved boorishly in Istanbul – getting rowdily drunk on the street, accosting
young women and baring their arses in public.[73]

Galatasaray knocked out Leeds and when they met Arsenal in
Copenhagen for the final, the city became a battleground between warring
English and Turkish fans.

Under their coach Fatih Terim, Galatasaray in the mid- to late 1990s struck a
winning balance between brilliant Turkish players, a productive youth system
and astute foreign signings such as Gheorghe Hagi, Gheorghe Popescu and
Taffarel. Galatasaray won the league four times in a row between 1996 and
2000 under Terim. They beat a talented Arsenal side on penalties to win
the UEFA Cup – becoming the first and only Turkish team to win a major
European trophy.

The Turkish sports minister at the time stated that Galatasaray's victory
would be 'an important step in Turkey's accession to Europe'.[74] By defeating
top European teams, Turkey was somehow proving its readiness to become
fully 'European' and join the EU project.[75]

In the early years of its tenure, the AKP appeared to strongly support
EU accession – making many legal changes and reforms in line with EU

law, including to restrict the power of the military. The military had also supported EU accession in the late 1990s, despite knowing it would lose some political power – betting that it would benefit from economic and political stability through EU membership.[76]

But the chances of Turkey joining the EU under current circumstances are minuscule. France and Germany are implacably opposed. Other accession countries had to complete one membership negotiation round. In 2005, Turkey's application was split into 35 chapters; each member state has a veto in each chapter, so, including two opening and closing steps of each chapter, with 27 members, Turkey would have to negotiate 1,890 potential vetoes.[77] Turkish public support for joining the EU has plummeted in recent years.

EU accession is now just a useful chimera, used by both the EU and Turkey as a rhetorical device for influencing domestic public opinion. UEFA is perhaps the only European organisation in which Turkey's membership cannot be questioned.[78]

In many South American countries, football is often described in terms of art. Brazilian football is compared to samba. Argentinian football is another iteration of the tango. Individual players are ascribed the irrepressible, flamboyant, hot-headed qualities of the artist: Maradona as maestro, Messi as impish magician, Brazil's hefty, heavyset Ronaldo as a bullocking, bruising ballerina.

Football is also war (minus the shooting, according to George Orwell[79]). There is a great Austrian term for a football fan – *Schlachtenbummler*: 'a person who travels from battle to battle'.[80]

War is certainly the dominant conception of British football: the trench, the parapet, laying siege and the preoccupation with beating Germany, linked to modern Britain's foundational myth – that Britain stood alone against the Nazis while the rest of Europe fell. England fans exalt when their heroes are bloody and battered, exemplified by Terry Butcher looking like some crusading knight, with his bandaged head, red seeping through the hastily wrapped fabric, his white shirt soaked in blood.

To some extent, Turkish football is spoken about in the tradition of conflict, but with its own historical, moral resonances. Historical myths are used for fan identities in the stands. Many Bursaspor fans see their club as representing the essence of the Ottoman Empire, and so they label Istanbul teams as 'Byzantine'.[81] 'It represents the current rivalry, the current inequality of power, through weird historical myths,' says anthropologist Can Evren. 'I think that makes football interesting in Turkey but also it makes it dangerous and it can be very politically loaded.'[82]

The past is particularly alive in the present in Turkey. Narratives are written over the bewildering complexities of talent, luck, circumstance, fine margins, inspiration, madness, weather, whatever. Historic battles are restaged in Turkish football. When Turkish teams play in Vienna, the media is filled with Siege of Vienna analogies, and the chance of revenge. Turkey was twice beaten 8–0 by England in the 1980s. 'They were national humiliations and they're sort of seen as a repeat of the defeat of the Ottomans by the British Empire in World War I,' says Evren.[83]

The story of Turkey is of a nation rising out of that defeat. Rather than the clichés of the South American artist, the Teutonic German machine, the tactical, canny Italian or the intricate, flamenco-footballer of Spain, the Turkish footballer should be a struggling, self-sacrificial fighter and an underdog. 'It's all about this idea of Turks being this group of people that never give up,' says Evren.[84] The red of the Turkish flag is meant to evoke the blood of martyrs[85] and in Turkish culture people are often expected to be ready to devote and sacrifice themselves for the collective, which is deemed more important than the individual.

In Euro 2008, the Turkish national team was heading for a first-round exit. They had lost their first match 2–0 to Portugal. In their second match against Switzerland, Turkey were trailing 1–0 at half-time. But early in the second half, Semih Senturk scored an equaliser and, in the second minute of injury time, Arda Turan grabbed the winner. In Turkey's final group-stage match they went 2–0 down to the Czech Republic and it again looked like they were crashing out, but they somehow found a way back to win 3–2 and qualify for the knockout stages.

They faced Croatia in the quarter-final – it was a tense match in which Croatia missed an array of chances. It remained goalless until the last minute of extra time, when Ivan Klasnić scored with a header for Croatia. They thought it was all over. But 60 seconds later Turkey's goalkeeper launched a long, desperate ball into the box; it bobbled around and then fell perfectly for Semih Senturk, who smashed a left-footed drive into the top corner. A buoyant Turkey beat Croatia 3–1 on penalties. Germany only narrowly defeated Turkey 3–2 in the semi-final.

'If you look at the Euro 2008 Turkish national team, it's the team that rises up from the moment everybody thinks they are defeated,' says Evren. 'This is the foundational myth of Turkish nationalist history.'[86]

To some extent, Fatih Terim embodies this sort of scrappy, underdog, terrier spirit. Terim has orchestrated many of Turkey's comebacks. Terim's self-appointed nickname of 'The Emperor' is apt, given his imperious persona. On the touchline he paces, scowls, broods – his mouth is often puckered in a cat's bumhole of disapproval. He has a penchant for flashy suits and open-necked *Saturday Night Fever* shirts. The journalist and Galatasaray fanatic Deniz Dogruer says Terim resembles José Mourinho in some ways: 'He is a fighter and a provocateur.'[87]

Terim is known more for his 'man-management' – delivering blistering tirades and foul-mouthed bollockings – than for much tactical sophistication.[88] He has become one of world football's best remunerated coaches – earning $3.8 million/year as Turkey's national team coach – and one of the most criticised.[89]

Turkey's qualifying campaign for Euro 2016 got off to a bad start. After three games they were joint bottom of their qualifying group alongside Kazakhstan. Terim promised that things would improve, and Turkey went on a great run – beating the Czech Republic and Holland. In the last game, against Iceland, Selcuk Inan scored a wonderful last-minute free kick to gain Turkey a 1–0 victory. Meanwhile, following Kazakhstan's unlikely away win in Latvia, Turkey qualified for Euro 2016 as the best third-placed side.[90]

Turkey suffered insipid losses to Croatia and Spain in their first two tournament matches in France. It seemed like they were out. But celebratory gunfire rang out in my neighbourhood when Turkey defeated the Czech Republic 2–0 in their final group match. Turkey were set to squeak through to the knockout round, taking the last spot for the best third-place team, if this makes sense. But in the 84th minute of a subsequent match between the Republic of Ireland and Italy, Robbie Brady reached a cross fractionally ahead of Gianluigi Buffon, and steered a header into the net, putting the Irish through and sending Turkey home early.

When Turkish teams are in trouble, they often turn to Yilmaz Vural. The 64-year-old has coached – at the time of writing – at least 27 different clubs over 30 years, which must be a world record in professional football. He is a kind of dogfight specialist – he has saved many teams from relegation at short notice. He has also been relegated 11 times, which must be another record. One season, two different teams he had coached were relegated.[91]

Vural is short and stocky, with a tremendous head of hair, gelled and combed back and fixed to the side, whitening at the edges. He teeth twinkle like a matinee idol's smile. 'I am one of the most popular entertainers in Turkey,' declared Vural when I met him, and few would disagree.[92]

Vural was born in 1953 and brought up in Adapazari, Sakarya – around 100 kilometres east of Istanbul. There were many artists and musicians within Vural's large, extended family. 'I'm a typical free spirit. I don't want to work in a standard job, nine to five. When I was a child and I was talking to myself, I was dreaming to be a captain of a ship, or an attaché in a different country.'

Vural spent many years in Germany and also played as a midfielder for Sivasspor when he was young, but he was always itching to get into coaching from a young age. His first big job was in 1986 at Malatyaspor. His teams have a propensity for being involved in matches with crazy scorelines. Often they overrun their opponents, or are themselves overrun.

If Vural had not made it in football, he would have been a theatre actor. Vural has also deployed his skills in several commercials, including for Lipton tea and, more recently, for condoms. Football is a perfect arena for his acting and oratory. 'Look at the most significant leaders of the world, they all direct the masses using their body language, their tone of voice. I'm doing exactly the same thing.' He claims to have the ability to come into a team and immediately lift the players with the right method. 'Sometimes you need to be a dictator, sometimes you need to be a democrat, sometimes you need to be laissez-faire.'

Vural is a livewire presence on the touchline; pleading, imploring, bol- locking, sometimes fighting. Many fans must be envious that he gets to slap footballers. He has a dire temper – in one match he kicked his own players up their backsides to get them back on the pitch after they had celebrated a goal too zealously. When he was coaching Ankaragucu they had an impor- tant match – they were in danger of relegation. He warned the players to be careful not to get any cards. They were winning 2–1. And then two players got sent off. Vural punched one of them in the face and tried to attack the other as he left the pitch. They lost the match 7–2. 'But this is just what is shown in the media. In the changing room afterwards we all kiss each other and we don't make it such a big deal.'

Vural might often get sacked but, as he points out, he is always hired again. Vural blames the football culture in Turkey. But it also seems that, while he offers an injection of energy and a short-term fix, he is seldom trusted over the longer term and is regarded as cheap to dispose of. He feels hard done by and it is easy to sympathise. In 2016/17 he steered Adana Demirspor to the play-off final of the PTT Lig. His tears showed how much it meant to him, as his team narrowly missed out on promotion to the top tier after losing on penalties to Alanyaspor. He was sacked soon afterwards.[93]

When Alex Ferguson blurted out 'Football – bloody hell' after winning the Champions League, or when Fatih Terim famously said in his chewy, idiosyncratic English, 'What can I do – sometimes? And it's the football, that's the football. Something happened. Everything is something happened,' they were tapping into the essential capriciousness of football.

Vural has said that there is no other sport 'as wicked and inconsiderate for not rewarding one for [their] efforts as football'.[94] Vural only regrets things he hasn't done. He has long craved the jobs and recognition that Terim has had. He feels he should have been given a shot at managing one of the 'Big Three', the Turkish national team, or abroad. 'Being Turkish and Muslim is another handicap across the world. European people are not considering us Turks inside the circle in Europe and they think we cannot do what they are doing, maybe they consider Turks or Muslims as less educated.'

When I met Vural, he was fasting for Ramadan for the first time in 20 years. 'I don't know why, maybe because I'm getting older,' he said. Then he patted his paunch and smiled ruefully. At 63, Vural says his craving for the biggest jobs in Turkish football will continue until his death. He is sure to keep approaching the game with the same chutzpah, brio and panache. 'Life is such a big stage and if you are not an actor, you will never be successful.'[95]

In June 2017, Vural took Goztepe to the Super League with a play-off win on penalties. It was his fourth promotion to the Super League. But Vural and the club parted ways during the summer. He won't wait long for another adventure.

Few accounts of Turkey avoid the cliché of the country as a bridge between East and West, Asia and Europe. But throughout much of its history the

Turkish republic has been more of a bastion, something defensive: a NATO bulwark against communism, a vigilant nation protecting its borders from 'enemies' within and without, a state resisting the diversity of its own people.[96]

This defensive mentality changed somewhat in the early years of the AKP, which sought to reach out to neighbours and historic enemies, and to build political friendships and trade links. The AKP took concrete steps towards reinvigorating the slow-moving EU-accession process

The AKP has used football as a tool in international diplomacy. In 2007 the Syrian dictator Bashar al-Assad hosted Erdogan and his wife in Syria in an attempt to build bridges. During the trip they attended a football match between Fenerbahce and the Syrian team Al-Ittihad. Erdogan and Assad later became close and even spent a vacation together.

In 2008, Turkey's AKP president Abdullah Gul became the first modern Turkish head of state to visit Armenia, for a football World Cup qualifier. The match acted as a precursor to – decidedly mixed – attempts to improve relations. In a sense, Turkey was finally becoming a bridge, envisaged by Erdogan as a mediator between Europe and the Muslim Middle East and beyond. Until it started to go sour.

The Syrian revolution broke out in 2011 and descended into civil war. Erdogan fell out with his erstwhile friend after Assad began deploying brutal violence against peaceful protesters. The AKP later supported, armed and funded rebel groups – including Islamists and jihadists – seeking to overthrow Assad. A diplomatic crisis ensued with Russia – which supports Assad – when Turkey downed a Russian fighter jet close to the Syrian–Turkish border in November 2015. Turkey was also laissez-faire about Turkish and foreign citizens crossing the Turkish border to access Syria and fight in radical Islamist and jihadist groups, including ISIS. Jihadists began re-entering Turkey and carried out devastating attacks in 2015 and 2016. Turkey became host to almost 3 million Syrian refugees fleeing the conflict. The EU signed a deal pledging money and a reinvigorated EU accession process in return for Turkey stopping refugees leaving for Europe. In a sense, Turkey has again become Europe's bastion: a sentinel preventing refugees fleeing war from reaching sanctuary in Europe.[97]

The pressures of neighbouring war, terrorism and a refugee crisis amplified an already fraught and violent situation in which the Kurdish peace process had broken down.

In the early years the AKP prioritised an Islamic, 'neo-Ottoman' identity that went beyond nationalism,[98] which helped to reach out to conservative

Kurds on religious grounds, and a liberal capitalist discourse to appeal to centrists.[99] Erdogan's ability to pitch an electoral 'big tent' is a winning strategy, even if he has to uproot the pegging and shift the coordinates at times. 'His greatest skill is to adapt himself or his ideology according to the time or the situation,' says Mustafa Hos. 'In a 100-metre sprint he can start running with a knife, and he can change the knife to a rose in the last 20 metres.'[100]

When the Kurdish political movement became an electoral threat in recent years, and he lost his liberal-inclined vote, Erdogan shifted his broad coalition and turned explicitly to red and raw Turkish nationalism. Erdogan won the 2015 election this way, but the price was ever more instability.

International football matches exposed these tensions. Attempting to hold a minute's silence at Turkish football matches is a foolish endeavour. However, before a Euro 2016 qualifier between Turkey and Iceland in Konya, it was still shocking to hear the scale of the massed boos, jeers and whistles during an attempted minute's silence for the victims of Turkey's biggest terrorist atrocity, the Ankara bombing in October 2015. Konya is perhaps Turkey's most conservative city – and most of the Ankara bombing victims were leftist or pro-Kurdish activists.

A month later, the day after multiple terrorist attacks in Paris, I headed to the enormous spacecraft, glowing with red neon, which also doubles as the 'Fatih Terim Stadium', home to Istanbul Basaksehir FK, for a friendly/ grudge match between Turkey and Greece. The Greek prime minister Alexis Tsipras was the guest of honour in this liminal territory of Istanbul, the target of another attempt to use football to improve relations. There were, however, no other Greek fans in attendance. It had not been deemed safe for them.

I sat next to a group of excitable young men who were astonished to discover that I was foreign. They offered me biscuits. Flags had been draped over every seat in the stadium – the lad next to me waved his with gusto, unaware that it trailed over my face with nearly every motion.

They vigorously booed the Greek players as they warmed up, and then they vigorously booed the Greek national anthem. Arda Turan stepped out of the line and implored the fans to stop. I thought about how awkward Tsipras and his counterpart must have felt at this clumsy effort to make friends though football. Before the match began the players assembled around the centre circle; they were wearing black armbands, their heads were bowed. 'Oh no,' I thought.

They attempted a minute's silence for the Paris victims. Nearly all of the fans around me were whistling, jeering and screaming: there were chants of

'The homeland will never be divided' and 'Allah / Bismillah / Allahu ekbar'.[101] The referee doggedly stuck to the whole 60 seconds.

The match itself was goalless and utterly devoid of action. Afterwards there was outrage and incomprehension at the booing.[102] The jeers were surely partly an expression of conservative-nationalist grievance.[103] Some sensed a double standard – that European teams don't hold a minute's silence when Turkish Muslim victims are killed in terrorist attacks.[104] There is a perception that some European countries support terrorism through the PKK. And many were probably not booing out of any political sophistication. Partly it may have been the natural belligerence of young football fans, an unthinking rambunctiousness whereby some jeer because it is Greece, because it is Europe, because they copy others, and many probably don't really know why they are doing it.

At the Turk Telekom Arena, Galatasaray fanatic Firat Tasvur was less than excited about the impending derby against Fenerbahce. He was literally feeling under the weather – it was April and the seasons had changed abruptly from cool to warm and, like many *Istanbullus*, he was suffering from headaches. But Firat had other, bigger worries on his mind. 'If I wasn't a season-ticket holder I wouldn't go to this match,' he said gloomily.

Galatasaray – champions the previous year – had endured a torrid season, languishing in eighth place and on their fourth coach of the campaign. They were playing a wretched, stodgy non-football – in the previous match I'd been to, a 1–1 draw with Lazio in the Europa League, the players seemed strangely enervated, like they were slogging through mud or battling a higher degree of gravity. It looked like a computer game in which normally skilled players lose power when played out of position. 'That's because we were playing five centre backs throughout the team and a right back as a right winger,' noted Firat. To make matters worse, Galatasaray had also been banned from Europe under UEFA's Financial Fair Play rules.

There was also a halo of dread around this match. It was a rearranged fixture, after the previous tie had been called off. In March, a bomb had exploded in Istiklal Caddesi, a major shopping street near Taksim Square, killing several people. The assailant was a jihadist, most likely linked to ISIS. The police cited intelligence that there was another plot to target the derby the following day – that three suicide bombers intended to detonate

explosives in the crowds leaving the match. The game had only been cancelled two hours prior to kick-off; so some fans were already at the stadium
and were afraid to leave and get back on the metro with suicide bombers
supposedly on the loose. It was the first time that the 107-year-old derby
had been cancelled.

The Istiklal bomb had been the latest of several attacks, some carried out
by jihadists, others by Kurdish militants. In March, a bombing in Ankara
by Kurdish militants had killed scores of people, including the father of
Galatasaray's striker Umut Bulut. Fenerbahce fans expressed their condo-
lences, and asked whether the ban on away fans could be lifted in solidarity.
The request was denied.

The derby would normally be sold out weeks in advance, but the arena
was perhaps only two-thirds full for the rescheduled match. One of the beau-
ties of live football is that it can be an escape from the worries of everyday
life – humdrum or otherwise. 'Now everyone is scared everywhere,' said
Firat. 'Nowhere is safe.'[105]

Erdogan has long been haunted by the spectre of Adnan Menderes. Erdogan
admired the executed prime minister and feared his fate. When the AKP
came to power in 2002, the Kemalist-dominated military was still the most
powerful political player in Turkey. It had forced the government of prime
minister Necmettin Erbakan's Islamist Welfare Party to step down five years
earlier in a so-called 'post-modern' coup, as the military used pressure behind
the scenes to shut down the party on Kemalist grounds. Erdogan, then the
Welfare Party's mayor of Istanbul, recited a poem by Ziya Gokalp during a
protest against the move. It featured the lines:

> The mosques are our barracks,
> The domes our helmets,
> The minarets our bayonets,
> and the faithful our soldiers.[106]

The sentiment was deemed incendiary and a challenge to Kemalism. Erdogan
spent four months in jail and was forced to resign as mayor.[107]

Erdogan joined the Virtue Party, the Islamist successor to the Welfare
Party. But the Virtue Party's Islamism was still too much for the judiciary

to stomach and it was dissolved in 2001. The party split into two strands: the Felicity Party (SP), whose strident Islamist ideas were largely driven by Erbakan's thinking, and Erdogan's more reform-minded Justice and Development Party (AKP), which advocated a softer Islamic identity, framed in a lexicon of liberal democracy.

The AKP came to power in 2002 in a landslide victory, but Erdogan could not enter parliament due to his criminal conviction. The law was altered the following year and Erdogan became prime minister in 2003.

In 2007 the AKP's Abdullah Gul was set to become president. It was a controversial move as not only would he would become the country's first Islamist president, but Gul's wife wore a headscarf. The military released a vaguely threatening statement on the eve of a presidential election, but Gul became president anyway, and the military did nothing. It blinked. The AKP narrowly survived a legal move to shut down the party on 'anti-secular' grounds – and later secured further legal and constitutional changes to weaken the military's political power.

In the AKP's second term, prosecutors also launched a massive operation to reduce the political power of the Kemalist-dominated military, through a series of prosecutions. In 2012 a court brought charges against Kenan Evren for leading the 1980 military coup. He was sentenced to life imprisonment, and died in a military hospital in 2015 at the age of 97. In a decade the military had gone from being the most powerful political player in Turkey to wielding almost no direct political power. Military tutelage gave way to AKP patrimony.[108]

The museum at Anitkabir tells the Kemalist-approved story of the founding of the republic, alongside a fetishisation of Ataturk's personal belongings. One room displays his medals, pistols and walking sticks; a second room is dimly lit, with Ataturk's more intimate belongings laid out in velvety cases, including an elaborate shaving kit, crystal vials of aftershave, brooches, prayer beads, a scanty dressing gown and a skilfully stuffed 'Fox', his favourite pet dog.

A library follows the museum, and finally there is the exit through the gift shop: Ataturk's image as domestic commodity in the form of badges, key rings, tea towels, jigsaw puzzles, watches and coasters. The repackaging of Ataturk for the domestic sphere is a relatively recent phenomenon, a nostalgia triggered in the 1990s by a growing challenge to Kemalist secular nationalism by Kurdish nationalism, neoliberal economics and political Islam, as religion has assumed an increasingly prominent role in Turkish public life.[109]

But Kemalism is malleable, ready for appropriation by left and right – everyone has their own personal Ataturk, including Erdogan. 'In [Erdogan's] initial ideology, Ataturk and republican Turkey is a parenthesis in the Ottoman history. He strongly rejects the heritage of Kemalism,' says Nicolas Cheviron. 'But then at the same time Ataturk is always a reference, he always has to position himself in comparison with Ataturk, he cannot get rid of the ghost of Ataturk somehow.'[110]

Erdogan has visited the mausoleum several times and written messages that he will further Ataturk's legacy. Erdogan as refounding father rejected Ataturkist elitism and his attitude towards religion, but inherited Kemalist traditions of authoritarianism, paternalism and a certain modernising zeal. Despite his Islamic moves, Erdogan has also defended the concept of 'secularism',[111] and finally he has embraced Turkish nationalism. 'I guess, psychologically, he cannot kill the father,' concludes Cheviron.[112]

The prosecutors who took on the military with Erdogan's blessing were mostly Gulenists – followers of Fethullah Gulen, an Islamist cleric living in exile in Pennsylvania, in the US, who spearheaded a vast education, business and media network.[113] Gulen and Erdogan, erstwhile allies, are now sworn enemies.

Gulen was born in a village near Erzurum, eastern Anatolia, in 1941. He began attracting followers as a preacher in the 1960s. Some regard him as a liberal Islamist, others as a cultish demagogue. He urges followers to live an Islamic way of life, defined by good manners, hard work, charity and inter-faith dialogue.[114] Gulen often appears to an outsider to be heavy, slow and frail in the rare interviews he permits, yet is apparently a charismatic, mesmerising, paternalistic personality to his followers.

Turkish Islamism had grown among pious Turks after World War II in reaction to a sense of cultural exclusion and repression, epitomised by the ban on headscarves in state institutions, and out of frustration felt by provincial, conservative businesses, who felt excluded from the elite commercial and political networks privileged by the Kemalist state.[115] Gulen's network included businesses comprised largely of the Anatolian bourgeoisie that grew after World War II and prospered in the opening up of the Turkish economy to international markets after the 1980 coup.

Businesses run by Gulen devotees financed a burgeoning education network in the 1980s that would eventually operate in over 180 countries. His movement was backed by powerful, sympathetic media outlets. Gulen also had political ambitions – his movement sought to place its followers throughout Turkey's key institutions: the civil service, education sector, judiciary, police and military.

Gulen has been in self-imposed exile in the US since 1998. He ostensibly left Turkey for medical treatment, but it's likely that he knew he was about to be prosecuted by the then Kemalist authorities. Recordings surfaced in 1999 of Gulen allegedly promoting an Islamist takeover: 'You must move in the arteries of the system without anyone noticing your existence until you reach all the power centres.'[116] Gulen claims his comments were taken out of context and doctored, but he has never produced a supposedly original version. In 2000 he was charged *in absentia* for advocating an Islamic regime. But his situation improved when the AKP came to power in 2002.

Gulen supported Erdogan's rise to power, striking an allegiance based on a shared commitment to liberal capitalism and Islamic morals, and a desire to transform the Turkish state. The Gulen movement provided skilled personnel who were invaluable cogs in the AKP machine, and their global network provided the government with diplomatic and business opportunities, particularly across the Middle East and in Africa.

With Erdogan's backing, Gulen's supporters in the police and the judiciary took on the power of the Kemalist military in a series of court cases that began in 2008. Investigators claimed that a clandestine Kemalist, ultra-nationalist group called 'Ergenekon' – which had supposedly evolved out of the 'Deep State'[117] – planned to stage a series of terrorist attacks as a pretext for a military coup. Thousands were detained and charged, including many critics of the Gulen movement and the government from across the political spectrum. Gulen was acquitted of his own charges in 2008.

It is now widely accepted that the Ergenekon prosecutions were largely politicised and characterised by fabricated and manipulated evidence.[118] Many now doubt whether 'Ergenekon' ever really existed as an organisation. The military became ever more staffed by Gulenists – at least until Erdogan and the Gulenists fell out definitively in 2013.

After Gulen had helped Erdogan curtail the political power of the military and much of the Kemalist opposition, there were no other serious rivals left. 'By 2010 there were only the two of them left and it was time to decide who was the boss, because this was really only an opportunistic alliance,' said Nicolas Cheviron, a biographer of Erdogan.[119]

Erdogan was never a Gulenist.[120] As both sides grew more powerful, they began to stray into each other's domain; Gulenists were becoming increasingly politically ambitious, while Erdogan had announced he was shutting down schools linked to the cleric just days before the corruption scandal broke.

The legendary Turkey and Galatasaray striker and captain Hakan Sukur was caught in the rift. Sukur scored 51 times in 112 appearances for Turkey, making him the nation's record goalscorer. His rampaging style of forward play earned him the nickname of the 'Bull of the Bosphorus'. Sukur scored more than 200 goals in three stints at Galatasaray, winning a glittering array of trophies – including successive league and cup doubles, and the UEFA Cup in 2000. In 1996 he scored 38 goals in one season, coming third in Europe's Golden Boot awards. He scored the fastest World Cup goal of all time, 10.8 seconds into a match against South Korea.

Sukur was known for his piety as a player. He was close to both Gulen, who was a witness at Sukur's wedding, and to Erdogan – who, as mayor of Istanbul, performed Sukur's first marriage ceremony live on TV. When Sukur retired from football he ventured into politics and was elected as an AKP member of parliament in June 2011. Sukur was an icon who could be depended upon to haul in the votes. But he remained close to Gulen.

With the impeccable timing of an innate goal-poacher, Sukur resigned from the AKP on 16 December 2013, the day before Turkey was rocked by a corruption scandal implicating those in the highest echelons of power.

Prosecutors close to Gulen accused suspects of bribery, fraud, money laundering and gold smuggling. Millions of dollars were allegedly found stashed in shoeboxes. At least 91 people were detained – all linked in some way to the AKP. Four ministers were forced to resign. Newspapers reported that another round of arrests was imminent, including that of Erdogan's sons, Bilal and Burak. In a leaked voice recording, Erdogan was apparently heard telling Bilal to urgently dispose of tens of millions of dollars. Erdogan denied the allegations and claims the audio was a montage.[121]

In a public statement Sukur had cited the government's recent closure of Gulenist prep schools as the reason for his resignation.[122] The former

AKP golden boy's actions did not go down well with Erdogan, his erstwhile chum. In April 2014 Sukur's name was taken down from stadiums named after him in the Istanbul districts of Sancaktepe and Esenyurt.[123] Later that year, during Erdogan's presidential election campaign at a rally in Sukur's home province of Sakarya, posters of both Sukur and Erdogan were hung behind the stage on which Erdogan was due to speak. Erdogan was looking radiant in his poster, beaming, with his hand over his heart. Sukur on the other hand looked foolish, his hand to his head as if he'd just been caught doing something shameful, with a caption reading: 'Brother, how will I look Sakaryans in the eye?'[124]

'We have no theft, insolence, or corruption. I can look Sakaryans and my country in the eye thankfully. It is important to be able to look Allah in the eye,' retorted Sukur on social media.[125] But Sukur failed to make it into parliament as an independent candidate in 2015, as his fortunes sank in tandem with the Gulenists'. By now the AKP had begun referring to the movement following Fethullah Gulen as the 'Fethullahist Terror Organization' (FETO).

In February 2016, it was announced that Hakan Sukur was being charged with insulting the president on social media.[126] He faces four years in prison if found guilty. Sukur is just one of the more famous names of a huge number of people accused of insulting Erdogan, including journalists, artists, academics, activists, regular citizens on social media – such as one man who had likened Erdogan to the *Lord of the Rings* character 'Gollum' – and, at one point or another, the leaders of all the major opposition parties.[127] Sukur – who denies the charges – was in the US and did not attend his first trial hearings. Sukur's problems would get more serious than a possible conviction for hurting Erdogan's feelings. In May 2016 the government officially designated the Gulen movement a terrorist organisation.

Euro 2016 followed the Turkish Cup and then came the ennui of preseason. Fans began speculating on what the open transfer window would bring. Then Turkey exploded into another political crisis that dragged football into its orbit.

Late on the evening of 15 July 2016, not long after strange movements of tanks and soldiers had begun, the Turkish prime minister Binali Yildirim announced that a faction of the military was attempting an uprising.

Yildirim insisted that the government remained in control and that the rebels would be punished.

Rebel soldiers stormed the AKP's Istanbul headquarters. They forced the state broadcaster TRT to read a statement announcing that the military had taken control of Turkey to protect the democratic order against Erdogan's erosion of secular values. They called themselves 'The Council for Peace in the Homeland', an oblique reference to a Kemalist maxim, and announced a curfew and martial law.

The rebels captured the Turkish military's head of command. Erdogan was on holiday in the Aegean resort of Marmaris – his hotel came under attack, but he had managed to escape not long before. Erdogan was on the run and needed to get on the airwaves. He eventually appeared on CNN Turk via a mobile phone app – the presenter held up the camera while Erdogan made a rallying cry to the nation: he called on people to take to the streets to face down the tanks: 'There is no power higher than the power of the people.'

Mosques burst into life at the ungodly hour, broadcasting multiple calls to prayer, calling people to take to the streets.[128] Erdogan's army of supporters responded. Thousands marched on Ataturk airport. They confronted tanks and soldiers. Rebel tanks opened fire on the parliament building in Ankara. Rebel and loyalist factions of the air force skirmished in the skies above the capital. All the opposition parties released prompt messages condemning the attempted coup.

I was in Izmir for a football conference. Despite being a bastion of the opposition CHP, as soon as Erdogan's call went out the streets became raucous with anti-coup protesters streaming towards Konak Square and hanging out of their cars – they resembled football fans except they weren't chanting, only honking and waving Turkish flags, their faces set in determination. They gathered in Konak Square and chanted against the coup.

Erdogan made it to his private jet and was harried in the air by a rebel plane, but the pilot – apparently unsure who was aboard – eventually veered off. Erdogan's jet continued on, circling, unsure where was safe to land. The masses in the streets were confronting soldiers, many of whom were young conscripts, afraid, unsure what they had been caught up in. Protesters seized back control of Ataturk Airport. Erdogan's private jet landed there at 3:20 a.m..

The police, bolstered with AKP loyalists during Erdogan's time in power, were helped by protesters in arresting rebel soldiers, including more than

40 in Taksim Square. In some locations gunfire broke out between rebel soldiers and loyalist military and police forces, and rebel soldiers opened fire on unarmed protesters, killing several people on the Bosphorus bridges. Rebels continued to pummel the parliament building and dropped bombs close to Erdogan's presidential palace. Rebel jets terrorised Istanbul, flying low and breaking the speed of sound to create sonic booms that shattered glass and made people think their neighbourhoods were being bombed.

As the night went on, the momentum shifted in favour of the government. Erdogan made a defiant speech at 4 a.m. which cemented the sense that the coup was being defeated.

At 6:40 a.m. the soldiers who had seized a Bosphorus bridge surrendered to the police and protesters with their hands in the air. Jubilant anti-coup protesters overran tanks and some attacked the soldiers, who cowered under their blows.

By 8:30 a.m. the kidnapped head of military command had been freed. He had been offered the opportunity to join the rebellion but had resisted. The coup had been defeated. The death toll had steadily risen throughout the night. At least 240 people, many of them civilians, were killed. Thousands were injured.

The general sense, among pro- and anti-Erdogan camps alike, was palpable relief that the coup had failed – that Turkey had been pulled back from the brink of military repression, greater bloodshed and a potential civil war between rebel and loyalist factions. Crowds gathered in the streets over several nights to wave Turkish flags and celebrate the defeat of the coup. A stage was erected in Taksim Square that blared out pro-government songs, including an infuriatingly catchy pro-Erdogan ditty that had been penned for his 2014 presidential campaign. A huge banner was hung over the derelict Ataturk Cultural Centre: 'The sovereignty belongs to the people.' It was a stunning reversal: three years after Taksim Square had been occupied by anti-government supporters, it was now full of mostly pro-Erdogan demonstrators.[129] Many liberals, and leftists, who had opposed the coup, felt uneasy at the largely conservative protesters in the streets. Some noted the irony in a president who had brutally suppressed public demonstrations and railed against the evils of social media, depending on them to save his skin.

Although the coup plotters had used Kemalist tropes, few were buying that. Suspicions fell on the Gulen movement. The government were adamant that Gulen and his movement were responsible, although some Turkish officials said privately that a Gulenist core was joined by other officers.[130] Gulen denied involvement and denounced the coup attempt.[131]

While most welcomed the failure of the coup, some likened Erdogan's attempts to consolidate power over the past few years as his own 'slow-motion coup'.[132] At the airport in the early hours of Saturday morning Erdogan had described the coup attempt as 'a gift from God'. Some feared he would use the failed coup as an excuse to further entrench his rule and crush dissent.

In the aftermath of the coup tens of thousands of people were arrested or dismissed from their jobs in the military, the police, the civil service, the judiciary, schools, universities and media outlets. Reports emerged of serious human rights abuses against detainees, including beatings and rape in custody.[133] Erdogan pledged to reintroduce the death penalty if ratified by parliament – a move that would officially sound the death knell of the EU-accession process. The government declared a state of emergency, allowing it to pass laws by decree.[134] In November 2016, it became apparent that 375 Turkish NGOs would be shut down under the emergency powers.[135]

'If the coup had succeeded, it would have been hell,' said the writer Akif Kurtulus, who is also the general secretary of the Aegean amateur football club Gumuslukspor. 'But now it's also hell for us.'[136] Many of his leftist friends had been jailed.

For Ravza Kavakci Kan, the AKP politician and a vice-chair in charge of human rights, the criticism of the government – particularly around the jailing of journalists – is unfair. 'In any democracy, someone that promotes terrorism will not be tolerated,' she said. 'So if a person is a journalist, if a person is a doctor, if a person is a politician, if a person is a maid – does that give them the right to break the law or promote terrorism?'[137]

But independent rights groups say it is very clear that many of those jailed have no link to violence or terrorism, and are in jail on trumped-up charges, as Turkey is now by far the world's biggest jailer of journalists.[138] Some figures, who had been targeted by Gulenist prosecutors and journalists when Gulen was allied to the AKP, now found themselves absurdly labelled as Gulen supporters by prosecutors or pro-government media.

'It's not a post-coup purge. It's a purge which happens post-coup. There is a difference. The government is not [just] cleaning the state or any other field from pro-coup people, or Gulenists,' says academic Daghan Irak. 'If they want to, they can declare anyone a Gulenist.'[139] For many, just asking awkward questions or doing human rights work is enough. In July 2017, the Director of Amnesty International Turkey, Idil Eser, was detained along with several other human rights defenders.[140]

Meanwhile, anger turned on Western governments, deemed to be more sympathetic to the victims of the purges than to the victims of the coup. Foreign leaders were lambasted for not visiting Turkey in the aftermath and for their lack of solidarity. AKP politicians began openly suggesting that the US was behind the coup and was protecting Fethullah Gulen. Putin reached out to Erdogan and the strongmen made amends.

The blood red of the Turkish flag, already common, became ubiquitous – strung across streets, projected onto buildings. Large, mostly conservative, crowds continued to rally in public spaces across Turkey in the weeks following the failed coup.[141]

The protests culminated in an anti-coup rally – perhaps 1 million strong – in Yenikapi, Istanbul, on 7 August 2016. Posters for the rally showed a striking image of a man, wearing a Turkish flag T-shirt, holding up his hand against a tank. Yenikapi Square became a billowing vista of red, like a vast poppy field. Erdogan declared himself a slave for God and ready for martyrdom. Some in the crowd brought banners and T-shirts pledging to die for Erdogan.

The opposition CHP and MHP were invited in a show of unity. The AKP's nationalist pivot, and renewed war on the PKK, have created a deepening de facto alliance between Erdogan and Devlet Bahceli, the leader of the ultranationalist MHP.[142] Kemal Kilicdaroglu, the leader of the main opposition CHP, said there was a 'New Turkey' after 15 July, using a phrase that stems from the Ataturk era, but more commonly used by Erdogan to invoke the AKP project. 'If we can further this power, this culture of rapprochement, we will all be able to leave our children a great Turkey,' said Kilicdaroglu.[143]

However, by October the state of emergency was extended and the AKP prime minister, Binali Yildirim, began likening the CHP's criticism of the post-coup purges to de facto support for Gulen.[144]

Rapprochement certainly did not extend to the pro-Kurdish HDP, despite it having strongly opposed the coup. Its offices were raided; it was accused again of supporting the PKK. In November 2016, several HDP leaders – including co-leader Selahattin Demirtas – were arrested in relation to terrorist propaganda. The HDP is now the third-biggest party in parliament; its seats will come in very handy.

The new football season kicked off as scheduled, though hardly as normal. Many were understandably rattled by the failed coup attempt. 'We were very close to being the next Syria,' said sports journalist Ugur Turker.[145] It was a commonly heard sentiment.

Besiktas's striker Mario Gómez, top scorer in the 2015/16 Super League season, cited the turmoil in his decision to leave Besiktas and return to Germany. At Besiktas's first home match of the season against Alanyaspor, the fans displayed a huge banner of a black eagle – the club's symbol – with a Turkish flag in its beak, that read: 'This land is our honour, democracy is our right.' But the fans were keen to stress their Kemalist leanings – a flag in the stadium called Ataturk 'The greatest Besiktasli'. After the national anthem they broke into a Kemalist chant.

Fans released messages of solidarity against the coup. The Turkish Football Federation announced the lifting of a ban on away fans at league derby matches for the first time since 2011, stressing a decrease in levels of violence, and the need for unity.

Many important figures had associated with Gulen during his period of AKP favour, but now anyone could be arrested under the pretext of being a Gulenist, and many vied to outdo each other in their florid denunciations of the cleric. The AKP Ankara mayor and Osmanlispor honorary president Melih Gokcek,[146] who had spoken warmly of Gulen in the not-so-distant past, epitomised the overcompensation, claiming that Gulen controls people using djinns,[147] and later speculating that Gulen has been working with the US to use technology to trigger an earthquake in Istanbul.[148]

Like all other institutions of the state, the Turkish Football Federation became subject to a purge: at least 94 people were sacked, including some referees and at least one Super League assistant referee, for suspected Gulenist links.[149]

A warrant was issued for the arrest of Hakan Sukur for supporting the so-called Fethullahist Terror Organization (FETO). A court authorised the seizure of Sukur's properties and possessions in Turkey, and Sukur's father was arrested. Galatasaray later revoked Sukur's club membership, along with that of over 2,700 other members suspected of having ties to the Gulen movement.[150]

Ismail Demiriz, an ex-Turkish international and teammate of Sukur who had made more than 250 appearances for Galatasaray, was arrested at his home in Istanbul. Demiriz's old teammate Ugur Tutuneker was detained and released pending further investigation. He said he had been 'tricked' by the 'treacherous group'.[151] A warrant was also issued for the arrest of Sukur's one-time strike partner Arif Erdem, who is apparently also abroad.

While lacking the sudden epochal shift of the 1980 coup, the failed coup of 2016 will have perhaps even more profound implications for Turkish society in the longer term, and therefore Turkish football. Everything is in flux and nothing is certain.

While Turkish schoolchildren sit in schools with walls decorated with painted panoramas of the War of Independence and busts of Ataturk, they will now study hastily drafted school syllabuses issued by the Education Ministry, which tell government-approved national myths of 15 July.[152]

Mustafa Kemal Ataturk, Ismet Inonu, Adnan Menderes, Suleyman Demirel, Bulent Ecevit, Turgut Ozal, Recep Tayyip Erdogan: throughout its history, Turkey has often been dominated by charismatic characters. But – apart from Ataturk and Erdogan – they in turn were dominated by the power of the military.[153]

On 10 December, a video released online showed a group of young men singing and strumming a guitar in a park next to the Bosphorus. Behind them, on the other side, a huge fireball mushroomed and lit up the sky. They stopped playing. Then the power of the blast snapped all the way across the strait and they scattered in fright: 'What *happened*?'[154]

Outside Besiktas's stadium, two hours after a match, a car bomb had exploded next to a police vehicle and a suicide bomber detonated a suicide vest in quick succession. They left carnage; at least 44 people were killed, over 100 were injured – many seriously. Police were the main targets – at least 30 officers died.

While the threat to the postponed intercontinental derby months before had been attributed to ISIS, this attack was claimed by Kurdish militants TAK (Kurdistan Freedom Hawks) – linked to the PKK.

'With God's help we will overcome [terrorism], and if we die we are martyrs,' said Erdogan. The park next to the stadium was almost immediately renamed 'Martyrs' Hill' by the local opposition-controlled municipality. But not everyone was happy with this language. The father of one of the victims said he didn't want his son to be considered a martyr; he would rather he was seen as someone who'd been murdered.[155]

That latest act of terrorism reinforced the sense that Turkey was still volatile, dangerous and out of control. Three weeks after the attack, in a part of Besiktas district not much further up the Bosphorus from the stadium, an ISIS gunman opened fire in the Reina nightclub, killing at least 39 and injuring dozens more. It was New Year's Eve, and that was how Turkey began 2017.

It's hard to recall Vinnie Jones scoring many goals, except maybe the odd, ugly toe punt or a clumsy own goal. But in *Reis* – 'Chief' – the hagiographic biopic of Erdogan released in 2017, one scene features Recep Tayyip Beckenbauer scoring with a spectacular overhead kick.

The film opens in a teahouse with a report coming over the radio that Adnan Menderes has been executed.[156] *Reis* goes on to depict Erdogan's early life and his rise to prominence, ending in 1999 when he was imprisoned. The film portrays him in a recognisable vein: as a tough, heroic, populist figure – championing the conservative, poor, pious masses that have long been repressed by the secular elite. At one point in the film Erdogan fearlessly defies death threats after refusing to take a bribe: 'A person dies once. If we are going to die, let's die like men,' he declares in a ripe and resonant voice – a line he has used in his actual speeches. In another scene he rescues a puppy from a well.

The film was released during the run-up to a referendum in April 2017 on changes to the constitution that Erdogan sought to vastly extend his powers – citing the various threats the country faces.

Football governing bodies are – at least according to the regulations of UEFA and FIFA – supposed to stay out of politics. However, the Turkish Football Federation's president Yildirim Demiroren openly supported Erdogan's referendum campaign, saying that he hoped Turkey would vote 'yes' to the proposed changes.[157] The federation allegedly suspended a referee in Sinop who called for a 'no' vote.[158] Major Turkish footballers, such as Arda Turan, Burak Yilmaz and former Fenerbahce legend Ridvan Dilmen, expressed strong support for Erdogan's 'yes' campaign.[159] The stars received criticism from some fans on social media – with many fans campaigning for a 'no' vote. Sol Acik, a left-wing Fenerbahce fan group, implied their support for Dilmen had died: 'We commemorate with deep sorrow and regret the death of Ridvan Dilmen 1962–2017,' they wrote on Twitter.[160]

Erdogan narrowly won with just over 51 per cent of the vote. The victory will change Turkey's parliamentary system to an executive presidency with sweeping powers, removing any credible oversight and effectively entrenching one-man rule and a political system that is shaped to fit Erdogan. The move also resets the clock on the two-term limit, allowing Erdogan potentially to rule until 2029.[161]

Erdogan dismissed the narrowness of the victory with a football analogy: 'It does not matter whether you win a match by 1–0 or 5–0; it only matters who wins the match.'[162] But politics is not football, and this was a victory secured by the ugliest of muddy goalmouth scrambles, and many believe this match was fixed.

The referendum campaign was held under a state of emergency, with the government enjoying a near monopoly on state resources, a cowed and controlled media, significant repression and intimidation of the opposition voice, and a xenophobic discourse that included Erdogan calling various European countries 'Nazis' in disputes over political rallies. There were also multiple accounts of voting irregularities and a last-minute change to the voting law to scrap a regulation on only accepting officially 'stamped' ballot papers that was meant to guard against fraud. The word 'hayir' – 'no' – became suspect in all kinds of contexts.

Yet the narrowness of the 'Evet' – 'Yes' – win under such circumstances shows there is huge opposition to the direction in which Erdogan is taking the country – Erogan lost the vote in the cities of Istanbul, Ankara and Izmir. Even the box office figures for Reis were disappointing, with just 67,000 viewers in the first weekend.[163]

A cult of personality has grown ever stronger around Erdogan, who is increasingly projected as the core of the Turkish political system – the 'Reis' who embodies the state. A pervasive narrative in much of the media and the government's discourse claims Turkey is essentially reliving events of the early twentieth century and that Erdogan is akin to a mythologised Ataturk in 1919, the only leader and saviour who can single-handedly protect the nation from the many enemies it supposedly faces, within and abroad.[164] 'Our president is like the piece which holds Muslim prayer beads together,' said the actor Reha Beyoglu, who plays Erdogan in Reis, at the film's premiere. 'If it breaks off, the beads will scatter.'[165]

The state-is-Erdogan narrative therefore demands vigilance, militarism and unquestioning loyalty to the 'Reis' for Turkey to survive; it articulates an exclusive version of what it means to be Turkish, with a heavy emphasis on 'traitors' and a xenophobic reading of the wider world.[166]

Erdogan has always sought allies in the state to achieve his objectives. The alliance with the Gulenists failed; now, ultranationalists and cranky Eurasianists are gaining influence, as are perhaps other religious orders such as the Suleymancis. It is not known who exactly is replacing purged officials, and if there is a new pattern or prominent grouping emerging, but it seems those chosen are likely cadres whose loyalty to Erdogan trumps any other concern, such as basic competence.[167]

What is the cost of embracing and resurrecting such frothy-mouthed nationalism? And what happens to a state and a legal system that is built to fit one individual – accorded vast, autocratic powers – once that person is no longer there? Clues and indications may be gleaned throughout football, as the various tensions and trends in Turkey are reflected in the sport.

Stadiums can become barometers of political temperature when other forms and venues of expression are repressed.[168]

In the café in Mesken, Bursa, the trauma of the 1980 coup was still felt by Dinamo Mesken's surviving veterans. After umpteen glasses of tea, we left the café en masse. The gaggle of old friends walked uphill, nattering away, and as we made our way through neighbourhoods of fading IKEA, pop-up-style apartment blocks, we could look down on Bursa laid out below, or up at soaring snow-peaked mountains looming ahead. We reached a football pitch enclosed in metal fencing. Players were warming up on the pitch, hands on haunches, cycling their legs in the air. Inside the clubhouse was a bright hubbub of chatter, as people sat at tables covered with soft pink tablecloths, smoking, drinking tea, playing cards. People upstairs were watching a televised match between Bursaspor and Besiktas, signalled by intermittent roars and the stamping of feet.

Ege Berensel's work on Dinamo Mesken had brought up buried, painful memories, but it also inspired surviving members to restart the team, something they still didn't deem possible in the 1980s and 1990s. It seems long ago now, but the AKP's early tenure was a time of relative liberalism, which opened up civil society and went further in rowing back on some of the painful legacies of the 1980 coup.

Vedat Vermez, Dinamo Mesken's goalkeeper in the late 1970s, helped Berensel trawl through archives, locate old members and dig up photos, and was instrumental in relaunching the amateur club – now known as Meskenspor – in 2008. Meskenspor began attracting significant support in the area and was active in the community, bringing people together, encouraging kids to play sports. Vermez still wanted to rename the club 'Dinamo Mesken' officially – 'to recreate the spirit of the football club,' he said.[169]

But the nickname that got them shut down in 1981 could equally be deemed an attack on 'national values' today. Under the post-15 July purge, it is again conceivable that some football clubs deemed to be politically suspect could be shut down.

'When the club re-formed in 2008 we showed that we weren't guilty,' said Omer Severgun, 53, a former Dinamo Mesken player. 'We care about friendship, respect, fair play – we grew up like this. This club is a very good example for the country.'[170]

Tunckanat Yegin was an administrator of the club in the 1970s, and at 69 he was the oldest member of the group. With shining eyes he warned me not to ask how passionate he is about the club, before answering the question himself. He said he was suffering from serious health problems: 'I feel an obligation to live because of this club. It's my family.'[171]

2

The Battle for Ankara

Among all the hardcore fans in Turkish football, perhaps the most fanatical are those of Ankaragucu – by far the most supported club from Turkey's capital city. For many fans, the club is their lives – and ambitious people have tried to harness its stature as a tool of power and prestige.

'Most Ankaragucu fans are really poor,' said Burak,[1] a member of an Ankaragucu fan group called Sokak – 'Street'. 'We lose everything in our lives, so we have to win something when we are supporting our team.' The ire of Ankaragucu can be dangerous, and their passion can quickly shift into violence; they are renowned across Turkey for hooliganism.

From the outset it was clear that Burak was a rascal. His face was usually fixed in a high-voltage grin, and he revelled in the notoriety of being a die-hard Ankaragucu fan. 'I fought so many times for my team,' he said, while knocking back beer in an Ankara bar. The worst time of his life was being banned from attending Ankaragucu matches for two years. In fairness, he did hit someone over the head with a rock. 'I had to injure them,' he insisted. 'They were attacking our bus. There were lots of drugs on board and if they'd found them it would have been very bad.'

Being banned was hell: 'I would hang out with my friends and then they would go to the game, and I would go to the police station and sign in,' he said, his grin dimming briefly. 'The worst kind of isolation you can get.' His love for Ankaragucu is unconditional: romantic, platonic and tribal. All his friends are Ankaragucu fans – he sees them as brothers, even if some of them are a bit crazy and wayward. One of his friends became famous for biting a mounted police horse, which bolted: 'We were talking about this for many years.'

I was in town for an early-season Ankaragucu match. Until relatively recently, Ankaragucu were used to playing the likes of Fenerbahce and Galatasaray in the Super League. In the 1999/2000 UEFA Cup they famously defeated Atlético Madrid 1–0 in Ankara, before losing the away leg 3–0.

But on a day shimmering with heat in Turkey's capital, they were taking on significantly less illustrious cross-city opponents in the third tier of the Turkish football league.

'Ankaragucu vs Keciorengucu is like Liverpool vs Scunthorpe,' said Jim Chalmers – a long-standing fan from Scotland,[2] who began going to Ankaragucu matches in the 1980s and became intoxicated by the passion of the fans. 'No disrespect to Scunthorpe,' he added.[3]

This club has long been mired in a crisis wrought by ambition and politics. As I followed Ankaragucu across a chaotic, dramatic season, it seemed at times that they were struggling to survive as much as to bounce back, and their recent story revealed something profound about the power of football clubs in Turkey.

Ankaragucu was originally formed in 1910 under another name by armament workers in Istanbul – the factory and the club relocated to Ankara during the War of Independence. It later became known as 'Ankaragucu' – 'the power of Ankara'. Alongside Ataturk's mausoleum at Anitkabir, the club became one of Ankara's biggest 'names'.

Ankaragucu share one the most legendary and enduring friendships in Turkish football with Bursaspor, their 'brother' team. In the early 1990s, Abdulkerim Bayraktar – a Bursaspor fan – began attending Ankaragucu matches as a student in the capital, forging connections between the clubs. The bonds between the fans grew stronger after Bayraktar was killed by the PKK during military service in 1993. The fans chant for each other's teams during matches, and both Anatolian clubs share a forceful Turkish nationalism, as well as antipathy towards Istanbul.

While Istanbul is Turkey's economic and cultural powerhouse, Ankara is at the heart of the centralised Turkish state. Ankaragucu's stature, position and history have often attracted the attention of Turkey's key political figures. At the time of the 1980 military coup there were no Ankara teams in the top division. In the 1980/81 season, Ankaragucu, then in the second tier of Turkish football, went on a giant-killing cup run, defeating Besiktas and Fenerbahce to reach the final. Ankaragucu's president, Sabri Mermutlu, suggested that the club should be promoted in recognition of the centenary of Ataturk's birth.[4]

Kenan Evren, the general who led the 1980 coup, also mused aloud that the capital city should have a top-flight team. The Turkish Football Federation – apparently by Evren's decree – altered the rules to allow lower-tier winners of the cup to gain promotion to the top flight.[5] After Ankaragucu beat Boluspor in the May 1981 cup final, Evren presented the team with their trophy, and they duly gained promotion.

The centre of Ankara feels haunted by the spectre of a half-forgotten utopia. A series of imposing, utilitarian state buildings line its long boulevards, alongside clipped and groomed parks. The city centre is almost Soviet in its fussy planning – the many footbridges traversing busy arteries are scarcely used by pedestrians, who prefer to dodge traffic in the road. Central districts like Cankaya are also home to many trendy bars, galleries and restaurants – a far cry from how many of the city's inhabitants live, in scrappy outlying districts like Kecioren, full of tower blocks and mosques. These peripheral areas house a largely working-class, often conservative and pious population – places where both the AKP and Ankaragucu find large (not necessarily mutual) support.

There was no animosity between Ankaragucu and Keciorengucu supporters – many Keciorengucu fans also support Ankaragucu. Kecioren's neat little stadium was 90 per cent yellow and navy – dominated by Ankaragucu supporters. Gecekondu – Ankaragucu's largest and most fearsome supporters' group – maintained a raucous display behind one of the goals, tirelessly chanting and pogoing in the hot September sun. The name 'Gecekondu' refers to the slums that were thrown up in the periphery and interstices of the city in the late 1940s and 1950s – and in later waves of urbanisation in the 1980s and 1990s – as Ankara's population soared.[6]

The match was high in industry and low in skill. Simple passes were shanked out of play. A black spray residue from pieces of rubber on the artificial pitch tracked the movements of the players' feet and the ball, when it was in contact with the pitch (several long balls searched out phantom players).

It remained scoreless until Ankaragucu snatched victory in the final minutes with a smartly taken goal. In the aftermath of the goal, some commotion broke out between the players, and when the final whistle went there was an unusual pitch invasion – men in suits, club officials, strode onto the field and fuelled the simmering aggravation. The Ankaragucu fans went from 0 to 100 in about three seconds, rushing down to the fences surrounding the pitch, screaming abuse at the opposing players as they left the field. Missiles were thrown, and a large man scaled and rocked the fence like an antagonised silverback in captivity.

Outside the stadium, all the tension was forgotten in the mad, honking celebrations. Fans hung out of car windows and chanted. Crammed buses, with bodies crushed against the doors, rocked with the passion of the terraces as they made their way through Kecioren's streets.

Kecioren is where it all began for the long-standing AKP mayor of the city, the colourful and somewhat crazed Ibrahim Melih Gokcek. He was born in the district in 1948 and became the local mayor in the 1980s, after the military junta of the 1980 coup gave way to a civilian government. Gokcek joined the Motherland Party led by prime minister Turgut Ozal, which took a keen interest in football, using the sport to boost the popularity and prestige of local and national politicians.

As mayor of Ankara, Gokcek's footballing interventions played a decisive role in Ankaragucu's strife – and the rise of a new, hated rival elsewhere in the city. Footballing shenanigans in Ankara say something important about political symbolism in Turkey and the rise of the AKP: a story of decline and eclipse – of dinosaurs, robots and Ottoman knights, of high-profile interventions and brawls, fans suffering for their much-beloved club, and football used as an instrument of power.

'Watch out for the dinosaurs!'

Melih Gokcek, mayor of Ankara since 1994, is a controversial figure. Some characterise him as a kind of mini version of his contemporary and boss Recep Tayyip Erdogan, with his neat side-parting and moustache, charisma and overbearing manner. Both men share interests in football and construction, a penchant for conspiracy theories, a passion for idiosyncratic prestige projects, and a supreme talent for conflict.

It's not clear how Gokcek has time to run Ankara, given his relentless social media activity. He typically posts in barrages of capital letters and his enemies and grudges are legion, running the spectrum from any regular citizen who annoys him, to foreign diplomats, to some in the higher echelons of his own party. Sometimes he exhausts all his foes into silence, and asks – triumphantly at first, and later rather more anxiously – 'Where have they gone?'[7]

'Watch out for the dinosaurs!' cautioned a friend from Istanbul when she heard I was going to Ankara. At first I thought that she was being rude about the inhabitants, whom she perhaps considered unfashionable and dated by Istanbul standards. But it transpired that she was referring to

Mayor Gokcek's municipality-funded 'Ankapark', a notorious amusement park filled with life-size dinosaur models.[8]

While the dinosaurs were tacky and comical, his giant robots were unnerving; one day a six-metre-high robot statue appeared on an Ankara roundabout – an intimidating Transformers-like machine.[9] When Turkey's Chamber of Architects and Engineers complained about the use of taxpayers' money on the statue, the mayor angrily warned them to 'respect our robot.'[10]

Gokcek's other hobbies include football. As mayor of Kecioren, he had used the neighbourhood football team to boost his prestige. In 1988 Gokcek held an emergency meeting at Hacettepe football club, without the knowledge of most club members, and got himself elected as club president by 48 votes to one. He changed the name of the club to 'Keciorengucu': 'the power of Kecioren'.[11]

After becoming mayor of Ankara, Gokcek became president of the city's municipal football team. When a legal change meant that mayors could no longer directly manage clubs, he simply became 'honorary chairman' and gave his son Ahmet an informal role at the club.

Melih Gokcek had been elected mayor of Ankara in 1994 as a member of the Islamist Welfare Party, at the same time that Erdogan was elected mayor of Istanbul with the same party. Islamist movements had emerged relatively unscathed from the political purges following the 1980 coup and were well placed to win power in many poorer municipalities and to step into the vacuums in local communities created by the decimation of leftist activism, which had been prevalent in the *gecekondu* areas.

Under the Motherland Party, municipalities had gained more fiscal autonomy from central government. The AKP's antecedents moved into poorer areas and began providing welfare and social services, and gaining support. Mayor Gokcek has made use of 'social aid': delivering aid packages of coal and food, and sometimes even kitchen appliances, to poorer residents, particularly around elections, while at the same time forging patronage networks between the municipality and large businesses in the city.[12]

Municipalities of all political parties – right and left – also focused more attention on football clubs, as the importance of the sport increased.[13] Football is a vital element in Turkey's nexus of power. 'When you are a president of one of the big clubs, every door opens,' says Ibrahim Altinsay, head of a production company and an ex-member of the board of Besiktas.

'You can be friends with the politicians, the banks, and the big companies. It gives you political power.'[14]

Football can also ensure loyalty and support from businesses and groups, whether big companies, politicians, important people in key neighbourhoods, or leading ultras and supporters' groups – a way of drawing them into a patronage network. At the higher end it can be connections and big business opportunities and benefits; at the lower end it can mean money, and help for small businesses, like those operating kiosks and car parks. Ambitious figures in Turkey are often also keen that football clubs are not used by rivals to challenge them or undermine their authority.

Meanwhile, the structure of Turkish football clubs requires that presidents have to win elections, while also giving them access to credit. Rather than being private companies, most clubs are member-based associations, in which the club's management are not personally liable for the club's debts. Ambitious presidents are tempted to borrow money, safe in the knowledge they can leave their successors with the burden.[15]

'All political parties have used football,' says football academic and writer Tanil Bora. 'The AKP is just doing it more energetically. They are penetrating deeply into all fields, not just football. It's not something new, but the dosage is very high from the AKP.'[16]

In 1999 Gokcek was re-elected as mayor with the Virtue Party, the Islamist successor to the Welfare Party. When that party was closed down, Ankara's mayor joined Erdogan in the AKP and was re-elected in 2004 and again in 2009.

Under Mayor Gokcek, Ankara's municipality club first reached the Super League in 2004, and in 2005 the football team was separated from the club's other sporting branches and renamed 'Ankaraspor'. But as a municipality team with a remote stadium, it attracted few fans. It was a frustrating situation for the ambitious mayor and Gokcek turned to Ankaragucu.

Ankaragucu had been struggling on and off the pitch, as a series of expensive and unwise transfers landed the club in a morass of debt, growing interest payments and spiralling wages. It had also frequently been led by presidents linked to rival political parties opposed to the AKP.

By 2009 Ankaragucu was in poor shape, battling relegation from the Super League. The club's president wanted to leave, and the mayor made a move. His son Ahmet ran unopposed and was elected club president. Despite Ankaragucu's long history, it has never won the national league – no Ankara team ever has. 'With its magnificent supporters and our support,

Ankaragucu may be the club to bring the trophy to Ankara,' said Mayor Gokcek.[17]

Gokcek had largely forgotten about the municipality team. 'Ankara's team will be Ankaragucu,' he declared.[18] There was some talk of merging the clubs – Ankaragucu's name, supporters, players and history would be aligned with the financial clout of the municipality. Although this idea fell through, several Ankaraspor players were soon transferred to Ankaragucu. 'Ankaragucu's name was very important for Gokcek – he wanted to take this brand,' says sociologist and Sokak member Mustafa Berkay Aydin.[19]

However, the football federation ruled that the mayor's move to install his son and take over Ankaragucu, while retaining links to the municipal team Ankaraspor, was a clear conflict of interest. The municipal team were relegated from the league.

Meanwhile, Ankaragucu's financial problems soared under Ahmet Gokcek's presidency, as wages and transfer fees on big money signings went unpaid. The club's debt ballooned from an already parlous 15 million TL[20] to 90 million TL.[21] Unpaid players terminated their contracts and left the club as free agents.

The ex-Aston Villa and England striker Darius Vassell was one of Ankaragucu's marquee signings in 2009 under Ahmet Gokcek's predecessor, Cengiz Topel Yildirim, who was linked to the opposition CHP. Vassell was mobbed at the airport by hundreds of fans, who gave him a hero's welcome – draping scarves over his neck, chanting his name and lighting flares. This was before he had even signed for the club – he was just in town to discuss a possible move. In a video uploaded to YouTube, a bewildered Vassell flinches as a firecracker explodes.[22]

The mayor's son Ahmet became president not long after Vassell joined the club. Vassell struggled to adapt to life in Ankara and documented his experiences online in articulate streams of consciousness: he was upset by the Eid sacrificing of a goat outside the stadium, and struggled with the amount of Turkish tea he was expected to drink. He was locked out of the stadium during a match. The club was in disarray, training sessions were cancelled. 'Lying awake in bed, the sound of the air conditioning is like the engine room to a train of stressful thoughts,' he wrote.[23] He was evicted from his hotel after the club failed to pay the bill. To his credit, Vassell stayed for the whole 2009/10 season but struggled for several years afterwards to get the wages he was owed.

The floundering club became mired in legal challenges by former presidents and board members, and in 2011 a court annulled Ahmet Gokcek's election. Successive presidents desperately tried to get the finances under control by offloading the club's best players. In 2012 a weakened team was relegated to the second tier of Turkish football for the first time since their engineered promotion in 1981, and to the third tier in 2013. The club was frequently on the verge of bankruptcy.

Many of Ankaragucu's fans held the mayor responsible for crippling their great club and accused him of holding an enduring grudge, using his influence to prevent the club from finding financial backers. 'I think that if Gokcek had lost the last [mayoral] election, Ankaragucu would be in the Super League now,' said Aydin.[24]

While Ankaragucu was in freefall, Mayor Gokcek's interest in the municipal club was rekindled; it regrouped and began rising back through the divisions after its enforced relegation. They renamed themselves 'Osmanlispor' – literally 'Ottoman sport' – in 2014, officially separated from the municipality (while retaining indirect links), and gained promotion to the Super League the following year. The rise and rebranding of Osmanlispor is symbolically important – partly embodying the spirit of the AKP and its attitude towards historical footballing and political elites. In its first season back in the top flight, the club was challenging for European qualification and had ambitions to win the league within five years. Meanwhile, Ankaragucu were toiling in the third tier.

A refrain among many football fans in Ankara is that Osmanlispor is a 'fake team', the mayor's plaything, the footballing equivalent of a giant dinosaur or robot. Some fans dubbed the club 'Gokcek Spor'. Burak – of the Ankaragucu fan group Sokak – also regarded Osmanlispor in a dim light. 'They are traitors to Ankara,' he said, before expressing the desire to see them drown in their own excrement. 'So many girls broke up with me in my life. If I got them all together, the hatred [I feel for them] would not come close to the hatred I feel for Osmanlispor.'[25]

The return of the Ottomans

Climbing to the hilltop citadel overlooking Ulus is like going back a century. Houses sag and slouch with age, locals wear clothes that wouldn't have been out of place under Sultan Abdul Hamid II, and stray dogs amble through tight, earthy streets. From the summit it's possible to see across the city to distant mountains in whose shadow Osmanlispor plays its football, near Yenikent, 40 kilometres from the centre of the city – the arse-end of Ankara, a wilderness of winter snow and summer dust.

Taking a free municipality bus that headed out of the city on a motorway, we passed vast military installations and an amusement park in which a diplodocus loomed. The suburbs fell away to small settlements and scrappy fields. When we finally arrived, the bus filled with a choking dust as it pulled into the stadium's car park. Huge statues of muscle-bound, turbaned Ottoman janissaries – Buddhist in scale – guarded the entrance to the stadium. A few stands sold grilled meat and soft drinks outside the ground. There was little else around.

The stadium could hold perhaps 10,000 people and was about 40 per cent full. Antalyaspor – Osmanlispor's opponents – had the 35-year-old ex-Barcelona and Inter Milan star Samuel Eto'o, whose touch and movement remained several classes above everyone else. But Osmanlispor had some pacey, willing forwards and were too much for Antalyaspor, eventually running out 3–0 victors.

If they lacked Ankaragucu's desperate fervour, the fans were still passionate inside the stadium – they kept up a racket for most of the match and each time they scored chanted 'Allah / Bismillah / Allahu ekbar' – 'God / in the name of God / God is great'.

When the municipal team was renamed Osmanlispor, it overhauled its brand, replacing the Anatolian leopard on the club badge with Islamic crescent moons. I met Mehmet Davarci, Osmanlispor's administrative manager, in the club's training ground in Batikent; the facility was all slick surfaces and sliding doors emblazoned with Ottoman knights. Davarci said that the name change was down to the club's secretive president, Sadik Dik, whom he said was fond of Ottoman history. 'And he doesn't just want [Osmanlispor] to be an Ankara team, he wants it to be Turkey's team, that is his dream.'[26]

Ankara was a strange choice for an 'Ottoman' team, having been the site of an ignominious defeat in 1402 by Timur [Tamarlane],[27] the only time an Ottoman sultan was captured in battle. In a match in August 2015, supporters of Genclerbirligi – an Ankara club generally associated with liberal and left-wing fans – taunted Osmanlispor with the chant: 'They're coming, they're coming, Timur's elephants are coming.'[28]

Interest in Ottoman culture, language and history has been revived under the AKP. Ottoman-era television shows have proliferated and *Conquest 1453*, which dramatises the Ottoman capture of Constantinople, was the country's highest-budget and highest-grossing film. Erdogan has increasingly referenced the Ottoman Empire, which is often taken by critics as an attack on the character of Ataturk's republic. In his pursuit of the trappings of greater presidential power, Erdogan is regularly derided by critics as wanting to become a 'sultan'.[29] His presidential palace – built on land within Ankara's Ataturk Forest – is certainly fit for a sultan. It is 30 times the size of the White House and is opulently furnished, with imported marble reportedly worth 3,000 euros per square metre and carpets worth £7 million. But the palace definitely, definitely does not have Saddam Hussein-esque gold toilet seats![30]

Guests have been treated to unusual welcomes. The Palestinian Authority president Mahmoud Abbas was made to pose for photographs with Erdogan on a sweeping staircase alongside guards dressed in Ottoman costumes – replete with chain mail, swords, spears and a couple of decidedly unconvincing moustaches.

It seems that Sadik Dik – or perhaps Mayor Gokcek, who after all has a son named Osman – wanted to sprinkle a little Ottoman stardust over the club, although it has not attracted too many fans of their own volition. Rival fans claim that the club pays and cajoles supporters into attending, and that many of them are public sector employees.[31] On the bus back to the city after the game against Antalyaspor, I witnessed a man come round and collect Passolig identity cards, in contravention of its rules.

A coterie of former Ankaragucu fans based in Kecioren also shifted allegiance to Osmanlispor, allegedly because of payments and economic incentives in terms of help for small businesses. These kinds of payments to buy the loyalty of prominent fans are prevalent in Turkish football; until recently many Ankaragucu fan groups had also long received money from the club.

Davarci denied that Osmanlispor pays people to go to the games, but admitted it does give free or cheap tickets to fans as it attempts to build a fan base, and that the municipality supports the club by providing free buses to the stadium. Davarci insists that Gokcek no longer has any direct link to the club, claiming that he is just a fan. This is not quite true, as the mayor remains the club's honorary president, while his son Ahmet is the club's 'Founding President' and continues to host footballing dignitaries, announce signings and harangue referees.

The use of Ottomanism is a deliberate AKP trope, designed to appeal to conservative, pious voters with both Sunni Islamic symbols and a swashbuckling aura of manly conquest. The AKP has successfully employed religion in its politics, so that many associate the party with Islam, while at the same time using a modern framing of religion and a creative, liberty-taking version of Ottoman history that encompasses fashion and consumption.

The main opposition Republican People's Party (CHP) is the party of Ataturk, but has struggled over the past few decades – partly because of its association for many with a Kemalist, social-democratic elite that suppressed many expressions of faith and failed to identify with the poor. 'Many people think the [CHP] are against religion. It's a very big problem for us,' says Aydin, who is also a member of the party.[32]

Osmanlispor are part of a cohort of tiny, little-supported clubs – such as Basaksehir, Kasimpasa and Akhisar – that are close to the government and which have thrived in the AKP era. 'Just like the AKP represents a new challenge to traditional elites in political terms, [Osmanlispor] is a new challenge to traditional elites on the soccer field,' writes the football blogger and academic John Konuk Blasing.[33] Many well-supported, historic teams such as Ankaragucu find themselves floundering in the lower tiers.

Many Ankaragucu fans support the AKP, but many do not. In addition to singing songs about how everyone is scared of them, how they are going to 'screw' the opposition's mothers, and their pride of being from Ankara, many of Ankaragucu's chants are nationalistic, and they like to sing 'We are Mustafa Kemal's soldiers.' 'It is sort of the politics of the apolitical. There is nothing party-political about it,' said John Angliss – Cider Kanka – another British Ankaragucu fan. 'They are all Turkish, all Muslims, broadly Ataturkist, all these things. They openly chant this, and if they get this chance they do it provocatively; it holds them together. If they chanted pro-AKP chants or anti-AKP chants it would break them apart, as some fans are pro-AKP and some are against.'[34]

In Ankara, though, it seems that Mayor Gokcek's popularity is on the wane. Erdogan seemed hesitant to endorse Gokcek as the AKP candidate in the most recent election after polls suggested declining support. Erdogan delayed his endorsement of Gokcek, before finally announcing his candidacy again, perhaps in lieu of other viable candidates, perhaps because the mayor's sheer longevity has given him leverage or clout within the AKP. Gokcek would point to his development of Ankara and his nomination for 'World Mayor' 2012 as evidence of his success. His critics accuse him of cronyism, haphazard development and gentrification, transportation problems and an allegedly poisoned water supply. His appetite for spats and controversy has not diminished: whether propagating conspiracy theories, calling a US official a 'stupid blonde' or suggesting that women who consider abortions should just kill themselves instead, burnishing his reputation as Turkey's Trump.

Gokcek controversially squeaked through the last election in 2014 – amid CHP allegations of vote stealing – after Turkey's Electoral Council awarded him the victory.

Gokcek is certainly unpopular among many Ankaragucu supporters. Even news that Ahmet Gokcek was settling a 22 million TL tax bill was greeted with suspicion.[35] Ali Imdat, the leader of ultras' group Gecekondu, nurtured a deep grudge against Gokcek – although he had supported him at first. 'It's very frustrating being the capital city and never becoming champions,' said Imdat. 'That hurts, so maybe we gave him our trust and our dreams.'[36]

What a difference a name makes

Osmanlispor's name change has myriad, often confusing precedents and parallels in Turkish football. Sometimes the reasons are sporting: When Goztepe, a famous old Izmir club, was languishing in the amateur leagues, the club decided to merge with a successful local municipal team, simply transferring Goztepe's name, colours, brand, founding date and fans over, and taking the municipal team's place in the professional league. And how is it possible that a team named 'Kayseri Erciyesspor' could win promotion to the Super League in both 2004 and 2005? Because they swapped names with the historically bigger team from the city, Kayserispor, in 2004.

Sometimes name changes are more ideological and symbolic: an old Ankara-based team adopted the name 'Turanspor' in 2015. Turan is the name of a Central Asian region, and Turanism is a pan-Turkic ideology followed by many supporters of the far-right, ultranationalist party in Turkey – the MHP. Turanspor started life in 1947 as 'Sekerspor' – literally 'Sugar Sport' – as the team of a state sugar factory. The factory was privatised in 2004 and the club went through various presidents and names, until club president Orhan Kapelman decided on a Turanist reboot.[37] The club discarded its badge – an Angora goat heading a football – and Turanspor adopted a new ultranationalist red and white badge with a horse rearing up inside a crescent moon, its rider brandishing a banner.

And Ankaragucu's last home match of the season was against a team from Diyarbakir that had controversially adopted the city's Kurdish name of 'Amed', becoming known as 'Amedspor'. The two clubs would meet in an explosive denouement to the season.

'A must-win'

While Osmanlispor were flying high in the Super League, Ankaragucu's season had stuttered. After January they failed to win in eight games and slid steadily down the table. The Round Ball in Ankara blog asked plaintively whether the football federation had banned them from scoring goals. The coach was sacked and replaced by a previously sacked coach.

Despite their predicament, Ankaragucu's average attendances far outstripped those at many Super League games, and their crowds were two or three times the size of Osmanlispor's. But a 1–0 away defeat by struggling Tepecikspor in February ended any realistic title hopes. The large travelling Ankaragucu support were served a spectacle which looked like '11 donkeys who had been poisoned by Raki running about a football pitch'.[38]

Financial problems mounted again and many of the players weren't being paid. The club was docked three points. Perhaps understandably, unpaid players lacked commitment and passion and the fans were getting on their backs. Many fans were back to calling for the president and board to resign, and the bile towards Ankara's mayor and jester-in-chief Melih Gokcek had risen up again.

Jim Chalmers has a habit of saying that every match is a 'must-win'. 'But this one *really is* a must-win,' he insisted before the final home match of the season, as Ankaragucu sat eighth in the table, needing a victory to stand any chance of qualifying for the play-offs. Long-standing Ankaragucu fanatic 'Maniac Kanka' Harun was boycotting the match and seemed heartbroken: 'I don't want to see those bastard players any more.'[39]

Ankaragucu's opponents were Amedspor, from the Kurdish-majority city of Diyarbakir. Tensions were running high after months of violence between the military and the PKK. Amedspor's fans were banned for security reasons. It was sure to be a fiery encounter.

Ankaragucu's 80-year-old 19 Mayis Stadium, with its rusty fixtures and rigging, was like a washed-up, storm-battered ship. Amedspor's players emerged from the away team's strange little trapdoor at the side of the pitch to a chorus of jeers and anti-PKK chants. The swathes of yellow and navy in the stands were streaked with blood-red Turkish flags.

Ankaragucu were unrecognisable in the first 20 minutes, working perfectly calibrated moves, pinning Amedspor back, and then taking an early lead through Hasan Ayaroglu's long-range left-footed drive. But as time went on Amedspor settled, and began to dominate possession. Ankaragucu's fluency began to founder; it was as if thought began to cloud clear minds, then deliberation took hold, then doubt. Ankaragucu hesitated on the ball and over-hit simple passes. The crowd was growing agitated. It wasn't long into the second half before the first signs of trouble. Gecekondu started pelting Amedspor substitutes with objects, and the police trotted into action, which only enraged the fans further, and they began pelting the police instead. The game was suspended for a few minutes until the police withdrew again and a semblance of calm was restored.

Amedspor grabbed a second-half equaliser from the penalty spot. Both sides pressed for the winner, both created chances, but it was Amedspor who took a 2–1 lead with five minutes left to play. A commotion broke out in the VIP stand in the aftermath of the goal. Men in suits grappled and threw punches with the abandon of an exaggerated Western saloon brawl, and it later became clear that serious violence had taken place. Amedspor officials had been attacked as they celebrated the goal – at least five were hospitalised, and one official was tipped head first off the stand and into the stairwell below. Photos later emerged of them looking bloodied and battered, and one had three cartoonish egg-sized bumps on his head.

The match limped on as a fight broke out among the players and the crowd began throwing objects again. When the final whistle blew for 2–1, Amedspor's players fled for the sanctuary of the trapdoor, while fans tore up seats and hurled them at the police. 'Ankaragucu's fans are its biggest strength and its biggest weakness,' lamented 'Posh Kanka', a long-standing Ankaragucu fan, after the match.[40]

The fans, club, media and football federation picked through the detritus of the defeat. Ali Imdat, the 45-year-old leader of the ultras' group Gecekondu, is a bit like an amiable pit bull: compact, with a shaved head and a loud throaty bark. He vigorously crushed my hand in greeting and presented me with an Ankaragucu scarf, but you probably wouldn't want to upset him. We met the day after the match, in his office in a scrappy Ulus backstreet next to a car park. The walls in his office were painted in yellow and navy. He was sipping tea from a tulip-shaped glass that looked thimble-like between his meaty paws, which he claimed he'd injured trying to stop the violence at the match.

He said that trouble was to be expected with the combination of despair at Ankaragucu's woes and the violence in the country. He harboured suspicions over the violence in the VIP area – he thought that maybe Ankaragucu officials wanted to distract attention from their own performance or to gain popularity by giving the Amedspor officials a beating: 'If fans did this they would face a lot of consequences, a lot of us already have criminal records. But these guys are "clean guys".'[41]

The next day, in the more salubrious setting of the club's training grounds, Ankaragucu's president Mehmet Yiginer was also digesting what had happened and, it seemed, trying to keep it down. 'Such events are always unpleasant and unacceptable,' he said. 'However, because of terrorism and the incidents in Diyarbakir the tension is high. This is just a reflection of it to the pitch,' he said.[42]

He claimed that no officials were involved in the violence. So who were the men in suits wrestling and throwing punches? 'They were just regular people who happened to be in the VIP area, not club officials.' This seemed extremely unlikely – who were these regular VIP pugilists? Video footage of the fracas showed Yiginer and others trying to restrain angry suited men, but most people were bent on fighting and it was inevitable that many were officials.

When the stakes are so high for the board, amid the emotion of wider violence in the country, it wasn't such a surprise to see them getting into scraps. As I thought back to the game at Kecioren near the beginning of the season, it wasn't even the first time I had seen officials getting into a fracas that season. These were people who, if forced to resign, would be cast out of a vital circle of power.

Yiginer said that the club's failure this season was primarily financial and complained that they could not get enough support from local businesses. He didn't know the exact figure of the club's debt, so he wouldn't give a rough figure, but insisted that two thirds of the debt had been paid under his presidency. This sounded like a rough figure. What was it, roughly? He didn't know the exact figure, so he wouldn't give a rough figure. This was going round in a bit of a silly circle.

Yiginer pointed out that he was paying down a debt he hadn't incurred. 'Six or seven managements came and each one damaged the club more financially. And I am the last one trying to solve the problems,' said Yiginer.

He also sought to blame the fans for the club's poor season. 'Sometimes even I can't understand them. Sometimes they support only their small groups, not the club. And sometimes they give full support, so it's changeable.' Yiginer suggested his unpopularity was partly down to his having ended the several-decades-long practice of paying money to the fan groups.

Yiginer is a businessman with links to the municipality (he was previously head of Ankara's taxi drivers' association and is now president of the city's Tradesmen and Artisans Union.). He is rumoured to be friendly with Gokcek, though he insists it is purely a professional relationship. Fans are calling for the club to sue the mayor and his son for their mismanagement but, while Yiginer didn't rule it out, he didn't seem too keen on the idea.

Yiginer cut a subdued figure and gave the impression that, while he cared about the club, he didn't much enjoy his job. When I asked what his best moment had been as president, he sighed: 'I haven't been through many positive things.' He thought for a moment and mustered a smile. 'The most enjoyable moments are when we win a match and we celebrate it together with the players. And when I can feel that all the fans are supporting the team and there is a beautiful feeling in the stadium. Other than that – no.'

Ankaragucu eventually finished ninth, the same position as the previous season, in the doldrums. The fans kept calling for Yiginer's head. Some started speculating that this would be the club's last season, that it could be killed off in the summer. Rumours circulated of CHP mayoral rivals to Gokcek taking an interest in the club. Meanwhile, Gokcek was making his periodic noises of reassurance to the fans, saying that the municipality was going to find financial backing for the club.

Across town, Osmanlispor finished fifth in the Super League – qualifying for the Europa League – and the municipality announced plans to build them a new stadium in the outlying suburb of Sincan,[43] much to the chagrin of Ankaragucu fans.[44]

And then, some weeks passed and everything settled into a preseason lull. Euro 2016 was a distraction. Despair shed some of its heavy drag. The fixtures for the coming season were drawn, the tables were stacked with zeroes. The cycle was beginning again in all its hope and madness.

In preseason Ankaragucu announced that it had formed a stock market company and, incredibly, had sold 20 million TL worth of shares, which had paid off much of the debt. It sounded too good to be true. But many of the fans didn't care – their spirits soared. By the end of the summer, the transfer ban had been lifted and the club began clearing out players and signed at least 13 new ones, most on free transfers.

The new season kicked off, and Ankaragucu won their first three games, their best start to a season for nine years. Morale lifted in the shadow of many of the same old problems. Then they lost a cup match – no bother, reasoned the fans, they could concentrate on the league. Then they lost their first league match, then a second. They were firing blanks again. Jim Chalmers returned to describing the next matches as 'must-win'.

The club means different things to different people, which are seldom less than vital: whether it is a golden ticket, a plaything, a modest livelihood, a lifeline, a family – or simply an adored football club.

Whatever happens to Ankaragucu, whether it bounces back, stagnates or slips further, many fans assert that it can never end because of their love and fidelity. Many feel like Burak when he says simply: 'It's my life. My friends are all Ankaragucu fans.'[45]

The fate of Ankaragucu shows the power of football and the temptation to use it as a tool of politics. The importance of football in Turkey creates a desperation – political, economic and social incentives for success that go way beyond sporting glory. The unusual structure of Turkish football clubs facilitates these ambitions, enabling all kinds of mischief and skullduggery. As the next chapter shows, the importance of football in Turkey has triggered accusations of corruption that have rocked the foundations of the sport.

Yet – perhaps echoing Turkey's wider political climate – many fans continue to harbour the desire for a strongman figure to take over and rescue their clubs. Gecekondu's leader, Ali Imdat, invoked the sense of loyalty he felt for Ankaragucu through his love of Ankara. 'If you're not a nationalist of your city, you're not a nationalist of your country, and God help you!' He had a hopeful, cryptic, somewhat messianic comment about the future. 'I think there will be a man who will come and change everything. Don't ask me who,' he said. 'Ankaragucu will never come to an end, someone will come up with a rescue plan. And if they end up playing in the street, we'll support them from the pavement.'

3

'We are watching a puppet show'

WIRETAP: 2 MARCH 2011 – 15:55
D: *Fenerbahce board member*
B: *Aziz Yildirim, Fenerbahce Club President*

D   'I'm on the other side.'

B   'We'll talk in the morning, that man is coming, I'll talk to you before he arrives, how is everything[?]'

D   'Everything is just fine... we have plowed all the 3 fields... I hope it will rain and our crops will grow.'

B   'Trabzonspor went a little bit err panicked, they've got panicked today, I've talked to Suleyman today, he sounded like a dead man... they are disturbed because we won't respond though.'

D   'At the moment it's okay my chairman now... it's quite fine.'[1]

By the midway point of the 2010/11 season, Trabzonspor had a built a nine-point lead at the top of the table. But in the second half of the season Fenerbahce went on a staggering run of victories, winning 15 out of 16 matches, reducing Trabzonspor's lead bit by bit until it had evaporated. Both teams were level on points going into the final match of the season.

Trabzonspor's final match was straightforward – they trounced Kardemir Karabukspor 4–0. Fenerbahce's match, away at Sivasspor, was trickier. Fenerbahce took an early lead, but Sivasspor quickly equalised. Fenerbahce took a 2–1 lead just before half-time and increased it to 3–1 in the second half. Sivasspor pulled a goal back, then Fenerbahce scored, then Sivasspor pegged them back again to make it 4–3.

Patrick Cox – a British Fenerbahce fan known as 'Amigo Patrick'[2] for his chant-leading exploits – was watching the game in a bar in Kadikoy, close to Fenerbahce's stadium, and remembers the final minutes vividly. Cox chewed off his nails, and the air was clotted with smoke and curses. Bar staff remonstrated with fans: 'You can't swear like that, where do you think you are? This is a nice place!'[3]

Fenerbahce held out for a 4–3 victory, 'and everyone went ballistic,' recalls Cox. Fenerbahce and Trabzonspor had both finished on 82 points, but Fenerbahce took the title as their head-to-head record against Trabzonspor that season was superior. Cox and the others spilled into the streets to join thousands of Fenerbahce fans in raucous celebrations. It was their first title in four years.

A few weeks later, on 3 July 2011, Cox was in a taxi on his way to the airport when a report came over the radio. His ears pricked up. With his then imperfect Turkish, he could make out something about Fenerbahce – something about arrests and Fenerbahce's president Aziz Yildirim. Cox was hearing breaking news of a match-fixing scandal on an unprecedented scale.

Sixteen of the 18 Super League teams were initially implicated in the allegations, including Trabzonspor, but Fenerbahce was singled out for playing a leading role. Scores of administrators and players at various clubs were arrested in raids of homes and club premises – including Fenerbahce's president.

Allegations of match-fixing and corruption have long marred Turkish football. Kenan Basaran – a journalist who has written extensively on match-fixing – said that nobody trusted Turkish football before 2011: there were always rumours about dodgy deals, and club officials were often accusing each other of fixing games. 'It was like the smoke of a cigarette; we see it but we can't hold it.'[4]

But not only was the scale of the 2011 allegations unprecedented, so too were the apparent quantity and quality of the evidence. Wiretaps, in some cases supported by photographs and money transfers, suggested that at least 12 Fenerbahce matches had been fixed, along with several others.[5]

The evidence suggested that players had been paid incentives to play well against Trabzonspor and to play badly in games against Fenerbahce or in matches that would help them – including an alleged $300,000 incentive paid to Ankaragucu, who lost 6–0 to Fenerbahce in the penultimate game of the season, and a payment to Bucaspor to go easy on Sivasspor, rivals for avoiding relegation, who would then be in a comfortable position in the last game of the season against Fenerbahce. Fenerbahce allegedly offered money to Sivasspor's goalkeeper to concede goals in that crucial final match: he conceded four, including one notably soft goal when a tame long-distance shot bobbled through his hands. Others had allegedly acted independently of Fenerbahce for their own gain, including Besiktas in its Turkish Cup victory.

All denied the allegations, except for Ibrahim Akin, an Istanbul Buyuksehir Belediyespor[6] player, who admitted to playing poorly in a league match against Fenerbahce for $100,000, and in the cup final against Besiktas – allegedly in exchange for two racehorses.[7] Akin later denied the charges and claimed his confessions had been coerced.

Trabzonspor fans vented their fury and demanded the return of their 'stolen' title and that Fenerbahce be punished. Meanwhile, Fenerbahce strongly denied the allegations, and their fans protested in the streets, at courthouses and during matches.

After the scandal broke, Fenerbahce's first home match was a preseason friendly against Shakhtar Donetsk on 21 July 2011. Aziz Yildirim's face was creepily ubiquitous, not unlike the scene in *Being John Malkovich* in which John Malkovich goes down the wormhole and arrives in a world populated only by Malkoviches: fans wore Yildirim T-shirts bought from the – Yildirim – club store, and Yildirim masks that were handed out by – Yildirim – stadium officials. And Aziz Yildirim's face scowled from posters hung around the stadium and the neighbourhood.[8]

In the first half, fans forced the media to leave the stadium – they had been enraged by coverage of the case. In the second half they invaded the pitch. Repeated attempts by the stadium announcers to clear the pitch failed, until they shouted: 'Anyone who doesn't leave the field is a Galatasaray fan!' This largely cleared the crowd, but by that point the match had been abandoned.[9]

The start of the following season was delayed by a month amid the riot of controversy. Fenerbahce fans chanted against the government, which many saw as aligned with the prosecutors and the judiciary. 'Fenerbahce's stadium became like a political arena, in every game. It was actually the first opposition [in the stadiums] against the government, before Gezi,' says Basaran.[10]

Fenerbahce fans typically felt they were being singled out for punishment, and some saw the allegations as a conspiracy to take over the club. Match-fixing is never just match-fixing in Turkey. For many, the notion that Fenerbahce and others could be innocent or that the prosecution had an ulterior motive was absurd. There were thousands of pages of wiretap transcripts, some of which were linked with other evidence, and corresponded to the outcomes of matches. It would be quite some conspiracy that would involve manipulating the innocent words of scores of prominent people into plots that corresponded to specific football matches. This seems extremely far-fetched. 'The thing is, you have to know Turkey to understand, there's so many things going on behind the scenes,' argues Fenerbahce fan Patrick Cox. 'It's not like England where $1 + 1$ equals 2. Here $1 + 1$ sometimes equals 3, sometimes 1, sometimes 10.'[11]

Like Besiktas and Galatasaray, Fenerbahce is one of the biggest institutions in the country, with thousands of members and tens of millions of fans, and is among Turkey's most valuable companies. Fenerbahce is seen by many as the wealthiest, most politically important Turkish club. While the club's presidents have been close to various political factions, the club has been seen as a bastion of Kemalism: labelled by some as the 'Republic of Fenerbahce', although its fan base is as diverse as Turkey. The financial, political and social clout of controlling such a club is immense.

Aziz Yildirim, a vastly wealthy and powerful businessman, was elected Fenerbahce's president in 1998 and has been in power ever since – an epoch in footballing terms. Yildirim was born in 1952 and made his fortune with a business empire that includes military contracts with NATO. In most photographs of Yildirim it looks like he is about to punch the photographer. Jowly, tubby, suited and bespectacled, he often looks like an over-aerated bank manager about to properly lose his rag. Yildirim is often found pontificating bitterly into a microphone, or berating someone in a jostling crowd; his public persona is of a brash, bellicose, arrogant bully, who adores Fenerbahce, and readily makes blustery threats and insults against referees, rival clubs and anyone who crosses his path. He is seen as a staunch Kemalist, with powerful connections within the military.

Like the vast majority of Turkish football clubs, Fenerbahce is a civic association, owned by members who elect a president, generally for two- or three-year terms. Presidents are generally hostage to short-termism and impatience, typically defenestrated after one or two terms. Aziz Yildirim is unusual in his presidential longevity, especially as he has not been wildly successful at Fenerbahce.[12]

To be a club president for nearly two decades, you have to be adept at electoral politics and patronage.[13] Yildirim discredited and kicked out major rivals from the club, battled hostile elements within fan groups, and likely helped supportive members and fans. But by 2011 the pressure on Yildirim was growing – Fenerbahce had not won a league title in four years. Yet he was still seen by many as Turkish football's most powerful president, the only figure with a modicum of independence from the government.

After the match-fixing scandal first broke, some Fenerbahce fans speculated that perhaps Aziz Yildirim had become too powerful for Erdogan's liking, pointing to reports that Yildirim had recently signed a lucrative helicopter contract against Erdogan's wishes. Perhaps, they reasoned, Erdogan wanted to depose Yildirim. But their suspicions later shifted to the movement led by the exiled Islamist cleric Fethullah Gulen.

Gulenists had already sought influence in many of Turkey's major institutions. The match-fixing prosecution was being led by officials linked to the Gulen movement. What if, some conjectured, the movement had seen an opportunity to take over or extend its influence over Fenerbahce?

Gulen and prime minister Recep Tayyip Erdogan had been allies – but the government saw that Fenerbahce's fans were turning against them, chanting anti-government slogans in stadiums. Meanwhile, under the surface, the government's relationship with the Gulen movement was shifting. The match-fixing crisis exposed severe cracks between them for the first time, in what would become an escalating feud.

By this point Turkish football was already beleaguered by financial crises, violence and political interference. The match-fixing scandal threw the sport into a full-blown existential funk. It seemed likely that scores of people would go to jail, that Fenerbahce would be relegated, and that Turkish teams would be banned from playing in Europe. Turkish football was on the verge of a nervous breakdown. Could Turkish football collapse? *Should* Turkish football collapse? And as the struggle ensued, tectonic shifts were taking place in Turkey's nexus of power.

WIRETAP: 11 MAY 2011 – 23:06
TT: An 'intermediary' in contact with, but not directly linked to, Fenerbahce
SS: A similar intermediary

TT 'Anything yet, nothing, is there[?]'
SS 'Yes there is... I am getting the wheat on Friday... I will have it... as I said before... we will send 4 men... I mean he will give on Friday... I'm giving you the ball, you've got the rest now.'
TT 'Okay, I'll sort that out later on.'
SS 'Tell your men to do something okay... or we will be f...d...'[14]

According to the match-fixing indictment, a Turkish police investigation into organised crime began in late 2010[15] and obtained a court order to tap the phone of alleged mafia figure and football agent Olgun Peker. A subsequent chain of communication led the police to tap various phones including, by February 2011, those of Aziz Yildirim and several of his contacts.

Yildirim and 92 other suspects – including some Trabzonspor officials accused of fixing matches in their favour, such as their president, Sadri Sener – went on trial in early 2012. Under tough new penalties against match-fixing, only just introduced earlier in 2011, prosecutors sought a punishment of over 100 years in prison for Aziz Yildirim.

This was a time in which the prosecution and the judiciary were heavily staffed with Gulenists. The prosecutor Zekeriya Oz had been hailed in the Gulenist media for his role in the Ergenekon cases, and he initially led the match-fixing investigations, until Mehmet Berk – also linked to the Gulen movement – became chief prosecutor.

Yildirim had been known to associate with several Kemalist military and ultranationalist figures, and prosecutors linked the match-fixing suspects to the so-called Ergenekon movement. But the defendants themselves also likened the case to the politicised Ergenekon trials brought by Gulenist prosecutors; defendants cast doubts over the validity of the wiretaps and there were concerns over due process; as in the Ergenekon cases, the match-fixing hearings were held in specially authorised courts by specially appointed prosecutors.

Fenerbahce's lawyers didn't dispute the authenticity of the wiretaps per se. Instead they argued that the wiretap evidence had been acquired illegally, and that the conversations in the transcripts were taken out of context or edited to appear incriminating; that references to ploughing fields or pouring concrete were actually innocent conversations about agricultural and construction interests that just looked bad alongside sporting allusions and flat-out footballing non sequiturs. They also questioned the timing of the match-fixing legislation. Before April 2011, match-fixing was not an offence under criminal law.[16]

Yildirim claimed that he was the victim of 'a plot to take over Fenerbahce'. Gulen denied any involvement and personally reached out to Yildirim a couple of times, but left room for doubt about the involvement of his wider movement and raised questions over the extent to which he retained control.[17]

Fenerbahce executives also attempted to link the allegations and the Gulen movement to their arch-rivals Galatasaray. The prosecutor Zekeriya Oz had been appointed to the Galatasaray board in March 2011 and Galatasaray was one of only two Super League clubs that had not been implicated in the scandal. Fenerbahce claimed that Galatasaray had cheerleaders in the Gulenist media, and linked several notable players from the 1990s and early 2000s to the Gulen movement.

To many, Fenerbahce's aspersions over the evidence were laughable. The coded-language argument often broke down as defendants struggled to provide evidence of legitimate business interests that could correspond to odd references to farming and concrete. The transcripts also featured players openly talking about receiving offers of bribes for fixing Fenerbahce matches – which seemingly left little room for ambiguity.

In July 2012, a court rejected Yildirim's arguments and found him guilty of match-fixing and forming an organised crime syndicate.[18] All Trabzonspor officials accused of match-fixing were acquitted. But – while sentencing Yildirim to more than six years in prison – the court also ordered his immediate release, since he had served a year in jail. If Yildirim could not successfully appeal his convictions, he would be barred from serving as a club official and his long reign as Fenerbahce president would be over.

While the criminal cases were unfolding, a divergence had opened up between the judiciary on the one hand and the government – and by extension the football federation – on the other. In the aftermath of the scandal, Besiktas had returned their Turkish Cup title but, to Trabzonspor's fury, the football federation allowed Fenerbahce to keep their league championship, although they were barred by the federation and then UEFA from taking part in European competitions. Erdogan – a declared Fenerbahce fan – further enraged Trabzonspor fans by saying that Fenerbahce should keep their 2011 championship because their fans shouldn't be punished for the actions of their officials.[19]

The government also made a series of hasty moves to amend the laws on football corruption, drastically reducing the severity of punishments for match-fixing convictions. Meanwhile, in early 2012, the Turkish Football Federation's president, Mehmet Ali Aydinlar, and vice-presidents, Goksel Gumusdag and Lutfi Aribogan, attempted to change the federation's regulations in order to prevent the relegation of teams found guilty of match-fixing.[20] They resigned after their move was defeated by federation members.

Three months later, the new government-approved football federation

president, Yildirim Demiroren – whose club Besiktas had also been implicated in the charges – cleared Fenerbahce and 15 other clubs of all wrongdoing relating to match-fixing.[21] Trabzonspor's fury grew.

While the match-fixing cases were making their way through the appeals
courts, Turkey was rocked by the corruption scandal in December 2013,
in which prosecutors linked to Gulen implicated senior AKP figures in
allegations of bribery, fraud, money laundering and gold smuggling – which
the AKP vehemently denied.[22] Gulen, Yildirim and now Erdogan all had
something in common – alleged misdeeds caught on tape and leaked to
cause maximum damage, which all claimed were manipulated. Erdogan did
not need this – he had a presidential election to win in 2014.

Erdogan and Gulen openly turned on each other. Erdogan accused Gulen
of establishing a 'parallel state' that was seeking to overthrow the government in a 'judicial coup', and began purging the judiciary and the police of
those suspected of being Gulen supporters. Media companies linked to the
Gulen movement were shut down or taken over. Prosecutor Zekeriya Oz,
and later Mehmet Berk, were among those removed from their positions.

In January 2014, an appeals court upheld Yildirim's convictions. In
February 2014, he surpassed Sukru Saracoglu's[23] record 16-year tenure as
president of Fenerbahce, but his legal options were dwindling. UEFA and
then the Court of Arbitration for Sport (CAS) also ruled that Fenerbahce
had fixed several games. His only chance was in gaining a retrial.

Meanwhile, in 2014, Fenerbahce launched a complaint with UEFA,
accusing Trabzonspor of fixing matches in its own favour in the 2010/11
season. The evidence: different sections of the same wiretaps Fenerbahce
had sought to undermine! UEFA and CAS both found that Fenerbahce
officials were guilty of attempting to fix several matches,[24] but that there
was insufficient evidence to find Trabzonspor guilty – mirroring the initial
verdict of the Turkish courts.[25]

In August 2014, a bruised but belligerent Erdogan won Turkey's presidential election, and his purging of Gulenists from the judiciary seemed to
be tipping the balance. Various courts and commissions moved to quash the
corruption allegations against the AKP over the course of 2014 and 2015.
Many of the Ergenekon verdicts were also thrown out.

In 2014 a change in procedural law meant that the way police had tapped
phones and acquired much of the wiretap evidence in the match-fixing case
was now considered illegal. But changes in procedural law can only be applied
retroactively to open cases, and Yildirim had been convicted. But, in Turkey's

freshly purged courts, Yildirim was granted a retrial on the basis that new procedural amendments had been made.[26] There was no legal precedent for such a move.[27] The change in procedural law could be applied retroactively to Yildirim's case because it was 'pending' again, and it also meant that the evidence had been fatally weakened – the wiretap evidence used to convict him was rendered inadmissible.[28]

On 9 October 2015, Yildirim and other suspects were acquitted of all charges in the match-fixing scandal, on the grounds of insufficient evidence, although the court did rule against Yildirim's claims that there had been a 'plot' or that the transcripts had been forged. 'From the first day to today you can't think of all these processes as independent from politics. Things that changed in politics, changed the case,' said journalist Kenan Basaran.[29]

Trabzonspor – pipped to the title by Fenerbahce amid the match-fixing allegations – were incensed. 'They established the reasoning starting from their ultimate goal, which is clearing those individuals. In order to clear the individuals, you have to render the existing evidence invalid,' claimed Trabzonspor's lawyer Erdem Egemen. 'In the first day of the investigation, those people were in jail. Now, they are shown as heroes. So from that point you can understand how Turkey deals with match-fixing. It's like a David Copperfield trick – you have everything, suddenly you don't have anything.'[30]

WIRETAP: 22 MAY 2011 – 15:00
JJ: Intermediary in contact with Fenerbahce
D: Fenerbahce board member

JJ   'Okay, I understand. We already knew that it would be like this. Will we be relaxed in terms of the other thing[?]'

D   'Yes Yes.'

JJ   'So, you made sure of your connections in the building site, right?'

D   'I'm telling you to watch the game relaxed.'[31]

In April 2016, police arrested dozens of people in connection with an alleged Gulenist plot to frame Fenerbahce for match-fixing.[32] Prosecutor Zekeriya

Oz remained at large – he is thought to have escaped to Germany. Mehmet Berk has been suspended as a prosecutor.

After talking about match-fixing for any length of time, battered by conspiracy theories, I would long to be alone in a darkened room, a damp cloth on my forehead and some kind of alcohol close to hand.

Did Gulenists really want to take over Fenerbahce? If so, did they manipulate evidence, or did they take advantage of genuine match-fixing evidence to push hard for an ambitious and politically motivated prosecution?

To what extent was Gulen fully in charge of his movement?

Did someone want to frame Gulenists by making it look like they were framing Fenerbahce?

Or, if Gulenists did want to oust Yildirim, did they do it with Erdogan's initial support or knowledge?

Or did Fenerbahce officials just concoct a convenient tale?

Or did someone want to frame Erdogan, by framing the Gulenists, by making it look like they were framing Fenerbahce?

Arrrguurggrghhhhh

Conspiracy theories thrive in authoritarian climates where transparency is limited and gaps open up to be filled by creative speculation, and where there is a long history of very real plots and coups, and very little in the way of media that is not a mouthpiece for some political faction. No wonder there are conspiracy theories about the Gulen movement when they say stuff about laying webs with the patience of a spider.[33]

'It was not a corruption case – it was a Fenerbahce operation,' insists Mustafa Hos, a leftist journalist who is a staunch critic of Erdogan and the AKP, and a fanatical Fenerbahce fan. 'It's a case to take Fenerbahce down. It was a plan to take control of Turkish football, by controlling Fenerbahce.'[34]

Hos believes that Gulenist prosecutors twisted evidence in the match-fixing trial, just as they fabricated evidence against him. Hos was accused by Gulenist prosecutors of making a phone call from his office at NTV that somehow started an operation which brought down a military helicopter. The evidence against him was produced from a time when he no longer even worked at NTV; the journalist who first wrote about these allegations is an alleged Gulenist now in jail, and the charges against Hos were forgotten with the purging of Gulenist prosecutors.

Some argue that UEFA and CAS could not make an informed decision on match-fixing, because the evidence given to them was not reliable. Ugur Turker, a prominent football journalist and Galatasaray fan, says that the evidence was likely manipulated rather than fabricated, 'because they are giving us some information, but withholding other information as well'.[35]

The Turkish Football Federation went further than anyone else I spoke to. First of all, Mete Duren, the federation's spokesperson, told me that match-fixing is not a serious issue in Turkish football, but that 'imaginary match-fixing' did take place. In the past, expounded Duren, many people had approached gullible club administrators, promising that they could influence the outcome of matches while, in reality, they were bluffing. 'If you really win the game, it looks like they did it. If the team lost then, well, the other guy didn't take the money or the asshole took the money and he didn't score it, or whatever.'

Assuming this is true for a moment, isn't it a problem that administrators are at least attempting to influence or think they are influencing matches? 'I believe that every team who wins a championship he won with his blood and with his strength and with his energy and I don't think that this was a big problem,' said Duren, obdurately.[36]

Contrary to the phantasmagorical 'imaginary match-fixing' that does not trouble the football federation, on planet Earth there is a very real and extensive history of documented match-fixing. Declan Hill, an investigative journalist and expert on match-fixing, is adamant that the evidence in the 2011 scandal is robust. 'It's very difficult to overestimate how corrupt Turkish football is,' says Hill.[37]

In the past few years there have been documented cases of match-fixing in Belgium, Croatia, Germany, Greece, Israel, Italy, Poland, Switzerland – Turkey! – as well as in at least 29 other countries.[38] Allegations of corruption and match-fixing have dogged Turkish football for at least four decades. There were Turkish Football Federation investigations into Turkish match-fixing in 2002,[39] 2004,[40] 2006,[41] 2008,[42] 2009[43] and 2010.[44]

There are essentially two 'types' of match-fixing in Turkey. The motive for one is sports related – for a club to win important games. The other, perhaps more common, type is related to gambling – to ensure that bets on the result are won.[45]

Hill argues that corruption in football is not linked to the wider culture per se – some countries that score well in corruption indexes may still be prone to match-fixing, and vice versa. Rather, specific circumstances lead to corruption in football. Match-fixing was rife in English football during the

1950s and 1960s because it was fuelled by illicit gambling and relative depriva-tion, as players were subject to a salary cap and had few employment rights.[46]

Match-fixing in Turkey is partly enabled by a paradox: the vital impor-tance of the game, whether for financial, political or social capital, aligned with the sheer scale of revenue washing through the sport – and the profound financial problems undermining and marring the Turkish game, which mean that many players, coaches and referees often go unpaid, and so become more open to corruption.

Another factor is the deep-rooted connection in Turkey between foot-ball and organised crime. Sedat Peker, a notorious alleged gangster and ultranationalist, has been a prominent name in football, corruption and the mafia over the past two decades.[47] Peker certainly has a colourful CV: as well as being convicted of forming an illegal organisation,[48] racketeering, robbery, forgery, false imprisonment and incitement to murder,[49] he was also a Fenerbahce 'amigo', and worked as a player agent – his name was on a 2004 indictment for fixing a game in favour of Fenerbahce against Besiktas.[50]

Sedat Peker's chief henchmen were allegedly his 'godson' Olgun Peker – who has been convicted of being a member of an organised crime group led by Sedat Peker – and Mecnun Otyakmaz. After Sedat Peker was imprisoned in 2004, Olgun Peker and Mecnun Otyakmaz allegedly continued to run multiple player agencies that allowed them to earn commissions on transfers and manipulate players into match-fixing.[51] Both got in on the presidential game: Olgun Peker was Giresunspor president from 2008 to 2010, while Mecnun Otyakmaz has been Sivasspor's president since 2004. A communi-cation trail from Olgun Peker allegedly led to Yildirim's phone being tapped.

Realistically, Trabzonspor have also been guilty of past match-fixing and corruption,[52] and accepting dodgy funds: Trabzonspor has been given money by Reza Zarrab, a Turkish-Iranian businessman named as an alleged high-profile crook in the 2013 corruption allegations and now facing money-laundering charges in the US. There have been past links suggested between organised crime – also including Sedat Peker – and Trabzonspor.[53]

In the end, love and hate cloud minds, and people often just believe what suits them. Those who insist the match-fixing evidence is manipulated will often readily believe in the veracity of Erdogan's corruption tapes, and vice versa.[54] Fenerbahce will dismiss wiretaps as false, unless sections of them implicate Trabzonspor – and vice versa.

Mete Duren of the Turkish Football Federation didn't believe the 2011 allegations at the time – incidentally, when he was spokesperson for Besiktas, who were implicated in the scandal – and then a year or two later it became obvious to him that it had nothing to do with cleaning up football. 'It was a totally political project to ruin the government let's say. Not to ruin football, not to clean football, but to ruin the government actually and to ruin the country actually.' I needed a drink. I asked Duren to unpack his logic. 'If you relegate Fenerbahce, everything will be a disaster. The broadcasting will go down, the whole of football and other teams cannot earn money and it will all be a big chaos. That's what was apparently the goal.' His evidence for this was that key prosecutors were Gulenists and had fled the country or been arrested. 'If it's a coincidence, I don't know,' he chortled.

Let's bring in the concept of cause and effect: the fact that these prosecutors fled the country or were arrested would suggest that they are suspected Gulenists, who had been targeted for arrest, notably after the 2013 corruption case against the government. However, their fleeing doesn't *necessarily* mean that they orchestrated the match-fixing plot to bring down Fenerbahce or the government. 'To be fair, this wasn't just any prosecutor. [Zekeriya Oz] was the point man in the most important prosecution that Gulenists were involved in – this guy had a record,' says James M. Dorsey, author of *The Turbulent World of Middle East Soccer.*

Dorsey says it's difficult to know what to believe when a prosecution has manipulated evidence that has been accepted by the judiciary. 'You can't, like in any other democracy, go through the court records and take that as some yardstick of what is true and what is not true, because you don't know what the paperwork is worth,' argues Dorsey. 'Now, did they fake it in the match-fixing case? I have no idea. But why should I take the evidence at face value, given the record? And particularly from [Zekeriya Oz].'[55]

Recep Ozcan, a Fenerbahce vice-president under Yildirim's predecessor Ali Sen – and a bitter enemy of Yildirim – casts doubt on whether it would be feasible for Islamists to take over the club. 'Eighty per cent of the Fenerbahce membership is Ataturkist, they support the CHP or MHP,' he said. 'If someone Gulenist wanted to take over, they couldn't get more than 20 per cent of the votes.'[56]

But journalist Kenan Basaran points out that the Gulen movement sought to capture major institutions, so it is reasonable to assume that they might try to influence major football clubs (whether the match-fixing evidence was authentic or not). Although the membership of Fenerbahce is staunchly Kemalist, the secretive nature of the Gulen movement means that links are not always obvious, and members may not have cared anyway back in 2011 when the Gulenists were ascendant. 'And this way they could have gained more control. Maybe not entirely taken over Fenerbahce, but taken more control,'[57] says Basaran.[58]

For many people linked to Trabzonspor, match-fixing is match-fixing – even if there were some wider political machinations taking place. In 2017 CAS upheld UEFA's ruling that it could not take any further action and could only intervene in matches played post-2013 – but CAS also made a striking statement, finding that there are 'serious doubts' over whether the Turkish Football Federation's disciplinary committee and arbitration body 'constitute an independent and impartial tribunal'.[59] However, Erdem Egemen, Trabzonspor's lawyer, is still doggedly pursuing a case with FIFA, demanding that the federation be forced to award the 2011 title to Trabzonspor, cover the club's losses and impose sanctions against Fenerbahce.

Meanwhile, Fenerbahce felt particularly vindicated following the July 2016 failed coup attempt, which implicated some Gulenist officials. Yildirim called for a probe into every championship since 1998 and said the club would consider filing compensation claims for losses amounting to $500 million.[60]

Turkey's supreme court still has to finalise Yildirim's acquittal. If it does, as it surely will in the current political climate, he will sit supreme again as the king of the club presidents. By 2018 Yildirim will have been Fenerbahce president for two decades, but that year an election is due, and Ali Koc, a businessman from Turkey's richest family, has announced he will stand. Koc has impeccable Fenerbahce and Kemalist credentials, and is even wealthier than Yildirim. If Yildirim does lose the election, he will lose some of his lustre, and he could become more vulnerable. A couple of years can be a long time in Turkish politics.

Five years on

On 3 July 2016, the fifth anniversary of the match-fixing scandal, around 30 protesters had gathered in Istanbul's Tunel Meydani holding banners against match-fixing. It was their 210th protest in Istanbul. The protesters were a group of mostly Trabzonspor fans who call themselves 'Clean Football Activists' – part of a kind of peaceful guerrilla activist network that gets up to various kinds of mischief in the battle against match-fixing. The group has taken its protests across the world. The organiser was arrested in Tiananmen

Square, China, after opening an anti-match-fixing banner. 'They released me once they realised it wasn't anything political.'[61]

Another protester, Burak Bektas, tried to enlist Pope Francis in the fight. 'I know the Pope,' Burak told me. You're mates? 'No,' he clarified, 'I mean – I follow him on Twitter. And I know that he always stands with weak and poor people. When he came to Turkey he rented a Renault Clio. So I wrote to him.'[62] Burak asked the Pope to intercede and support their struggle, but he didn't write back.

Perhaps no one has racked up more miles in protest than Ibrahim Erturk, who is Turkish but has lived in Germany for the past 35 years. Erturk has travelled around 50,000 kilometres across eight countries as part of his protests, and handed out more than 10,000 leaflets. He has protested six times in front of UEFA headquarters, three times in front of FIFA. On the fifth anniversary he recalled the moment he heard about the arrests. 'I was very proud of my country when I heard the news, seeing that anyone, even someone like Aziz Yildirim, could be held accountable,' said Erturk. 'Now I lost all my trust in my country.'[63]

Burcin Aydogdu is a lawyer and academic in his late thirties, in an affiliated group that has bombarded UEFA and other organisations with tens of thousands of letters and emails protesting match-fixing.[64] 'I was eight years old when I saw the last championship,' recalled Burcin. 'It was 1984, I remember it. I had the poster of that winning team on my wall. But this [new generation] haven't seen any championship—' He abruptly stopped talking and his eyes filled with tears. 'I can't express how it feels,' he continued after some time. 'Trabzon is a little different, they hadn't won the championship for 27 years. Normally an Istanbul club wins the championship and people celebrate in every city, in every district – except Trabzon,' he said.[65]

Trabzonspor is not in the 'Big Three', but is part of the 'Big Four' – it enjoys privileges that most clubs lack. 'Yes, it has a little part in the crime,' admitted Burcin. 'Trabzonspor gets more [TV revenue] and that may be one of the reasons the club is not protesting as much, and they have political connections as well.' The activists have faced indifference from their club. 'The relegation of Fenerbahce would have caused such a big financial crisis that Trabzonspor itself would be affected negatively because the money in the market would have decreased,' said Burcin.

Burcin believes they are struggling for something almost philosophical about justice and power. For them, too many people are drawn to raw power, whether that is to Fenerbahce, Aziz Yildirim, strongman political leaders like

Erdogan – or even Trabzonspor in Trabzon. 'This match-fixing case is connected to politics, but politics itself is not about ideology, it's about power.'

The institutions that are supposed to be arbiters of fairness, such as the football federation and referees, are seen as compromised by politics or corruption. In Turkish football there is little sense of legitimate competition between independent units on a level playing field. Instead, Turkish football is characterised by socially loaded rivalries and alliances, argues anthropologist Can Evren: 'Every loss easily gets translated to a story of political conspiracy.'[66] Many of the big non-local rivalries in Turkish football relate to past allegations of match-fixing.[67]

Truth is a scare commodity in Turkish politics, like the cigarette smoke of match-fixing that cannot be grasped. The impact and fallout of the match-fixing allegations are more concrete.

The sense of grievance following the 2011 match-fixing scandal is total; every team sees itself as a victim in this saga in one way or another, including Fenerbahce. Average Super League attendances fell from an already low 14,058 in 2010/11 to 11,250 following the match-fixing allegations,[68] and they would fall much further following the introduction of the Passolig e-ticket system in 2014. Some disillusioned Fenerbahce and Galatasaray fans admit to only watching two matches a year – Fenerbahce vs Galatasaray and Galatasaray vs Fenerbahce – because the sense of competition has been so denuded that all that is left is a duopolistic rivalry.

Kenan Basaran argues that the 2011 case was a wasted opportunity to finally get to grips with match-fixing in Turkey and clean up the sport, but claims that the case had weaknesses and the prosecution had political motives. 'Because of that bad experience it's really hard to actually go after match-fixing again and bring match-fixers to trial.'[69]

There is a widespread belief that match-fixing continues. 'They don't have a credible whistle-blowing system. They don't have a proper and effective system to ensure that the players get paid. Nothing has fundamentally changed in Turkey,' argues Declan Hill,[70] while Deniz Dogruer, a journalist, football blogger and Galatasaray fanatic, says that the biggest crisis in Turkish football remains linked to injustice: 'We still think we are watching a puppet show.'[71]

A fan is, by default, someone who suffers. There can only be one champion each season, one cup winner. Even those who triumph are typically put through the wringer. But when the rigging of systemic injustice is glimpsed, it is unbearable, and the sickness it engenders metastasises.

There has been a rivalry between Fenerbahce and Trabzonspor since the mid- to late 1970s, when they were the two best teams in the country. The rivalry had been spicy, occasionally violent, but generally healthy and had enlivened Turkish football. But the match-fixing case turned rivalry into dire, intractable enmity.

Many accuse Trabzonspor fans of being stuck in 2011. 'Would you just move on if it happened to your team?' asked a Trabzonspor fan, who has worked as a scout for the club. 'Now I wish there had never been a match-fixing investigation, that we never found out about this.' He said it had spoiled his fun, his passion, his experience of being a fan. Now he 'knows', he can't let it go – he said he enjoys being a scout, unearthing new talent, but he takes no joy from supporting Trabzonspor. In fact, he takes a kind of masochistic pleasure from reliving the 3 July scandal: 'We are still playing that season – this is how I enjoy football now.'[72]

It has now been more than half a decade since the scandal broke. Corruption allegations, combined with parlous finances, violence, under-performance and political interference, have created an unparalleled, multi-faceted sense of malaise in Turkish football – and Trabzonspor is a classic case, illuminating a cocktail of woes. The club also reveals something important about inequality in Turkey and the fraught relationship between Anatolia and Istanbul.

Trabzonspor descended into a spiralling crisis in the years following the scandal. Its presidential elections, held in early December 2015, were set to be the most dramatic and important in the club's history. There was a sense that, if the wrong candidate was elected, this great but faltering club could founder.

Rebels of Anatolia

The port city of Trabzon is defined by stark geography, hemmed in and compressed between the Black Sea and crowding mountains, which rise into a vast snow-bound massif, isolating the city from its Anatolian hinterland. Pedestrian access to the sea is curtailed by thundering ribbons of roads.

Trabzon was a wealthy and cosmopolitan city throughout much of the Ottoman era. But as Trabzon's port declined, so did the fortunes of the city. By the time the Turkish republic was founded, Trabzon was stagnating.

Trabzon is known for its hazelnuts, tobacco and tea, but is now most famous for its football team.

People from Trabzon are often stereotyped as having quick tempers and a propensity for violence. Trabzon sees itself as a city with a unique spirit – energetic, funny, tough and pugnacious – down-to-earth people rebelling against the hegemony of Istanbul through their sporting prowess. Trabzonspor has been the only Anatolian club to consistently challenge the Istanbul footballing elite.

Trabzonspor – a composite of several local teams – was formed in 1967 and soon rose through the divisions, gaining promotion in successive seasons. Their 1970s heyday was fired by locally produced stars such as goalkeeper Senol Gunes – now Besiktas coach – who once kept 12 consecutive clean sheets.[73] Trabzonspor became the first Anatolian side to win the national league, becoming champions six times between 1976 and 1984 in what became known as the *Trabzonspor Efsanesi* – 'The Legend of Trabzonspor'. Subsequent years were leaner for the club, but Trabzonspor won the Turkish Cup several times and frequently challenged for the championship.

Yet, by the end of 2015, this great Turkish club was in a profound crisis. 'It's to be or not to be,' said Emre Akturk, a sports journalist for *Sabah* newspaper and general secretary of the Trabzon Journalists' Association.[74] Clearly, all is not well when Shakespearean tragedy is invoked at a football club – even if the reality was more often akin to farce.

Trabzonspor was in dire financial straits. Attendances had plummeted and the club was sliding down the table. The club's members and fans were divided, conspiracy theories abounded, and there was a smouldering sense of injustice from the 2011 match-fixing scandal. An empty white plinth stands in front of the six championship trophies on display in Trabzonspor's museum, waiting for the trophy Trabzonspor believe is rightfully theirs.

Three candidates for the club presidency vied for the gargantuan task of turning the club round in a feverish election environment. The presidential front runners, Muharrem Usta and Celil Hekimoglu, were neck and neck, but they were being stalked by the volatile incumbent, Ibrahim Haciosmanoglu – recently sanctioned by the football federation for holding a referee hostage! – who was said to be scheming behind the scenes to engineer another victory.

Akturk said that permanent obscurity, relegation or even extinction was possible if the club was not swiftly brought under control. 'If the club members elect the current president again the club will go [under], that's for sure,' said Akturk.

Haciosmanoglu is bellicose and grim-faced, with a greying widow's peak. He is a wealthy businessman, whose main commercial interest is in construction, and he has also repeatedly been linked to the mafia.[75] Haciosmanoglu was elected president of the club in May 2013, partly on the basis of a grand promise: that he would use his political connections to have the 2010/11 title stripped from Fenerbahce and awarded to Trabzonspor.

Haciosmanoglu's detractors claim that his presidency has been disastrous. The club's debt doubled under Haciosmanoglu to reach 400 million TL.[76] The long-standing practice of shelling out millions on 'blockbuster' signings to buy (often ageing) foreign stars on lucrative contracts intensified under Haciosmanoglu as the club struggled in the aftermath of the match-fixing scandal.[77] In the summer of 2014 alone Trabzonspor spent at least €62 million on players, recouping just €11.2 million in sales.[78] The wages of just three players – Oscar Cardozo, Kevin Constant and Stéphane Mbia – equated to roughly 30 per cent of Trabzonspor's annual income.[79]

The club turned to loans to finance its shopping frenzy. Trabzonspor owed more than 75 million TL to Turkish banks. Interest on debts stretched a gaping budget deficit. By the end of 2015, many of the players had not been paid for almost a year. Despite being named in Turkey's top 100 most valuable brands, Trabzonspor had not been able to attract a shirt sponsor for the previous two seasons.[80] The club had churned through several coaches in that time.

A few years ago, the club was regularly attracting attendances of 20,000 and sometimes filling its 24,000-capacity Huseyin Avni Aker Stadium. In recent seasons average attendances of around 7,500–9,000 have been more typical. 'It started from the season after the match-fixing [scandal],' said Ahmet Hamzacebi, a 30-year-old member of Trabzonspor's Vira ultras' group. 'The attendances began decreasing after fans saw that Turkish football is unfair.'[81]

Attendances tend to be much better for matches against Fenerbahce, which have become increasingly vitriolic and marred by violence. In March 2014, a match between the two sides was abandoned at half-time when Trabzonspor fans began throwing objects onto the pitch after Fenerbahce had taken a one-goal lead. Trabzonspor fans had been further enraged before the match after discovering that police snipers had been placed on surrounding buildings.[82]

In April 2015, the Fenerbahce team bus came under gunfire on the Surmene–Arakli highway close to Trabzon; the driver reportedly suffered non-fatal gunshot wounds in the attack.[83] In April 2016, a match in Trabzon between the two sides was abandoned in the 91st minute when a Trabzonspor fan jumped onto the pitch and rugby-tackled and punched the fourth official. Fenerbahce had been winning 4–0 at the time. 'If there is injustice in sport, if the government or the Turkish Football Federation doesn't give you your rights, then violence is normal,' said Hamzacebi.

Trabzon has staunchly backed the AKP in recent general elections, and Erdogan is eager to be seen helping the club. As prime minister he altered coastal development laws to enable Trabzonspor to build a new 40,000-capacity stadium on land reclaimed from the sea (Trabzon's AKP municipality wanted to name the complex after him[84]). Erdogan – draped in a Trabzonspor scarf – personally laid the new stadium's cornerstone.

Less overtly, in as yet unproven allegations, WikiLeaks cables claimed that Erdogan had installed his friend and former Trabzonspor captain Faruk Nafiz Ozak as Trabzonspor president in 2005 and secretly funnelled millions of dollars to the club in order to buy players, boost Ozak's popularity and overshadow Trabzon's mayor, who was then a member of the opposition CHP.[85]

Trabzonspor is a club with great political significance because it is the biggest institution, employer and symbol of the city – and the city represents a key Black Sea voting bloc. 'Being president of Trabzonspor is like being president of Trabzon. Not just Trabzon, but places like Kocaeli and other areas near Istanbul that have a large diaspora from Trabzon,' says Erdal Hos, a journalist and academic. Hos says that the club's president is more important than the city's mayor. 'Because as Trabzonspor president, not only do you have access to money, you have access to politicians. You can pick up the phone and call the prime minister, and he has to take your call. And the president of Trabzonspor has more influence with the general public.'[86]

Trabzonspor's incumbent president, Haciosmanoglu, irritated some by continually boasting of close personal links to Erdogan and appearing with him in public. Trabzonspor abstained in the 2015 Turkish Football Federation's presidential elections; however, it emerged that Haciosmanoglu had wanted to back the government's choice and vote for Yildirim Demiroren, who is an unpopular figure in Trabzon due to his failure to strip Fenerbahce of the 2011 league title. Five Trabzonspor board members resigned in protest at Haciosmanoglu's stance, with the club's former vice-president Sebahattin Cakiroglu posting on Twitter: 'If I don't spit in your face Haciosmanoglu I have no honour.'[87]

The parlous finances, political posturing, divisions and failure to gain the 2011 championship under Haciosmanoglu were compounded by deeply embarrassing incidents in October 2015. After a contentious 2–2 draw with Gaziantepspor, Haciosmanoglu – enraged that Trabzonspor had not been awarded a late penalty – ordered his staff to lock the referee and his officials in the stadium until morning. Four hours later Haciosmanoglu was persuaded to order their release by the personal intervention of President Erdogan.[88]

After the incident Haciosmanoglu made a weird, rambling statement in which he said he was 'ready to die' for Erdogan, and then added misogyny to his litany of misdemeanours by saying, 'Nobody has the power to make us live like a woman,' a reference to his belief that the refereeing team was part of a broader conspiracy against Trabzonspor. 'To live like a woman' became a trending topic on Twitter. Haciosmanoglu later apologised for the incident, noting: 'My mother is a woman.' The football federation subsequently gave Haciosmanoglu a 150,000 TL fine and a nine-month 'full-term pregnancy' suspension for his shenanigans.[89]

Haciosmanoglu was going into the election in pretty bad shape, but he still had a few tricks up his sleeve, attempting to amend the club's voting regulations to give voting rights to a new cohort of around 1,300 members, largely regarded as Haciosmanoglu cronies.[90] The move was blocked but many wondered what else he would try.

Visitors to Trabzon during the first few days of December would have been forgiven for thinking that a general election was about to take place in the city. One contender, Muharrem Usta, was ubiquitous: his face was on campaign posters in Trabzonspor while colours of claret and blue lined major roads on billboards, lamp posts and the sides of buildings. In the posters Usta's folded arms prominently displayed a gleaming watch and wedding ring. Usta had set up a huge campaign office in Ataturk Alani, in the heart of Trabzon, that blared Trabzonspor songs into the square for hours each day – songs that became earworms, tormenting and strident. Video screens and banners projected ambitious promises, including a pledge to make Trabzonspor champions in 2017, the year of its 50th anniversary.

Usta, 50, is a wealthy, Trabzon-born, Istanbul-based businessman who is said to have close personal connections to Erdogan. Usta is a partner in Medical Park, a lucrative private hospital group in which, it has been claimed,

Emine Erdogan, the wife of the president, also has a financial stake (although the Erdogans deny this).[91] Usta had been criticised in Trabzon for Medical Park's sponsorship of their arch-rivals Fenerbahce. It was widely acknowledged in the city that Usta was the preferred candidate of the government.

Usta would not admit to having the direct support of the government, but said he would use his business acumen and his contacts in political and economic circles of Istanbul and Ankara to boost the club's annual income from 80 to 130 million TL, secure sponsorship and renegotiate loan terms.

Yigit Oguz Duman, a management consultant in Usta's team of prospective board members, denied that winning the league in 18 months' time was just an empty slogan or that it could trigger more dangerous spending. 'Success is a very critical point,' he said.[92] He was vague about how such a rapid turnaround would be achieved, except by getting the finances under control and improving the management of the club.

Usta and his team are most comfortable speaking in a corporate lexicon of business and marketing. Their longer-term ambitions included turning Trabzonspor into a national and global 'brand'. 'Trabzonspor was the second favourite team of most Turks. There was a sympathy and a love for this brand – because it was a local [Anatolian] team fighting against a very powerful Istanbul aristocracy,' said Duman. 'We have to revitalise this brand.'

Trabzon's diaspora was vital to Usta's campaign. Trabzon and its surrounding area have seen huge levels of emigration over the past few decades, mostly to Istanbul and nearby areas, but also elsewhere in Turkey, and to Europe and North America. Usta was betting that there are now more Trabzon members outside the city, and that they would be more likely to vote for him. Usta's team painted their rivals as parochial – especially his main challenger, Celil Hekimoglu. 'Hekimoglu is trying to manage [just] from Trabzon which will limit the club's vision,' said Duman, 'and in the end we would just be an ordinary city team.'

Celil Hekimoglu, 51, had a more low-key campaign office located on the less salubrious main road bypassing Ataturk Alani. He was a visible presence across the city in campaign adverts and posters, but his visibility was dwarfed by Usta's, pointing to a gulf in funding. Hekimoglu is also a businessman but is based in Trabzon – his main commercial interests are in distributing parts of cars and aeroplanes.

'Hekimoglu's team has the story of Trabzonspor, the philosophy, the tradition, the knowledge, the experience,' said Hakan Kulacoglu, who was part of Hekimoglu's team of prospective board members and was widely tipped to become vice-president under a Hekimoglu presidency. 'The Usta team is a big business group that is not close to Trabzonspor.' He said that a football club could not be run in the same way as a typical private company. 'We need to have our president and members based here in the city for the success of the team. This is something about spirit.'[93]

Hekimoglu's slogans invoked the 'Spirit of the 1970s', tapping into the romance and nostalgia of the club's glory days. He had the support of legendary player Ali Kemal, who appeared on some of Hekimoglu's campaign posters in his 1970s pomp of eye-wateringly tight shorts and a lavish mane of hair.

Hekimoglu's team was a bit more circumspect. 'Everyone wants to make Trabzonspor champions! But I'm not sure it is a logical or realistic target for next year,' said Kulacoglu. 'I think Mr Usta developed a slogan for this congress because he is a different kind of businessman [to Hekimoglu] – he likes commercials and advertisements. We are more realistic and we know Trabzonspor.' Hekimoglu's team was preaching patience – they said it may take three or four years to win the league. But that may not be exciting enough for fans and club members who are eager to taste glory after barren years.

The differences were more in terms of presentation and positioning. In terms of policy, there was little difference between the two front runners. Both pledged to invest in the youth team and scouting networks; to pay players through (even more) loans from their wealthy board members; to raise revenue through developing the new stadium. Both were happier talking about boosting revenue than cutting costs, though they promised to end extravagant signings and bring the wage bill under control. Both were committed to pursuing the 'stolen' 2011 championship.

Unlike his two rivals, there was scarcely any trace of the incumbent candidate across the city. Haciosmanoglu eschewed campaign offices and banners and slogans for media appearances. He said he'd learned from his mistakes and needed more time to fix the problems at the club. He pledged to raise a colossal amount of revenue – 167 million TL/year – through huge projects to develop the new stadium complex and a commercial development in Istanbul, but it was all a bit vague.[94] (Haciosmanoglu's team would not provide an interview.)

The day of reckoning was 6 December 2015. Outside the venue, as members milled about, it was hard to find anyone who would admit to supporting Haciosmanoglu. I asked some men standing near to a solitary, empty gazebo with a banner bearing Haciosmanoglu's unsmiling face if they supported the current president. They looked at me as if I'd just pulled down my trousers to reveal a tattoo of Aziz Yildirim's face. 'No. We don't want anything to do with him.'

No one would admit to being a Haciosmanoglu supporter, but at the congress meeting the day before he'd had voluble support and – astoundingly – the congress had passed a vote of confidence in the previous year's financial performance. Perhaps there was a phenomenon of 'shy' Haciosmanoglu supporters, as there are 'shy Tories' – people who won't admit their voting intentions because they suspect they might be doing something considered shameful.

On a television mounted on a tea van outside the venue, Necati Selvitop, a presenter on a local channel, interviewed member after member expressing their support for Usta or Hekimoglu. Finally, one man said he supported Haciosmanoglu because he thought the president was honest and that he'd fought hard against the Turkish Football Federation. Selvitop agreed: 'Maybe our president sometimes does crazy things, but he does it for Trabzonspor.'

Trabzonspor members gathered in the stands of the Hayri Gur Spor Salonu, Trabzonspor's basketball stadium. Notices advised members that it was forbidden to enter the arena carrying guns. Trabzon's mayor Ahmet Metin Genc presided over proceedings from the stage, his voice bossing and booming over the sound system. Huge Turkish and Trabzonspor flags were hung above the stage alongside a giant portrait of Ataturk. On the basketball court below were 20 ballot booths.

It seemed obvious who would win: Usta had the most money, his face was plastered all over town, and he had the support of the government. But it wasn't as simple as that: candidates had to cultivate relationships behind the scenes and curry the favour of key members who could influence large voting blocs. Local boy Hekimoglu was a popular figure in the city, but then Usta's team estimated that 60 per cent of the members came from the diaspora and would vote for their man. It was too close to call, and few wanted to write off the wily Haciosmanoglu.

On stage, each candidate made a final pitch for votes. Hekimoglu sported a claret blazer and took to the stage to a raucous reception from his supporters. He started a little hesitantly, frequently looking down at the lectern, and struggling to project his voice, which broke and squeaked at one point, but he grew in confidence. 'I will bring us together as I am one of you,' he pledged. He said that anyone could stop him in the street and ask him questions. Hekimoglu urged patience regarding the economic problems and said that the club's finances would be available to members in real time on a smartphone app. He got stuck into policy, before ending on some fist-pumping slogans: 'We will show our power to Istanbul again!'

Next up was Muharrem Usta. 'You sponsored Fenerbahce and we will never forget that!' heckled someone from the crowd. Usta remained unperturbed: he had the polished, rapid patter of a businessman delivering a sales pitch. Usta recited 'Selam Trabzon'uma' – 'Hello my Trabzon' – a poem by Mahmut Gologlu, and then gave a shout-out to fans all over the world. 'Trabzonspor is the only universal company of Trabzon. We can't only run this club from Trabzon,' he insisted. He eschewed policy detail for feel-good slogans: 'We can't unite without success; we will win our eighth championship [sic] in our 50th year!' He told members not to worry about the financial troubles, that he had a plan. 'We will take the club on a journey with glories, cups, championships!'

Finally, it was the incumbent Ibrahim Haciosmanoglu's turn. Initially speaking in sombre, lithium-dull tones, he claimed that his childhood dream had been to become the president of Trabzonspor: 'Thanks to God, I got this chance,' he intoned. 'Two years ago Trabzonspor's members gave me this sacred mission.' He said his fight against match-fixing had been undermined by some Trabzonspor members who'd opposed him; that the state of the club's finances had been exaggerated by his critics; that the slowing economy and weakening Turkish lira had compounded the poor financial state he had inherited. He pointed out that the club had reached the Turkish Cup final and the Europa League under his presidency, although he failed to mention that they had lost in the final and had been knocked out of Europe in the preliminary rounds by a team from Macedonia.

Haciosmanoglu referred to conspiracies within Trabzonspor's membership, the football federation, Fenerbahce – steadily working himself into a rage. He mentioned criticism he'd received for holding a referee hostage. 'I did it for this city's honour!' he erupted. 'Nobody dishonours this city!' He ignored the mayor when he told him his time was up.

'Be sure we will get our cup – our struggle against match-fixing will continue full-throttle,' he said, by now fully animated and puce-faced. 'They made an operation against me because of my fight against match-fixing!'

'Your time is up Mr President,' repeated the mayor.

'Actually, we are very nationalistic. We love our country,' continued Haciosmanoglu, taking no notice of the mayor. 'But when Turkey qualified for France 2016 we wrote to UEFA and told them to kick Turkey out of the cup!'

The mayor interjected for the third time and they began to argue. 'Please let me finish my sentence,' Haciosmanoglu retorted angrily. The mayor told him again to finish. Haciosmanoglu jabbed his finger and continued railing against enemies, while jeers broke out in the crowd. At some point, he abruptly finished and left the stage.

Members started spilling onto the basketball court to get to the voting booths. Over several hours 7,395 members cast their votes. By 4:30 p.m. the voting had ended and the count began. Hours passed; boredom settled like a fine dust. Claret and blue flags, balloons and pendants strung to the basketball scoreboard gently rippled and swayed; there was a soft babble of voices. The only significant noise came from the cheerful Hekimoglu contingent, who periodically broke into chants. When I opened my bag the sickly-sweet smell of Usta's lacquered promotional bumf wafted out.

I wondered who would win this vital race: the polished, corporate Usta who was close to Erdogan; the more parochial, 'spirit'-invoking local boy Hekimoglu; or the scheming, truculent Haciosmanoglu.

By 5:30 p.m. early results had begun to be conveyed by observers from the stage as the votes were counted. Hekimoglu was leading Usta by 100 votes after four boxes, while Haciosmanoglu was trailing in distant third. Usta's team was sanguine – they thought that the first boxes would mostly consist of Trabzon resident voters, and as the diaspora votes were counted their man would take the lead.

By 8 p.m. there were only five boxes left and the confidence of the Usta supporters had evaporated – Hekimoglu led by 150 votes. In the crowd, Haciosmanoglu burst into tears and was consoled by a group of his supporters. As the tension rose, scuffles threatened to break out. I felt glad that everyone's guns had been confiscated.

Fifteen minutes later the agitation was growing further, and shouts traded between the stage and the crowd suggested that Usta and Hekimoglu were almost level with two boxes left to count, that it was too close to call, that the lead was inching back and forth between the candidates.

At 8:49 p.m. the mayor had the microphone in his hand and, clearly relishing his role, thanked everyone, let a dramatic pause fill the auditorium, and then, with considerable bombast, announced that Usta had won by 12 votes. Several recounts followed, dragging the event late into the night. By 10:30 p.m. it was clear the result would stand, and Hekimoglu conceded defeat.

On the highway back into the city centre, Usta supporters hung out of car windows shouting in glee, horns blaring, as if celebrating an increasingly rare Trabzonspor victory.

Football on the verge of a nervous breakdown

Trabzonspor's travails are stark, but they are not particularly unusual – more an extreme, bloated example of a fairly common predicament. When the sports economist Tugrul Aksar talks about Turkish football, he generally speaks in terms of cliffs, snowballs, rot, black holes and 'hitting the wall'. Aksar has speculated that Turkish football could soon collapse, and some have suggested that might not be such a bad thing.

The history of professional Turkish football has often been the history of financial struggle, but the financial problems have ballooned over the past 15 years to reach unprecedented levels. In the year 2000, revenues in Turkish football were around €150 million and debts were around €60 million; by 2015 revenues had risen to €700 million, far eclipsed by debts of around €1bn.[95] In terms of revenue, Turkey's Super League is usually ranked sixth highest in Europe,[96] but in terms of indebtedness it far exceeds divisions of a similar size, such as in Holland, Portugal or Russia.[97]

'In Turkey, many football clubs should have gone bankrupt but the state doesn't want them to,' said 'Ahmet', a prominent sports lawyer who did not want to give his name for fear of repercussions. 'If the president of a club was the president of a firm, they would go to jail. But if you are a president of a club you are a hero, and if you leave the club in ashes nobody asks: "what did you do?"'[98]

English football clubs are hardly paragons of morality or austerity, but at least they are held to a degree of financial accountability and their directors are legally responsible for their club's debts. In Turkey, the club-as-association bears responsibility for the debts, allowing presidents to come in, load up the club with loans and walk away with no liabilities, shaking it off as if they've woken from a bad dream and leaving subsequent administrators to grapple with any financial fallout. Players often go unpaid, sapping their motivation and making them more open to corruption.

Much of this debt comes from expensive transfers, which have been sustained even as many clubs floundered in financial strife.[99] In the last two decades Turkey became one of football's premier destinations for ageing footballers hoping to eke out a few more years on lucrative salaries, under puny tax rates of 15 per cent.[100] The Turkish Super League has the oldest average player age in Europe.[101]

While transfers excite fans, there is also a lot of money to be made from inflated fees. Player agents have confirmed that Turkish football transfers are rife with scams and irregularities – club presidents, board members, agents and other hangers-on often take sizeable cuts and commissions from transfers, while numbers are often fudged between clubs and accounts.

There is a sense that football is too big to fail: the AKP government has taken unprecedented levels of economic intervention in the sport, to underwrite football, prop it up and inflate it with capital – leveraging credit to the clubs from friendly banks and repeatedly deferring their tax debts.[102] 'It didn't hit rock bottom yet because the system also digs the bottom deeper!' says Ibrahim Altinsay, head of a production company and an ex-board member of Besiktas.[103]

The state also wields power through the football federation. 'We talk as if the Turkish federation is autonomous, but it's not,' says Ahmet. The government has a decisive role in appointing members and uses its influence through the football federation to cajole and secure sponsors. The sponsors of professional football tend to be linked to the state.

Dire, public financial shame is no impediment to career success in Turkish football governance, as long as you are chummy with the government. The wealthy businessman and current football federation president Yildirim Demiroren assumed his role with the backing of the government, despite an abysmal track record as president of Besiktas, during which time the club's debts soared and the team was implicated in the match-fixing scandal and returned a trophy.

Most economists agree that the value of the football broadcasting revenues has been wildly inflated by the government. The government pressured Turk Telekom to compete in the 2014 bid, forcing Digiturk to increase its bid from $321 million/year in 2010 to $450 million/year.[104] Digiturk – a company which was linked to the Turkish state until Qatar's beIN took it over in 2016 – has struggled to recoup its investment. In November 2016, Digiturk beat Turkcell to win a new broadcasting tender for $500 million/year ($600 million/year with tax) until 2022/23.[105]

When revenues are boosted, clubs don't tend to spend on unsexy accounting measures, like repairing balance sheets or paying off debts, or on sensible longer-term development, such as investing in youth academies. Increased revenues tend to go on acquiring more expensive players and coaches on high salaries. The bitter rivalries that pervade Turkish football fuel competitive spending by presidents.

Turkish clubs are now struggling to comply with UEFA's increasingly stringent 'Financial Fair Play' (FFP) rules and can only obfuscate their financial shame so much. In the spring of 2016 Galatasaray was given a one-year ban from Europe for vastly exceeding the permitted level of losses under the FFP rules.[106] UEFA has also issued warnings to Besiktas, Fenerbahce and Trabzonspor to reduce their debt.

Some economists draw parallels between the debt-driven model of Turkish football and trends in the wider Turkish economy. Turkey's economy boomed in the AKP's first terms, posting record levels of sustained economic growth which fuelled a significant improvement in social welfare and health outcomes, especially for poorer segments of society. There was huge investment in infrastructure.[107] However, in recent years the economic dream has soured: growth has slowed, the lira has weakened, inflation is rising, youth unemployment is high and debt is growing. 'Turkey has a significant current deficit and Turkish football has a significant current deficit. We cannot close these gaps,' says Tugrul Aksar.[108]

Even economists who are broadly supportive of the government agree that, financially, Turkish football is in its worst ever shape. Sebahattin Devecioglu, a sports economist, blamed some of the problems on the struggling wider economy: 'When the economy is bad, football is the first thing sponsors cut.'[109]

Turkey should be one of the strongest footballing nations in Europe: it has a huge, young, football-crazed population. But, by most metrics, Turkish football has become less successful over the past 15 years. Galatasaray won the UEFA Cup in 2000, but since then no Turkish side has reached a major European club final. Turkey has not qualified for a World Cup since 2002, when it came third. In UEFA's country ranking for club football, Turkey has stayed fairly stable over the past 15 years, usually ranked 10th or 11th in Europe. It is poor value for money. Corruption, financial strife, lack of green space, short-termism, meddling and interference, and neglect of youth development and education have led to chronic underachievement. Many of Turkey's recent national team players are from the Turkish diaspora, born and raised in western Europe. 'When you look underneath the football populism, there is nothing,' says Mustafa Hos.[110]

Most Turkish clubs remain civic associations.[111] In the era of modern football, clubs designed largely to be non-commercial social clubs with multiple sports branches have become worth millions of dollars.[112] Some have created separate commercial enterprises linked to the clubs that can be floated on the stock market in order to raise revenue[113] – this double system can provide scope for much creative accounting. The economics of the clubs have far exceeded their legal structure.

Mustafa Erogut is executive director at Istanbul Basaksehir FK, which is part of a new experiment in Turkish football. In 2014 the club shifted from a municipality-owned association to an ownership model. Eight shareholders bought the football branch of the club from the municipality and are legally responsible for the club's debts.

'The ownership model helps executives to make long-term plans,' says Erogut. 'Because when you don't own the club, and you have the election pressure on you, you just think about next Sunday.'[114] Associations are more likely to buy expensive, older, more established, players to gain short-term success, and neglect youth development. Basaksehir are currently building a huge youth-development academy.

Becoming a private firm also makes the club's finances more transparent, as it is compelled by trade laws to open its books to an independent auditor every three months.[115]

Erogut also works for the Turkish Union of Clubs and has seen a draft of the government's long-awaited 'law of clubs'. He claims that a mandatory ownership model and personal liability for debts are important components.[116] It's easy for a small club like Basaksehir, with few members, limited debt and very few fans, to shift models – it is much harder to convince members at big clubs to surrender their prestige and power, and to convince new owners to take on some of the colossal debts floating around Turkish football, and to drink from a dirty bucket that may have been passed down over several terms.

The drawbacks of the ownership model are also obvious. As British football has shown, private ownership does not preclude huge indebtedness or clubs being used by wealthy owners as vanity projects or as ways to launder money, process debt or promote their other ambitions. Under the ownership model, an unpopular president at a failing club can remain in power.

Perhaps there is a third way: clubs could vastly expand their membership and, while retaining an electoral structure, the length of presidential terms could be expanded so that longer-term planning is possible, the clubs could be made more transparent, and the presidents and board could become legally liable for the loans they take on. The clubs could become truly fan-owned.

The ruling AKP remains hugely ambitious with regard to football and has stated it wants to make Turkey the world's fourth-biggest league by 2020, surpassing Italy and France.[117] It seems like hubris when Turkish football's long-brewing economic and political strife is becoming headier and more potent over time. At the end of the 2016/17 season it was announced that – despite UEFA and FIFA regulations and warnings – the debt of the 'Big Four' clubs had reached record levels, with their revenues lagging far behind.[118]

The journalist Ugur Turker praises the government's economic record: 'This government solved a lot of things – to improve the life standard for Turkish people: in health, in public transport. People can touch this, they can see the improvement.' He says their legacy in football is similarly positive: 'They didn't let any sport go bankrupt.'[119]

That the government should be credited because Turkish football didn't collapse is a somewhat backhanded compliment, and it ignores the government's role in the mounting problems. It has had more than 15 years to legislate financial regulation of the sport, even as many clubs have struggled or collapsed.[120]

Some argue that football is only too big to collapse until the government is too weak to support it, and then the failings could become too big for football not to collapse. Emir Guney, director of the Sports Studies Research Centre at Kadir Has University, says that if the government loses an election and its economic influence, or if a serious recession means there is no longer any money for football, then the system could collapse. 'It could hit rock bottom,' says Guney 'which maybe is also the solution to these problems because we need to start from scratch.'[121]

When asked to name a hopeful trend in Turkish football, Ibrahim Altinsay replied: 'It's close to the bottom, that's the good news. It's close to bankruptcy.'[122] Altinsay says the government should have taken drastic action in the aftermath of the match-fixing scandal and in light of the financial strife, to shut down the clubs and start again with the same names but a cleaner structure.

But it's not clear that measures to clean football would even work without wider systemic change, given that the institutions tasked with reform – the Ministry of Youth and Sport, the government, the Turkish Football Federation – are often not trusted by fans.

There remain many beautiful things about Turkish football – carnivalesque drama, red-raw passion, awe-inspiring spectacles, some great players and exciting talents, a rich history that colours the present. Football is also a dynamic site of struggle and an agent for change, as we shall see in subsequent chapters. But the professional sport is also imperilled, faltering, on the verge of a nervous breakdown. It would take a brave and credible government indeed to make the radical changes that are necessary in Turkish football.

Declan Hill says that Turkish football has huge potential, if only they could fix and clean up the sport: 'What an extraordinary gift they could bring to the world.'[123]

4

Stadium Sagas

It's easy to feel cheerful in Izmir's soft Aegean light, inhaling blasts of salt-seasoned air, while strolling along the Kordon, a promenade that runs for miles along the city's seafront. Izmir feels wide open, with the mountains that line its curving, sweeping bay like a pair of outstretched arms.

On a bright mid-October day, I walked north along the Kordon, taking care to avoid being hooked by fishermen who heedlessly flung their rods back and snapped the bait forward into the choppy, copper-tinged water. One fisherman sat smoking, sideways and cross-legged on the wall, barely paying attention to his line, looking like a dapper Greek gentleman with his bushy white moustache, flat cap, shirt and tie. A man dressed for the office and the ocean.

I reached Konak Square, in which clouds of pigeons broke, shifted, re-formed and settled around the clock tower as they were indulged by feeders or terrorised by children. A young boy in full Galatasaray kit stood on the threshold of the ornately tiled Yali Mosque. An image of Mustafa Kemal Ataturk gazed from the municipal building overlooking the square. Ataturk's image is ubiquitous in Izmir – the city is a rare, major bastion of the struggling main opposition Republican People's Party (CHP), first formed by Ataturk. Kemalist, CHP-supporting, liberal/'infidel' Izmir today embodies some of the resistance to conservative AKP hegemony.

The AKP partly built its domination through economics – particularly through the construction sector, which some argue has been used to reward supportive businesses and voters at the expense of opponents, and to form a loyal, conservative and Islamic middle class. Football stadiums are now a major component of this approach: in recent years the AKP government has embarked on an astonishing and unprecedented programme of mass stadium building, perhaps only matched in scale by China.

Not far inland from Konak Square is the site of Izmir's historic Alsancak Stadium, one of Turkey's oldest football venues. The struggle over the stadium became a battle between AKP ambition and dissenting fans who wanted to protect the stadium and its cosmopolitan heritage.

Izmir was a cosmopolitan city known as Smyrna before the War of Independence. Some conservative Ottomans referred to the city as 'Gavur' – meaning infidel or heathen – due to the large numbers of non-Muslims living there at the time.

As in other major Ottoman ports, football was introduced to Izmir by the British in the late nineteenth century and was soon taken up by other non-Muslims such as local Greeks, Armenians and Jews. Football has been played on the site of Alsancak Stadium since at least 1910, when a local Greek team, Panionios, owned the land.[1]

Much of Izmir's cosmopolitanism was subsequently obscured or lost. A few days after Mustafa Kemal's Turkish army had driven the Greek forces out of the city in 1922, a fire started in the Armenian neighbourhood of Basmane and spread to other parts of the city, almost totally destroying the Armenian and Greek quarters. 'Let it burn, let it crash down,' responded Kemal when he heard of the fire.[2]

Panionios relocated to 'New Smyrna' in Athens after the mutual ethnic cleansing of Greek and Turkish communities in both countries in 1922 – euphemistically called 'population exchange' – following the Greek army's defeat.

Several Turkish football teams had already been formed in Izmir by the time of the war, some of which embodied growing Turkish nationalism, and many more teams proliferated in the new republic, attracting passionate support. One of Turkish football's fiercest rivalries is between the Izmir teams Goztepe and Karsiyaka. Their enmity is illustrated by the city's geography: the respective neighbourhoods directly face each other from opposite sides of Izmir's bay. A 1981 match between the clubs holds the world record attendance for any non-top-flight match at over 80,000.[3]

Despite their bitter rivalry, both teams – along with several other Izmir clubs – shared a home in Alsancak Stadium.[4] In 1959 Alsancak Stadium hosted the first ever game in Turkey's national league, between Izmirspor and Beykoz 1908.[5] The authorities, however, had been talking about demolishing the stadium for years.

The threatened demolition of Alsancak Stadium has had a remarkable impact on football fans in Izmir. Supporters of several Izmir teams set aside their bitter rivalries and came together in 2012 to form Turkey's first football supporters' network, called Taraftar Haklari – 'Fan Rights'.[6] 'Trust between the supporters was built through the stadium issue,' said Burkal Efe Sakizlioglu, the president of the group. 'Everyone has memories of the stadium and an emotional connection.'[7]

The supporters feared that the government would follow a recent template and capitalise on Alsancak's prime location. Under the AKP, old stadiums, traditionally built in the centre of cities, have typically been demolished or slated for destruction, and new arenas have been built far outside city centres. The sites of the old stadiums in prime locations are often given over to shopping malls.

In 2012 fans from various Izmir teams held street protests against the demolition – around 1,000 people turned up to one demonstration. It may have been the first time that supporters of different clubs in Izmir came together as football fans in the street. They formed a platform along with 40 local civil society organisations and made a documentary about the history of the stadium. Local CHP politicians lent their support.

Yet, in August 2014, the stadium was officially condemned for destruction.[8] Altay football club owns the stadium and rents it to the other teams. The Provincial Sports Directorate announced that tests had confirmed that the stadium, and an office building housing Altay's club administration, were at risk of collapse in the event of an earthquake.[9] The demolition of the stadium began abruptly a year later, just days before the start of the new season in August 2015, leaving the teams of Alsancak Stadium homeless.

In mid-October 2015, only the floodlights, pitch and net-less goalposts remained. At first glance, the green of the grass appeared vivid against the brown earth where the stands had stood, but on closer inspection the pitch was yellowing, and a hose lay strung out and idle on the grass.

The ground where the stands had stood had been raked by the teeth of a huge machine, which had prised up stones from the pavement. A man picked his way through clumps of earth, looking for something to salvage. There were more dogs in the area than people. A huge hydraulic digger stood as if at attention, waiting to be relieved. A row of cypresses at the far end of the pitch looked nakedly tall, the base of their trunks painted white, giving the impression of football socks pulled up tight over skinny shins. Two palm trees huddled close to one floodlight, as if hoping to remain inconspicuous and escape the destruction. The site had an eerie quiet, charged by over a century of football.[10]

Taraftar Haklari accept that the government is probably right when they say that the rickety old stadium was not earthquake-proof. However, the fans felt ignored and that their concerns to protect the city's footballing heritage were not heeded. 'They didn't connect with the platform of 40 civil society organisations, they didn't get any sense of what we want or need, or what we think are problems,' said Sakizlioglu.[11] They simply pressed ahead with the demolition.

Not only did the authorities demolish the stadium just days before the new season, but the Turkish Football Federation then promptly amplified the farce by fining three of the teams for not having a stadium.[12] It felt suspiciously like punishment for some of the fans. The football academic and blogger John Konuk Blasing has written that the AKP has also 'made no secret of its disdain for "heathen" [*gavur*] Izmir'.[13]

The supporters' network believe that the government has been neglecting Izmir in a perverse bid to both punish CHP voters, and attract votes through suggesting the economic possibilities if only they would switch to the AKP – a kind of 'trade' was how Ata Akil, a member of the network, perceived it: 'You vote for us first and then we will solve your problems.'[14] He said that Antalya had 'given in' and voted for the AKP. Now, investment in Antalya was increasing, and Antalyaspor also had a brand-new stadium, which was set to host the 2016 Turkish Cup final.

While Alsancak Stadium had been demolished, the battle to save the site for football was not over. The sagas surrounding various new football venues in Turkey show a mixed picture for the AKP of success, farce and dissent.

Monuments to power

As mayor of Istanbul, Recep Tayyip Erdogan had been involved in the development of the city's Ataturk Olympic Stadium, which was opened in 2002 – it was the first new stadium to be built in Turkey after the 1980 military coup. Erdogan had overseen significant infrastructure improvements in Istanbul as mayor, and when the AKP came to national power in 2002 they prioritised the construction industry – building airports, bridges, roads, hospitals, transport networks – and thousands of mosques – in a nationwide infrastructure boom.[15] Over time, a stadium-building programme gathered pace to become a frenzy. The AKP government is currently overseeing the construction of 26 new stadium projects in 24 cities, with several more set to follow.[16]

Galatasaray opened their new 'Turk Telekom Arena' with a match against Ajax in January 2011. Erdogan turned up to the opening, likely anticipating a warm and grateful reception for helping to construct the shiny new arena – but he was met with boos and whistling from the crowd when his presence was announced on the big screen, and the protests intensified after a speech by Erdogan Bayraktar, the chairman of TOKI – Turkey's Housing Development Administration.[17] Erdogan left the stadium in a huff before kick-off, and later labelled the fans 'ungrateful' – pointing out that the state had paid for the stadium, which had been built by TOKI.

TOKI has emerged as a major player in the government's stadium-building schemes, and Galatasaray's new stadium became a template for much of the stadium-construction frenzy that followed.[18] TOKI brokered construction tenders for the Turk Telekom Arena, acquired land for the complex on the outskirts of the city, and sold the land of the old 'Ali Sami Yen Stadium' – named after the founder of the club – in the central Istanbul neighbourhood of Mecidiyekoy, for the construction of a shopping mall.

Galatasaray's new stadium is an awe-inspiring arena, with sheer-drop stands and bone-rattling acoustics, but it's situated in a bleak, soulless non-space next to a traffic-throttled ring road. The site around the stadium is marred by concrete, ditches and potholes. Galatasaray's famous slogan 'Welcome to Hell' is now often more apt for those sitting for hours in congestion outside the stadium, or idling to get out of the makeshift, bottlenecked car parks in the surrounding area, rather than the famously intimidating reception waiting within.

In many of the new stadiums, the local municipality (or more rarely the national government) takes on credit from the state to build a stadium.[19] Often they work in partnership with the Ministry of Youth and Sports and with TOKI, who coordinate and control the construction supposedly to maximise efficiency and to acquire the government's desired outcomes.

Typically, the municipalities own the stadiums and rent them to the clubs – usually for a nominal fee, perhaps 1 TL per season.[20] The clubs gain the revenue from the stadium such as sponsorship and ticket sales. The municipality typically makes money from development of the old stadium's land. TOKI gets a cut of this income and, theoretically, capital flushes back into the state's coffers.

It might seem strange that TOKI – initially designed to coordinate social housing – is so heavily involved in stadium construction, but for the government it has the perfect expertise and positioning to play the role.

The AKP amended scores of procurement laws and building regulations to enhance TOKI's powers. The political and economic use of stadiums by the AKP is nothing new – stadiums have been political structures in Turkey since the 1930s, helping to create alliances and patronage between clubs and politicians. But the scale and ambition under the AKP is unprecedented.

Mass construction is a key AKP growth strategy, something that can power the economy, and is the most visible, tangible, tactile way in which they can prove that they get things done. Onsel Gurel Bayrali, an economist who studies Turkish football stadium construction, says it is part of a wider trend of 'monumentalism' in the construction industry, particularly in Anatolian cities – helping turn ideology into matter.[21] 'People in Malatya, for example, say "oh yeah [the AKP] are working." How can they understand that? They constructed a soccer stadium. It's a kind of monumental project.'[22]

The AKP has become notorious for its mega-projects, many of which have drawn criticism and protest for their lack of environmental concern or their over-ambitiousness. The government is spending $100bn in construction projects in Istanbul,[23] building what is set to be the world's busiest airport, as part of plans to turn Istanbul into Europe's major transport hub, and a third Bosphorus bridge that was criticised for destroying fast-shrinking forestland and which has been underused since its opening. Erdogan describes, with pride, a pet project to build an enormous canal linking the Sea of Marmara with the Black Sea as one of his 'crazy projects'.[24] Turkish companies that construct projects such as stadiums and airports effectively at home are then put forward for tenders abroad.[25]

Bayrali argues that the AKP's use of the construction industry also helps it to build a loyal business class that is largely Anatolian, conservative and Islamic, which can overshadow rival traditional Kemalist elites. 'There is a shift in power blocs,' says Bayrali. 'Other industries are controlled by the Kemalist bourgeoisie,[26] so the AKP wanted to create an alternative by promoting the construction industry.'[27]

There are ideological factors at play with the naming of new football stadiums. Many old 'stadiums' were named after Kemalist politicians or former club figures. Until Erdogan's recent diktat against using the 'un-Turkish' term,[28] the new venues tended to be called 'arenas', partly reflecting an Americanised corporatisation, and the names often reflect the shifts in corporate or political power: Besiktas's 'Inonu Stadium' – named after the second CHP president of Turkey – was demolished and replaced by the

'Vodafone Arena'. Fenerbahce's Sukru Saracoglu Stadium has been renamed 'Ulker Stadium', after a major, conservative food manufacturer.

Afyon, Antakya, Antalya, Bursa, Diyarbakir, Elazig, Eskisehir, Giresun, Kayseri, Konya, Rize and Sakarya all have or had stadiums named after Ataturk that have been or will be renamed.[29] Kasimpasa SK now play in the renovated 'Recep Tayyip Erdogan' Stadium – the president grew up in the neighbourhood.

Under the AKP, the power of the MUSIAD association – which represents mostly small and medium businesses, usually conservative, pious and Anatolian – has risen at the expense of TUSIAD, the association that generally represents the 'secular' elite and has often found itself at odds with Erdogan. The bids for key construction projects, including many stadiums, are typically closed auctions for companies close to the government. However, this practice is not limited to the AKP. Municipalities controlled by the opposition CHP – such as Izmir – have also been accused of favouritism in awarding construction contracts to friendly firms.[30]

'After the 1980 coup, there was an ideological transformation in Turkey which provided an opportunity for political Islam,' argues Bayrali. 'Islamic understanding and neoliberal understanding harmonised, and a new terminology was created: "Homo Islamicus". It was the title of a magazine published by MUSIAD in the early 1990s. Before 1980, political Islamists often promoted austerity and railed against conspicuous consumption and individualism – many believed that Muslims should not be rich, and were sceptical of the private sector and free market. 'But Homo Islamicus created an opportunity to adopt political Islam into neoliberal understanding. They say that Muslim people can do business, they can become rich, they can consume – but based on Islamic rules.'[31]

This materialised further under the AKP and the understanding of Islamic consumption has changed. Religiously conservative people became more likely to go out to alcohol-free restaurants and cafés, to shop and consume conspicuously, and religious clothing became more imbued with fashion, such as the headscarf – long a solely religious and political symbol, which has also become a fashion accessory that indicates wealth and social status.

Islamist parties also focused on providing welfare; they boosted investment in local services, made possible by increased fiscal autonomy gained by municipalities in the 1980s under the Motherland Party (ANAP), and provided gifts and other material benefits (such as fridges or washing machines) through charitable bodies that were often funded by wealthy

Islamic businessmen, and tied implicitly to political parties. The idea was to improve the lives of poor, struggling people and garner votes.[32] The Motherland Party was not as popular as the AKP because it didn't embody religion as skilfully, and the Welfare Party was never as popular as the AKP because it didn't incorporate liberal economics and politics into its programmes. Neither could create the AKP's powerful economic, Islamic networks at the top, middle and bottom of society.[33]

There are both Keynesian and corporatist elements to the AKP's massive programme of stadium construction: Keynesian, in that building stadiums in numerous cities brings a degree of work to often far-flung, deprived areas; corporatist, in that the main beneficiaries are a coterie of friendly construction businesses that enjoy a mutual political and economic circle-jerk with the government.

The AKP government came to national power following years of corruption by its predecessors. They gained admiration for an ability to get things done, building with a greater aura of determination and honesty. But over their tenure, AKP politicians have also become plagued by allegations of corruption and cronyism – the construction industry in particular is reportedly rife with bribery, nepotism and fraud.[34] Much of the 2013 corruption allegations centred on construction.

And for all the AKP's talk about ordinary people and representing the underdog, it has also removed many labour rights and protections; Turkey is now second only to China in terms of fatalities at work.[35]

Critics say that TOKI is opaque, unaccountable, massively indebted, and that it allows the government to play politics with construction – helping to transfer rent to friendly firms, entrenching centralised power at the expense of municipalities, and enabling gentrification and cronyism. The government points out that TOKI has built a huge number of worthy projects, including half a million homes, 700 schools and 100 hospitals since 2003.[36]

I approached TOKI for an interview and provided them with questions on their request. I thought the questions were perfectly reasonable, asking TOKI to address some of the criticisms made against them and inviting them to advocate for their successes. However, when my translator followed up with a contact at TOKI, their spokesperson complained that 'foreign journalists don't understand anything' and embarked on a lengthy diatribe. When my translator suggested that TOKI could explain this to me in an interview, they gruffly said they would see and rang off, never to be reached again.[37]

The government argues that, by embarking on this mass stadium-building programme, it is spreading wealth around the country and improving the fortunes and prestige of Anatolian teams, which in turn will make Turkish football more equitable.

Konyaspor could be considered an example. Konya is generally regarded as the most conservative city in Turkey: women without headscarves are fairly uncommon, most shops close for Friday prayers, and alcohol vendors are scarce in the extreme – although I did spot 'Night Club Number One', which from the outside looked like a tyre outlet in an industrial retail park and made me dread to think what 'Night Club Number Two' was like.

Konyalus are rightfully proud of their city, which is full of ancient, beautiful mosques, phenomenal restaurants, tranquil gardens and squares, and the Mevlana museum – Rumi's former lodge of the whirling dervishes, now hosting the tomb of the Sufi mystic poet. I found Konya very friendly – I got a hero's welcome each time I returned to the hotel, and once even had my beard tickled under the chin by the man on reception, who chuckled and said 'haji'[38] indulgently. Konya staunchly backs the AKP and has thrived; it has a well-tended feel, a new tram with features like a smiling face glides through the streets, and the renovated souk is bustling and full of character.

Konyaspor has traditionally yo-yoed between the first and second tiers of Turkish football, but in the past few years has been on a markedly upward trajectory. The club's new 42,000-capacity Torku Arena was opened in 2014, and the city has been rewarded with key Turkish international matches, play-off finals and the Turkish Super Cup – the equivalent of the Charity Shield. 'We used to have a poor stadium and we were known for having poor support,' said Ibrahim Apali, the 36-year-old leader of Nalcacililar, Konyaspor's biggest fan group. 'But in two years, since the stadium was built, we have developed fast. And because of Mevlana museum, the image of the city is changing.'[39]

Many Konyaspor fans believe the investment in their city and the stadium, along with their respected coach Aykut Kocaman, explains their increasing success. In 2015/16 they finished third in the Super League – their best ever result – qualifying for Europe for the first time in the club's history. The following season they sold over 26,000 season tickets – only Besiktas sold more[40] – and they won the Turkish Cup, the first major trophy in the club's history.

Nalcacililar have embraced ultras culture – bouncing up and down non-stop for 90 minutes, making an unceasing racket, creating an impressive spectacle with colourful scarf-waving shows, and expressing their pride in the team and 'Seljuk' identity in chants, banners and choreography. Apali has tried to stamp out violence, swearing and drinking in the group, though there are still a few naughty boys among the fans. He says the support is geared to boost the team on the pitch, and the 'brand' of the club – the fan group has a headquarters that is full of Konyaspor merchandise.

The government has built a huge Mevlana cultural centre in the city, which hosts Sufi dancing, hawks Rumi paraphernalia, and sells politics with giant pictures on the wall of Erdogan and Ahmet Davutoglu – the Konya-born, former AKP prime minister.[41] Rumi could surely never have imagined that, centuries later, his lodge would draw devotees and pilgrims from across the world, that hordes would come to stare at his tomb though the prism of strange machines, that a cultural centre would be created in his name, the great leaders of the age depicted on the walls, making political capital. And the stadium is another monument in the city – the Mevlana and the arena put Konya 'on the map'.

Smaller cities are hoping to do something similar with their stadiums. Akhisar Belediyespor is a municipality team which reached the Super League in 2012. They had a great season in 2015/16, almost qualifying for the Europa League. The club's president is also the AKP deputy mayor of the city. Few people had heard of Akhisar, in the Manisa province in west Turkey, until the rise of the football team.

The municipality sees the football team as the most valuable 'brand' in the city, and is using the club as a vehicle to boost development. The AKP municipality plans to build a new stadium in Akhisar to stimulate economic development, hoping that commerce and retail develop as a result, and selling the land of the old stadium to build a shopping centre, and pay off the municipality's considerable debts.[42] While increased fiscal autonomy for municipalities in the 1980s paved the way for the rise of Islamic parties, now that the AKP is in power, it has been steadily taking that power back for the central government, and municipality funding has been cut.

The new stadium project in Akhisar is taking a long time, which shows some of the stratification of the AKP – that its regional branches are sometimes not totally in sync with central government. Akhisar municipality chose not to involve TOKI in the stadium process so that they won't have to share the economic rents, but as a result they believe that it will take at least twice as long to build the stadium.[43]

The new stadium and the success of the team can make or break the little city. 'I think that, if Akhisarspor gets relegated to the second league, probably the municipality loses the next election,' says Bayrali. 'It's that serious.'[44]

Stadiums have also been used to develop – often conservative – urban peripheries. The Istanbul suburb of Basaksehir, home to a mixture of middle- and working-class people who are typically from conservative, religious parts of Anatolia or central Istanbul, is an AKP stronghold – the creation of the neighbourhood was one of Erdogan's projects while he was mayor of Istanbul.

The football team in Basaksehir has gone through several names and iterations – it is currently called Istanbul Basaksehir FK and has a recently constructed stadium that is a major factor in the tiny club's growing success. They finished fourth in 2014/15 and 2015/16, qualifying for the preliminary rounds of the Europa League. In 2016/17 they mounted a serious challenge for the double, and finished second in the league and runners-up in the Turkish Cup. 'A small club with big ambitions,' says Mustafa Erogut, the club's executive director.[45]

To get to Basaksehir's 'Fatih Terim Stadium' from central Istanbul I took the metro to the end of one line, then to the end of a second, then to the end of a third. Then I took a bus. Basaksehir is a frontier planet of sleek, gated communities with names like 'Ak Residence', alongside scrubby undeveloped valleys, wide, mostly carless boulevards and clusters of dingier-looking generic apartment blocks. In rows of shops, blue TEKELs – the state-sanctioned alcohol vendors common in central areas of Istanbul – were conspicuous by their absence. Basaksehir's new stadium, brand new, shiny and metallic, looks like a spaceship landed on the outer fringes of the city.

Basaksehir started life as a team of Istanbul Metropolitan Municipality in 1990. They broke from the municipality in 2014 and formed a private company. The club's president Goksel Gumusdag had high ambitions to develop the club when he first became involved around a decade ago. 'He thinks Basaksehir is a new, important location in Turkey. There are around 500,000 inhabitants – which is higher than the Icelandic population,' said Erogut – a large pool of potential supporters and players.

'It's not just football. It's social responsibility,' says Erogut. While they want talented kids to join the academy, they also want to give less talented kids the opportunity and space to play football, in a city that is often bereft of green, open space – the space out on the margins of the city is enabling them to create 11 full-size training pitches. Basaksehir are developing education facilities that can teach more academic kids skills in marketing, media and sponsorship.

Basaksehir's stadium is a big part of their success. While it was being built, they played in the nearby Ataturk Olympic Stadium and got crowds of 30 or 40 people – not thousand! – literally 30–40 people, most of whom were friends or family of the players. The crowds were sometimes bigger when I played for Barton Rovers in the South Chiltern Minor League.

Unlike many such projects, Basaksehir's stadium was built quickly and efficiently, within 16 months. The club benefitted from close links with the government – Basaksehir's president is related to President Erdogan by marriage.[46] Kalyon, the contractors that built the stadium, have close personal ties to Erdogan.[47] As mentioned in the Introduction, Erdogan displayed scintillating form in an exhibition match during the stadium's opening ceremony in 2014 – scoring a first-half hat-trick and ensuring a much friendlier reception than at Galatasaray by strictly vetting all the attendees. Erogut, who is normally quite stolid, becomes heady and coquettish when talking about Erdogan: 'We like him, and we think he likes us!'

Erogut enthuses about the economic figures under the AKP: stable banks, a steady currency, high GDP growth, IMF debt clearance, growth of big global brands like Turkish Airlines – and infrastructure. 'Turkey came from one point to another in 15 years,' he said. 'Sports also followed this – and I think we have one of the best stadium infrastructures in Europe.'

In two years the club has gone from having 30–40 fans to attendances of 2,000–5,000. The club gives talks in schools and offers cheap tickets and promotions. It hopes to have attendances of 10,000 in its roughly 18,000-capacity stadium within a few years. The club has become a social and sporting space in a conservative community – which makes the AKP municipality look good.

Burak Bilgili, 27, is the co-founder and spokesperson of the Basaksehir fan group 1453 Basaksehirliler (1453 is the year of the Ottoman conquest of Constantinople). He moved to the area with his family around 15 years ago from the more central conservative neighbourhood of Fatih. 'It's good to live in Basaksehir because it's more peaceful compared to [central] Istanbul. Everyone knows each other, we don't have any security problems, we are all friends. There is a community.'[48]

In late September 2016, I went to a Basaksehir match against Osmanlispor, another pro-AKP team. Basaksehir sat top of the league, with a 100 per cent record from four matches, including a win over Fenerbahce. Osmanlispor were fifth. The stadium was mostly blighted by the spectacle of massed empty seats, in orange, grey and blue. Perhaps 3,000 had turned up. In my stand I spotted the same number of people – one – wearing a Besiktas shirt as I did wearing Basaksehir colours. In the away end, the Osmanlispor fans were orchestrated in raucous tandem – they bounced, chanted and flailed their scarves in military unison.

In my stand, the main sound was a moist threshing of seeds, the occasional round of applause, the odd groan as a pass or shot was shanked into orbit. Most of the people seemed to be curious onlookers rather than fans. Basaksehir's fan group 1453 Basaksehirliler was quiet or absent from this match – at subsequent matches around 50 of them offered voluble, lively support.

Some fans don't like this club because they see it as synthetic – created from the top down, benefitting from past links to the municipality[49] and direct help from the local and national government, enjoying success that eludes many great, historic, well-supported clubs. The club counters by asking why a huge new district shouldn't have a football team and points to the government support for many other clubs.

At least Basaksehir is cheap – a ticket set me back a mere 15 TL. Later that night Besiktas were taking on Galatasaray in the first 'Big Three' derby of the season. I had wanted to go to the match, but the cheapest available tickets I could find cost 400 TL, or 26.66666 Basaksehir matches. I decided to watch the game in a *meyhane* in Besiktas.

The scene could not have been more different from Basaksehir. Besiktas was populated in black and white; it was like every Besiktas supporter in the country had descended on the district, torrents of fans making their way through the streets, lighting flares, drinking beer, taking shots of tequila from an ad hoc stall, eating meze on outdoor tables, chanting, fists raised, mugging and gurning for photos, fingers clenched to look like eagle talons. Shops pumped out Besiktas songs. Besiktas came back from 2–0 down to draw, and when they equalised there was pandemonium: chairs were scattered, flares – seemingly produced from thin air – mingled with the neon light of bar signs, casting narrow streets in a fiery glow. People grabbed onto each other in sheer delight. Basaksehir has some way to go yet.

Look on my works, ye mighty, and despair

Some of the concepts for Turkey's new stadiums are impressive and somewhat idiosyncratic. Bursaspor's new stadium has been built to resemble a crocodile – the team's mascot, favoured by Bursaspor fans because it is green and ferocious. There is a huge green band around the stadium, and an entrance designed to look like a crocodile's head is under construction. The new stadium in Trabzon has been built on an artificial island, on land reclaimed from the sea beneath the city's imposing hills. Gaziantepspor's new stadium is covered in a mosaic-style design (Gaziantep is home to the world's largest mosaic museum).

However, with a few exceptions like Basaksehir, the stadium-building programme has not gone smoothly. Many of the projects have faltered or stalled as the firms undertaking the work have experienced financial problems, often relating to the wider downturn in the economy, or have found the projects to be more technically challenging than anticipated, littering the country with half-finished white elephants.[50] A surge in stadium openings followed the June 2015 election in which the AKP failed to win a majority for the first time in its history. But, in the rush, many of the newly opened stadiums are technically uncompleted and essentially remain building sites, and the surrounding infrastructure is often poor.

Bursaspor's new 'Timsah' – crocodile – Stadium on the banks of the Nilufer River broke ground in June 2011 and was scheduled to be completed by 2013, but the deadline was pushed back and back. Erdogan eventually officially opened the stadium with a symbolic kick-off in December 2015. 'Dear people of Bursa, now you have a stadium as glorious as the city,' he announced. Some fan groups boycotted the opening, criticising it as a political event that vetted and sidelined fans and the team – the opening game was played by political 'celebrities' of the municipality and national government. Many spectators left during the match, unable to bear the tedium. The rushed opening was betrayed by a pipe bursting, causing a ceiling to collapse.[51]

When I went to a match at the Timsah Stadium in early February 2016, we had sat in heavy traffic and then charted a haphazard course through poky back roads in an attempt to reach the stadium. There are no official car parks, just people using empty plots and their initiative. The atmosphere in the stadium was vibrant, with the Teksas supporters' group behind the goal providing a crashing spectacle, bouncing up and down, sometimes vibrating from side to side. But the stadium was less than half full, the concourse beyond the stands was dusty and vacant, and the area outside the stadium was pure asphalt, vast and bleak. Moreover, the skeleton of the crocodile's head was far from completion.

Despite some architectural quirks, many of the stadium interiors have a similar feel. Inside most new stadiums you find yourself in a mostly indistinguishable, albeit fairly impressive, big round bowl. Whether these new stadiums can help weaken the hegemony of the Istanbul 'Big Three' is doubtful – after all, the Istanbul big teams also have their new stadiums.

If part of the idea is to reward voters with shiny, outer-city new stadiums, it is ironic that many fans don't want them, or remain unimpressed. Gaziantepspor consistently have attendances below 5,000, but their new mosaic-clad arena, opened in January 2017, has 36,000 seats with the potential to increase to 43,000. It is far outside the city.

'The biggest problem is transportation. Most supporters are not well off and they can't afford to travel,' said Tevfik Okan Enlicay, a member of the Gaziantepspor fan group Genclik 27. 'We love being in the city centre, it's the heart of the city, and it helps bind people. The stadium is a gathering place – you can meet there and eat kebabs and see your friends,' he said. 'In the new stadium we'll just go to matches and we won't gather there and socialise. So it will kill our group and our spirit.'

They worry that the old stadium will be knocked down to build a shopping mall in a city centre that is already full of malls. Genclik 27 is resolutely apolitical, in a city that staunchly backs the AKP. But they are roused into anger by the stadium issue. 'The stadium will be built to increase the value in a rich area. At the moment it's "nowhere's town",' says Mehmet Emin Uzumcu, another member of the group.[52]

Gaziantepspor's old stadium probably looked like a wreck to the appraising eye of the authorities, with its decrepit stands, dust-ingrained seats, pillars that obscure the view, a sandy perimeter track, and a shabby ragtag of shops and stalls underneath the arches. But Genclik 27 were happy with what they had – or at the very least wanted a new stadium to be built on the same location. This is something that the government and the football federation cannot fathom, or don't care to fathom: that many fans cherish their history, and prize access and community.

The pattern is being repeated across the country. Many of the new stadiums being built in Turkey are vast and seem set to hugely exceed their likely attendances, often compounded by their locations far from the city centres. Average Super League attendances in 2015/16 were just over 8,000, and these averages are pushed up by the 'Big Three'.[53] The economic burden of maintaining such huge, poorly attended stadiums could be a serious headache for future municipalities – colossal burdens that could become Ozymandian wrecks.[54]

But the larger the stadium, the greater the prestige and the higher the cost, meaning more money can be doled out. The vast programme is also linked to the government's ongoing ambitions – so far unsuccessful – to attract prestigious international competitions such as the European Championships and the Olympics. At the opening ceremony of Besiktas's new stadium, Erdogan – the Fenerbahce supporter draped in a Besiktas scarf – stated that the new stadiums across the country made Turkey's future hosting of the Olympics a mere 'formality'.[55]

'They wanted to erase its history'

When I visited Izmir again in July 2016, the site where Alsancak Stadium had stood was encircled by metal fencing. The rubble had been cleared and the daunting machines had left. The goalposts and the floodlights remained in place, and sprinklers half-heartedly sprayed a pitch that was as threadbare as a cricket crease. It wasn't yet clear what would happen to the site. 'We want restoration – we don't want a "new", modern stadium,' said Burkal Efe Sakizlioglu of the supporters' network Taraftar Haklari, who insist that the stadium should be rebuilt with the same characteristics as much as is possible, while ensuring that it is earthquake proof.[56]

In 2016 Izmir did not have any teams in Turkey's Super League; some major clubs languished far down in the lower depths of Turkish football. Sakizlioglu linked the struggles explicitly to a lack of attention and investment: 'The problem is not only with the football teams, it's with Izmir as a city. There are fewer opportunities in Izmir.'[57] Two other new stadium projects have been mooted in Izmir, but they haven't got off the ground, apparently because the CHP municipality and the AKP government can't come to an agreement.

In fact, a new stadium has been built in recent years in Izmir – for the club Bucaspor. Buca became the only AKP municipality within Izmir in 2004 when Cemil Seboy – a former Bucaspor club president – won local elections. A new stadium was built for Bucaspor, and it opened in 2009.

Having long been mired in the third tier, over time it developed a well-respected academy and reached the Super League in 2010.[58]

The panoply of Izmir teams has given the city a rich, vibrant footballing culture and history, with charismatic clubs and fans, but perhaps the sheer number of teams has also impeded the city's footballing glories.[59] Izmir teams have never been hugely successful – under any government. On the other hand, Izmir clubs like Goztepe and Karsiyaka continue to command huge, passionate followings that dwarf most clubs in Turkey and they should have been more successful.[60] One of the reasons that Izmir has such a vibrant football culture and range of clubs is the city's cosmopolitan history, which Taraftar Haklari want to honour.

The territory that became Turkey was hugely diverse under the Ottoman Empire, and this was reflected in football. Among the first Anatolians to take up football were Greeks in Izmir. The Orpheus club was founded in 1890, which later split into two clubs that became strong rivals: Apollon and Gymnasio, which later became Panionios in 1898. Panionios relocated to Athens and remains one of Greece's strongest teams.[61]

Maccabi, a Jewish Istanbul team, was formed in 1909. There were many Armenian teams and players. The football historian Mehmet Yuce found that the earliest reported Fenerbahce match was in March 1908 against Kumkapi, an Istanbul Armenian team.[62] The first football club in the Trabzon region was probably Sporting Trabzon, a club set up in 1904 by Bogassian Effendi, an Armenian tradesman, with many Armenian players and supporters. Greek and Armenian players also played for the big Istanbul sides. In Izmir the most famous Armenian club was the Hay Vorsordats Club ('The Armenian Hunters' Club').

Several Turkish-Muslim teams were formed in Izmir to take on non-Muslim rivals in the city. Karsiyaka was formed in 1912, and took the colours of red and green to represent Turkish nationalism and Islam. Altay was formed in 1914 to encourage Turkish youth to play sports.

With the outbreak of World War I, football continued to some degree – for Turkish Muslims at least. 'Because the [Young Turk] Progress and Union Party [CUP] saw sports as gymnastics for war,' says Yuce.[63] Many Greek and Armenian clubs stopped playing.

In 1915, with the Great War becoming increasingly desperate for the Ottomans, the fear of Russian victory grew. The authorities increasingly believed their large Armenian population to be mostly aligned with the Russians. In the spring of 1915, a series of horrific events took place, as part of an attempted extermination and clearance effort – what many now refer to as the Armenian Genocide. As many as 1.5 million Armenians and hundreds of thousands of Assyrians were killed.[64] Most Armenian property and wealth was seized. Most of the killings and deportations of Armenians occurred across Anatolia. In Istanbul, some Armenian players could carry on their lives: Karnik Arslanian, for example, played for Fenerbahce until 1919. But many intellectuals and community leaders were rounded up, and several Armenian sports figures were murdered, including Shavarsh Chrissian – the editor of *Marmnamarz*, the Ottoman Empire's first sports magazine, which was published in Armenian.

The official Turkish position remains, in spite of overwhelming evidence to the contrary, to deny that a genocide took place – insisting that the killings were not official policy and that the deaths were part of widespread violence in which many Turkish Muslims also died.[65]

Turkey underwent a dramatic demographic transformation. Izmir went from having an estimated non-Muslim population of 62 per cent in 1900 to 14 per cent by the late 1920s, while Istanbul's non-Muslim population fell from 56 per cent to 35 per cent, and Erzurum went from 32 per cent non-Muslim to 0.1 per cent after almost its entire Armenian population was expelled or killed during the genocide.[66] Still, in the late 1920s and 1930s, matches between the Istanbul clubs Pera – largely Greek – and Taksimspor – largely Armenian – became huge derbies, drawing crowds similar to Fenerbahce vs Galatasaray.

Minorities were subject to pressure, harassment and wealth taxes in the early years of the republic. In 1955 thousands of Muslims – incited by false rumours that Ataturk's childhood home in Thessaloniki, modern-day Greece, had been attacked – converged on Istiklal Street in Istanbul. Soldiers stood by as rioters burned and looted shops, places of worship and homes belonging to Greeks, Armenians and Jews. Many people were beaten and raped in the pogrom, and several people were killed. Impoverished, and fearing further violence, most remaining minorities left Turkey. Out of the hundreds of thousands of minorities in the 1950s, 65,000 Armenians, 17,000 Jews and just 2,500 Greeks remain.[67] A handful of minority football teams – such as Beyogluspor and Taksimspor – endure.

The AKP has often adopted a softer approach to minorities than its predecessors. The dialogue regarding historic violence towards Armenians has become more open, Armenian churches have been restored, and relations with Greece have been greatly improved.[68] At the same time, the AKP has also used racist, xenophobic language. Erdogan once claimed that his family originated from Batumi, Georgia. But in a 2014 interview he complained about people questioning his background: 'I was called a Georgian. I apologise for this, but they even said [something] worse: They called me an Armenian. But I'm a Turk.'[69]

The AKP government has also increasingly come under criticism for prioritising Sunni Muslims over other sects, and favouring capital over heritage and the environment – continuing and intensifying a long-standing practice of uprooting and gentrifying poor and minority communities. Some accuse the AKP of seeking the 'Dubaisation' of Turkey, with its proclivity for ostentatious skyscrapers, refrigerated malls and privatised space.[70] The sociologist Daghan Irak has drawn a link between the potential supplanting of Alsancak Stadium with commercial interests by the AKP, and historic uprootings in Turkey's history.[71]

In 2014, the AKP government passed a law that gave landlords the power to evict their tenants without cause, after ten years of residence. The law has led to the eviction of many small, historic businesses in prime locations, popular with tourists – particularly in central areas of Istanbul. Restaurants and shops that have been operating since the late nineteenth century have subsequently been closed to make way for hotels or chains. The law does not specifically target non-Muslim minorities, but members of the dwindled Armenian, Greek and Jewish communities are among Istanbul's oldest merchants and are often most at risk of eviction.

In Izmir, the battle to save Alsancak Stadium, and the desire to protect their heritage, triggered a recognition among Taraftar Haklari of the city's diverse history. Taraftar Haklari plan to open a museum at the stadium which would reflect the cosmopolitan history of football in the city. 'Every culture must be in the museum, not only Turkish,' stressed Sakizlioglu. Taraftar Haklari are in contact with supporters of exiled Panionios, the Greek team that originally owned the land, who are eager to be part of the project and want to donate items to the museum. 'In our opinion, the AKP didn't like the multiculturalism of the stadium,' argued Sakizlioglu. 'They wanted to erase its history.'

In 2017 Altay's president pledged that the club would be playing in a new stadium on the site by 2018, and later in the year Turkey's prime minister Binali Yildirim confirmed that a new earthquake-proof Alsancak Stadium – albeit flashy and modern – would be constructed on the site. It was a rare victory for football fans – such as Taraftar Haklari – in their long-running war against what they see as AKP gentrification.

In 2013 Taraftar Haklari and other football fans participated in seismic anti-government protests in the streets. The epicentre was in Taksim Square, Istanbul, where history, construction, gentrification and football jarred up against each other to shake the foundations of the government.

5

'Everywhere is Taksim, everywhere is resistance'

The spectators are divided into two sections. Each would encourage the [players] of its own side, and keep swearing at the enemy. Everyone says whatever they want to. Everyone shouts and bawls at will. A freedom of expression, and thought, at full speed... Those who want to understand democracy in a specific sense should go to Taksim Stadium. I, for my part, spent a beautiful and lucid two hours there.[1]

This account of a football match in the 1920s by the great Turkish poet Nazim Hikmet does not sound much different to today's spectacle. Taksim Stadium was Turkey's premier football venue at the time; it hosted Turkey's first international game in 1923. In 1940 it was demolished and turned into Gezi Park, as the locus of Turkish football shifted down the hill to Dolmabahce Stadium. Taksim – Istanbul's most famous square – has always embraced collective emotions, writes the artist Emre Zeytinoglu.[2]

Gezi Park, in the north-west corner of the square, is a scrappy mishmash of concrete, patchy grass, playgrounds, fountains, crumbling steps, ad hoc coffee shops, stained and worn benches, half-hearted flower beds, and perhaps more than 600 trees – a rare and awkward and precious green space on the overdeveloped European plateau of the city. Gezi Park's users represent downtown Istanbul in idling microcosm: office-workers, tourists, refugees, dedicated drinkers, couples, hawkers, families, tea sellers, solitary readers, sex workers.

As mayor of Istanbul, Recep Tayyip Erdogan had supported a decades-old plan for a mosque to be built in Taksim Square. The project ended up being aborted after the 1997 military intervention – many Kemalists had seen it as an attempt to impose an Islamist identity on a symbolically vital square that features a monument dedicated to Ataturk.

In 2012 Erdogan – then prime minister – announced that the park would be demolished to make space for a reconstruction of the Ottoman-era Halil Pasha artillery barracks. The run-down barracks had been transformed into Taksim football stadium in 1921.

In Erdogan's vision, the reconstructed barracks was expected to house a shopping mall, luxury apartments and possibly a museum. Historic buildings and green spaces in Istanbul have repeatedly been slated for destruction under the AKP. Any protests were typically dispersed or ignored, and the land was developed.

Protesters at Gezi Park defied this trend, and many of its fiercest foot soldiers were football fans. Football became an unprecedented site of rebellion, triggering a fierce backlash from the government, and a hugely symbolic struggle over the character of Turkish football fandom. As the government wanted to gentrify Gezi, some say they wanted to gentrify football fans.

'The "looters" are coming'

The Besiktas ultras' group Carsi – 'bazaar' – formed in the early 1980s and took their name from the marketplace in Besiktas, a central district next to the Bosphorus, just down the hill from Taksim Square. 'Look out for a heavyset bearded guy,' said Yener Ozturk, a long-standing member of the group in his mid-thirties, before we arranged to meet next to the eagle[3] statue in the heart of the district. We settled in a pub to talk over pints of Guinness, an apt drink for a fan of Besiktas, who play in black and white.

Carsi are often associated with left-wing politics – their logo features a version of the anarchist 'A' and they are known for social activism: delivering books, clothes and school supplies to earthquake victims, donating blood, and speaking out against racism, fascism, animal cruelty and environmental destruction. Yener may look tough with his heavy-metal beard, all-black attire and arms patterned with tattoos, but he is also a big softy: when not watching football, he spends many of his weekends volunteering at an animal shelter, feeding and playing with the cats and dogs.

While Galatasaray's origins were among the aristocratic elite of the Galatasaray High School, and Fenerbahce were originally associated with the bourgeoisie, Besiktas sought to position themselves as the working-class underdogs. 'There is a saying – "*Besiktas ic sesidir*": "Besiktas is your inner voice,"' said Yener. 'You have to be willing to help other people, treat them

the way you would want to be treated, help the less fortunate if you can –
that's just the way a lot of people here were brought up.'[4]

Despite their left-wing associations, Carsi have members from all backgrounds, with views across the political spectrum. Carsi are held together
by their particular love for Besiktas, expressed in poetic intensity, longing,
melancholy and humour in banners and songs: 'I saw you on a rainy day /
You were wearing your striped jersey,' begins one Besiktas song:

> I was stricken that moment, I fell in love
> The meaning of life was black and white
> The line that separates death from life
> Cannot separate black from white
> Even if all roads end in death
> No one can come between lovers.[5]

With such love come corollaries – disappointment, bitterness, betrayal.
Players who fail to demonstrate sufficient passion are told to take off their
shirts and play naked. Carsi congregated under the Kapali – the covered
stand – in their old Inonu Stadium, where the acoustics would amplify
a formidable din. Besiktas can plausibly claim to be the world's loudest
football fans – they hit a record 141 decibels at their final match in the
stadium in 2013.[6]

Carsi can also be fiercely antagonistic and irreverent, known for their
humour – particularly when it comes to their most hated rivals, Fenerbahce.
Besiktas have a famous song, known as the 'Fener Opera', in which they
pledge to stop swearing, before the chorus rings out: 'But one last time /
suck my dick, Fener.'[7] Some of Carsi's most famous chants include 'Carsi is
against everything,' and 'Carsi is against itself.'

Carsi's main weapon might be humour, but they have also often battled
rival fan groups and clashed with the police. 'Before the whole Gezi thing a
lot of Carsi fans owned gas masks,' said Yener, 'so we were used to all that.'

The decision to raze Gezi Park had been officially made in February 2013,
but a protest movement to save the space had been growing over several
months. On the evening of 27 May 2013, bulldozers demolished a park wall
and began uprooting trees. A crowd gathered and set up a peaceful protest
camp to try to prevent any further destruction. Erdogan was belligerent
from the outset: 'Even if hell breaks loose, those trees will be uprooted.'[8]
Over the next few days the police cleared the camps, but the protesters just

set them up again. Yener stopped in at the sit-in on 30 May: 'It was just 30 to 40 hippies in tents having beers, nothing out of the ordinary.'

Just before dawn on 31 May, the police used extreme violence to clear the encampment and set fire to tents – several protesters were hospitalised with head injuries or breathing difficulties. The police sealed off the park; they probably thought it was all over. But something inside many people snapped. Hundreds and then thousands and then hundreds of thousands took to the streets to chant anti-government slogans – not just in Istanbul, but in many cities across Turkey. They fought running battles with the police in streets echoing with the sound of firecrackers and clouded with endless volleys of tear gas. Protesters began digging up paving stones and building barricades.

On the first day of the protests Carsi were hesitant, unsure whether to join. But they saw the brutality on TV: the police tear-gassing and chasing children and old people through the streets, pursuing protesters and spraying water cannon and tear gas wherever they took refuge: into restaurants, hotels, a hospital. Police vehicles crushed bodies, police batons cracked skulls, projectiles made contact with heads and eyes.

'We thought – we can't just stand still and do nothing,' said Yener. Thousands gathered in Besiktas on the second day of the protests and marched the short way up the hill to Taksim Square. 'The roads were blocked by the cops but when they saw us [coming] they moved,' he laughed.

Erdogan had derided the protesters as 'capulcu' – 'looters' – and protesters happily appropriated the name. 'The capulcu are coming,' chanted Besiktas fans as they entered the square wearing their black-and-white jerseys. Many held Carsi scarves.

Thousands of fans from other football clubs also joined the protests. The Taksim demonstration was the first time that significant numbers of fans from different Istanbul teams set aside their history of mutual loathing to unite in protest. Fans of Besiktas, Fenerbahce and Galatasaray protested together, chanting: 'Down with fascism: Cim Bom,[9] Fener, Carsi!'

'It was one of the best things I've seen in my life,' said Yener, 'because I never expected to see a Fenerbahce fan in arms with a Galatasaray fan walking down the street together. I saw a Fenerbahce fan take off his jersey, rip it, and tear it round a bleeding Galatasaray fan's leg.' The phenomenon was dubbed 'Istanbul United' by some in the media.

Football fans joined protests across the country. In Ankara, Ankaragucu fans joined Genclerbirligi supporters in the streets. In Izmir, supporters of bitter foes Goztepe and Karsiyaka joined forces with supporters of other clubs in a kind of 'Izmir United' protest. In Adana, the vicious rivalry between Adanaspor and Adana Demirspor was – mostly – set aside as they also joined forces in the streets, although limited skirmishes also broke out between the two sets of supporters.

For some, the coming together of fans was symbolic and epitomised the blurring of borders that had brought all kinds of people to the streets. Like the leftists, feminists, LGBT activists, Kurdish groups and others who came together in the Gezi protests, many football fans were experienced and adept at facing the fury of the police in the streets. Football fans fortified barricades, helped with first aid, adroitly dealt with tear gas and battled the security forces. Besiktas fans hot-wired a bulldozer from a construction site close to Inonu Stadium and used it to harry the police. The protesters successfully occupied Taksim Square and Gezi Park, creating a festival vibe in their hard-won, shared space. They sang songs, gave speeches, cooked, prayed, made art, held debates and workshops, and practised yoga.

The argument that Carsi and other football fans 'saved the day' was overblown and perhaps belittles the many others who instigated the pro-tests before football fans turned up. However, there's little doubt that football fans were among the most effective street fighters of the protests. Football fans swelled the numbers, raised morale and injected an element of abandon.

A court's decision on 31 May to temporarily suspend the demolition of the park failed to quell the uprising. Beyond the initial aim of saving Gezi Park, and outrage at police brutality, a range of other grievances came to the fore during the protests, mostly relating to Erdogan's growing authoritarianism.

Among those present were Kemalists and some nationalists angered by the AKP's increasing promotion of Islamic values in education and throughout wider society; those enraged by the AKP's support of Islamist and jihadist groups fighting in the Syrian civil war; feminists angered by Erdogan's retrograde attitudes towards women; LGBT people who had suffered under the AKP's growing social conservatism; anti-capitalist Muslims angry at the AKP's economic policies favouring big businesses; Kurds; environmentalists;[10] urbanists; yoga practitioners; the list goes on and on. Some were upset by hostility shown towards Alevis, epitomised by the naming of the third Bosphorus bridge after 'Selim the Grim', an Ottoman sultan infamous for massacring Alevis.

Many were alarmed by the AKP's growing intolerance of dissent and freedom of expression. Turkey has historically been a repressive state for journalists, but under Erdogan media repression has become increasingly severe as thousands of websites have been banned, social media has been periodically suspended, media outlets have been seized by the government or shut down, and ever greater numbers of journalists have been harassed, sued, arrested and jailed.[11] The extent to which the media has been cowed by Erdogan was epitomised by CNN Turk's decision to screen a documentary about penguins instead of covering the outbreak of the protests.

Many found Erdogan's abrasive manner infuriating, with his propensity for hubris and bullying, his total rejection of criticism, his eagerness to control people's private lives and his divisive rhetoric. Many were angered by the government's restrictions on alcohol: Erdogan has described anyone that drinks as an alcoholic and once claimed bafflement as to why people drink wine when they could just eat the grapes.[12] Alcohol is symbolic for many of Kemalist values.[13]

'We have never seen any democracy in Turkey,' argues Gokhan Karakaya, who was, until recently, a member of the largest Galatasaray ultras' group, ultrAslan.[14] 'Whoever leads the country always tries to impose their beliefs. But [Erdogan] did it the most.'[15]

Above all, says Gokhan, antipathy towards the police, stoked through their regular violent encounters, brought football fans together. 'Be sure that most supporters hate police in Turkey,' he said. 'Religious, nationalist, left-wing – it doesn't matter. They hate police.'

While the protests revealed the depth of the animosity towards Erdogan and his government, he also enjoys huge support. Counter-Gezi protests formed in which thousands gathered to show their backing of the government. Erdogan railed against the Gezi demonstrators, calling them alcoholics, spies, traitors and the stooges of foreign powers.

Over time the Gezi protests gradually lost their force. Opposition parties and groups sought to join and capitalise on the protests, leading some Carsi members to become disgruntled and leave. Everyday life and work loomed again. After a couple of unsuccessful violent attempts, the police finally succeeded in clearing the park and the square on 15 June 2013. Millions had taken part nationwide, thousands were injured, and at least 11 people died.

Yet, sporadic protests continued throughout the summer. Despite the divisions among the protesters, it felt to some as if a political and cultural movement – albeit messy, contradictory, inchoate and divided – had begun to emerge. And, for the moment, the park had been saved. Meanwhile, football became an unprecedented site of rebellion.

The backlash

'With Gezi park, and with the government's growing intervention, stadiums became like political arenas. You could not have found a stadium without political chanting after 2013,' argues Emir Guney, director of the Sports Studies Research Centre at Kadir Has University. '[The Gezi protests] created a notion of togetherness against the system.'[16]

The government was rattled by the Gezi protests and sought to quell resistance among football fans by outlawing 'political' chants and banners in stadiums. Yet the measures only stoked defiance: 'Everywhere is Taksim, everywhere is resistance,' chanted Carsi and other groups. 'The stadiums are the one place that the government cannot control totally because it is the one place where masses will come and chant,' says Guney. Meanwhile, pro-government groups began to emerge, including a conservative, anti-Carsi Besiktas fan group calling themselves 1453 Eagles.[17]

Carsi gained unprecedented popularity in the wake of the protests: its logo became ever more visible and its numbers swelled. But it also came under severe pressure from the authorities, exacerbating divisions among leading members. A group of 35 fans – including several Carsi members – were accused of attempting to stage a coup. The defendants faced life sentences if convicted. The trial was just one among many, in which thousands of people were accused of various crimes relating to the protests, many on charges of 'terrorism'.[18] Scores of football fans across all clubs were arrested in the aftermath of the protests.[19] Less than a year after Gezi, the government also attempted to tighten its control over football fans by rolling out a controversial e-ticketing identity-card system, which in turn stoked more resistance.

Turkish football is steeped in the significance of numbers. Many fan groups feature meaningful dates and numbers, and many fans break into chants during the minute of the match that corresponds to their city's licence plate number. The 34th minute of football matches became a political flashpoint: rebellious fans began chanting Gezi slogans during that minute, as it is the Istanbul licence plate number. AKP supporters, such as those at Kasimpasa SK, began chanting pro-government slogans in the same minute.

And fan groups such as Galatasaray's ultrAslan, some of whom are unhappy with the politicisation of supporters, have broken into noisy apolitical chants in the 33rd minute in a kind of pre-emptive drowning-out strike.

One number is a particular signifier of controversy. Mention '6222' to Turkish football fans and it will often provoke an instant groan and rant; it is the number of the Ministry of Youth and Sports' law on the 'Prevention of Violence and Disorder in Sports'. The number '6222' is regularly invoked by many supporters and critics as a kind of shorthand for all that is wrong-headed with the government and the Turkish Football Federation's approach to football fans. The government, and the football federation, counter that the law was necessary to tackle a range of profound problems in Turkish football, including fan violence.

Under law '6222' the football federation introduced a controversial Passolig e-ticket system to the Super League in April 2014. Spectators of matches now have to buy a Passolig card to attend matches in the top two tiers of Turkish football. The football federation claims the system allows it to identify and ban perpetrators of violence and those who use violent and offensive language, prevent gate-crashers, crack down on black market ticket sales, and encourage more women and children to attend matches.

But many fans are unhappy with financial and political aspects of the card. The Passolig card is a multi-use bank card issued by Aktif Bank – getting a card means being forced to become a customer of the bank, whether you like it or not.[20] Aktif Bank is a subsidiary of Calik Holding, which was formerly headed by Erdogan's son-in-law Berat Albayrak, and whose chairman Ahmet Calik is known to be close to Erdogan.[21] 'How convenient!' said Yener, the Carsi member. 'Not only are you paying to get ID'd, you're also paying them. It's like a double insult.'[22]

Aktif Bank shared personal details with third parties – including various private companies – and with government ministries. Many fans also see Passolig as a political tool to control football fans, by identifying people chanting anti-government slogans, and to stamp out dissent from the stands.

The introduction of the Passolig card triggered an instant backlash in the streets and the stands. In April 2014, 'Istanbul United' reunited, as fans from various clubs again joined forces in the streets to protest against the system. Widespread discontent and boycotts of the system led to a precipitous fall in attendances – to an average of around 7,000 in 2014/15, down from almost 14,000 in 2013/14.[23] Emerging Turkish football fan networks, such as those featured in the previous chapter, have challenged the Passolig system in the courts.

Passolig operates at the intersection of authoritarian surveillance politics and the commercialisation of football, which some argue encapsulates the nature of the AKP government quite well. Some see Passolig as an attempt to fundamentally alter the character of Turkish football fandom, a symbolic struggle of huge political and social significance, and a breaking point.

Since Passolig is fundamentally justified in terms of addressing violence, it is important to put the disorder into some perspective – just how violent is Turkish football?

Crazy in love: violence and Passolig

The Turkish authorities were worrying about violence in football way back in the 1930s, assigning observers to intervene in fights, usually between players and officials, and holding weekly meetings to improve relations between clubs. Many early republicans had often disdained football, fearing that it would lead to divisions and rivalries in the young country, and, in a sense, their fears were justified.

The professionalisation of football in the 1950s was a key factor in the rise of football violence.[24] An injection of money into the sport raised the stakes and stoked competitiveness. By the 1950s football had become hugely popular in Turkey and allegiance to a club became an ever more important part of one's identity. There was a heightening of emotion surrounding football. With more pride and money at stake, violence in football increased, and the locus of violence shifted to the terraces. 'The image of the footballers reflected in the press turned from being that of a "beyefendi" (gentleman) to that of a "delikanli" (those with wild blood),' writes the academic Sevecen Tunc.[25] The press began likening football matches to cockfights.[26]

Turkey's worst ever footballing disaster occurred in Kayseri in 1967. The disaster highlighted the role of social, cultural and economic factors in some footballing rivalries: the neighbouring cities of Kayseri and Sivas were competing to be the dominant social and economic power of central Anatolia in the 1950s and 1960s.[27] Kayseri was regarded as wealthier and had a large population of Alevis, a religious minority who practise a mystical form of Islam linked to Shi'ism. Alevis are typically associated with the political left. Sivas is largely a conservative Sunni city. The violence of the 1960s and 1970s also included a sectarian dimension to some extent. Football provided another arena for their city rivalry.

At a crunch match in 1967, Sivasspor, playing away, brought 5,000 fans to Kayserispor. The game was awaited eagerly. Mutually insulting slogans were daubed on the trains that travelled between the two cities. Clashes broke out in Kayseri on the day before the match as the Sivasspor fans descended on the city.

On the day of the match, 21,000 crowded into the stadium in a fractious atmosphere. Various weapons had been confiscated from the fans, including knives, chains and cudgels. After Kayserispor scored an early goal, a fight broke out between the players and soon spread to the stands, as both sets of supporters hurled rocks at each other. A group of Sivasspor fans rushed towards the exits and the pitch in a panic to escape the falling debris – the police pushed them away from the pitch and a crush formed against the fencing. 'When the human wave drew back, the scene was horrific: 40 people were dead and at least 300 were injured,' wrote Yigit Akin.[28] The match was abandoned and the players fled to the dressing rooms.[29]

The tragedy shocked the nation, and the football federation empowered clubs and the authorities to take more measures against violence, but the Kayseri disaster did not herald a great change in football violence or governance.

Football violence in Istanbul was at its zenith in the 1980s, with years of so-called terrace wars. At that time, the 'Big Three' Istanbul teams all played in Besiktas's Inonu Stadium, while other grounds were being renovated. Hours and even days before a derby, fans would fight over control of the terraces and Carsi made it their mission to occupy the *kapali* stand. They used fists, boots, sticks and rocks initially, and tooled up with flick knives, meat cleavers and doner kebab knives as the violence escalated over time. Eventually they were using Molotov cocktails and guns.

Fans raided rival premises and ambushed each other, destroying property and beating rivals in tit-for-tat violence. In 1991 a Besiktas fan was kicked to death by Galatasaray supporters. Soon afterwards the leaders of the fan groups negotiated a truce of sorts, putting an end to the conflict away from matches and de-escalating the violence to what was deemed a more reasonable level.[30]

Throughout the 1990s and 2000s, violence around football matches continued. Fans would trash toilets and rip up seats, and generally scrap in and around the stadium. In the penultimate week of the 2012/13 season – just a couple of weeks before Gezi and 'Istanbul United' – a Fenerbahce fan was stabbed to death by Galatasaray supporters.

Much of the violence is spontaneous and has triggers – insults, perceived injustices or humiliating losses. Lots of the fighting revolved around personal enmities built over time: some of it is fuelled by suspected match-fixing, such as the vicious hatreds between Besiktas and Bursaspor, or Fenerbahce and Trabzonspor.

Ata Akil, an amiable 35-year-old Izmirspor fan, was banned from attending Izmirspor matches for a year after taking part in a pitch invasion and fighting with rival fans. 'When I saw [rival team] supporters running onto the pitch and attacking [Izmirspor's] players, and the police not doing anything, I shouted for everyone to get on the pitch,' he recalled. 'During that match there had been lots of bad language, they threw stones, we threw stones – whatever, no problem. But at the point when they were attacking our players, that's when I got mad.'[31]

Akil was caught on camera and identified a week later. He had to sign in at a police station during the first and second halves of every home match during his ban:

> But the police station was too close to the stadium. So in the first half I'd sign in at the police station, and then go into the stadium and watch the rest of the first half. At half-time I'd leave, sign in at the police station again, and then go back to the stadium to watch the second half. This is Turkey.

'You're conscious of the responsibility you've got,' recalled Gordon Milne, Besiktas's coach in the late 1980s and early 1990s. He says Turkish fans were different to English hooligans, who were more focused on fighting for fighting's sake. 'The majority here were normal people who just got that wound up about what had happened,' said Milne. 'I always felt – Christ – you only needed something small to set it off, and if results weren't right, then you'd get trouble.' He never felt that sense of responsibility in England. 'No, here you were sitting on a powder keg.'[32]

Until 10–15 years ago, large, hostile welcoming parties would greet away fans arriving in many Turkish cities, stoning their buses. 'They are defending their cities, and when we go there we were trying to conquer their cities,' said Gokhan, the ex-ultrAslan member.[33]

Often violence is justified by the hot-blooded, *delikanli, arabesk* love that fans have for their clubs.[34] The journalist and commentator Ugur Turker made an argument that I heard a lot. 'This is the situation in Turkey: we don't love "football", we love our teams. We want our team to be successful, to be champions, nothing more,' he said.[35]

Journalist Volkan Agir recalls being slapped at a Galatasaray match because he was trying to watch the game, rather than chanting. Agir says that many fans – particularly of the big teams – make their club their identity. 'If you cannot win in your company, or your family life, or in social life, you create a connection with a winner,' he said. The club and the fans offered a community. 'They are not football crazy – they are crazy of winning, or leading, being part of something.'[36]

Fan violence is often triggered and inflamed by club presidents and officials, and I have seen this first-hand – officials punching each other in the VIP section, running onto the pitch to confront the referees or opposing players, or using insulting language to refer to rivals. Heavy-handed, rough treatment at the hands of the police often stokes violence, much of which takes place outside stadiums, beyond the view of Passolig. 'In Turkey you will see fights in parliament, in traffic jams, everywhere – it's about society, not just about football,' argues Deniz Dogruer, a football journalist.[37]

Footballers sometimes get caught up in violence. In August 2015, the windscreen of Fenerbahce midfielder Mehmet Topal's car was hit by a stray bullet in Istanbul. Luckily, Topal's car has bulletproof windows and the midfielder was unhurt. This was not even the first time Topal had been shot at. He was on the Fenerbahce team bus that was attacked by gunmen earlier that year close to Trabzon, in which the driver was injured.

The Besiktas winger Gokhan Tore found himself embroiled in controversy, accused along with a friend of threatening two national teammates with a gun over an argument concerning his ex-girlfriend.[38] In an apparently unrelated incident in 2014, Tore was shot in the shoulder while at an Istanbul nightclub at 4 a.m.. Tore claimed to have been an innocent bystander, unwittingly caught up in another dispute. Fortunately, the bullet just grazed him and he was back in training after a short convalescence.

Violence finds its way into other Turkish sports. In May 2016, a wheelchair basketball match between Besiktas and Galatasaray in Germany was abandoned after fighting between the fans.[39]

Many criticise the authorities for their failure to understand the roots of conflict and look at the bigger picture, and their lack of dialogue with fans, preferring instead to impose discipline from the top down, whether that is by baton, tear gas, water cannon or the Passolig card and the law. Over time the police and authorities became more organised – passing stringent legislation to deal with troublemakers and organising away fans' travel to and from stadiums. In 2011 away fans were banned from attending derby matches between the 'Big Four' teams. The '6222' law was many years in the making, and was finally passed in 2011.

'[6222] punishes fans from the beginning, cuts off all communication lines, and is based on punishment only,' says Basar Yarimoglu, a management committee member of FSE (Football Supporters Europe) and a founding member of Taraf-Der, a supporters' rights group set up in Ankara in 2013 in opposition to the '6222' law. '6222 is the biggest problem,' says Yarimoglu. 'Passolig is a kind of child of it.'[40]

Yarimoglu argues that the authority invested in individual police officers on match days, to scrutinise banners or flags, for example, means there is no system in place and cuts communication between clubs and fans. Supporter Liaison Officers (SLOs) are supposed to bridge communication between clubs and fans, but Yarimoglu claims that SLOs in Turkey tend to be members of the clubs' management committees, rather than real fans. '[They're] just a puppet for the clubs.'

For all the anecdotal incidents of violence, the level of disorder in Turkish football should be kept in perspective. Emir Guney says that, while there is a problem with fan violence in Turkish football, it is significantly smaller than the hooliganism problem that marred English football in the 1970s and 1980s. 'It is manageable,' says Guney. 'The fans are not violent just to be violent – they are violent because they want to be heard, and because the government and the federation oppress them with laws and regulations.'[41]

Violence in sport is a complex phenomenon – when it's not brutally simple – and it's not clear that the government or the football federation have the wherewithal or desire to understand its roots and manifestations. If violence is the failure of language, then it is instructive that there is so little dialogue in Turkish football between the fans and the authorities – whether that is the football federation, the police or politicians.

Some argue that the opinions and grievances of fans could be aired and addressed through the formation of an umbrella supporters' organisation. 'If the fans will feel that they are listened to and that things are changing, most of them won't act violently,' argues Guney. 'Some people will always act violently but then it will be easier to act on the small [violent] minority, rather than against the whole population which is against their system!'

Instead, football is a battlefield between many fans and the authorities. The biggest per capita rebellion against Passolig was at Genclerbirligi – regarded as Turkish football's least violent club. '[Genclerbirligi] were never punished because of violence and the biggest resistance against Passolig appeared amongst them, so it's really a big question mark for the football authorities,' says Basar Yarimoglu, of FSE and fan network Taraf-Der.[42]

Their decidedly mixed experience of resistance became a stress test for the culture of dissent among football fans.

Genclerbirligi: the rebellious ladies and gentlemen of Turkish football

Genclerbirligi fans are an unusual entity in Turkish football: they don't fight, and they don't swear in their chants. 'Sociologically, I think we are the "good boys" of the city,' said Erdem Ceydilek, a member of the Genclerbirligi fan group Alkaralar.[43]

Genclerbirligi – 'Union of Youths' – was formed by students from Ankara Boys' High School in 1923. The club almost went bankrupt in the 1980s but recovered under the eccentric stewardship of club president Ilhan Cavcav.[44] They won the Turkish Cup in 1987 and 2001 and, after coming third in the previous season, went on a dramatic UEFA Cup run in 2003/04, knocking out Blackburn Rovers, Sporting Lisbon and Parma, before losing to the eventual winners, Valencia, in the fourth round.

Genclerbirligi has always had a relatively small fan base and has traditionally been regarded as the team of students, intellectuals and Ankara's liberal and leftist elite. Around the year 2000, Genclerbirligi typically drew home crowds of around 1,000; they would converge behind the goal.

Over the next decade or so, success on the field, and efforts by the fans, built support for the club, and they started filling out the stand at the side of the pitch. The club gained some glamour from the popular television series *Behzat C*, whose title character is a charismatic detective from Ankara who is a big Genclerbirligi fan.

The notion of shifting footballing allegiance is anathema to the vast majority of Turkish football fans: support for a club is often an inheritance, the club name spelled out in DNA sequence. A football fan who changes teams is often referred to as a '*donme*', a pejorative term for someone who has converted or changed, now most typically deployed as a derogatory reference to transgender people.[45]

There is a practice – alluded to in a TV commercial – of football fanatic fathers painting the penises of their babies in the colours of their favourite teams and taking photographs, to be shown to the child when they grow up. A painted penis suggests a (somewhat forced) fidelity to the club's colours from birth.

There have probably been very few, if any, baby penises painted in the red and black of Genclerbirligi. Many Genclerbirligi fans are proud '*donmes*', often formerly fans of one of the Istanbul 'Big Three'. Some shifted allegiance because they wanted to support a team from their home city, while others were attracted to the club because of its political stances. The team's black and red colours are fitting for the anarchists, communists and socialists that comprise much of their fan base.

They still manage to wind up opposition fans without swearing: when away fans of one of the 'Big Three' Istanbul clubs chant 'You're sons of bitches' at Genclerbirligi, they fire back 'You're sons of Istanbul' – a sly dig at the many fans who come from across the country, including Ankara, and support a 'Big Three' club, rather than their local team.

Ankara was a laboratory for the pilot phase of the '6222' law in the years leading up to 2011. Thousands of Ankaragucu fans were given banning orders. Genclerbirligi were targeted because of their banners. At one pre-season tournament, Genclerbirligi brought flags to represent the nations of their foreign players: Burkina Faso, Costa Rica, Sweden – and also Ghana. 'The police came and said, "Why are you flying a PKK flag here?" I think they were referring to the Ghana flag,' recalled Ceydilek. 'The next day there was the final game of the tournament and it was obvious that there were hundreds of plainclothes police around us.'

After Gezi, the government unrolled nationwide bans on expressions of 'politics' in stadiums – by which they meant no left-wing or oppositional politics, argues Ceydilek. '[But] the national anthem is a political act and [it's played] before every league game.'

By the time of the Gezi protests, Genclerbirligi were attracting 5,000–6,000 supporters; after Gezi it peaked at around 9,000. After protesting in the streets, many Genclerbirligi fans continued their resistance in the stands – chanting 'It began in Taksim, the fight goes on' and 'political slogan' in response to the ban on expressions of politics in stadiums. 'Being a Genclerbirligi fan became one of the symbols of having an oppositional voice,' said Ceydilek. The protests lasted for a year – then the Passolig card was introduced.

Individual fans and some entire fan groups from teams across the country boycotted matches in the wake of the introduction of the Passolig system.[46] Genclerbirligi fans overwhelmingly agreed to boycott the system; per capita it was the most dramatic and disciplined boycott in the league. Attendances fell by more than 90 per cent.

The Passolig boycott arguably claimed a major scalp in January 2015 when Ulker – a food brand and major sponsor of Turkish football that is close to the government – pulled much of its funding from the sport, citing concerns about violence, dwindling crowds and the e-ticketing system: 'No one wants their information to be collected, even by the state; this is disturbing.'[47]

But many club administrators express their support for the system, even citing the fall in attendances as inevitable and welcome in the short term. 'Thanks to Passolig there is less violence now – because of the identity and face recognition,' said Osmanlispor's chief administrator Mehmet Davarci. 'The ones who are refusing to go to the stadiums are the ones who would cause violence there.'[48] This, however, is utter tosh – as demonstrated generally by the sheer numbers of those boycotting the system, and specifically by Genclerbirligi's boycott.[49]

Genclerbirligi stuck to the boycott over 2014/15, but misgivings grew among some fans. Boycotts by fan groups of other teams were often less organised and attendances began to creep up among other clubs. Alkaralar worried that the boycott in isolation was ineffective and that it would only hurt the club, that attendances would never recover. Many decided to stick to the boycott, but others – such as Alkaralar – decided to abandon it in 2015/16. 'Now it's meaningless to boycott because the games are sterilised and there is no other place for us to raise our voices,' said Ceydilek.

'It sounds contradictory to criticise Passolig and get a Passolig card, but it's only one component of industrial football – and we watch games on TV, we buy the official shirt of our team,' says Ceydilek. 'We will be glad if it's cancelled but for now there is a saying in Turkey: "You are the only one playing the drum" – it's only you and your little community.' The split in fan groups over Passolig boycotts has caused rancour, illustrating how Passolig has both triggered resistance, and divided it. 'They call us traitors,' said Ceydilek.[50]

'Alkaralar are scabs,' said 'Hakan',[51] a fan linked to the left-wing Genclerbirligi supporters' group KaraKizil, who remain committed to the boycott. 'They betrayed every single other fan in Turkey.' He has been friends with many of them for 15 years and says he will remain friends with them. 'But I don't know why they did this.'

I met Hakan and his friend, KaraKizil member Ozan Uzun, in the same pub I'd met the Alkaralar fans the day before. Again, beer after beer was brought forth in iced glasses, easing a headache from the previous day. Hakan had a moustache that drooped over his lip and absorbed the froth of his beer.

Hakan believes that Alkaralar's position is 'delusional': that they can't resist the system by participating in it – after all, political chanting and banners are banned.[52] Hakan and Ozan also feel betrayed by Alkaralar because many KaraKizil members are also involved in Taraf-Der, which is fighting the Passolig system through the courts. The perceived betrayal by Alkaralar is ascribed to their more liberal politics. 'The only left-wing group in Turkey is KaraKizil,' insisted Hakan.

There are six or seven supporters' groups within Genclerbirligi. 'I am a member of another supporters' group actually,' said Hakan. 'Our name is "we are sons of bitches." There are only two of us.'

Isn't this against the non-swearing rule?

It is. But it helps to stop all the Genclerbirligi fans in *Maraton* [stand] from swearing [back] against the 'you're all sons of bitches' [chant]. Because if one of us is in the stands when the opposition starts to chant 'you're all sons of bitches', we start celebrating! We claim to be the most known fan group in Turkey. There is only two of us because of the law. You can establish a gang with three [or more] people under Turkish law, but two people are [considered] 'individuals'. It's not an organised crime.[53]

Is it you two?

'No it is me and another guy,' Hakan replied. 'He was supposed to show up today, but he didn't.'

'I'm not crazy like that,' added Ozan.

'We also like to steal banners from [fellow Genclerbirligi fans] and take naked pictures with them,' continued Hakan. 'Everybody knows my ass.'

You'll have to send me some photos.

'Oh. You wanna see my ass?'

I steered the conversation back to Passolig. For them, fan violence in Turkey is spontaneous and has clear triggers. 'Fan violence is promoted by the people from the club – the chairman, or the people who want to be chairman. There is no organised fan violence,' said Hakan, who argues that

Passolig is not actually necessary in what they deem to be a surveillance society. Their stadium was already full of high-definition cameras before the Passolig system was introduced. 'So they know even when you pick your nose,' said Hakan. 'They know the identity, not only of yourself, but also of your right ear!'

Although Alkaralar had returned to the stands, the attendances remained pitifully low, the atmosphere was lacklustre, and the club was struggling for form on the pitch. What if Genclerbirligi get relegated or fold?

'Fuck this Genclerbirligi. Cut off my tail and I will grow another one!' replied Hakan.

Ozan admitted that Passolig had somewhat disrupted political activism among fans. 'If there was no Passolig we would still be in the stands fighting against the law against violence in sports, but now because of Passolig we are not there.' But he insisted that KaraKizil remain active on the streets.

As I was leaving the pub to meet Alkaralar and go to a Genclerbirligi match later that night, Hakan shouted after me: 'Don't be a part of the crime!' I looked back, and held up my hands in apology and helplessness, and they were laughing.

'Berkin died like that'

Yusuf Murat Ozdemir is also a Genclerbirligi fan and a member of KaraKizil. His life changed forever during the first hour of the first day of the Gezi protests, which had spread to his home city of Ankara, where he was studying computer science at university.

Murat, then 26, joined the protests in solidarity with Gezi and against the AKP's authoritarianism. He was angry with Ankara's AKP mayor Melih Gokcek for the city's increasingly chaotic public transportation, for the city's allegedly poisoned water supply and – in echoes of Gezi – for the mayor's role in the destruction of green space for construction projects.

Murat was with a group of KaraKizil friends at the back of a peaceful protest. Some of his friends wanted to buy beers, but Murat didn't think it was appropriate to drink alcohol during a protest. 'It was a good thing that I didn't drink, because if I'd drunk beer I would not have been accepted for surgery the same day,' he recalled.

Murat and his friends were close to the American Embassy and wanted to get back to Kizilay in central Ankara, but the police had blocked off the road. The police started to fire tear gas on the group, and everybody ran. Murat had run perhaps 50 metres from the police lines when he turned and glanced back for moment, and something crashed into his left eye.

> After I got shot I saw tear gas and the canister in front of me. There was lots of excitement so I didn't feel much in that moment. After half an hour it started to burn. But for half an hour I just kept running. I didn't just run away from the police, but also I ran to the hospital because cabs wouldn't take me because I was bleeding.[54]

The hospital cleaned away the blood and covered his eye, and then sent him to another hospital. He had an operation that same day. 'I really didn't notice that I couldn't see out of my left eye for a few hours.'

Murat counts himself as both incredibly unlucky and fortunate. 'If I hadn't turned back maybe I would have been shot in the back of my head and that would have killed me. Berkin died like that,' he said, referring to Berkin Elvan – a 14-year-old boy in Istanbul, a bystander to the protests, who was hit in the head by a police tear gas canister and later succumbed to his injuries.

Murat's glasses may have absorbed some of the impact of the canister, but the shattered glass shredded the nerves in his eye. In his first operation the doctors removed the shards of glass – at the last moment the surgeon found the final piece, saving the eyeball. Eleven days later Murat had a second operation which removed the eye's fluid and injected silicon to prevent shrinkage. A third operation removed the stitches. He will probably need a fourth operation as the body typically starts to reject silicon as a foreign body after a few years. If they have to permanently remove the silicon, the eye may start shrinking and they might have to remove the eyeball. 'My doctor said, "If you see the light, you will probably see with your eye like you used to,"' says Murat. 'The problem is – I don't see the light. I don't see anything.'

Murat was depressed and traumatised after the shooting and, although he is feeling much better, it is still raw enough that he doesn't want to go into details. He missed out on jobs because his eyesight loss meant he couldn't be trusted with carrying and using expensive equipment. He had difficulties reading, he struggles to play football. His left eye often gets dry and bloodshot, and burns. His right eye is a deep brown, but his damaged eye is tinged with cyan.

As time passes, Murat is adapting better. His friends are a massive support. While he was in hospital he had a huge number of visitors, many from Genclerbirligi, so many that he lost track – perhaps 100–150 in one day. 'That's very supportive actually. And it's also very dangerous because they can bring in some viruses or bacteria!' he says, laughing. 'The doctors got angry with me.'

At a Genclerbirligi match thousands of fans wore eye patches in solidarity with Murat and the many other protesters who were hit in the eye by tear gas canisters. 'I observed them – after five minutes they started to remove them, they couldn't follow the match,' he says with a laugh. 'But this protest was very beautiful.'

Genclerbirligi fans also made banners in support of Berkin Elvan. Tear gas is supposed to be fired high in an arc, so that it drops relatively gently out of the sky, but the police repeatedly fired the canisters laterally and directly into crowds, using them as missiles to injure and maim. The police claimed that Murat was hit in the eye by a stone thrown by protesters. However, the medical reports were unequivocal – they stated that Murat was hit by a tear gas canister that had been fired directly.

Murat is pursuing criminal charges cases against the police, and a claim for compensation. His lawyer has asked for the names of the police officers on duty that day, but the police claim they don't know, so his case is stalling. 'We have to wait. But I don't care any more. Because I don't expect any justice from this country.'

For Murat it is not just about the police officer who shot him, or even Erdogan or the AKP, it is systemic. 'Because people think that they have to worship someone, they have to find their leaders and sacrifice their lives for their leaders, their governments,' said Murat. 'Tayyip Erdogan is a figure today but 30 years ago there was another figure; 50 years ago there was another figure who was important for those people… two things are responsible for this. The first is religion and the second is nationalism.'

Perhaps in a few years, if Murat can keep his eyeball, then new technology may have developed that can make a difference to his eyesight. Nevertheless, Murat's life is back on track. He is working again and plans to study for a PhD in the US.

Murat has attended some protests since he was shot. A year after Gezi he was at university when protests broke out against the mayor's plans to build on more green space close to the campus. 'I saw the tear gas,' recalled Murat. 'I didn't go home. I waited there, but far at the back. There was

500 metres, maybe more, between the police and me. But I was still able to see them.'

Courts and coups

Many of the fans in KaraKizil were part of the Taraf-Der supporters' network that was fighting the Passolig system through the courts, supported by Izmir's fan network, Taraftar Haklari.

Many fans felt that an early Passolig commercial was patronising and insulting to fans, portraying some of them as boorish and stupid. 'This is how Passolig thinks of [typical] Turkish fans,' says Dincer Tomruk, a lawyer and football fan who has represented the supporters' groups. Their campaign against the advert succeeded in getting it pulled from the air. 'That was our first victory as a group.'[55]

The supporters' rights networks then took Aktif Bank and the football federation to the consumer court, arguing that the sharing of personal information breaches consumer rights, and also registered a complaint at the competition agency, arguing that a system run by one bank over a term of ten years contravenes competition laws.

Despite numerous requests for comment, Passolig refused to defend or advocate for its own system, and I spent months chasing Aktif Bank to respond to the concerns of fans, who are, by default, also their customers. A PR agency working for the company eventually told me that Aktif Bank was not willing to talk because it is producing a coffee-table book about Turkish football and it wants to open a football museum. I asked why that precludes the bank from talking to me. 'They are probably worried because they wouldn't have total control over what you write,' she said. 'We don't know what you are going to say about the government.'[56]

Aktif Bank's silence is not surprising: it has a huge financial and political stake in the Passolig cards, with a monopoly on running the e-ticket system that brings significant commissions – though it gives half back to the clubs – enjoying privileges such as highly favourable interest rates on loans and sponsorship deals, and gaining huge numbers of new customers. Several matches are restricted to the holder of a specific 'club' Passolig card – allegedly to prioritise fans and stop rival fans from accessing the stadium, but in practice anyone can buy multiple cards, as long as they pay a fee each time.

Mete Duren, the spokesperson of the Turkish Football Federation, said that the system had been shaped by Aktif Bank. When the law was set to be implemented, many of the clubs baulked at having to bear the considerable cost of installing the high-definition camera systems, as did many companies. Aktif Bank was apparently also not keen, but suggested ways in which the agreement could be made 'feasible', including introducing the banking and purchasing elements. 'They did a big favour to the clubs by taking over all the costs of the instalments and the equipment,' said Duren.[57]

Duren says that the system has weeded out troublemakers and encouraged football lovers to come to the matches. 'We had the feeling that every year we were losing more and more real football fans,' he said. He claimed that the huge fall in attendances after Passolig was mostly linked to clubs ending the practice of handing out free tickets to fans that could be sold on. 'The black market entrance into the stadium has stopped,' he said. 'I can't say it is zero but at least it has been decreased I would say 90 per cent.' His only evidence for this is the word of the clubs, but privately many fans and some clubs admit that this practice has decreased but is still widespread.

I certainly found that it was easy to purchase tickets on the black market – the electronic system may make it easier in some ways, because now you can – perfectly legally – transfer tickets from one card to another without having to meet. The Passolig system can track ticket transfers, but not whether money is changing hands.[58]

Some fans are gradually returning to the stadiums – average attendances have risen to over 8,000 – and others are not troubled by the system, particularly those broadly supportive of the government.[59] But I met many fans who continue to boycott the system.

The football federation says it has reduced violence, and announced that away fans would be able to attend derbies in 2016/17 for the first time since 2011. While the cameras may indeed present a deterrent, and the sharp reduction in attendances reduced the potential for trouble, violence inside the stadiums still takes place. During the final match of the 2015/16 season, fans of relegated Eskisehirspor set fire to parts of their own stadium and invaded the pitch![60] It is noteworthy that Passolig has not been introduced in less popular, less lucrative sports – such as basketball – in which violence is also an issue. Outside the big derbies, section closures and stadium closures remain common.

Despite its ostensible identification with the poor, the AKP has become infamous for its gentrification, Gezi Park being just one example. Some argue that the Passolig system is part of an ongoing attempt to gentrify fans. 'We are not wanted,' says Genclerbirligi fan and Taraf-Der member Hakan. 'They want customers, not fans.'[61]

In this sense, Turkish football is following trends in other countries – notably England – which have sought to socially engineer fandom and make football stands more 'middle-class', largely by pricing out lower-income supporters, curtailing 'unruly' behaviour and commercialising the match-day experience with adverts and invocations to consume.[62]

The anthropologist Yagmur Nuhrat believes that the AKP has intensified and entangled neoliberal and neo-conservative trends that emerged in Turkey in the 1980s:

> We see this in urban regeneration projects, and regulations pertaining to families and reproduction, and education – and we see it in football. And it's never been so wholesale and it's never been so bodily for so many people and displacing so many people and changing their everyday lives.[63]

Nuhrat speculates that a limited number of cheaper – though not cheap – seats are retained to keep some of the passionate following for branding purposes:

> They need those people because it's a part of the whole package – they need it to remain as a spectacle so that other people can come in and watch them. They're the fire of the show, but they need to be contained in a specific section of the stadium where the tickets cost less.

The commercialisation of football throws up huge hypocrisies. When Besiktas fans threw their scarves on the pitch during a match in 2011, to donate them to earthquake victims, the football federation fined the club – but then later sold footage of the incident to Coca-Cola for an advert.

The constitutional court ruled that the concept of e-tickets is constitutional but that the selling of personal information is unconstitutional. The competition authority will review the case again in 2019. The consumer court ruled in March 2016 that the Passolig card could continue, but that there could be no sharing of data with 'third parties'. But the constitutional court had previously ruled that Aktif Bank itself is a third party, so what happens next is confusing. The lawyer Dincer Tomruk sees this as an ongoing fight, likely to drag on for years: 'Even if the decision was in our favour, we don't have confidence that the decision will be applied properly,' he said, pointing to increased government influence in the judiciary and the football federation.[64]

Meanwhile, as the battle against Passolig went through the courts, a group of 35 fans – including several Carsi members – went on trial, accused of attempting to stage a 'coup' against the government during the Gezi Park protests. During the first hearing, in December 2014, a leading Carsi member and defendant, Cem Yakiskan, said that Besiktas had not even been able to topple their unpopular club president – now football federation president – Yildirim Demiroren for years, let alone the government, adding, 'If we had the power to stage a coup, we would have made Besiktas champions,' to laughter inside the court. Outside the courtroom, fans from different clubs again protested together in support of the defendants.

'It's just senseless. How can a group of football fans bring down the government? Come on, seriously. We don't have assault rifles, tanks, or jets or anything – how are we going to do that?' said Carsi member Yener, who believed the trial was a blatant attempt to cow rebellious fans. 'If they put a leash on Besiktas, that's going to be a big positive for them.'[65]

After several hearings, the 35 members were acquitted in December 2015 of attempting to overthrow the government, and of forming and managing criminal and terrorist organisations. But the strain of Gezi, its aftermath, and the trial exposed cracks in the group, increasing the pressure on Carsi to curb its rebellious behaviour.

The gentrification of Carsi?

I met Cem Yakiskan, 50, in his bar in the heart of Besiktas. There were photos of Charles Bukowski and a poster of the assassinated Armenian journalist Hrant Dink on the wall, and a model wooden boat with its sails painted in Besiktas colours. Yakiskan was bespectacled, with greying, thinning hair, and pale-blue eyes. He looked more accountant than anarchist. In a sense Yakiskan embodies the gentrification of the once working-class area: he had started out working in construction, then in a market selling fruit, before becoming a textile producer, managing a store, and opening his bar in 2012.

'I was born in this district. When I was a little kid we didn't really have anything else to keep ourselves busy, other than playing football and watching football,' said Yakiskan. 'And during the times of the military coup in the 1980s we *really* had nothing else to do. The only entertainment we had was football.'[66]

Yakiskan claims that the essence of Carsi was a spirit:

If you feel the spirit of Carsi inside you, then you are a member. What is this spirit? You have to be fair to people, you have to treat people as equals, you have to care about everything around you – including animals and trees and nature.

Carsi began as a loose gang, as Yakiskan and his friends hung out and fought in the terrace wars together. They had to stick together for their safety outside the stadium. 'Now anyone can get a hat and scarf and they can become a member of Carsi, and people financially benefit from it,' said Yakiskan. 'It became a commercial brand and that's not at all what our goal was.' Yet, there is a prominent Carsi logo painted on the wall of the outside area of Yakiskan's bar, so it seems he too benefits from the brand.

Yakiskan denies there is a leader but sees himself as a leading member. He helped arrange the truce that ended the worst of the violence, worked to turn the group's focus on to social projects, and says it was inevitable Carsi would end up at the Gezi protests: 'But when people started stepping back we were left [exposed] at the front. That's why people started seeing us as the leaders.'

He projects nonchalance about the trial. 'I grew up on the streets, I'm used to these kinds of accusations and battles. But I have two children – my children and my wife were more affected by this.' Yet the trial was a financial blow – he had to pay for bail and legal fees, and many people stopped coming to his bar. The police started turning up and hassling the customers; he claims there were attempts to blackmail him. It is not over for Yakiskan as the prosecutors continue to appeal the acquittals.

Yakiskan denies that the trial has weakened and intimidated Carsi. 'I know a lot of people who would go in a heartbeat if Gezi happened again, and I am one of them.' Yet, other leading members of Carsi had opposed the group's involvement in Gezi, leading to feelings of rancour and betrayal.

Yakiskan's old comrade Alen Markaryan was there with him at the beginning of Carsi, but they no longer talk. Markaryan has also moved up in the world – he owns a hot and stifling *meyhane* in a district some way up Barbarossa Hill, ten minutes' drive from Besiktas. He was both large and diminutive: a small head and thick arms, small hands, short in stature but with a barrel for a torso, a limited neck.

Markaryan is perhaps the most famous Carsi member of all time – remarkable in that he is of Armenian descent and famed mainly for his exploits as the foremost 'amigo' – chant-leader – a position he has now largely given up.[67] In 2011 he was shot in the leg after a dispute with another Carsi amigo.[68] He has also been banned from going to the matches for much of the past five years. 'Because if you go to the middle of the stadium, and you can silence the fans with one gesture, that's authority. So when [the authorities] see that, they try to stop you.'[69]

Markaryan said he wouldn't even want to share a page or appear in the same book as Cem Yakiskan, but had agreed to talk to me because a friend had asked him to. Markaryan had been bitterly opposed to Carsi heading to Gezi, or getting involved in any politics:

> You have one duty and that is to defend Besiktas. Before [Gezi] I had already distanced myself, but [when Gezi happened] I distanced myself completely. I have a phrase that I often repeat: 'Until you get to the gates of the stadium, you're a Turk, you're a Kurd, you're an Alevi, you're a Sunni, you're a Muslim, Christian – anything you want to be. But once you pass the gates you only have one identity and that's Besiktas.'

Why did you distance yourself from Carsi before Gezi? 'Platini said that he quit football because his brain could still dominate his legs but his legs could not carry out the movements of his brain. It was something similar.'

Markaryan didn't attend the trial hearings but said that when Yakiskan and the defendants were cleared he felt relief. But he was also pleased that the trial had, as he saw it, disrupted Carsi's involvement in politics. 'A movement had begun, and the trial stopped it,' he said.

Carsi ultra Yener Ozturk said that, on the opening day of the new stadium, one of the best aspects was Markaryan's appearance; it was the first time he had seen him in years. Just before kick-off Markaryan walked onto the pitch, briefly remonstrated with a security guard, got his way, strode into the centre circle, and put his arms in the air, vibrating his hands. 'Ooohhhhhh,' went up a thundering cry from the stands. Markaryan gestured for yet more volume – 'OOOHHHHHH' – and held it there, and held it some more, and then brought his finger to his lips. 'Shhhhh,' said 40,000 people and a momentary hush settled. Markaryan brought his arm down and 40,000 screamed: 'One, two, three: Besiktas!' and they clapped in rapid staccato: 'Besiktas!' and the crowd became a huge bursting, billowing sheet of movement, as tens of thousands jumped up and down.

Carsi had been on best behaviour that day, purposely avoiding any controversy. They were worried about stadium bans, fines, escalating clashes and more court cases. 'We just don't want to deal with it again,' said Yener. 'Who wants to go jail for the rest of their lives over football? Because it is just football. No one wants to risk anything I guess.'

Did that mean that the government had won and put a leash on Besiktas? 'Maybe a little bit. But it's a short-term thing – next season it'll be back to normal I'm sure,' said Yener. 'We'll go back to cursing and see what happens. But this year no one wants to [screw] it up. Because it's so close, and we haven't been this close in a while.'[70]

Turkey's invincibles

Despite being one of the 'Big Three', Besiktas has always seen itself as a kind of underdog compared to its more gilded rivals. But in the late 1980s and early 1990s, with Englishman Gordon Milne as coach, Besiktas went through its most glorious era. Milne was back in town for the opening of the new stadium and reflected on his time as Besiktas coach and how Turkish football has changed.

Milne played for Liverpool under Bill Shankly and was capped several times for England. He went on to manage Wigan Athletic, Coventry City and Leicester City, gaining a reputation for attacking, direct football. By 1987 he fancied a new challenge, preferably abroad – perhaps in France or Spain. He heard about an opening at Besiktas through England's assistant manager Don Howe. Milne had to admit he'd never heard of Besiktas. 'Don talked about the passion, and how they're football crazy, how the president's a good guy.'

Things started moving very fast. Besiktas rang him that evening and invited him over. The next day, Milne was sitting in the Hilton looking down on the Bosphorus and Inonu Stadium below. He couldn't fail to be impressed. Milne is now 79 years old, but could easily pass for 20 years younger. We were drinking tea on the veranda of the same hotel he first visited all those years ago.

Milne got to work right away but it was not the most auspicious start. Besiktas hadn't shown him the training facilities – probably for good reason. 'They were very primitive,' said Milne, recalling a training pitch of earth and sand, full of potholes. Many of the showers were broken. Then there was the problem with money. 'Players weren't getting paid on time. They never paid me on time – that never bothered me because the chairman Suleyman Seba was a fine man and I trusted him.'[71]

Milne decided not to bring any English staff over – he didn't want any cliques forming. He relied on his Turkish translator, Ali – who perfectly translated exactly what Milne said – and a Turkish assistant manager, Bahattin Baydar. Milne never mastered Turkish, which helped him in a way. His language limitations and the poor training facilities forced him to adopt a simple but effective coaching style. He remembers an early training session: 'They're trying to pass the ball and the ball's bobbling, and the wind's blowing sand in everyone's faces – nothing's working. So I had to bring it back to real basics,' recalls Milne.

Milne was aware that Besiktas were impatient for success and, unless he delivered quickly, he would soon be out of a job. 'The first year we didn't achieve anything. We finished second, but that's nothing here and then the natives were getting restless.'

Not speaking Turkish also helped him avoid much of the criticism that was brewing in the press and the stands. The media attention was intense. 'I can remember in my last year at Leicester, coming out of the dressing room after a game and there would be six reporters with a pad and a pencil writing down what you said about the game. I came here and there was 60 with microphones and recording machines.'

Milne recalls how Bill Shankly used to deal with the press:

At home, on a Sunday, if the newspapers were all over the kitchen, Liverpool had won because he'd read them all. If they were folded all neatly in a nice pile, they'd lost. He wouldn't read them. And I think if I'd understood [the papers in Turkey] it would have affected my mentality and how I'd operated.

Milne got the club to build a grass training pitch and better facilities. Despite the language barrier, Milne was forging strong bonds with the players. He wasn't afraid to drop big name players. 'We won the cup in the second year, and that kept me afloat.'

In the third season everything fell into place. The front three of MAF – Metin (Tekin), Ali (Gultiken) and Feyyaz (Ucar) – ran riot. They once scored all the goals in a record-breaking 10–0 demolition of Adana Demirspor. The captain, Riza Calimbay, was a brilliant player, the engine of the team – 'a little workhorse'.

Milne also had a calm demeanour that he tried to transmit to the players – they were often hyped up in the days leading up to the games, and their personalities were fiery. As they got closer to winning the league, Milne saw how much it meant to the players. 'In a way they were probably keener than me to win it. That always struck me – how important it was to them. The satisfaction I got was, when we did it, seeing them.' He was also pleased to repay the faith that the president had shown in him. The team was high on belief – Milne remembers Calimbay saying that Besiktas would win the league the following season, no problem. They did. Then they won a third title in a row in 1991/92, finishing the season unbeaten – a feat never emulated in Turkish football's top flight. Milne reflected:

> When you're on song you take it for granted, you're just doing it, you're not thinking too much, it's instinctive, and you don't want that rhythm to be broken. The train's on the line and sometimes it only takes a little thing to nudge if off and it can be difficult to get it back on again. So [Besiktas] had that rhythm.

By 1994 Milne had been at Besiktas for nearly seven years, an eternity in Turkish football. Although he believed he could have won the league again, he also felt it was time for a change. In the early 1980s, Milne had coached the young Gary Lineker at Leicester City, and in 1994 Lineker had just transferred from Tottenham Hotspur to the Japanese team Grampus Eight, who were looking for a coach. Seba gave his blessing to Milne to leave. It was a bit of a wrench. 'In a way I couldn't get away quick enough cos I thought "I could get too sentimental here and change my mind."'

Milne was not as successful in Japan. When he got there, Gary Lineker was injured. They had a three-foreigner rule and three Brazilians – then the club went over Milne's head to buy two Serbians. 'So now I've got three Brazilians, two Yugoslavs and Gary [Lineker]. If Gary's fit then I play Gary, and then I have war with Brazil or Yugoslavia because somebody's going to be left out.' The board kept interfering, Milne resisted, and not long later he was sacked, in Japanese style. The team were preparing to go to Australia for a tour. The board told him: 'We'd like you to take the team to Australia. After Australia, you take a little holiday.'

Bursaspor came in with an offer and Milne jumped at the chance to return to Turkey. He spent a season there and it was going well, until Seba started to talk about a return to Besiktas, which turned his head. Milne left Bursaspor but the Besiktas job didn't materialise, perhaps because of other board members. 'I always felt that I let Bursa down a little bit,' he admitted.

Trabzonspor swooped in and offered him a job in 1996. 'That was an experience. You know, Trabzon's in Turkey but it's a state on it's own is Trabzon,' laughed Milne. He remembers travelling to the airport and being dumbfounded as board members handed over guns at passport control. 'And they had this passionate crowd that could react on their own team in two minutes,' said Milne. Their team bus would often be stoned by their own fans, sometimes even if they'd only drawn.

Milne left Trabzonspor after one season, returning to the UK and working as Newcastle United's director of football alongside his old friend Bobby Robson until 2004. Milne returned to Besiktas for a brief stint as director of football in 2006, tasked with bringing through young players, but he felt unable to do his job because of the interference of board members. Milne was also always conscious of politics being in the background, in a way that it wasn't in England – machinations over kick-off times, appointments of referees, politicians identifying with the club:

I kept away from politics. If politics gets involved in football it tarnishes it forever. It's the innocence of football that to me keeps the interest anywhere in the world. Get a ball down and you can play anywhere can't you? Wherever you are, whatever nationality you are you can meet someone and play football. And, OK, I might be romantic, but that's how I see it... the majority of people enjoy football because it's a relief from bloody politics isn't it?

Suleyman Seba – who had been a Besiktas player and scored the first ever goal at the Inonu Stadium – was Besiktas president from 1984 to 2000; he passed away in 2014 at the age of 88. Milne attended Seba's funeral and remembers his old friend fondly. Milne returns to Turkey regularly, where he is adored by Besiktas fans and even regarded warmly by their rivals. His son is married to a Turkish woman. I spoke to Milne in April 2016 – he was in town for the opening of the Vodafone Arena.

Milne recalls Inonu Stadium vividly. It was very different from the identikit 'bowl' arenas that characterise modern football. He would sit on the bench and gaze out of the stadium at trees and the buildings beyond. Some fans are nostalgic for Inonu. 'But it was a mess underneath, the toilets – urgh – poky rooms, concrete, metal gates that go through here and there, it was a bloody marathon to get in and out of, and hostile for a visiting team: if you're coming from bloody Real Madrid then, Christ Almighty, it's like you've gone back to the bloody stone age here, [they're thinking] "What's this?"' chuckled Milne. 'It was like a dungeon underneath and then you'd come up the steps and onto the pitch.'

The run-in

Besiktas just needed a point from their last home match of the 2015/16 season against Osmanlispor to wrap up the title with a game to spare, putting an end to seven years' bad luck. Black-and-white hordes descended on Besiktas; it became hard to keep track of friends amid the uniformity of colours. Buzzing bug-like drones hovered above the crowds. The neighbourhood was under clouds of smoke from countless flares and fireworks; the district echoed with explosions, and there was the smell of cordite and sulphur in the air. Besiktas won 3–1 and their fans revelled across the district.

The streets echoed with one chant in particular:

> Siyah!
> Beyaz!
> Sampiyon!
> Besiktas![72]

These were happy days at Besiktas – back in their home, traditions rekindled, a first league title since 2009. Besiktas flags and banners turned up all over the city.

But they were not happy days in Turkey. The grievances that led to the Gezi uprising have only grown. There is simmering discontent amid swathes of the population. The authoritarianism of the government has only become more severe. Many anti- Erdogan voters – who constitute roughly half of the population – feel their circle getting smaller; the space they feel comfortable in is shrinking.

The Gezi protests rattled the government. They exposed its insecurity and its determination to impose what it sees as the will of the majority. Anti-government protest is viciously crushed. With all the regular news of media outlets being shut down, it is sometimes surprising that there are still so many left to repress. Football fans have been pursued through the courts in the hundreds.

When I had met with a group of various Izmir fans, we laughed about some of the more absurd bans on football banners under 'Law 6222', and the other pressure they were subject to, but once the laughter subsided an Izmirspor fan, Ata Akil, said something good-natured, but pointed: 'Turkey is a great place if you're a visitor – you can have a great time and you can have a laugh at everything that goes on here. But it's different if you're a citizen,' he said. 'When you are forced to live it, it's bullshit.'[73]

The fear among many is that polarisation, rancour and division have become necessary conditions for Erdogan to maintain his grip on power, using antagonism and demonisation of opponents as tactics to shore up support amid the government's growing struggles.

The future of Gezi Park remains unclear. On the anniversaries of the uprising the police occupy the streets in force, ready to shut down any protests in a moment. 'One of the subjects that we have to be brave about is Gezi Park in Taksim,' said Erdogan on 18 June 2016. 'I am saying it here once again: We will construct that historic building [the Ottoman barracks] there.'[74] In February 2017, construction quietly began on the long-planned mosque in a corner of Taksim Square. No protests materialised – only a few cheering supporters turned up. Since the failed coup in summer 2016 and the following crackdown, there has been a reversal – Taksim has been more often occupied by pro-government supporters.

For the moment, Gezi Park is still there, enjoyed by those who prize the rare green(ish) space. Gezi is more than just a park in Taksim Square – it is a symbol and a spirit, a proto-movement as motley and diverse as Carsi. It remains to be seen whether the authorities can gentrify Gezi Park, and whether they can fully gentrify football fans.

'Gezi brought all kinds of people together but after that we separated again, we couldn't understand what those days meant. It's the same for the supporters also,' said Galatasaray fanatic Gokhan Karakaya. He describes Turkey now as a police state, and believes that the state's violence has cowed opposition among football fans and in wider society: '[Erdogan's] army is the police.'[75]

Football fans may be divided, but anthropologist and Besiktas fanatic Yagmur Nuhrat does not think that the Gezi effect has ended: 'I think it's something that is still very available for people to draw upon whenever there's a protest.' Nuhrat says that Besiktas fans are currently trying to reconcile their self-image, as underdogs and rebels, with a craving for success. 'I found for the first time actually some self-censorship and self-policing,' she said, when talking about the new stadium.[76]

It was inevitable that a diverse alliance like Gezi could not hold – LGBT people couldn't unite with the far right, Kurds couldn't hold together with ultranationalists, feminists with many football fans, and leftists with their multiple sects and schisms. Football fans couldn't maintain their unity.

But there are some gains. The lawyer Dincer Tomruk says he stays motivated in his fight against the Passolig card because of their small victories, his love of football and the 'Gezi spirit': 'Many people still believe in what we did and accomplished back then.'[77]

The Gezi protests may also have boosted civil society in Turkey, forging links between different issues and groups. Emrah Akman, a member of Taraftar Haklari, thinks that a cultural change is taking place. He says that most Turkish people across the political spectrum traditionally wanted a strong leader. 'I guess people [at Gezi] stopped wanting a strong leader and discovered their own power.'[78] Different people saw they could come together, partly epitomised by the alliance between football fans; they encountered and heard each other for the first time.

The emergence of the supporters' rights networks like Taraf-Der and Taraftar Haklari could be significant. They are small groups, they are still developing, they are overwhelmingly – but not all – leftist, but it shows a trend: some football fans in Turkey can set aside their rivalries and are increasingly organising for their rights. Taraf-Der and Taraftar Haklari are working together to try to get Turkey's first national umbrella fan rights group off the ground, that can represent the concerns of all fans, regardless of political ideology, and can gain official recognition from the Turkish Football Federation.

'But the missing link is Istanbul,' says Basar Yarimoglu of FSE and Taraf-Der.[79] Not only are there tensions between fans of the major Istanbul teams, but there are also tensions between fans within their own clubs: differences due to politics, relations with the club management, and personalities. It shows the limits to 'Istanbul United', when fans supporting the same team are so riven.

The authorities may feel they are winning the battle over Passolig as attendances rise slowly, painstakingly, although they remain way below pre-Passolig levels and average figures are dragged up by the large attendances attracted by a few teams. Many Carsi members hate the Passolig system, but they now have the cards – their love of Besiktas outweighs their hostility to the system.

The battle for the soul of Turkish football is ongoing: Passolig endures, Gezi Park endures and Carsi endures, albeit not quite as before, subject to political repression, division and struggling with its own form of gentrification.

I asked Carsi's Cem Yakiskan if he'd wanted the so-called 'Istanbul United' phenomenon to last. He started to smile and shake his head before I'd even finished the question. 'No, I never wanted that. We are socialists, but – as socialist as we are – we are fascists for Besiktas!'[80]

6

Kurdish Cup Specialists

On a bright January day, a group of football fans dressed in a tropical array of colours had gathered in Sirinevler Square, on the outskirts of European Istanbul. Most wore the green, red and gold of Amedspor – the biggest team in Diyarbakir, the largest city in the predominantly Kurdish south-east. After I'd said I was writing about Turkish football, one fan corrected me with a grin: 'No! This is Kurdish football.'

The group were in high spirits. Amedspor, who play in the scrappy depths of Turkish football's third tier, were in the midst of a thrilling and unlikely cup run. Later that afternoon they were taking on the high-flying Super League side Istanbul Basaksehir FK.

Most were members of the Amedspor fan group Barikat, which was formed in 2014 by Bilal Akkulu to support the club through ultras culture. 'We want Amedspor to be for Kurdish people what Barcelona is for the Catalans,' he told me.[1]

'Barikat' is a provocative name, meaning 'barricade'. Amedspor's cup run had coincided with the breakdown of the peace process between the Turkish state and the PKK – a Kurdish armed group that Turkey, the US and the EU classify as terrorists. While Amedspor went on their cup run, Kurdish militants were building barricades and battling the security forces in cities across the south-east. The renewed violence in the Kurdish region and beyond was among the worst in a three-decade insurgency, in which more than 40,000 people have died. Inevitably, the tensions of the conflict found their way into football.

Much of the controversy centred around Deniz Naki – Amedspor's star player and political renegade. Naki's body is a billboard for his identity. Although Amedspor's 26-year-old playmaker was born and brought up in Germany, his family are Alevi Kurds originating from Dersim. He wears the number 62 on his shirt (Dersim's licence plate number). On his left hand is a tattoo of Alberto Korda's Che Guevara image. He has tattoos in capital letters on both forearms – 'Azadi' ('freedom' in Kurdish) inked on the left, 'Dersim 62' on the right – which he can hold up and display in pride, defiance or provocation as necessary. Blue letters on his knuckles spell 'Naki'.

Naki has a knack for controversy; he whips many conservatives, Turkish nationalists and Islamists into a froth of rage. Whilst playing for the Ankara club Genclerbirligi in 2014 he was attacked on the street after he had declared his support on social media for the Kurds fighting against ISIS in Kobane, a Kurdish city in Syria just across the Turkish border. Naki no longer felt safe in Ankara after the attack, and returned to Germany. But Barikat contacted Naki and played a role in persuading him to join Amedspor, in the less-than-salubrious Spor Toto 2 league.

While Amedspor had struggled for consistency in the league, their cup form had been truly inspired. They had qualified for the group stages after two knockout rounds, which included a narrow extra-time victory over the talented second-tier side Elazigspor. In the group stages they remained unbeaten, qualifying for the next knockout round with a game to spare. Amedspor's match at Basaksehir's stadium would be a spicy confrontation to settle first and second place in the group and decide who each team would play in the final 16.

The Amedspor fans bundled into a couple of buses and headed towards Basaksehir's stadium. As we neared the ground, Bilal told everyone to 'stay together' in case of attack by rival fans. Basaksehir is close to the ruling AKP and its fans are known for their conservatism. When we arrived there were no Basaksehir fans in sight – only a man hawking Amedspor merchandise who gave chase when he spotted the bus. Smoke plumed from a cart selling barbequed meat as scores of Amedspor fans milled around and got their bearings.

Forty-five minutes before kick off, huge queues had formed at the away fans' ticket office – a tiny portacabin, which looked incongruous compared to the inter-galactic engineering of the new stadium a couple of hundred metres away. After 20 minutes the queues had not noticeably diminished – they were checking every person's identity against a security database before issuing them with a ticket. It seemed like an obvious attempt to needle the Amedspor fans.[2]

With five minutes to the 2 p.m. kick-off, there were still a couple of hundred people stuck outside, and it was clear they would miss much of the match. At 14:03 a huge cheer erupted from the crowd – Amedspor had taken an early lead. The joy swiftly turned to anger – they were missing this. Tensions rose and fell – most people waited patiently, some screamed and ranted, one threw dirt through the grille. A minibus full of glowering police officers inched through the crowd. Minutes later the queue parted to make way for a bulky water cannon truck.

Amedspor led 1–0 at half-time and the crowd at the box office slowly drained away and into the stadium. A group of ferrety teenage Amedspor fans celebrated finally getting a ticket by chanting something unwise, and the police seized on them, booting them up the backsides, shoving them against a corrugated fence, and administering a few slaps and kicks while pulling open their shirts and trousers to search them. The much-chastened lads were eventually allowed to go on their way.

By the time we got our tickets and navigated the lines of tight security to enter the stadium, an hour of the match had been played. An almighty roar arose from within. We hurried up the stairwell and into the away section in the upper tier of the stadium in which the 500 or so Amedspor fans were crowded, chanting and pogoing in a frenzy. The scoreboard read 2–0 to Amedspor.

'We will win as we resist,' chanted ecstatic Amedspor fans. 'The barricade is here.' They sang 'Everywhere is Sur, everywhere is resistance,' referring to a district of Diyarbakir under heavy bombardment, and the same song for Cizre, a city that had seen some of the worst of the conflict.[3] And they sang: 'Don't let children die, let them come to the match.' The rest of the stadium was virtually empty, with perhaps 50 Basaksehir fans dotted across the stands.

Basaksehir pulled a goal back, and their onslaught on the Amedspor goal intensified. Amedspor fans were shouting themselves hoarse. A police officer stood on the touchline with a camera trained on the Amedspor fans, but as the game neared its end he was becoming distracted by the match, filming less and less, until the camera hung uselessly by his side in the final few minutes as he'd turned to watch the game.

When Basaksehir's Semih Senturk equalised in the fourth minute of injury time, their substitutes exploded onto the pitch with the force of shaken champagne, reeling and cavorting and gesturing 'up yours' to the Amedspor fans, while Senturk and a teammate faced the Amedspor fans, stood to attention, and gave a military salute in a clear gesture of Turkish nationalism.

JANUARY 28, 2016
Turkish Cup group stages (final match)
Fatih Terim Stadium, Basaksehir

Medipol Basaksehir **2—2** Amedspor

SENTURK 67, 90+5   CAPAR 3, 58

When the match was finished, the Amedspor fans were funnelled into a narrow corridor to leave the stand – the last-minute equaliser had felt like a loss, and tensions were peaking. Bilal and others tried to calm some who were becoming overly excitable. One man scaled a pipe in the corridor and ripped a CCTV camera from the wall – several took advantage of the opportunity to score graffiti into the wall: 'Cizre', 'PKK'. One man scored something rude and immediately spotted a young girl looking, implored her to look away, and stood sheepishly in front of his handiwork. The police saw some of what happened and were not impressed.

To exit the stadium, the fans ran the gauntlet of robotic riot police. But the mobile, marauding football police in jeans and stab-proof vests were more dangerous – all enormous, bearded, baton-swinging, screaming, their faces puffy and flashing with rage. They grabbed certain fans by the arm – including Bilal – and hauled them behind the police lines while scattering and dispersing the rest by striking at them with batons.

More than 100 were detained. A few weeks later I saw Bilal again: he had been held for more than 24 hours and beaten round the head, while one friend had his arm broken. He claimed not to have been given food or water for 20 hours. They had been banned from attending matches and now faced charges of making terrorist propaganda.

Basaksehir topped the group with their injury-time equaliser, and Amedspor went through in second place, setting up a knockout tie with Bursaspor – a club known for their staunch Turkish nationalism and which has had several run-ins with Kurdish football teams in the past. It became, for many, Turkey vs Kurdistan.

Behind the barricades

'This pot makes the best tea. I could fight for 300 years if I drink this tea,' said the young man flashing a grin and heaving a huge fire-blackened pot from the flames. 'You have to try it.' He was sitting on an old armchair behind a barricade in Diyarbakir's historic district of Sur with other young Kurdish fighters from the YDG-H – the Patriotic Revolutionary Youth Movement – a self-styled neighbourhood defence force that is broadly considered to be the urban youth wing of the PKK.[4]

It was late November – just as Amedspor were in the early stages of their cup run – and the group had declared the area an autonomous zone. They had dug up cobblestones to create trenches, built barricades from sandbags, and pegged huge sheets and tarpaulins across streets to provide screening from snipers. The fighters were preparing to defend the neighbourhood against imminent moves by the security forces. The scene was being repeated in several Kurdish-majority towns and cities across the region – in Cizre, Nusaybin, Silopi, Silvan, Varto, Yuksekova and elsewhere.

The Marxist–Leninist PKK launched an armed struggle for Kurdish independence in 1984. In the early years of the conflict, the military battle was fought primarily in rural areas and militants were typically said to have 'gone to the mountains'. Over time the armed conflict also spread to urban areas, and the military struggle opened into a wider contest within politics and culture, which inevitably encompassed football.

Kurds make up the fourth-largest ethnic group in the Middle East, but remain stateless. Some 25 to 35 million Kurdish people live in a region that straddles Turkey, Syria, Iraq, Iran and Armenia. Kurds make up around 15 to 20 per cent of the Turkish population, forming the country's largest minority group and the world's largest Kurdish population.

Kurdish nationalist rebellions – such as the 1925 Seyh Said uprising – were violently crushed by the new Turkish republic. The Turkish state often denied the very existence of Kurdish people and suppressed Kurdish politics, culture and language. Kurds were often euphemistically referred to as 'Mountain Turks'. Some claimed that the word 'Kurd' was onomatopoeic, representing the sound made by 'Mountain Turks' as they crunched through snow.[5]

In the late 1960s, as football was blossoming across Anatolia, it was only fitting that Diyarbakir, the largest Kurdish-majority city, should have a major club. Diyarbakirspor was formed in 1968. Its badge combined two famous symbols of Diyarbakir: the city's dark basalt ramparts and a sliced watermelon. Diyarbakirspor was, in some ways, Amedspor's precursor as a Kurdish standard-bearer. Diyarbakirspor gained successive promotions to reach the top flight for the first time in 1976.

Diyarbakirspor became a political instrument. Politicians such as Nurettin Dilek, the centre-right Motherland Party mayor of Diyarbakir in the mid-1980s, believed that they would gain votes and prestige if they could associate themselves with a successful Diyarbakirspor team. 'Diyarbakir has symbolic value as the major Kurdish city,' argues the journalist Faruk Arhan, who has written two books on Diyarbakirspor. 'If [the authorities] can control Diyarbakirspor, it helps them to control Diyarbakir and the Kurdish population in the region.'[6] Arhan has documented political intervention over several years, such as the pumping of money into the club, arranging of transfers and match-fixing by paying off referees or rival players.

The authorities also hoped that success on the pitch could be a distraction from the violence in the region, which reached its height in the late 1980s and 1990s. There have been over 50 Kurdish rebellions since the founding of the Turkish state, carried out by groups with various ideologies, but the PKK's rebellion has been the largest and the most enduring.[7]

The PKK was formed in 1978 by Kurdish students at Ankara University, and Abdullah Ocalan emerged as its leader. The PKK thrived partly because of its ruthlessness. Ocalan – who also goes by the avuncular nickname of Apo – built a cult of personality, and was merciless in killing any defectors or perceived rivals within the organisation, and in decimating other groups. 'PKK out!' became the favoured term of abuse towards Diyarbakirspor and its fans. Ocalan – densely moustachioed in the manner of a mid-1980s Liverpool player – is a Galatasaray fan, apparently because the club's red and yellow colours, along with the green of the pitch, form the Kurdish tricolour.[8]

The PKK killed hundreds of soldiers and those deemed to be supporting or sympathising with the state. They abducted children and forced them to serve in their ranks. Defectors faced execution if they attempted to flee. The PKK disrupted state education, killing teachers and burning schools, and enforced strict moral codes – banning the consumption of alcohol and pornography in some of its strongholds to save the local population's energy for the struggle.

The state's tactics were also brutal. They set up death squads that disappeared and tortured thousands, repressed Kurdish political parties and attempts to express Kurdish cultural rights, and torched villages and towns, displacing hundreds of thousands. In a sense, the Turkish state actually put Turkish Kurdistan on the map: by creating a state of emergency region (OHAL) in south-east Turkey, in which martial law replaced the rule of law, it marked out a visible Kurdish territory.[9]

The PKK weakened from its high point in the mid-1990s. Its inflexible socialist zeal and the enduring domination of Ocalan and his cult of personality stunted the organisation, and it failed to win the loyalty of many Alevis, pious Sunni or Zaza Kurds, or to create viable political institutions.[10] After being depleted on the battlefield in the mid- to late 1990s, and following Turkey's capture of Ocalan in 1999, the PKK increasingly sought compromise and negotiation with the Turkish state.

Diyarbakir's police chief, Gaffar Okkan, became known for his relatively enlightened vision of security, as he clamped down on corruption among the police, and targeted the Islamist Kurdish Hezbollah militants, who had previously attacked left-wing Kurds with impunity. Okkan also believed that linking the success of Diyarbakirspor with the state could be a way to counter the rise of Kurdish nationalist parties that had been growing in strength and popularity since the early 1990s – he was a high-profile supporter of the club. But Okkan was assassinated in 2001 – his assailants were never caught.

Arhan says that there was a concerted attempt to gain promotion for Diyarbakirspor in Okkan's memory. His many interviews from this period with club officials, players and fan groups suggest that referees and rival players were bribed on a large scale to get Diyarbakirspor promoted again in 2001.

The AKP came to power in 2002, and as a government was the most sympathetic in Turkish history to Kurdish grievances and rights. The AKP stressed unity between citizens as Muslims, rather than as primarily Turks, and relaxed many restrictions on Kurdish language and media, invested money to develop the south-east, and curtailed some of the more brutal practices of the security forces. The AKP hoped peace would create a grateful and loyal Kurdish constituency. Many pious and socially conservative Sunni Kurds regard the secular socialism of Kurdish nationalist parties as anathema, and voted for the AKP in large numbers.

At a political congress in 2009, Erdogan described Turkey as a mosaic, and listed a diverse range of people who represented the unity of the Turkish nation, which included some surprising choices, such as leftist poet Nazim Hikmet and the Kurdish singer Ahmet Kaya. It drew a furious response from some nationalists, including an MHP politician who asserted that Turkey was not a mosaic but rather a piece of whole and indivisible 'marble'.[11]

But the decline of the military's political power provided opportunities for the AKP's 2009 'Kurdish Opening', which sought to improve minority rights and prepare the conditions for the end of the conflict with the PKK. Turkish nationalists were livid, accusing the AKP government of jeopardising Turkey's territory and national identity. Yet, the limited moves contained in the 'opening' did not go far enough for many Kurds. It was an indication of the scale of the chasm that the AKP was trying to bridge.

Local AKP politicians also wanted to win control over Diyarbakir's municipality and, like their predecessors, saw a thriving Diyarbakirspor as a way towards achieving this, and associated themselves with the club. But Diyarbakirspor fans were becoming more political, attending protests against unsolved murders and 'disappearances', and increasingly chanting pro-Kurdish slogans in the stadium. There were instances where they booed the Turkish national anthem. 'The Kurdish political movement realised that football could be a field of struggle,' says Arhan. Kurdish nationalist parties were winning local elections and Arhan believes that the AKP cut its support of the club when they realised it would not help them politically. 'The government favours in 2001, turned into fines by 2009.'[12]

Some incendiary matches cemented a footballing enmity between Bursaspor and clubs from Diyarbakir. A match between Diyarbakirspor and Bursaspor in Bursa's Ataturk Stadium in September 2009 descended into violence as Diyarbakirspor's players, officials and fans were subjected to verbal and physical attacks by Bursaspor fans chanting 'PKK out!' – many Diyarbakirspor fans were injured.

Some Diyarbakirspor fans wanted revenge. The return match in March 2010 was abandoned after 17 minutes as the Diyarbakirspor fans pelted Bursaspor players and the referee with rocks. Diyarbakirspor was fined and ordered to play five home matches behind closed doors.

These matches were the turning point. Fines compounded financial problems. The club became deeply indebted, and players went unpaid. Diyarbakirspor could not afford to travel to some away matches. The club dropped rapidly through the leagues in successive relegations, and folded in 2013. 'If the AKP had won the municipality, Diyarbakirspor would be in the Super League right now – without any doubt,' believes Arhan.

In late 2012, Erdogan – then prime minister – initiated a secret dialogue with the imprisoned Ocalan. It was a brave and risky move that could have left Erdogan open to charges of treason. In March 2013, the AKP announced an official peace process with the PKK, which was intended to definitively end nearly three decades of conflict. 'War is easy, peace is hard,' noted Erdogan at the outset of the process. Ocalan called on the PKK to impose a ceasefire, and it complied.[13]

As the PKK mostly withdrew to northern Iraq, and its rural presence diminished under the ceasefire, the group sought to consolidate its presence in urban areas, forming the loosely structured groups that became known as the YDG-H, which were comprised of local youth[14] and leaders in contact with the PKK's broader structure of command.[15]

Following the demise of Diyarbakirspor, another team emerged as the strongest side in the city, with support from the municipality run by a party affiliated to the pro-Kurdish Peoples' Democratic Party (HDP). The municipality team was formed in 1990, and in 2014 the club decided, uni-laterally and controversially, to change its name from Turkish to Kurdish: from Diyarbakir Buyuksehir Belediyespor to 'Amedspor' – 'Amed' is the Kurdish name for Diyarbakir – and to adopt the Kurdish colours of green, red and yellow.

The Turkish Football Federation did not accept the proposed changes and fined the club; the sensitivity and bickering over names and colours shows the enduring power of language and symbols in Turkey. However, the club was permitted to adopt the official name of 'Amed Sportif Faaliyetler' – 'Amed Sporting Activities'.[16] In a major upset, Amedspor beat Galatasaray 2–0 at the Istanbul club's Turk Telekom Arena in a January 2015 Turkish Cup match – a week after they had been fined by the football federation for changing their name. After the match, Amedspor's president Ihsan Avci stated that his club was not 'Diyarbakir's team but Kurdistan's team, the people's team'.[17]

In 2015 the pro-Kurdish HDP took a bold decision to contest that year's general election as a party. The Turkish parliament has a 10 per cent vote threshold that political parties must reach in order to take up their seats – partly designed to keep Kurdish parties out of parliament. The HDP and its predecessors typically won 5–6 per cent of the national vote, but the HDP had seen its support surge in recent years. HDP's co-chair Selahattin Demirtas is a rare phenomenon in Turkish politics: a match for Erdogan in terms of charisma, he is youthful and charming, and has a propensity for breaking into song and poking fun at Erdogan. Like previous pro-Kurdish parties, the HDP draws significant support from those who are sympathetic to the PKK. Demirtas's brother is a PKK fighter. However, the HDP has taken a consistent line against violence, and has mostly sought to distance itself from the group.[18]

The HDP pushes for autonomy and cultural rights for Turkish Kurds but is also a home for minority ethnic and religious groups, such as Armenians, Roma, Syriac and Yezidi, that have traditionally been excluded from the dominant conception of Turkish nationalism, and the HDP has also fielded more female and LGBT candidates than other parties. It is by far the most diverse party in the Turkish parliament. It has made a strong bid for the non-Kurdish vote among leftists, liberals, LGBT people, feminists and any other 'Gezi' type voters who are against the AKP and have tired of the insipid opposition provided by the CHP. The party has also gained many conservative Kurdish voters from the AKP, who were upset with the government's hostile stance towards Kurdish groups fighting the so-called Islamic State in Kobane.[19]

If the HDP ran as a party and surpassed the 10 per cent threshold, it would gain funding, prestige and power, but the move was a gamble because, if a party falls short of 10 per cent of the vote, its votes are forfeited to the second-biggest party in that constituency. In areas where the Kurdish nationalist parties excel, the second-biggest party is usually the AKP. Erdogan and the AKP desperately wanted these votes. A simple majority would have given them a fourth consecutive term in government but they needed a 'super-majority' of two-thirds in order to achieve Erdogan's dream and force through a new constitution, against opposition from other parties, that would award significant new executive powers to the (supposedly) ceremonial presidency.

Erdogan had once envisaged reaching an accommodation with the HDP. It would support his proposed constitutional reform in return for increased autonomy and rights under the changes.[20] The HDP was initially amenable, but many of its supporters found the notion of an all-powerful President Erdogan toxic in the extreme, and so the HDP cooled its enthusiasm. By early 2015, Demirtas had publicly vowed to scupper Erdogan's ambitions, taunting the president that he would never achieve his dreams as long as the HDP existed.

Erdogan heard this taunt, and perhaps concluded it was correct. His attitude towards the peace process soured. In 2005 he had gone to Diyarbakir and announced: 'The Kurdish problem is my problem.' In February 2015, he made a speech and said, 'What Kurdish problem? What have you not got? What else do you want? For God's sake, what don't you have that we have? You have everything.'[21]

That month there had been an apparent breakthrough in peace process talks in which the government had agreed to concessions towards the Kurds, while Ocalan called for the PKK to begin discussing disarmament. But Erdogan publicly and casually disavowed the process in March 2015. He ramped up the Turkish nationalist rhetoric.[22]

The election took place in June 2015 and the HDP exceeded expectations, winning 13.3 per cent of the vote and becoming the first pro-Kurdish party to enter parliament as a political party. The ultranationalist MHP also did well, while the CHP more or less flatlined. The strong showing of the HDP and the MHP denied the AKP even a simple majority in parliament. Turkey found itself with no AKP government for the first time in 13 years. Indeed, it had no government whatsoever. Many saw this as a hugely positive outcome – weakening single-party hegemony, electing record numbers of female parliamentarians and opening the potential for a more inclusive and deliberative democracy. The various parties began discussing terms for coalitions. And then everything fell apart.

The summer of 2015 was a summer of violence, and the Kurdish cease-fire definitively broke down. On 19 July 2015, a bomb exploded in Suruc, a Turkish town on the Syrian border, killing 33 mostly leftist activists, and injuring more than 100. The activists had been heading to Kobane, to help rebuild the city. The bomber, 20-year-old Seyh Abdurrahman Alagoz, was an ethnic Kurd from Adiyaman, and reportedly had links to ISIS.[23]

The PKK accused the Turkish government of abetting the attack and killed two Turkish policemen in retaliation. The violence escalated rapidly. Turkey began an aerial bombing campaign against PKK targets in northern Iraq, and embarked on a security crackdown across the Kurdish region – including the mass arrest and prosecution of Kurdish politicians, activists and citizens, and blocking of Kurdish-language news sites.

In August 2015, the PKK instructed the YDG-H to impose no-go areas in several cities across the south-east, which would be declared autonomous zones.[24] Meanwhile, some municipalities run by the DBP – affiliated to the HDP, but considered more hardline and closer to the PKK – also declared autonomous municipalities. The Turkish government announced a series of curfews[25] in order to reassert control but was frustrated in its attempts to definitively retake control of some neighbourhoods, and resorted to the use of tanks and artillery in order to pound the militants into submission, causing many civilian deaths and casualties. The PKK maintained a steady rate of violence against the security forces.

The AKP was well poised to make political capital out of the breakdown of peace. It announced its intention to stop negotiating with the HDP and PKK, and to find an alternative Kurdish interlocutor. It used inflammatory nationalist rhetoric and secured a response – there were scores of attacks on HDP offices and other Kurdish targets across the country by nationalist mobs.

Kurdish football clubs were caught up in controversy. Batman Petrolspor was fined by the football federation for breaking its regulations after its players and officials released white doves and called for peace before the club's first game of the season in August 2015.

Erdogan exercised the presidential prerogative – for the first time in history – to call a snap election on 1 November 2015. The AKP had tried peace and lost votes. Now it would see if war could gain victory, hoping to play on fears of instability to lure far-right nationalists from the MHP, while encouraging conservative Kurds to return from the HDP. As president, Erdogan was supposed to be above the political fray. But he campaigned hard for the AKP, booming, 'It's me or chaos,' as swathes of the south-east became mired in conflict. Civilians were being killed, injured, maimed and displaced. Anyone taking to the streets under curfew – for food, water, to get medical attention – risked being shot on sight. During curfews in September, at least 22 civilians died.[26]

On 10 October 2015, a peace rally held by leftists, including many HDP supporters, outside Ankara's central railway station was bombed by terrorists linked to ISIS – 102 people were killed, making it the bloodiest act of terrorism in Turkey's history.[27] The HDP suspended its rallies and accused the government of complicity in the violence.

In the south-east many HDP officials and their affiliates were arrested or prevented from campaigning in certain areas deemed to be security zones. The AKP directly linked the pro-Kurdish parties with the PKK, and intensified a crackdown on critical media, seizing control of opposition outlets the week before the election, and exploiting the largesse of the state to dominate the airwaves.[28]

The AKP vote surged by almost 10 per cent in the snap election as they gained 5 million votes to secure a decisive majority. The ultranationalist MHP was the biggest loser, haemorrhaging votes to the AKP. The HDP's vote also fell significantly but, crucially, the party remained within the parliamentary threshold by a matter of decimal points.

The AKP had engineered a stunning reversal in just a few months and had returned to government, although it was still short of a supermajority.

However, the violence of the previous months only intensified in the aftermath of the election. Barricades kept being thrown up while Erdogan said he would crush the PKK once and for all.

Diyarbakir's old city district of Sur had seen some of the most intense violence. Sur is encircled by ancient, dark, basalt walls, thought to be the world's second longest after the Great Wall of China.

It's possible that tourists, ignorant of the news, could have followed their guidebook to Diyarbakir in November 2015. In the old city they could have passed an intimidating cluster of armoured police cars, but that would have given way to a more genteel setting, a yellowing tree standing out against the grey basalt of Ulu Camii, and old men, many wearing baggy *salvar* trousers, sipping tea and chatting in front of the mosque.

Tourist signs would lead them to the Surp Giragos Armenian church, less than 100 metres away. They might have ventured beyond the adjacent Seyh Matar mosque, with its famous four-legged minaret, and rounded the corner. But then they might have started to feel like something was awry. They would notice that there were suddenly very few people on the street, that craters had been dug in the road, that holes like gaping mouths had been punched into some of the buildings, and walls had been punctuated with haphazard full stops. And at the end of the street they would see a structure, a wall of sandbags with a face wrapped in a *keffiyeh* poking over the parapet. The head on the other side of the barricade was just the torso of a mannequin, but the fighters from the YDG-H had created another enclave within the city walls.

Some of the fighters looked very young. One, wearing a tracksuit, looked about 15 years old: his scarf kept slipping down to reveal a soft, smooth face. Every so often he would remember and tug it back up again. What are you expecting to happen, I asked? 'We are expecting anything. We will resist and we will die if necessary,' he answered automatically.

The leaders were a little older. Osman – not his real name – was a bearded fighter in his early twenties; he wore military-style fatigues, carried a rifle and had stuffed a pistol into his jacket pocket. He walked through the neighbourhood, identifying weak points, ordering more barricades to be erected at key positions and adding graffiti to the walls: 'YDG-H', 'PKK', Kurdish flags and stars, stencils of Ocalan and his moustache.

A cat shrank by against a wall next to a barricade manned by female fighters with grenades stocked in their belts. The women were more diligent with their face masks, lifting them up only slightly to accommodate sips of tea. A few residents milled about on the streets, including old people and children, but the area was overwhelmingly shuttered and many streets were deserted. Many residents had left the neighbourhood when the fighting began.

After making his rounds, Osman arrived at the barricade with the world's best teapot, and sat fiddling with his gun and mucking around. A metallic clang rang out as he fired an empty chamber at his friend, and then he settled down and began speaking about what it meant to create an autonomous zone.

The barricades went up for the first time just after the June election, and had been cleared several times. 'When the AKP lost that election, they became so aggressive towards the people of this neighbourhood. Because these people didn't vote for them, they wanted to take revenge.' The residents had become especially fearful of a special unit of police – nicknamed the '*Esedullah*' – who wore beards and long hair, and were considered by residents to be hardcore Islamists. They left menacing graffiti following their raids. 'They use bad words, came into the streets, took people into custody, and tortured them,' said Osman. 'That's why these barricades were built, for our protection.'[29]

Osman denied any formal links to the PKK and described himself and the other fighters as locals defending their neighbourhood. But he used terms taken straight out of Ocalan's lexicon of 'democratic confederalism'. Whilst in prison Ocalan moved away from calling for Kurdish independence and Marxism, and towards the idea of autonomy within Turkey, apparently inspired by his readings of the anarchist thinker Murray Bookchin. Osman said that they wanted to create their own systems of justice, health, education and security, adding: 'But – this is very important – with the state. We want confederalism as part of the state. But the mentality of the state needs to change regarding self-autonomy.' Osman suggested that confederalism meant autonomy for regions across Turkey, such as in the Black Sea. 'This is not only about Kurds ruling themselves.'

Osman said they had created their own clinics in the neighbourhood run by retired doctors and those with first-aid knowledge, but accepted that they were not professional and could not treat serious injuries, but were hoping to develop them over time. They were opposed to prisons and believed in 'educating' people who had committed crimes – he claimed – usually by detaining them for a week or so, and forcing them to read books that explained the errors of their ways. A man who had beaten his wife was recently 're-educated' and then told to take her on holiday for a week to make amends.

Osman said there was no age limit for fighters, and he saw no issue with children being on the front line. 'Everyone here is a target for the AKP mentality. They see all the Kurds as terrorists – that's why it doesn't matter if they are children or old men, they can be on the front lines,' he said. 'People need these skills because they are attacking all the people – old people and children.'

This particular ramshackle experiment seemed doomed to failure against the superior might of the state. It had been imposed against the wishes of many residents, who did not want their neighbourhoods turned into war zones despite the harassment and brutality of the security forces.[30] Yet the barricades had also been surprisingly durable, and some residents did offer support.

Ihsan Sevintek, 44, owned a general store just metres from a barricade. Sparrows darted in through the open door, scoped out the shop, and darted out again. There was a hole in the top of the shop's front window which Sevintek claimed had been caused by a police projectile. He said it was the fourth time his window had been damaged – each time he had to pay for repairs himself, and he would just leave this hole for the time being, anticipating further clashes.

After the last curfew, there was a week without barricades and Sevintek said that the police came into the area every night, forcing people into the street in their underwear, questioning, humiliating and often arresting them – accusing them of supporting militants. 'I want to tell you something important,' he said. 'Don't think that Kurds want to depend on ditches and barricades. Kurds have democratic wishes – we want to speak our language and we want our rights. We have waited for rights in a democratic way – but when cobras [armoured security forces vehicles] come here and state forces attack us, they have to use ditches and barricades as a solution.'[31]

The military burned Sevintek's village near Lice in the 1990s – his family lost everything and, like many others who migrated to urban areas across the country, Sevintek pitched up in Diyarbakir. With urbanisation came a rising Kurdish consciousness and a growing demand for Kurdish rights that was often largely supportive of the PKK, but was not wholly shaped by its ideology. All kinds of culture became increasingly political – music, theatre, cinema and football.

Sevintek had become an Amedspor fan:

I was born as a Galatasaray fan but when I saw our local team playing big clubs, and what happened when they shouted 'PKK go to hell' at our players and supporters, you start questioning this – and at some point I thought, I want to start supporting my local team. I hate nationalism – of all kinds – but I understood that I should support my local team.

He mentioned the penalties against the club for pro-Cizre chants. 'When the government treats us all as terrorists and judges all of us, it affects every aspect of life – so of course this finds its way into sports.'

'Amedspor' had become freighted with binary labels that varied according to viewpoint: terrorism/resistance, separatism/self-determination, patriotism/treachery, 'Azadi' vs the disintegration of Turkey.

Sur was back under 24-hour curfew within a week of my visit, ushering in the most intense and violent phase of the conflict so far. The militants were proving to be surprisingly resilient – holding out against superior firepower in narrow streets, through IEDs, booby traps and snipers.[32]

By January scores of locally elected pro-Kurdish politicians had been arrested, among them 18 HDP-affiliated mayors – including the co-mayors of Diyarbakir – who were replaced by government-appointed trustees. The mayor of Van was sentenced to 15 years in jail for being a member of the PKK. Human Rights Watch described the moves as unprecedented.[33] Thousands of Turkish academics who had signed a petition lamenting the impact on civilians of the state's violence in the south-east, and calling for the resumption of peace talks with the PKK, were being investigated under terror charges. Several were later jailed.[34]

Reporters for pro-Kurdish outlets have been routinely detained and subject to violence and harassment by the security forces. Dozens of Kurdish outlets have been banned and websites shut down. Reporters at mainstream news outlets knew to self-censor, and access to the conflict areas for media and human rights workers was severely curtailed.[35] As usual, civilians bore most of the suffering. In Cizre more than 170 people were killed – either by grenades, shells or rockets – while sheltering in basements, allegedly alongside wounded rebels – the majority of the bodies were too charred to identify.[36]

Historic sights in Sur, including Surp Giragos Armenian church and the 500-year-old Seyh Matar mosque, were further damaged. Pro-government TV stations showed daily footage of coffins, draped in Turkish flags, of soldiers and police who had been killed by Kurdish militants.

After the Basaksehir match, Senturk's military salute had drawn criticism for being provocative and incendiary. Amedspor fans saw it as anti-Kurdish, and therefore racist, and as celebrating the Turkish military, which has killed scores of civilians in recent months and reduced parts of Diyarbakir and other cities to rubble.[37]

Some Turkish nationalists defended Senturk and argued his gesture was important to show solidarity with the soldiers who were being killed by the PKK. Burak Bilgili, the general coordinator of the Basaksehir fan group 1453 Basaksehirliler, said:

> We don't want politics in the stadium. Obviously, Basaksehir is a district that mostly supports the government, and the majority of our members may support the government, but there are all views in our group and we don't treat them differently. We don't allow politics in the stands. But there are certain values – like patriotism, respecting the nation, the flag – and we don't allow members to disrespect them.[38]

He said that they didn't have a problem with Amedspor as a club, only with some of their fans, and argued that Senturk's salute was above politics and a reaction to terrorism. 'That gesture is a common value of Turkey, so we don't see it as a political reaction.'

In short, as Amedspor progressed to the next round of the cup to face Bursaspor, both sides felt provoked. Some Bursaspor fans wanted their coach Hamza Hamzaoglu to drop their many foreign stars and only field Turkish players for the match.

Turkey vs Kurdistan

Amedspor supporters were banned from attending the match in Bursa for security reasons. Only Bursaspor Passolig card holders could attend. I was forced to watch on TV.

Amedspor's players ventured into the belly of the beast: figuratively (the only fans were Bursaspor supporters, raw and loud with nationalist fervour) and literally (Bursaspor's recently opened stadium has been built to resemble a crocodile). The normally green and white stands were awash with red Turkish flags.

Bursaspor established an early dominance in possession, but almost midway through the first half Amedspor launched a counter-attack amid a white noise of jeers, reached the byline, and cut the ball back into the box. There was a scramble, and a Bursaspor defender poked the ball loose from the area – it fell to Amedspor's Ercan Capar, who struck it through a thicket of limbs, into the bottom-left corner to give Amedspor the lead.

Bursaspor suddenly had the jitters, while Amedspor were cool in possession, sitting deep but breaking quickly. Deniz Naki was central to everything, busy in the space behind the strikers, linking play, creating mischief and drawing plenty of fouls. Hamza Hamzaoglu, Bursaspor's coach, looked perplexed, his arms flapping against his sides. Amedspor went into the break 1–0 up.

In the second half, as Bursaspor probed for the equaliser, Amedspor snuffed out their attacks and broke quickly. Naki found himself through on goal after a hectic run through midfield, but rolled the ball just wide. On 65 minutes, another Amedspor counter-attack found Naki on the edge of the area, and he drilled the ball with the side of his foot into the goal to make it 2–0. The Bursaspor goalkeeper, on all fours, punched the ball into the ground.

In the dying minutes of injury time Bursaspor got a goal back. They had one frenzied minute to find an equaliser. For Bursaspor the seconds were fluid, draining unstoppably. For Amedspor they were huge blocks of time, solid and yielding stubbornly.

In the 95th minute an Amedspor player launched the ball high, every moment in the air precious respite from Bursaspor's attacks. The ball came down to earth, only to be floated towards empty space towards the corner flag...

JANUARY 31, 2016
Turkish Cup – Last 16
Timsah Arena, Bursa

Bursaspor **1–2** **Amedspor**

DE SUTTER 90+4

CAPAR 20
NAKI 65

The referee blew the final whistle and Amedspor's players celebrated, while the crowd vented its fury. The players shook hands and the Amedspor players ducked and hurried from the pitch under a cascade of missiles thrown from the crowd. A line of riot police trotted onto the pitch, and the feed cut abruptly to the next cup tie.

Clashes broke out in Diyarbakir as the police used tear gas and water cannon to disperse crowds who had taken to the streets to celebrate Amedspor's win.

Naki was back in controversy. While celebrating Amedspor's victory on the pitch, he displayed a defiant 'V' sign: 'V' for peace, or 'V' for victory – it depends on your reading. After the match he took to social media: 'We dedicate this victory as a gift to those who have lost their lives and those wounded in the repression in our land which has lasted for more than 50 days.'[39] Naki was referred to Turkish football's disciplinary board.

A tweet – later deleted – from an account using Amedspor's name read: 'We dedicate the 2–1 victory at Bursaspor to the guerrillas resisting in Sur and Cizre and to the altruistic people of Kurdistan.'[40] The club strongly denied any links to the account. The next day, 40 heavily armed anti-terrorism police raided Amedspor's headquarters in Diyarbakir and seized computer hard drives.

The draw for the quarter-finals was made that same day: Amedspor were drawn against Super League leaders Fenerbahce. The quarter-finals would be played over two legs and the first match would take place a week later in Diyarbakir.

It quickly became clear that Amedspor fans would not be able to attend the biggest match in their club's history. Hours after the draw, the federation announced that the match in Diyarbakir would be played behind closed doors and that the club would be fined 25,000 TL as punishment for the supporters' 'ideological propaganda' – for their chanting during the match with Basaksehir. Two days later, the federation announced that Naki would be banned for 12 matches and fined 19,500 TL for making 'ideological propaganda' and for 'unsporting' behaviour. It appears to be the lengthiest ban given to a footballer in Turkey.[41]

For Tarik Capci, 43, a journalist and former member of Teksas – Bursaspor's largest fan group – the punishment was fair. He didn't believe Naki's homilies to peace for a second. 'If there was an active terrorist group in England today and they were killing people, and at the same time people supporting them said they were asking for peace – do you think you would find that peace sincere?' asked Tarik.[42]

Visiting Diyarbakir in February for the first leg of the quarter-final was very different from my last visit in the previous November. There would be no sipping tea in the shadow of Ulu Camii: much of Sur remained under curfew. Many of the young fighters I had met in November had probably been killed. The security forces had set up checkpoints and fortified positions at the gates in the old city walls. Seyh Said Square on the edge of historic Diyarbakir was surrounded by metal police fencing, although a few small boys played football inside the cordon. In the evening the muffled thud of explosions came from the old city.

On the morning of the match, Diyarbakir was eerily quiet and most shops were shuttered. The HDP had asked businesses to close for three days in protest at deaths in Cizre. Most of the municipality was also on strike. In some streets the rubbish was already spreading across the road; lettuce and orange peel were crushed into pancakes on the tarmac by passing cars.

The municipality's press office said that there were 600–700 police stationed around Amedspor's stadium, on the outskirts of the city. I preferred to watch the match with some ordinary people from the city and ended up at the Golge Park café, in the shadow of the old stadium in the centre of Diyarbakir. There was a soft burr of men talking, the tinkling of tulip-shaped glass as they stirred sugar into their tea, and the clink of rolling plastic dice.

On widescreen TVs the coverage was starting. Mascots held flowers. Both sets of players posed in front of a banner saying 'Don't kill the kids, let them come to the matches' – a surprising show of solidarity from Fenerbahce, given that this was the kind of 'separatist ideological propaganda' that had got Amedspor fans banned from the match.

Amedspor's 1,500-capacity stadium was empty except for a few dozen club officials and police. The club had draped huge banners covered in the images of fans over some of the stands facing the camera, which gave an odd impression of frozen, distorted, bloated spectators. Around 100 Amedspor fans had protested outside the stadium and been driven back by the police.

The match kicked off and the Amedspor players stood locked in place – a protest at the sanctions against the club. Fenerbahce knocked the ball around harmlessly in their own half for 30 seconds until the protest had ended, and the match came to life.

Few people in the café held out much hope for Amedspor against the might of the Super League leaders, especially while missing their talisman

Deniz Naki. In the opening minutes Fenerbahce dominated possession but Amedspor looked organised and composed. The pitch was rough-looking, with yellowy patches like piss stains from a giant dog. Amedspor's impressive technical ability had been honed on this bobbly surface – it was like the pitch had little air pockets under it that would gently push the ball up every couple of metres. The camera work was inhibited at such a small ground – it was difficult to see the ball on the far touchline, and when the action went into the near-right corner a pillar drifted into the shot. Every so often there was the roar of a fighter jet passing overhead.

From nowhere, a goal! A speculative long-range shot from Amedspor was parried by Fenerbahce's goalkeeper, Fabiano, straight back to Amedspor's striker Sehmus Ozer, who forced the ball into the goal from ten yards out, and the café erupted in cheers. The joy was short-lived – four minutes later Fenerbahce slotted in an equaliser.

As the half progressed, it became clear that Amedspor looked a little flat without Naki's scurrying menace behind the strikers: they missed his ability to hold up the ball and spark attacks. Fenerbahce struck just before half-time as their hulking striker Fernandão nodded in a simple cross from the right, his marker lagging a metre behind, to make it 2–1 to Fenerbahce at the break.

At half-time I spoke to a group of men sitting at the table behind. They were civil servants and didn't want to give their names: 'These days you can get into trouble for a Facebook "like",' said one with a smile. They thought the punishments were unfair. 'Is there anywhere else in the world where a footballer makes a peace sign and gets banned?' asked one.

But they also thought the punishments had raised awareness of the team and the political situation in the south-east. They were hoping Amedspor could come back and salvage a draw. 'But in this bad political situation even losing 2–1 would be a great result.'

It was a crisp, sunny day. Fenerbahce's coach, Vitor Pereira, shielded his eyes against the glare. The shadows of the players began to lengthen. The camera showed the stand behind the goal on the left, swathes of red and green seats empty except for a few police officers idling under the setting sun. It seemed likely that Amedspor would run out of steam and ideas, and that Fenerbahce would use their nous and skill to press their dominance and steadily crush their opponents. But Amedspor looked the hungrier team and started to exert sustained pressure. As in previous cup ties, Amedspor were only becoming stronger as the match went on.

Perhaps Fenerbahce didn't fancy fully exerting themselves in the second half, on this contoured pitch, a patchwork of many micro-surfaces, in this fraught city, in a cup quarter-final tie that they thought they'd won. Like everyone else, they underestimated Amedspor.

On 67 minutes Amedspor launched a move reminiscent of their goals against Bursaspor, breaking through towards the byline, and pulling the ball back for a runner from deep: this time Naki wasn't there but Ibrahim Coskun was. '*Buyrun!*' – there you go! – shouted the men in the café. And Coskun slotted the ball in from the edge of the area: 2–2!

The café erupted, the men jumped to their feet and high-fived. 'I don't normally care about football!' shouted a giddy civil servant.

The café had barely settled when the left-footed forward Yusuf Yagmur once again ran at the Fenerbahce defence, jinking one way, then another, forcing a little space, and unleashing a clean strike across Fabiano and into the top right of the goal. This time the café erupted like the terraces – the civil servants were on their feet, pumping their fists in glee.

Fenerbahce regrouped and shook themselves back to life. Five minutes later, Fenerbahce's Raul Meireles clipped a ball over the top and an Amedspor defender and Fenerbahce forward Volkan Sen tussled over possession. Amid the tangle of limbs, the ball finally settled at Sen's feet and he steered it past the goalkeeper to make it 3–3.

Fenerbahce regained ascendancy and Amedspor hunkered down to defend. In the dying minutes and, against the run of play, Amedspor found themselves in a goal-scoring position. '*Buyrun!*' screamed the café in unison… and the shot was scuffed, the referee raised his hand and blew the whistle for full time. Amedspor had secured a famous draw against the top-ranked team in the country, humbling a third Super League side in a row, even without their star player.

FEBRUARY 9, 2016

Turkish Cup Quarter Finals – 1st leg

Seyrantepe Diski Stadium, Diyarbakir

Amedspor **3—3** Fenerbahce

OZER 10	CIVELEK 14
COSKUN 68	FERNANDAO 44
YAGMUR 70	SEN 76

After the match I left the café and made my way out to the fringes of the city, to meet up with Deniz Naki at the club's training facilities. Tarmac turned into muddy tracks servicing the construction of a dense sprouting of apartment blocks where many wealthier residents would surely move to be far from dangerous central neighbourhoods like Sur. A man showed us the way and chatted about the match. Normally he was a Fenerbahce fan he said, but he was gutted that Amedspor had not won. 'Fener are just a football team. But this is my land.'

We found the man at the centre of the storm slouched at a 45-degree angle in front of a television, which was replaying highlights from the match. Naki had watched the match alone at the training ground. He was thrilled with the result, if frustrated that it hadn't been a win and that he had not been able to play.

Naki was bearded, and his hair was gelled and fixed as precisely as if set in stone. He looked more youthful in real life. On the pitch Naki buzzes with energy and aggression. Off the pitch he was calm, boyish, a little shy even, or perhaps he was just on best behaviour. Amedspor's lawyer sat in on the meeting.

He had been called a terrorist and an infidel, fined thousands of lira, and banned for 12 matches, but he said he would do the same again. 'I am a professional footballer, but I can't accept injustice anywhere,' he said.

Born and brought up near Cologne, Naki began his career at Bayer Leverkusen and played for the German under-twenties. He transferred to the Hamburg side St. Pauli, whose fans are famously left-wing. When he scored in a match against Hansa Rostock, whose fans had been performing the Nazi salute, Naki celebrated by facing the Rostock fans and drawing his finger across his throat. At the end of the match he planted a St. Pauli flag in the centre circle. Naki was banned for three matches.

After his spell at Genclerbirligi, he had offers from teams in Belgium, Holland and Germany, but opted for Amedspor with a sense of mission. 'I don't ask for money, I don't ask for anything – I just want to carry this team into the Super League to give it honour.'

I put it to Naki that many people feel like the pitch is not the place for politics and that his gestures were provocative. 'There is a war now and children are being killed. And it's so clear who's killing the children – it's the state. For me, [Senturk's] military salute supports this slaughter, but my sign is asking for peace,' replied Naki. 'It might be political, but it is a different kind of political position. But the problem is – when I do [the 'V' sign] I'm a "terrorist", but when you make this sign then it means "peace", because I'm a Kurd and you are from England.'[43]

The violence over the past few months has affected Naki and he has sought out its civilian victims. In Cizre he visited people who had lost relatives to the violence, including a family who had kept the body of their dead child in the fridge because they couldn't take the corpse to the cemetery under curfew.

I asked Naki to clarify his position on the PKK and the young people fighting in the region's cities, but he preferred not to comment as he said it was dangerous to give clear political opinions one way or the other: 'We are in such a critical period that even people calling for peace can be arrested or killed.'

Soran Haldi Mizrak, Amedspor's lawyer and spokesperson, is a busy man. He also said that the club did not take a position on the PKK, and claimed it was not a relevant subject for a football team. 'But a certain proportion of society and our fans support both the PKK and us. This should not be our problem.'[44]

Some will take that as tacit support for the PKK, but probably the best way to characterise Amedspor is as an HDP team – they have consistently come out against violence, they espouse a soft form of Kurdish nationalism, and they seek to appeal to leftist and liberal Turks. 'Of course, we do believe in self-determination, every society has this right. But we want this to be achieved through ideas, rather than war and clashes,' said Mizrak. 'The name "Amed" means we have a stance that involves responsibility to society. You can call it kind of a socialist team.'

Amedspor oppose 'industrial football' – they want to keep ticket prices low and to focus on developing local talent. They have cultural and educational activities promoting chess and folk dancing, and run summer camps and support children who are struggling academically: 'We want footballers to have good minds,' said Mizrak. Football's popularity makes it a useful tool, according to Mizrak. 'This makes it possible for Kurdish voices to be heard better across the world.'

Despite their notoriety, they don't have a huge number of active fans. The Barikat leader Bilal Akkulu complains that many Kurdish people don't support Amedspor – they struggle to sell out their tiny stadium, which is understandable when many people have more urgent, pressing concerns than football. 'Sporting success would be a game-changer in this sense,' he said.[45]

Istanbul has become the world's largest Kurdish city, and Barikat reflect the urbanised, diaspora existence of much Kurdish youth. Most of their members live in Istanbul and other western Turkish cities. As well as supporting the team through an ultras' culture of banners, chants and pogoing, they organise meetings, forums and conferences, and claim to oppose all violence. 'Amedspor and Barikat are the football branches of the Kurdish freedom movement,' he told me. 'We wanted to build a different sort of fan group which is against swearing, violence, sexual discrimination and racism.'

They created a women's ultras' offshoot – Mor Barikat[46] – in 2015. Mor Barikat is a distinct organisation – when they chant, the Barikat members are expected to be quiet and listen respectfully.

But there are many fans outside Barikat who don't embrace the ultras' culture and say that politics is hurting the club. 'Those who blame us for being political, they often also have a political stance – like being pro-government,' says Dilek, a member of Mor Barikat.[47]

The leader Bilal Akkulu denies any direct connection with the PKK or a shared ideology, though he admits that some beliefs may overlap. Bilal says it is difficult to control all the fans – when they chant PKK slogans it is hard to stop them.

The sanctions against Amedspor have taken a toll. They have been fined around 214,000 TL this season by the football federation – Amedspor is a small club that is mostly funded through federation support, through sponsorship, by the municipality and from personal donations. The sanctions amount to 10 per cent of the club's budget.

Amedspor's antecedents Diyarbakirspor were forced under by financial pressure. Amedspor are hoping to avoid that fate by attracting more sponsors and by asking for more private donations. They are also asking the fans to tone down their behaviour – at least at big games where they are under the most scrutiny.

Over the course of the season, the club has faced increasing hostility at away matches, which rattled some players and motivated others, including Naki, who ascribes their inspired cup run to the added concentration and motivation from playing big sides. Before one away match, every hotel in Sivas refused to host the team – Amedspor eventually found somewhere to stay, 35 kilometres from the city.[48] Mizrak was among several officials who were later attacked and hospitalised by Ankaragucu officials during a league match in April 2016.

Both Naki and Mizrak mentioned Tahir Elci, the lawyer and president of the Diyarbakir Bar Association, who was shot in the head and killed in Sur in November 2015, moments after making a televised call for peace with the PKK.[49] As someone who has already been attacked in the street and vilified across the national media for weeks, Naki is a potential target – especially in cities outside the region. 'I will be recognised on the street and there will be danger but how can I live with fear?' asked Naki. 'But I am not afraid. Otherwise, I would go back to Germany and be safe there or I could just go upstairs and hang myself. So I reject fear.'

At 26 years old, Naki was probably approaching his peak. It's clear that he has the talent to play at the highest level. He said that while his main aim was to help Amedspor get into the Super League, he would consider other moves in the future – but only to raise the profile of Kurdish issues. He is considering going into politics after football.

Everyone at Amedspor is keen to point out that the team has players from a range of ethnic, religious and political backgrounds: Turks, Kurds and Alevis, HDP and AKP supporters. But, as Diyarbakir has become the de facto capital of Turkish Kurdistan, so Amedspor has assumed the standard of footballing Kurdishness. 'There are almost 40 million Kurdish people in the region and we represent them – in some way,' said Naki. 'We are perceived as the Kurdistan team here, that's the reality.'

Back in downtown Diyarbakir, we learned that a 17-year-old boy had been killed in clashes that afternoon while trying to march to Sur. The sting of tear gas lingered in the evening air.

In March, as the military prevailed in cities across the region, and curfews were lifted, the scale of the devastation became more obvious. Many of the neighbourhoods in Cizre had been under curfew for 79 days, and those in Sur for over 100 days. Some neighbourhoods looked like Kobane or Gaza in the aftermath of a war: intimate and often abandoned domesticity was glimpsed through buildings shorn of their facades; brick walls had been punched through rooms by militants; mounds of rubble stood in place of houses; gutted apartment blocks slouched like collapsed wedding cakes; the carcasses of cars lay on the streets; birds' nests of rebar were torn out of ballast. There were uprooted trees, scatterings of shell casings, fire-scorched surfaces, melted glass and the stench of bodies buried under rubble. Entire neighbourhoods had been emptied out. Thousands of families were homeless.

The military had claimed to only target militants, but there was stark evidence that the violence was total and indiscriminate.[50] Human Rights Watch found that some of the violence and deaths occurred in areas that were not behind barricades or where no armed groups had been operating.[51] It found credible reports that the security forces had deliberately killed civilians who were waving white flags or trapped in basements – including children.[52]

The sociologist Cem Emrence says that, in many cases, the political character of neighbourhoods determined many counter-insurgency operations. 'Places where [the AKP] had a realistic chance of increasing its vote share were left out,' he said.[53] Strongholds of pro-Kurdish political movements were battered. 'In Nusaybin, you don't stand a chance. In Yuksekova you don't stand a chance. In Cizre you don't stand a chance. So in that respect there was a strong political logic attached to it.' Just as villages had been cleared by scorched-earth fire in the 1990s, now restive urban communities were also being cleared. The government pledged to rebuild the shattered cities and was beginning to offer compensation to displaced people, but some feared it would use it as an opportunity to gentrify and cleanse the strongholds.

Kurdish militants were expanding their violence outside the region. A massive car bomb in Ankara in March 2016 killed at least 29 people, and injured many more – responsibility was claimed by TAK (Freedom Falcons of Kurdistan), an offshoot of the PKK.[54] By June 2016 the PKK had mostly returned to fighting in rural areas.

The parliament passed a law stripping the HDP of immunity from prosecution, and prosecutors began preparing legal files accusing Demirtas and other HDP politicians of supporting the PKK.

Meanwhile, Amedspor returned to the drudgery of the third tier, with one eye on the impending second-leg clash against Fenerbahce. The return tie took place three weeks after the first leg in the rather more sedate environs of Kadikoy, Istanbul. If Amedspor could humble Fenerbahce at their own stadium, they would qualify for the semi-final, and European qualification beckoned as the other sides had likely already qualified through the league. The thought of Amedspor competing in the Europa League was mind-boggling.

The second leg was on a dreary early March evening at 6:15 p.m., a stale time for a match but the TV schedulers preferred to shunt it back to make way for the Konyaspor vs Besiktas tie, which meant that many people would not have time to get there after work. And there would again be no Amedspor fans for the biggest match in their club's history. The authorities had decided it was too great a security risk. Gaggles of Fenerbahce fans were drinking beer in Yogurtcu Park, across from the stadium.

There were so few Fenerbahce fans – just a few thousand – that they didn't bother to turn on the huge electric heaters for the match, even though the evening was cold enough for breath to be visible. Fenerbahce had invited 45 children from Sur to attend the match as a gesture of goodwill.

There were more Turkish flags than usual in the stands and Amedspor got a few jeers when they came out of the tunnel. When the national anthem was played, several fans displayed the ultranationalist 'wolf' symbol. Fenerbahce chant-leaders were poised on their podiums, eagerly waiting for the national anthem to end so they could launch the crowd straight into 'Martyrs never die, the homeland will never be divided.'

For the first time in the tournament, it looked like a third-tier side whose race was run. Fenerbahce took a 2–0 lead in the first half. Amedspor pulled a goal back, but in the dying minutes the ball pinged around their box like a piece of exploding popcorn until Fenerbahce prodded it into the goal to wrap up the tie.

At the final whistle, Amedspor's players left the pitch hastily amid some low-level abuse. There was no reason to hang around, no fans to salute on the club's biggest occasion. It was a sad and hurried end to an astounding cup run. It took the mighty Fenerbahce to finally stop Amedspor: 6–4 on aggregate. And everyone at the football federation probably breathed a big sigh of relief.

MARCH 3, 2016

Turkish Cup Quarter Finals – 2nd leg
Sukru Saracoglu Stadium, Istanbul

Fenerbahce **3—1** Amedspor

(6—4 on aggregate)

TOPUZ 31	ICER 77
FERNANDAO 40	
NANI 88	

In October 2016, a Turkish court announced that Deniz Naki was being charged with 'promoting terrorist propaganda'. The indictment featured several social media posts, which were accused of 'creating enmity and hate between two different sections of society', 'glorifying terrorists and terrorism' and 'presenting security forces as committing massacres against the region's people'.[55] The indictment also featured a photograph of Naki wearing traditional Kurdish clothing at a Newroz – Kurdish New Year – celebration, which prosecutors claimed was the outfit of a Kurdish militant.

Naki accepted that he had posted the messages, except one from September 2015 that sent a greeting to the 'heroes' of Dersim, after two PKK militants had been killed fighting security forces. Naki claimed that message could have been posted by a friend in Germany who has access to his account. He insisted that the other posts were messages of peace. 'I want fraternity, unity and equality for everyone in this country.'[56] If convicted, Naki faced up to five years in prison.

In November 2016, several HDP parliamentarians were arrested – including the co-leaders Figen Yuksekdag and (Erdogan's nemesis) Selahattin Demirtas – on charges relating to terrorism that they vehemently deny. They remain in prison at the time of writing.

Meanwhile, despite the shock to the military from the July 2016 failed coup, the violence in the south-east continued unabated. The government will face a dilemma. The PKK cannot win on the battlefield, but neither can they be eradicated, and Kurdish political consciousness remains a growing force. But pursuing peace and delivering Kurdish autonomy lose key nationalist votes. This is the genius and tragedy of Erdogan: he created an unprecedented opportunity for peace, then he retreated to nationalism and squandered it.

On the pitch, Amedspor started 2016/17 brightly. Naki was back after his suspension and had scored four goals in his first few games. In November 2016, a court acquitted Naki of all charges, but the prosecution appealed and in April 2017 he was given an 18-month suspended prison sentence – putting him on probation for five years.

It is an awfully long time to stay out of trouble. Naki said he will appeal the verdict: 'I gave a message of peace. I said I was against the war and I have been punished for this. I am someone in love with peace and I will always give this message. I am ready to pay the price whatever it is.'[57]

7

The Rebel Referee

Halil Ibrahim Dincdag fell in love with football as a child. He was a talented central midfielder but as a teenager he suffered a slipped disc. As he struggled to come back from injury he realised he would never play at a high level. 'I wanted to find a way to stay inside the football world, so I began refereeing in 1995,' he told me.[1] Dincdag dreamed of becoming an official in the Turkish Super League.

He realised he was gay by the time he'd started secondary school, although he kept his sexuality secret. Trabzon, where Dincdag grew up in the 1980s and 1990s, is a conservative city: 'In those years, if you'd revealed you were gay, people would force you out of the city or kill you.' His sexuality would later shock the nation.

I first met Dincdag in October 2015, when he was about to turn 39. He was well into the sixth year of a legal battle with the Turkish Football Federation. He wore red-rimmed glasses on his beaky nose and had a neat shadow of stubble. He was folded and self-contained, and his hooded eyes had a hawkish vigilance.

Homophobia is pervasive in Turkey and is particularly endemic in Turkish football. Many of the insults chanted at football matches are laden with homophobia or sexism. '*Ibne hakem!*'[2] – 'faggot referee!' – is a common insult heard at football matches of all levels across the country, the Turkish equivalent of the English fan's refrain 'the referee's a wanker!'

Dincdag would tune out these taunts – every referee gets them. Off the field, he was always animated by injustice. 'I was always opposing the leading figures of the referee circles in Trabzon. If I thought they were doing something wrong, I would stand up and tell them they were wrong. I was also supporting my colleagues when I felt they were mistreated,' he said, grinning at the memory. 'I became kind of the leader of the rebel referees in Trabzon.'

Dincdag refereed around 80 matches a year and his ratings were high, but his rebellious stances earned him high-ranking enemies. He claims that the head of the referees' association in Trabzon had threatened to 'kick the arse' of anyone who tried to promote him to the national leagues. 'He really didn't like me!' said Dincdag gleefully.

After 14 years in the Trabzon amateur leagues, Dincdag still harboured dreams of becoming a professional referee, although his hopes were fading with time. Nevertheless, he was content in his life. He loved refereeing and his job as a presenter on a sports radio station. He didn't have a partner, but he had a couple of gay friends and they would meet and talk freely. His family were not aware of his sexuality and would never have guessed. Dincdag says they were always very loving and caring, but he was still unsure how they would react if he came out. They are very devout – his brother is an imam in Trabzon. He considered telling his sister, but decided against it: 'I was happy with my job and with my life and there was no need to mess everything up.'

Life was neatly compartmentalised. But in 2008 he was called up for mandatory military service. The military, football and his sexuality collided, and Dincdag's life was pitched upside down.

Outed

The general perception in Turkish society has long been that being a man means being a soldier. Military service is mandatory for men – women are exempt – and many see it as a male, patriotic rite of passage. But as a child Dincdag wondered why people were forced into the military, encouraged to fight, kill and even die. As he got older he understood that violence, the harsh rules and discipline in the military, and being subordinate to others were inimical to how he wanted to live. He decided at a young age that he didn't want to serve.

For university graduates, military service is typically around six months long, while for non-graduates it is generally 12 months. Dincdag had deferred military service in 2006, but by 2008 he could no longer put it off. Becoming a conscientious objector or evading military service could mean a lifetime of periodical hassle, arrest and imprisonment, with stark implications for his career and making it hard to buy a house, get a loan, stay in a hotel or even access medical treatment. He would lose his refereeing licence. Wealthy people can use their connections to avoid service or get an easy posting far from the violent flashpoints in the country's south-east. Some pay fines of several thousand Turkish lira every few years to evade service. These were not options for Dincdag.

But the Turkish military regards homosexuality and transgenderism as psychosexual disorders – so if gay conscripts can 'prove' their sexuality, they are usually exempt from military service on 'medical grounds'. If Dincdag could get an exemption on the basis of his sexuality, he could avoid serving and resume his life.

Once he was called up, the following few months were racked with anxiety and trauma as he reported his sexuality to the military. He was sent to military hospitals to be examined, and given a month-long medical exemption. When this expired he was told to report to his division. Dincdag was terrified – there were more than 100 men in his barracks, and violence in the military – including rape – is commonplace towards those suspected of being gay. Dincdag's friend was raped by seven men in the military when they realised that he was gay.

When Dincdag refused to go, some officers were sympathetic – one assigned him two guards to protect him in the barracks. 'One night I was ill, and this officer was in charge,' recalled Dincdag. 'He got really angry with the guards!: "How did he get ill?"' Dincdag stayed for a week in barracks in Sivas under protection but the strain was taking a toll – he broke down and threatened to commit suicide. A military psychologist sent him to a psychiatric unit where most of the patients were schizophrenic. It was like a prison, with bars on the windows. He was not allowed to leave. The staff left the ward at night and Dincdag says that he and two other gay 'patients' barricaded themselves in a room for their own protection as other patients tried to force the door.

Dincdag says he was spared some of the humiliating and degrading questions and requests that are sometimes posed to 'test' sexuality in the military's medical facilities – such as requesting video evidence of the patient having gay sex, or asking whether they played with guns or dolls as a child. Gay conscripts have reportedly been asked whether they like football, which serves as another barometer of straight masculinity for the military.[3]

Nevertheless, he was asked endless questions; it was a gruelling process. Dincdag was told by medical staff that he didn't 'look gay', that he was too conventionally masculine. 'They also told me: "You have a good physique, you can serve as a solider."' They asked gossipy questions about whether he'd ever had a partner while working as a referee. After ten fraught days and barricaded nights on the psychiatric ward, Dincdag was finally given an exemption on medical grounds. A long struggle lasting several months was over and Dincdag felt immense relief. He returned to Trabzon and resumed refereeing and his old job. Life settled back into familiar routines.

But the respite only lasted a month. The referees' association in Trabzon asked Dincdag for his military service report, which showed that he had been exempted from military service on medical grounds. It didn't mention details. The association told Dincdag he could no longer serve as a referee as he had a certified health problem. When Dincdag protested that he was in perfect health, the association pressed him for details. In desperation he showed them a longer report that detailed his exemption on psychosexual grounds due to homosexuality.

The association were shocked – they sought advice from the national referees' association within the football federation. Their response was the same: Dincdag could no longer work as a referee because his 'medical condition' invalidated his licence.

In May 2009, Dincdag officially appealed against the decision. Two days later, the first article about him appeared in the press, although he was unnamed, with a headline in *Fanatik* newspaper: 'Gay referee wants his whistle back'.[4]

The leak had to have come from within the football federation. The media went into a frenzy and the stories proliferated. Dincdag fled to Istanbul, afraid that the media were going to track him down in Trabzon and start hassling his family, who still knew nothing about his sexuality. The national press had acquired his phone number and were calling constantly to ask for interviews.

The newspaper articles were becoming increasingly specific; *Haberturk* journalist Fatih Altayli wrote a piece that used Dincdag's initials, referring to him as 'Trabzon District referee H.I.D.' He may as well just have named him. It was clear to Dincdag that his sexuality, previously known to just a couple of friends, was being outed to the nation.

Dincdag stopped running and began doing what came more naturally – fighting. He decided to appear on national television and defend himself. It was a shocking moment for many people. On the way to meet Dincdag for the first time, my translator chattered excitedly about the television appearance, which he vividly recalled more than six years later, because it had been so unprecedented.

Waiting backstage in the studio, Dincdag anxiously turned over what he was about to do in his mind. He hoped that by telling his own story on television he could take back a measure of control. TV was the most powerful way to do this: he hoped that his visibility would help people relate to him, to see him as human. On the other hand, it held risks – the more people recognised him, the higher the risk of attack. And he worried how his family would take the news. 'This felt like a life or death decision,' he remembered. 'I felt like I had come to the end of the road – that I would die or I would be reborn.'

Dincdag appeared on *Telegol*. Initially the channel wanted to blur Dincdag's face – he asked them to show him, as he now wanted everything out in the open. 'The crowds shout "fag" at referees whose decisions they don't like,' said Dincdag.[5] 'Well, here I am.' He spoke about what he had been through. After Dincdag left the TV station he was under huge strain: 'I was in a tunnel, and I couldn't see the end.' He waited for the fallout.

The first family member to call was his sister – she said his mother had been shocked and upset, but that she wanted to talk to him. 'My mother said, "No matter what people say, you're our son. We love you, we support you – stay with us."'

In the following days he spoke to his mother every day, but he avoided the male members of family. His father and brother had tried to call but he was afraid of how they would react. When he eventually spoke to them, they were just as supportive: 'Don't give up fighting,' his father told him.

Once it was clear he had the backing of all his family, Dincdag felt enormous relief: 'My family was supporting me, so what other people said didn't matter.' If they hadn't supported him, Dincdag says that he might not have survived: 'I would have considered suicide.' He would need their support to get through the ordeal of the following years.

Aftermath

Dincdag's TV appearance put the Turkish Football Federation on the defensive. The federation vice-president Lutfi Aribogan denied that Dincdag's sacking was related to his sexuality, and called his behaviour the 'emotional' response of a referee who lacked the talent to be promoted to the professional leagues – an absurd claim, given that their official decision to remove his licence had been on 'health' grounds unrelated to his performance. Oguz Sarvan, the head of the referees' board, scurrilously implied that Dincdag's lawyer, rather than the federation, had leaked his name to the media.[6]

After the TV appearance, Dincdag lost his job at the radio station where he had worked for 12 years. 'They told me that my presence at their radio station was completely in contrast to their broadcast principles.' Most of his friends supported him, although a few cut off contact. People would stare at him in public, while some would come up and express support. Others were more threatening – he received death threats for years. A gang from the Black Sea region sent emails to Dincdag and his lawyer, telling them where they'd been to prove they were following them, and promised to kill him.

Dincdag was swallowed in a deep depression. 'After appearing on TV I lost 33 years – I lost my life, my occupation, my experience.' He applied for more than 150 jobs, but all of the applications were unsuccessful. 'People would Google me and see the news. I even applied to wash dishes in a restaurant but they rejected me. I was only surviving with the support of my family.'

In 2013 his mother died. Dincdag was devastated. The following year, he was diagnosed with testicular cancer. He underwent surgery and radiotherapy, and is now in remission.

Unable to work or referee, Dincdag has devoted himself to his legal struggle and activism. He opened a lawsuit against the football federation in 2009, suing it for 110,000 TL for violation of his private life and discrimination. Turkish justice is usually protracted – by October 2015 there had been 18 court hearings in his case.

'This is a case for all the people who were alienated or marginalised by the system, who were kicked out of the circle,' believes Dincdag, who says that teachers, government employees, police officers and all kinds of people have reached out to him with their stories of homophobic discrimination.

'My trial caused a huge crack in the wall of homophobia in Turkey and, if we win the trial, we will totally destroy the wall of homophobia,' said Dincdag. 'If we destroy homophobia in football, homophobia in other sectors of society will also be destroyed.' He still hadn't given up hopes of returning to refereeing, but he needed to win his case.

Dincdag felt like he had been given a death sentence, but had escaped and emerged stronger. 'Those who violated my rights will end up in court and they will get a red card!' he told me. A verdict was due by the end of 2015.

A turning point?

Burcu Karakas, a journalist who has written extensively about Dincdag's experiences, says that his case was a turning point in terms of lesbian, gay, bisexual and transgender (LGBT) rights in Turkish football and society. 'After Halil's case people started talking about homophobia in football for the first time,' says Karakas. 'It opened a debate.'[7]

Dincdag's television appearance shocked the nation, and triggered some hostility and homophobia, but it also made many stop and reflect. His humanity and courage gained him admiration and respect. Karakas says that Dincdag would not have experienced such sympathy 20 or 30 years ago, as attitudes towards homosexuality have softened in recent decades. A significant LGBT-rights movement first emerged in Turkey in the mid- to late 1980s.[8]

Karakas argues that, paradoxically, homophobia can be challenged through football precisely because it is a site of huge prejudice, the domain in which men 'practise their manhood' through displaying conventional norms of masculinity. If Dincdag had been a singer or an actor, there would probably have been less fuss and his case would have had less of an impact, because LGBT people, such as the famous actor and singer Zeki Muren, are more accepted in the considerably less macho world of show business.

Derogatory football chants in Turkey often equate weakness with femininity or submissive sexuality. The journalist and conscientious objector advocate Onur Erem says that a cultural distinction between being sexually 'passive' and 'active' is often made in the military, and in wider society, that dates back to Ottoman and Byzantine times. 'It's a kind of tradition that goes way back in these lands: that if you are a person who is penetrating, it doesn't matter what you are penetrating – it shows your masculinity.'[9] The penetrated are submissive and, if they are male, are worthy of contempt, and are expected to conform to a feminine or camp stereotype.

When fans label rivals *'ibne'* or *'yavsak'* – 'sissy' – they are primarily insulting their manliness, over their literal sexuality. A Besiktas song about Galatasaray goes:

> C'mon, a blow job Galatasaray
> Take it in your mouth Galatasaray
> Your administration, footballers and fans: they're all sissies
> Assmongers Galatasaray: ass, ass, ass![10]

Fans of Besiktas, who play in black and white, also deride their rivals Fenerbahce (yellow and navy) and Galatasaray (yellow and red) as 'colourful', implying flamboyance and 'gayness'. Besiktas's rivals are just as homophobic. Galatasaray fans chant that 'a real man would not support a team with wings.'[11]

When fans chant, 'What's up with you ref? You seem to be shaking your hips' or call the referee 'ibne', they are also often calling into question his fairness and competence, by insulting his manliness.[12] Shortly after Dincdag's TV appearance, the former referee Erman Toroglu argued that Dincdag shouldn't be given his job back: 'I reckon [gay referees] would have a tendency to give more penalties to good-looking, tough footballers.'[13]

Many fans see themselves as well-defined, stock macho characters who are diametrically opposed to the 'ibne': like the *delikanli*, which literally translates to 'crazy-blooded' but also describes a male ethics: a young man who is tough, courageous, honest, no-nonsense, charismatic, down-to-earth, rough and ready – but fair.[14]

Bawer Cakir ticks quite a few boxes that could irk certain chauvinists in Turkey: he is a gay, Kurdish, left-wing journalist. As a child in the early 1990s, he was taken to watch Fenerbahce by his football-mad uncle. The football stadium seemed, to him, to be a place where men vent their rage and frustration. 'The main problem about football culture is that it's like a gladiatorial arena. This culture is like a vomiting of masculinity and when I was in the stadium everyone was screaming, "Fuck your mother, motherfucker." There wasn't any single second I didn't hear this kind of thing,' recalled Cakir.[15]

Cakir loved the sport but was put off by the culture, so he began to see football as his enemy. But as he got older he got into punk music and zines, and discovered that there were football clubs popular with leftists, like Hamburg's St. Pauli – whose fans take strong stances against homophobia and sexism. He began to re-engage with football, and he started finding things to admire about other clubs' stances on LGBT issues – Barcelona, Liverpool, Livorno, Borussia Dortmund. He also lived in Argentina for a few months and became a Boca Juniors fan, and he admires Maradona and the Argentinian national side: 'They beat England many times. The Hand of God, darling.'

He also mused on football's 'gay side': '22 guys, sweating, fighting: football is one of the most homoerotic sports in the world – after scoring they touch each other's asses, there's kind of like a big orgy, they kiss each other... it's very strange that they totally refuse this reality. They never recognise it.'

Cakir argues that homophobia was imported from the West, and insists that men in the Middle East used to touch each other's balls as a greeting.

It's certainly true that many countries in the world that criminalise homosexuality are in the British Commonwealth, and took their law from repressive British legislation, which was viciously homophobic in the imperial era. The British exported football, and football culture. 'Football is part of this colonial culture too.'

Sexualised language is prevalent in Turkish stadiums, in a way that it isn't in most other Muslim-majority countries. Itir Erhart, an academic who researches gender and football fandom, is a Besiktas fan. Erhart believes the football stadium is the most masculine space in Turkey. She used to sing sexist and homophobic chants with gusto, without really considering what she was singing. She had an epiphany when she was in her mid-twenties during a game against Fenerbahce, in which she was shouting at the opposition fans and suggesting they do something that was not anatomically possible for her. 'It's almost like I saw it as being a genuine fan; like everyone swears, so I swear,' she said. 'At that moment I was like – oops – why am I doing this? It's vulgar, it's sexist, and I'm not even a man. And I realised it was my strategy to be part of the stadium.'[16]

Erhart stopped singing sexist and homophobic chants. 'These chants or this kind of language is not confined to football only, but in football it's very aggravated.'[17] There are fans who deny they are homophobic, but still sing these chants. The nature of Turkish patriarchy varies from many other Muslim countries in the region – women are more visible in public, they attend football matches but are generally expected to not be overly feminine. 'In Turkish culture, anything feminine is to be looked down on. So you could be like a man who doesn't fit the stereotype or you could be a woman, it doesn't matter. Femininity is denigrated,' she says. 'That's part of everyday discourse and heavily reflected in football.'

Unlike in many other Muslim-majority countries in the region, there are no anti-LGBT laws in Turkey. Homosexuality has been legal in Turkey since the foundation of the republic in 1923, and was legal in the Ottoman Empire from the mid-nineteenth century. Turkish society is generally more liberal and pluralistic than many of its neighbours. Paradoxically, this may make homophobia more prevalent in the streets and in the stadiums, believes James M. Dorsey, author of *The Turbulent World of Middle East Soccer*. 'In some ways it is also a testament to Turkey because [homosexuality] is public,' he says. '[In Turkey] it's going to be more of an issue for those who don't like [homosexuality], rather than [in Arab countries] which, in their perception, is non-existent.'[18]

While there have been some positive changes in Turkish society over the past 20 years, Cakir says that little has really changed in the stands. 'Because men – heterosexual men – don't want to let gay people in because this is their area, this is their world,' says Cakir. 'It is a kind of pagan ritual to go to the stadium together and [swear] and they don't want us there, because we can kill the party.'

But football's widespread appeal across Turkish society may also make it an effective vehicle to challenge prejudice, although much of this potential is latent. 'Ninety-five per cent of the population like football and people talk about football every day. Many people only read about football – they don't care that the police kill someone somewhere or arrest academics – but they care about every unimportant detail about football,' says Cakir. 'For example, if the president of a football club said something [positive] about Halil Ibrahim [Dincdag], it would change many things, very fast. But the problem is, they can't.'

Karakas believes that Dincdag has given some LGBT people hope. 'He's still alive and he can walk on the street,' she says. Of course, not everyone is as brave and persistent as Dincdag, and many cannot rely on the support of family and friends. 'I can't say that people now accept homosexual referees or players,' says Karakas. 'It's not the case.'

I wonder what would happen if a Turkish footballer came out now. 'Everything would be over for this person, for their career,' said Cakir. 'It doesn't matter what the fans think about him – the president of the club would tell them to leave – "You are not good for us." It's about morality and saleability – football is a product and they need to sell it.' Having a gay player could be bad for business.

It is, however, now more possible that a player could come out as gay in retirement and gain acceptance, though Cakir believes they would need to have been very successful and otherwise conventional to command respect. 'Society would accept someone if they look like them and they did some good things for the nation or country,' believes Cakir, who adds that this attitude is also prejudiced. 'Why do we have to be perfect?'

Homophobia is a problem in football all over the world, not just in Turkey. It is extremely difficult for LGBT professional footballers to come out anywhere. Although gay British rugby players such as Gareth Jenkins have come out, no footballers in the UK have been out, while playing, since Justin Fashanu. Fashanu was the first £1 million black player when he moved from Norwich City to Nottingham Forest in 1981. Fashanu faced difficulties with his manager Brian Clough after he found out he had been going to gay bars.[19] After Fashanu came out publicly in a 1990 tabloid interview, he was subject to abuse by fans. He committed suicide in 1998.[20]

The American footballer Robbie Rogers has come out as gay and is playing for LA Galaxy in the MLS (Major League Soccer). He played in England for Leeds United before coming out and said in an interview with *Howler* magazine that the main issue now in the UK was not so much the fans as the players, in a macho, often homophobic dressing-room culture.[21] The *Guardian*'s 'secret footballer' takes the opposite view.[22] Rugby is also more progressive in terms of gay referees. While Nigel Owens – arguably rugby union's most respected referee – publicly came out as gay, no professional football referees have come out in the UK. Jesús Tomillero, a gay Spanish referee, received death threats after his return to football.[23]

Dincdag remains the only high-profile LGBT figure in Turkish football. But because of his case, the next referee who comes out as gay will have an antecedent. Dincdag says he has spoken to gay referees who have officiated in the Super League. He also claims to know of gay Super League footballers.

Homophobia in Turkish football and society long predates the AKP. But Karakas argues that the AKP's social politics is constructed partly on a particular conception of masculinity and Turkishness: 'In terms of policy, as long as you are a [straight] man, a Turk and a Sunni Muslim – then you are OK!'[24]

The AKP came to power in 2002 balancing a socially conservative agenda with a liberal democratic rhetoric of tolerance and pluralism which, perhaps grudgingly, encompassed LGBT rights. Early on in the party's tenure, Erdogan said that LGBT people 'must have legal protections in terms of their rights and freedoms'.[25]

Bawer Cakir participated in the earliest Gay Pride march in Istiklal, Istanbul, in 2003, when there were only a few dozen people attending. 'People were looking at us like we were in a zoo – strange, freaky creatures. But that moment was a big, big step.'[26] It grew into the largest Gay Pride march in any Muslim-majority country, with tens of thousands attending by 2014. LGBT people have become a more visible and confident presence in many cities in the past 15 years, and organisations advocating LGBT rights have proliferated – even in small, conservative Anatolian cities.

Yet, in over 15 years in power, the AKP has failed to introduce legislation that prohibits discrimination on grounds of sexuality, and its rhetoric has steadily shifted over the course of its tenure to outright hostility and moral condemnation. In 2004 justice minister Cemil Cicek justified his decision to remove the term 'sexual orientation' from the draft Turkish Penal Code, 'because gender already covers it'.[27] In discussing the 2007 constitutional amendments, AKP politician Dengir Mir Mehmet Firat suggested that legal rights on sexuality were an issue for the twenty-second century.

AKP politicians have repeatedly stated their opposition to gay marriage. Cakir argues that this 'threat' of marriage is used as an excuse for inaction on gay rights by the AKP. He says that, in general, LGBT people in Turkey are not asking for marriage: 'We just want to exist.'

In 2010 Aliye Kavaf – the AKP minister responsible for families – said: 'I believe homosexuality is a dysfunction, a disease. It is something that requires treatment.'[28] While campaigning for the May 2015 general election, prime minister Ahmet Davutoglu said: 'Homosexuals caused the destruction of the Tribe of Lot and yet the HDP nominates them.'[29] The notionally social democratic, Kemalist CHP and the leftist, pro-Kurdish HDP have fielded openly LGBT candidates and both parties have some politicians who espouse clear policies in support of LGBT rights.

Activists argue that the AKP's increasingly sexist and homophobic rhetoric has fuelled bigotry and violence across the country. Research suggests that violence against women has soared,[30] and violence and discrimination against LGBT people remains pervasive under the AKP.[31]

In July 2016, Muhammed Wisam Sankari, a gay Syrian refugee living in the conservative Istanbul district of Fatih, was reported missing. Two days later his mutilated, decapitated body was discovered; friends could only identify him from his clothing. Five months before his murder he had also been abducted and raped by a local gang, according to Sankari's flatmate.[32]

In August 2016, Hande Kader, a 23-year-old transgender woman, was murdered. She had been repeatedly raped and mutilated. Like many transgender people, who find it virtually impossible to get other jobs, Kader had done sex work. She was last seen getting into the car of a client. As the rights group Transgender Europe notes, 'No country is safe for trans people.' However, according to the group's data, Turkey has by far the highest trans murder rate in Europe.[33] Violence and harassment have made suicide prevalent among transgender people in Turkey. 'There are very few trans individuals who die of natural causes – nearly none,' said Kemal Ordek, the president of Red Umbrella, an association that defends the rights of transgender sex workers, in an interview with the BBC.[34]

Kader was also a brave activist – she faced down the police in the streets when they attacked peaceful Pride marches. Gay Pride in 2015 was shut down at the last minute, apparently because the event coincided with Ramadan.[35] Police water cannon inadvertently created rainbows as they violently broke up the event. The following year Gay Pride and Trans Pride were banned in advance on security grounds following a spate of terrorist bombings and threats from far-right ultranationalist groups – although much larger gatherings, such as the 'Democracy Watch' demonstrations following the failed coup, passed safely under heightened security. Again, those who attempted to protest during Trans Pride and Gay Pride 2016 were violently dispersed and many were arrested. Erdogan was accused of hypocrisy after having a publicised iftar dinner during Ramadan with the transgender singer Bulent Ersoy, hours after police had broken up an LGBT rally with tear gas.[36]

Much has changed and much has remained the same since Dincdag was sacked in 2009. Military service is still compulsory. Many gay men who declare their sexuality to the military are still abused and humiliated and, in proving their sexuality, they face possible consequences for their future employment, and are forced to accept their sexuality as a 'sickness'. Many gay men just do their military service and 'pass' as straight.

But there are changes taking place in Turkish society. 'There are lots of people – including lots of men – who are questioning patriarchy and objecting to this patriarchy, both in society and by the army,' says journalist Onur Erem.[37] 'In the 1990s, people would have made fun of them, called them "gays", but today heterosexual people also debate these topics, so there is progress. But on the other side violence against women is increasing because of Islamist policies of this government.'[38]

Life under AKP rule has been a paradoxical mixture of progress and polarisation for many women and LGBT people, growing space amid a growing threat – a kind of flourishing under siege.

'Everything in football is about the government now and the political situation,' argues Cakir. 'If we cannot change the political situation here, we cannot change anything about football.' The AKP government has a firm grip on the football federation, and the federation's agenda and concerns generally reflect those of the government. The federation doesn't have specific policies addressing homophobic chanting, beyond generic laws designed to punish swearing and abusive chants.

'Unfortunately, that is the Turkish way of cursing. It has nothing to do with homophobia,' claimed Mete Duren, the Turkish Football Federation's spokesperson, who defended the lack of a policy to tackle homophobic or sexist chanting. 'We cannot educate football fans,' he said. 'We can only punish.'[39] Duren said that the federation cannot punish individuals, it can only punish a club, and said that clubs should exercise their right to sanction abusive fans.

While the government and the federation fail to implement legislation or policies to tackle homophobia, some activists are using football as a tool to combat homophobia, transphobia and sexism.

Gezi football

LGBT activists featured prominently in the Gezi protests, making speeches and resisting police attacks on the front lines. Like football fans, many LGBT activists are experienced in dealing with violent confrontations with the police. For many Gezi protesters it was the first time they had seen or heard openly LGBT people. Prejudices and misconceptions were undermined, bonds and connections formed. For many LGBT activists, it was their first opportunity to articulate their concerns and issues on a grander public scale.

Though the Gezi 'movement' has fractured and splintered, it has fostered a degree of increased recognition, at least among more liberal elements of society, of the way in which concerns of class, gender, race, religion, sexuality and other factors intersect.

A Gezi dividend has emerged in football – especially where activism and football converge. On a chilly October night in 2015, I attended the opening games of the second season of the Ozgur Lig – 'Free League' – an alternative football league created by activists in Ankara earlier in the year. A player for Karsi Takim – '"Against"' Team' – told me that the league represented 'Gezi football', bringing different groups of people together, such as anarchists, Kurds and LGBT people.

The league opposes industrial football, sexism, patriarchy, homophobia, transphobia and racism, and seeks to promote grassroots football and political opposition to the AKP. Matches are seven-a-side and by the second season the league had expanded from 14 to 19 teams.

Sportif Lezbon play in the Ozgur Lig and claim to be Turkey's first openly LGBT football club. Although Sportif Lezbon predominantly comprises lesbians and bisexual women, people of all genders and sexualities play for the team. Selin Yildiz, 25, was one of the founders of Sportif Lezbon.

Selin grew up in Istanbul playing football in the street and at school, often against boys. She had to be tough in order to thrive. 'Sometimes during the matches I was hurt but I couldn't show it, because people would say things like "Don't play like a girl." It's an insult.'[40]

Her father was proud of her footballing skills, recalls Selin: 'Only my mother sometimes made comments like "Why don't you help me with the housework rather than playing football?"' Selin continued to neglect dusting for football, and she excelled – in 2005 she joined Kartalspor, a professional women's team in Istanbul.

By the age of 13 or 14 she had started to realise that she was attracted to girls: 'I thought it was a kind of illness and I would recover,' recalls Selin. 'At the same time, deep down, I knew it wasn't something temporary.' Selin didn't dare come out while playing for Kartalspor – she later learned that some of her teammates were lesbians but their sexuality was not discussed openly. 'My coach was always talking about there being "no lesbians in my team",' she says. Selin played for Kartalspor for two years but she drifted away from football as her studies took precedence.

The idea of Sportif Lezbon began when Selin and a group of bisexual and lesbian friends went for a picnic and played a match. They had so much fun that they decided to form teams, but their matches were disorganised and only close friends and activists were playing. They wanted to take a daring step and create a team that could openly encourage and support LGBT people, and challenge prejudice in football and society. An opportunity arose in the newly formed Ozgur Lig.

Sportif Lezbon believe that football can be a site of radical politics, to challenge prejudice, conventional ideas and violence. 'Football is the world's most popular sport,' says Selin. 'And it's also a kind of bastion of masculinity; when you say "football", people think of men. So we want to turn it inside out – not only to challenge sexism and homophobia and transphobia, but also to oppose other harmful ideologies.'

'I joined the team because I wasn't happy about it all being lesbians! I wanted trans people to be represented,' said Demhat Aksoy, a 22-year-old transgender woman. Demhat is a member of Pembe Hayat – 'Pink Life' – an LGBT activist group. 'If you're an activist you don't have the chance to be in the closet. Trans people like us can be beaten or killed every day.' She was beaten by family members when she was younger. 'Now they have just about accepted me as a "gay man" – for them it's somehow preferable to being transgender.'[41]

Sportif Lezbon aim to attract more players and supporters, and they hope to play in a future LGBT Olympics. They also want to use the club to reach out and support LGBT footballers across the country. Selin knows professional lesbian players who like the idea of Sportif Lezbon but feel that they can't join or support the team publicly because they feel they have to keep their sexuality secret.

In addition to their exploits on the pitch, Sportif Lezbon use humour and wit as weapons. Their name is an echo of the famous Portuguese club Sporting Lisbon and, as homophobic chants are a staple of Turkish football, Sportif Lezbon have made humorous chants, slogans and banners a key part of their arsenal of dissent.

Some are tricky to translate because they involve slang, rhyme and wordplay, and often subvert Turkish pop songs. Others are pretty straight-forward: 'Lesbians on the pitch, boobs in the air'; 'Truck driver lesbians [slang for 'butch'], come and play'. And they have a chant which is deployed as affectionate abuse of opponents: '[name of team or individual], come here, do fisting with the lesbians'.

Tanju Gunduzalp, a 45-year-old journalist and player for Solteki – a team featuring a mixture of players from a leftist newspaper and a cycling club – argues that anti-LGBT attitudes are not limited to conservatives in Turkey: 'Socialists have their own prejudices and this includes homophobia. This is why Sportif Lezbon is an important team.'[42]

He was watching a game between FC Bakunin and Tasra with 'teammate' six-year-old golden retriever 'Itir', who had just been dashing madly back and forth across the pitch before the match. Gunduzalp claimed Itir is a player for Solteki. 'Actually she would be a good goalkeeper, if only she would stay in the goal,' he mused. He conceded that a few people were afraid of the dogs at first, 'but most got used to them.' Gunduzalp said that there were now three or four dogs 'playing' in the league and, for him, the idea was based on fun and irreverence. 'The concepts of competition and winning are inherently masculine and patriarchal and we are fighting against this,' he said.

But the league has serious activist aims and has made significant progress in terms of gender balance: only three teams had female players when the league was launched, but by the end of the first season only one team didn't have any female players.

Although Sportif Lezbon haven't faced any negative attitudes within the league, it was the first time that many players on other teams had met and played against openly LGBT people. 'Our goalkeeper is now famous for having conceded goals against every sexual orientation,' remarked a player from KaraKizil, a group of left-wing Genclerbirligi fans.

Ozgur Lig partly took its inspiration from some of the alternative leagues with a similar ethos that have been set up in Istanbul, including Gazoz Ligi, Efendi Lig and Karsi Lig. Sportif Lezbon have inspired LGBT teams to form, including Atletik Dildoa and Queer Park Rangers, who formed in Istanbul in late 2015.

Halil Ibrahim Dincdag referees in some of these alternative leagues in Istanbul, from which he earns a small income. To some extent, these alternative leagues are often leftist echo chambers that can be easily ignored – some believe that they don't have much traction beyond their bubbles. But, as homophobia exists among the left, many of the players are not yet 'converted', and sometimes it is important to rouse the converted into action.

Some argue that, rather than challenging the heteronormativity of Turkish football, inviting Dincdag to referee in activist leagues relegated him to a 'gay sphere', and that a more significant change in society would be reflected by Dincdag officiating in mainstream football again and being accepted.[43]

Dincdag says that the Swedish official Anders Fisk is his favourite referee. 'Currently there is no referee in Turkey I can admire – they should admire me!' he boasted.[44] Dincdag is not short on ego or hubris. He draws a mixed reaction from other LGBT activists, partly because he can be prickly and perhaps also because he does not subscribe to standard political positions. Anyone hoping to pigeonhole Dincdag will be frustrated.

He might referee in 'Gezi football'-style alternative leagues, but he didn't like the Gezi protests. 'I stood up against this government and this system in 2009 – they are very late!' He went to Gezi demonstrations a couple of times, but stopped going when political parties became more prominent. 'It started as a popular movement but it was transformed into a tool of political movements in Turkey.'

Dincdag is not too keen on Pride – he said it was important to attend the events and create awareness, but regarded it as being more about fun than politics, and didn't think it was a good idea to hold it during Ramadan.[45] 'Having a conflict with religion and tradition is not a helpful thing at all for the LGBT movement,' he said. 'In Gay Pride if you are getting naked during Ramadan you are just making a castle out of cards and then someone will flick it and it will collapse.' At the same time, he was miffed that no one had offered him a prominent role in this year's events – he felt ignored by the younger LGBT generation. He mentioned an award he received in Berlin in

2014 for his struggle: 'But in Turkey only one LGBT news website covered this story; it's not considered an important topic in Turkey.'

It seems that he has to be at the centre of everything. He was even considering setting up his own alternative football league that he said would unite all different political factions and ideologies. 'I'm trying to remember the slogan, it's very complicated,' he said, looking towards the ceiling. He said it will be called the 'Peace League' and the logo will be three whirling dervishes. Then he remembered the slogan: 'It's based on a quote by Mevlana [Rumi] – "whatever you are, come"... "whoever you are, play football."'

Dincdag claims not to support any political party and says he has only ever voted in constitutional ballots. 'I am opposed to discriminations like left wing and right wing. The LGBT movement cannot be stuck somewhere on a political spectrum. I carry democratic, socialist, conservative, nationalist values – a combination of all of them.' He becomes much more strident when talking about politics, rapping and thumping the arm of his chair in emphasis. 'If someone stereotypes something as "fascist" or "communist" or "anarchist", I extract them from my life.' He says he is religious and practises a form of Sufi Islam.

Dincdag says that the only person he would vote for is himself. 'Maybe you can do another interview with me when I become a candidate in the parliamentary elections,' he says. We both laugh. But he says he is serious, that he could join any party, so long as they support his struggle and stand him in winnable seats. 'I'm a mosaic, carrying humanitarian values. I am carrying all the colours of the rainbow.' He laughs when I suggest he tone down the rainbow rhetoric if he wants to join the AKP or the MHP.

Eventually it emerges that Dincdag has held talks with the opposition CHP: he claims they wanted him to join the party but he was too tied up in his lawsuit. Once the lawsuit is over he will consider joining a party. 'Politicians are lying to the people. I promise freedom, no one will stop others living their freedom. This is a revolution – my trial is a revolution,' he says. 'I will win this trial and then I will go to the parliament with this victory.'

The verdict

In late December 2015, after more than six years of legal struggle, a court found in favour of Dincdag and ordered the football federation to pay him compensation of 23,000 TL.[46]

We caught up again in June 2016. Dincdag was pleased that he had been proved right and hoped that the verdict would set a precedent. At the same time, it was a very late decision. The discrimination has cost him the foundations of his life, and he intends to appeal the meagre level of compensation, which was less than a quarter of what he had asked for. 'I felt happiness and pain together,' said Dincdag of his feelings on hearing the verdict.[47]

If he had served in the military for six to 12 months, he might be a professional referee by now, or at least would have avoided a lot of trauma, but Dincdag claims he doesn't regret his choices because he had to fight for his beliefs. 'But of course I would have liked to have lived my life without making my homosexuality a matter of public discussion!'

Six years of struggle, with very little money, the death of his mother and his health worries have taken a toll – he is exhausted. He now wants to buy a house in Turkey and to find a serious relationship. He hasn't had a partner for a while, he can go years without seeing anyone, and he has never had a long-term relationship. 'Actually, I receive many invitations for dates! But it is a sort of trust issue.' My translator, who is married, tried to console him with a Turkish saying: 'If you're single, you're a sultan.' Dincdag doesn't agree. 'I want to love someone and be with someone. But my boyfriend must be courageous and fearless like me!'

He hasn't lost hope of becoming a referee, but it seems like he has lost some of his drive. 'The [refereeing] administration has changed [personnel] in these six years but the mentality has not.' He now dreams of becoming a politician and of landing a role at FIFA or UEFA as their Turkish representative in combating homophobia in sports. 'If I become a referee, this will [only] mean I won this struggle for myself,' he reasoned. 'But, if I become an administrator in a federation, this will mean that I fought for LGBT people in Turkey and I can carry on the struggle this way.'

With his big mouth, bravado and bravery, Dincdag could be a major asset to any political party or institution. He could also be a major headache. He matches a huge heart with prickliness, and he is incapable of running any political line. He is a keen unifier, and a singular man. He is a perennial, incorrigible rebel.

8

Free Syrian Football

When the revolution broke out in 2011, Firas al-Ali was playing in Damascus for Al-Shorta, and for the Syrian national team. 'Society treated me like a superstar,' he told me. 'When I went to the shop just to buy something it would take me four hours to deal with the attention from fans!'[1] Syria was football crazy, and regular attendances of above 30,000 put Turkish Super League averages to shame.

With his previous club – Al-Taliya of Hama – Firas won the Syrian Cup twice and reached the quarter-finals of the Asian Football Confederation Cup (AFC), Asia's version of the Europa League. Firas is a winger and a free-kick specialist whose left foot would impress Gareth Bale. Al-Taliya's fans recorded a song for him, which sounds better in Arabic, but goes something like: 'When you run on the pitch, the fans boil over, your crosses are so beautiful, Firas al-Aaaaliii!'

I first met Firas in March 2016, when he was 29, in a Syrian café in Gaziantep, southern Turkey, where he was in exile, about 250 kilometres from where he was born. Firas had brought along his six-year-old son, who was sporting a fake leather jacket and wore a long fringe swept across his head, like a 1950s biker. Firas was dressed more casually, brownish hair turned dark with gel and styled a bit like Cristiano Ronaldo, Firas's footballing hero. Firas had the cobalt-blue eyes of a Siamese cat.

As a footballer, Firas witnessed some of the nepotism and corruption of Bashar al-Assad's dictatorship first-hand – players who were picked because of their connections with the regime rather than their talent. Firas had felt critical of Assad, but he had kept quiet, as did most under the terror of Assad's *mukhabarat*, the secret police.

But when the revolution broke out, Firas joined the protests, covering his face to hide his identity. Firas couldn't stop talking – he got into arguments with teammates who had continued to support Assad, even as the dictator's security forces bore down on peaceful protesters with extreme violence, brutality that soon ensnared his family. His 19-year-old cousin was killed at a protest – the bullet entered his eye and came out of his head. His niece was killed – completely vaporised when a barrel bomb fell directly on her house.

As months went by, the protests continued and the repression intensified, giving way to an increasingly complex, factionalised civil war, as the opposition took up arms. Firas's hometown of Kafr Zeita, near Hama, became associated with the rebel Free Syrian Army (FSA). Despite being a police officer, Firas's brother was arrested because of his connections to the rebellious town. Meanwhile, Firas remained in Damascus, where he would hear gunfire during training. The stadium was converted into a military base for the regime.

While on a training camp with the national team he watched from the window of his hotel as smoke rose from shelling across Damascus. One day he found out that his 13-year-old cousin had been killed by the security forces. Half an hour later he joined the rest of the team for dinner – one teammate mocked the protesters and Firas lost it: he had to be pulled off him. Firas couldn't take it any more; it was time to defect.

At dawn the next day, he sneaked away from the training camp, from the city, from his career, and set out for Kafr Zeita, some 300 kilometres north of Damascus, but the national team – preparing visas for a tournament in India – had his passport and military service documents. 'At every police checkpoint there was a risk that I would be detained and taken for military service,' said Firas. 'The thing that saved me was that the soldiers at the checkpoints were football fans – they knew me and I didn't have to show my ID, otherwise they would have taken me, because I didn't have any papers.'

Firas spent around seven months in Kafr Zeita, while the war raged and his money dwindled. 'The roof of my house made me a footballer!' Firas told me, while describing his town. As a child he'd set up a small table on the roof and would fire endless shots and passes at the target each day, until he could hit it almost every time, and had practically destroyed everything else on the roof in the meantime. When he broke something, his dad would get angry and twist his ear, but the next day would buy him a new football or pair of shoes. Firas played on rough, sandy ground and was forever going through balls and shoes. 'My family's financial situation was not great,' said Firas, 'but my father had the feeling that I would become something special.'

Kafr Zeita was subject to heavy bombardment by Assad's forces. It started with shelling around six times a day. Then the shelling increased and they started to drop bombs from helicopters. It wasn't safe to hide in the house;

they had to flee to nearby farms and fields, returning when the helicopters left. They had a radio that alerted them before an incoming attack, but they had very little time. 'If [my brother] didn't have a car we would have stayed in our house and died,' said Firas. Rockets destroyed his family's houses, life became unliveable, and Firas went from unemployed footballer to refugee – taking his wife and three kids, and his parents, and crossing into Turkey – it was 2013, and the Turkish government was still maintaining its open-door policy to Syrian refugees.

While his family went to Karkamis refugee camp, Firas wrangled over a contract with the Jordanian Super League team Al-Hussein. He spent a successful season there but being away from his family for a year proved hard and he returned to Turkey to collect them and bring them over to Jordan. While he was in Turkey, the Jordanian government changed the visa requirements for Syrians. Firas and his family were turned away at the airport and returned to the camp. 'I surrendered to bad luck,' said Firas.

The days of receiving daily adoration and an annual salary of over $100,000 – a fortune for most people in Syria – seemed unimaginably distant. 'I moved from a five-star environment to one with no stars. The camp and being a refugee, how can I talk about it? Everything is difficult, from the simplest thing. Even leaving the camp is difficult.'[2]

There are seven of them in a three-by-three-metre tent, sleeping next to each other on mattresses on the floor. The bathroom is the length of a football pitch away, and feels much further at night. Only when his family sleeps can Firas have some time alone for his thoughts. By the last three or four days of the month, the money they've been given by the camp has usually run out.

Karkamis is the smallest camp in Turkey and there is not much crime, unlike in some of the bigger refugee camps. But there are dangers – photographs on Firas's phone showed towering black plumes coming from burning tents in the camp, likely caused by electrical faults or cigarettes, infernos which can rapidly spread and burn through dozens of tents at a time.

Firas and his immediate family were relatively safe, but when Firas prepared to talk about his arrested brother he sighed and swallowed and looked down at the table. When he looked up again, the blue in his eyes had faded. Three years after his arrest, they received news. A government officer had leaked 750 photographs of dead prisoners, and Firas's brother was among them. In the photo, his neck was covered in bandages. 'Maybe they cut his throat,' said Firas. All they knew for certain was that he had been killed 45 days after being arrested.

Firas had been fortunate to avoid his brother's fate. His fame as a footballer had got him through regime checkpoints, but many footballers and other celebrities who spoke out against Assad's regime became targets. Several players have been arrested for supporting the opposition. Mosab Balhous, a goalkeeper for Al-Karamah and the national team, was arrested and jailed for sheltering armed gangs and possessing suspicious amounts of money. However, he was later released and became the national team's captain after publicly supporting Assad. The under-16s captain Mohammed Jaddou claims he was threatened both by the rebels and by the regime – he risked his life several times to reach Europe, including spending five days at sea.[3]

Dozens of players and coaches have been arrested and killed in a war that has claimed hundreds of thousands of lives. In October 2016, it was reported that Jihad Qassab, a 40-year-old former Syrian national team captain and defender for Al-Karamah, had been tortured to death in prison, two years after being arrested by the regime, which claimed he had been making car bombs for the rebels. Renowned players such as Omar Al-Somah and Firas Al-Khatib now play in Gulf leagues and had resisted call-ups from the official national team.[4]

But no footballer was more prominent in the rebellion than Abdelbasset Saroot, the so-called 'Singing Goalkeeper of Homs'. In 2011 Saroot, then 17, was Syria's under-twenties goalkeeper and played for the country's dominant side over the previous years, Al-Karamah, based in Homs – one of the epicentres of the uprising. Saroot led protests, inspiring crowds with patriotic, religious and political chants and songs. Saroot became a fighter in various armed groups, was injured several times, and became a major target of the regime, surviving assassination attempts that killed family and friends.

Firas never considered taking up arms – he hates violence and confrontation. 'When I heard about my brother, yeah I wanted revenge. But who killed my brother? I don't know. I just know that the person responsible is in power – Bashar al-Assad,' he said. 'I have an idea that God is here, he exists, so if the killer of my brother didn't take his punishment in this life, he will take it in another life.'

Assad – a member of the Alawi sect, linked to Shia Islam – has attempted to stoke sectarian fears in his bid to keep power. Firas's brother was likely arrested by the Shabiha, a mostly Alawite militia that supports Assad. But

Firas, who is a Sunni Muslim, still has Alawite friends, including some who support the dictator. 'I'm not guilty for what happened and my Alawi friends are not guilty for what happened. The guilt is with some people in the government and the other side.'

Amid the privations of Firas's life, football still keeps him going. He runs a football academy in the camp for around 200 kids. The pitch is bare, rocky ground. They have one football and use stones for training cones. 'But when I see the kids are happy I forget that I am a professional player with a lost career,' he said with a smile.

Firas is also involved in a struggle to set up an alternative Syrian national team in Turkey that can rival and displace the official Syrian national team run by Assad's regime and recognised by FIFA. 'I can't fight with a gun, so I will fight with football and the talent that God gave me.'

The alternative national team

As in Turkey, the popularity of football in an authoritarian climate has always made Syrian football political. Since 2011, Assad's regime has used the sport for propaganda – a successful official Syrian national team and league give the impression that the country is still functioning, although, because of the war, Syria plays its 'home' games in countries such as Malaysia and Oman. The former coach Fajr Ibrahim staunchly backed Assad in public – Ibrahim and the midfielder Osama Omari even appeared at a press conference wearing Bashar al-Assad T-shirts. Ibrahim claimed he was proud of Assad because 'This man fights all terrorist groups in the world, he fights for you also,' whilst also having the gall to claim he wants to keep politics out of sports.[5] Fajr's T-shirts and homilies could not save him from being sacked in 2016, and the Syrian FA offered the vacancy to José Mourinho, who strangely declined the offer.[6]

Syria has never qualified for the World Cup Finals, but despite losing many players the team has done remarkably well recently, getting beyond the third round of qualifying for the Russia 2018 World Cup with a series of impressive results against the likes of China and South Korea, and only losing narrowly to Australia in a play-off. They have maintained a national league, although few people attend the matches, which are typically played in Damascus or Latakia, and the clubs face dire economic straits.

Syria played its first official international match in Turkey in 1949 (they lost 7–0). In 2015 in Turkey, near to the border with Syria, a group of rebel footballers founded an alternative – run by the General Commission of Sport and Youth in Syria, a non-governmental organisation opposed to Assad and broadly aligned to the Free Syrian Army, which manages football in parts of Syria and Turkey. They sought to recruit players from inside Syria – some players took considerable risks to join them, but many were unable to defect because of the threat that they or their families would be detained, tortured or killed. The team held trials close to the Syrian border. Two players even returned from Europe to play with the team.

After the revolution broke out, the Turkish government supported the overthrow of Assad. Turkish authorities armed and financed several of the groups fighting the dictator, including radical jihadist and Islamist groups.[7] The alternative national team was given a place to train in Mersin by the Ministry of Youth and Sports. They gained sponsorship from humanitarian organisations that allowed them to provide the players with accommodation, food and transport. The full squad came together in Mersin in May 2015 and began training regularly and playing friendlies. They applied to FIFA to be recognised as the official Syrian national team.

Football has been used in this way before: in 1958, during Algeria's war of independence, the National Liberation Front (FLN) formed a team, which became the precursor to the Algerian national team formed after the country won independence from France. The Palestinian national football team was recognised by FIFA in 1998, and the Palestinian Authority uses football to resist Israeli occupation and fight for Palestinian rights and independence. Football is also a tool used by the Kurds: both in Iraqi Kurdistan, which fielded a team in the 'alternative' World Cup run by CONIFA,[8] and in Turkey.[9]

However, towards the end of 2015 there was a split in the alternative Syrian team: the majority of players and staff parted ways with the coach and a few other players. The funding ran out by the end of the year. FIFA declined their application. Everything ground to a halt.

When I met Orwa Kanawati, the president of the Turkish branch of the General Commission of Sport and Youth in Syria, in Gaziantep in March 2016, they were still trying to get the alternative team up and running again, but finding sponsorship was proving hard. Kanawati was bitter about being rejected by FIFA but said it was important to develop the alternative team so that it could be poised for any changes in the war. 'What if Bashar al-Assad falls now? People who support him now will disappear,' said Kanawati. 'Maybe FIFA doesn't accept us now but they might support us in the future, because we don't know what will happen.'[10]

After the alternative national team stalled, Firas went back to running his academy in Karkamis, and trying to stay fit in the cramped confines of the camp. Many of the other players went back to scraping a living in informal, menial jobs.

Bashar al-Assad's position is now much stronger than when the alternative team was first formed. Increased Russian military support has entrenched his rule over areas under regime control and he has been making gains against the rebels on the battlefield. The alternative team is deeply affected by the wider political situation. In recent months, the Turkish stance towards Assad has softened since he no longer looks like being overthrown, and the Turkish government is more concerned about the growing power of Kurdish groups on its border. By the summer of 2016, the team was still negotiating for sponsorship. A planned tournament was cancelled after the failed military coup. A potential sponsor from Qatar fell through, after the official Syrian national team was drawn in the same group as Qatar in the final qualifying rounds for the Russia 2018 World Cup.

'Look, this Syrian alternative national team with this [Free Syrian] flag on the chest is not something small or normal. It represents democracy and freedom and civil society,' said Firas when I had first met him, as they struggled to resurrect the team. 'It's like a dream to have this here in Turkey. But you can't say that it's real, it's [still] a dream.'

Months later, on a sunny October day, we headed north out of Hatay, down in the corner of Turkey close to the Syrian border, on a road that wound over hills, through villages plotted with olive groves, towards great triangular mountains in the distance. After some time, we turned off onto a side road, and a caged artificial pitch came into view. A slender white minaret poked up among the trees just beyond the pitch, looking like a rocket about to be fired into space. On the pitch, a group of Syrian players were swinging their arms and legs and warming up. A bus pulled up and Firas al-Ali stepped off. He was wearing a woolly hat and a Besiktas tracksuit. I didn't know he was a fan. 'I'm not – it's just the cheapest!' he laughed. He had turned 30. The skin around his eyes was lined – he looked older than when I last saw him back in March.

Over the summer, Firas had been offered a one-year contract with a Kuwaiti team but he turned it down. Turkey's open-door policy towards

Syrian refugees was now over – Syrian refugees trying to cross the border illegally are now likely to be shot at, and heavy visa restrictions are in place. Firas wouldn't have been able to bring his family to Kuwait and was worried that, once the contract had finished, he would be stranded, unable to return to Turkey. A team from Kirsehir, in the centre of Anatolia, had also offered him a deal: they would pay for his football licence and his residence permit, and he would get a salary of $150/month.[11] As a professional player he had earned more than 50 times that amount. He couldn't leave his family in the refugee camp for such a pittance. Firas is afraid to sign for teams in Iraq or Lebanon in case he is kidnapped and delivered to the regime in Damascus.

Firas was outside Hatay to play a friendly for his new team – Fateh Helfaya, named after a village close to Firas's – as they warmed up for the start of a new season. While the alternative national team remained stalled, a new league had been formed for Syrian players in southern Turkey. The league had some support from the Turkish Football Federation and each team was being supported by Syrian businessmen in Turkey – Fateh Helfaya was being sponsored by a Syrian telecoms shop in the nearby town of Kirikhan.

The league aimed to give talented young Syrian players the opportunity to be spotted by Turkish teams, and to keep the less talented ones active and fit. The league – with 26 Syrian teams – would also provide a base of emerging talent for a future alternative Syrian national team. Most of the players were fitting football around their jobs, working as taxi drivers, as barbers or on building sites. Refugee camp residents are normally given a few days every few months to leave the camp, but Firas was something of a celebrity and for him they were making an exception. The team's sponsor was paying for his travel. Firas was both player and coach.

The Syrian teams could only find a slot to play early on a Sunday morning. The game kicked off – Fateh were taking on a team called 'Sar'. Firas was wildly better than everyone else, but he was still rusty. He slipped a couple of times on the greasy artificial pitch, with its cloying rubbery smell. He walloped a couple of free kicks out of the pitch enclosure. But he soon found his touch. He was switching between wings – at one point he picked up the ball on the right touchline, on the halfway line, pushed the ball past a flying tackle and nipped round the other side, raced through, cut inside onto his left, drifted until he had almost reached the left corner of the penalty area, and unleashed a brutal shot that was parried by the goalkeeper. Firas was orchestrating the game, maintaining a running commentary of encouragement, instructions and admonishments to his teammates.

It was 3–1 to Fateh Helfaya at half-time. Firas couldn't score. But in the second half he was getting better and better. He put a beautifully weighted cross into the box that was fluffed by the striker. 'Argh, get to the car!' shouted Firas with a cheeky grin. He injured the opposition goalkeeper with a cannonball of a shot to the solar plexus. Then he scored one goal after his attempted rabona bounced back to him and he hit the rebound into the top right, and put another into the same corner with his laces. I think Fateh Helfaya won the game 6–4 – it was hard to keep track.

'*Mabrouk*, you played well,' I told Firas after the match. 'What – me? That was the worst I ever played.' We got into the minibus and drove towards Kirikhan, where the team's sponsor is based, with Syrian '*habibi*' music blaring out from the sound system. On the right were muddy plains, on the left were mountains crowned with wind turbines that turned thickly. We reached Kirikhan and found a restaurant.

Firas enthused about the new league, set to begin in November. 'There is a system, from bottom to top,' he said. It had helped compensate for the failure of the national team. Rather than being organised from the top down it was now working with people using their initiative from the grass roots.

As the violence in Syria continues with no end in sight, it's likely that a huge number of Syrians in Turkey will become a permanent, or at least long-term, diaspora. Syrian refugees have become bargaining chips in an obscene diplomatic game between the EU – desperate to prevent greater numbers of refugees fleeing war from seeking sanctuary in Europe amid a politically toxic, racist climate – and Turkey, which has done more than any other country to harbour refugees, while at the same time eagerly using them as leverage to soften EU criticism of the AKP's escalating human rights abuses.

Turkey has accepted more Syrian refugees – over 2.7 million – than any other country.[12] Syrians in Turkey are usually in a form of legal limbo – they have a special legal status as 'guests' with temporary protection and are not afforded refugee status[13] or a standard residency permit, nor can they claim asylum or, generally, become Turkish citizens.[14]

Syrians living in Turkish camps are given the bare minimum to survive, while the 90 per cent of Syrians who live outside the camps in Turkey are left to fend for themselves and often struggle to access housing, healthcare and education.[15] Until recently, Syrian refugees could not work legally. A legal change in January 2016 theoretically loosened work restrictions, but formal work remains extremely hard to come by. While recognising that Turkey has spent huge sums on hosting Syrians fleeing violence, a June

2016 report by Amnesty International found that Turkey is not meeting the basic needs of most Syrians and is not providing them with effective protection.[16] Turkey has recently gone through its own period of instability and heightened violence, and many Syrian refugees felt acutely vulnerable during and after the failed coup. People do not exhaust their resources and take risks on perilous boats for nothing.

Many Syrians resisted learning Turkish as they thought they would be heading back to Syria before long. Few Turkish people speak Arabic, English or French, and so they struggle to communicate. Syrians are generally hugely segregated, and while many Turkish people sympathised with Syrian refugees and welcomed them warmly, Syrian workers have taken informal but scarce, low-paid jobs, and large Syrian groups living in overcrowded properties have pushed up rental prices, stoking resentment among some Turkish people towards their guests.

Football has become a way to make life more bearable for Syrian refugees and to help them integrate. A recent proliferation of grass-roots football projects has emerged throughout Turkey. The alternative sports commission oversees Syrian teams and youth football academies in several cities, including Bursa, Gaziantep and Hatay,[17] and a project in Kahramanmaras which aims to bring Syrian and Turkish players together. There are numerous Syrian teams in Izmir. A project has been proposed to create a league in Antalya with teams made up half of Syrians, half of Turkish players.[18] The Balkanised ramshackleness of Syrian football in Turkey somewhat reflects the nature of the opposition – the FSA has become a vast ragtag of groups, with various ideologies, and it's not really clear if it exists as a coherent entity.[19]

We were about to wrap up the interview, when two men approached our table. 'Salam aleykum,' said one, who held a walkie-talkie. 'W-aleykum is-salaam,' we trilled in tandem. The man with a walkie-talkie had a forehead as lined as a musical score; his companion hung back, silent and grim. They asked what we were doing, what we were talking about and where my press pass was. I had been denied a press card on the grounds that the ministry didn't recognise publishing houses. Three Syrians and I tried to explain in broken Turkish what we were doing. 'You'll have to come to the station,' said the man with the walkie-talkie.

We sat in an abject line on a bench outside the police station, while the officers disappeared inside with our identity cards. I felt guilty I had dragged them into this, and angry at whoever had been stupid and paranoid enough to call the police, irritated at the police for harassing us, afraid that I was going to be deported, and ashamed for feeling afraid about such a thing when I was sitting with these refugees who had been through war and trauma. After half an hour an officer returned, handed back our identity cards, and warned me: 'Don't do any more reporting.' It was hardly *Midnight Express*, but we were relieved to leave.

'Ahhh, now do you feel freedom?' said my Syrian translator, with a broad smile. 'Now you have experienced just a tiny part of what we have to put up with in Syria. At least the police here treated us kindly. In Syria my head would have been kicked 100 times by now.'

We were keen to get out of Kirikhan. I was heading away from the border to Hatay, while Firas made his way back along the border to the refugee camp. We shook hands and parted ways.

Earlier that day, Firas had been reminiscing about his favourite goal. He was playing for Al-Taliya away at Al-Ittihad's stadium in Aleppo, one of the world's oldest cities, now largely pounded into rubble. There were 70,000 people in the stadium, most were screaming on Al-Ittihad, who needed a win to wrap up the title. Al-Ittihad were winning 3–1 at half-time. But Al-Taliya got a goal back in the 82nd minute, and then equalised in the 89th minute. In the second minute of stoppage time, Firas ran at the defence and, from a seemingly impossible angle, swept the ball into the net at the near post. 'I shot and I saw the ball crossed the line, and I ran: but the fans didn't make a sound,' he recalled, 'and I thought, "No, it's not a goal... but I saw it." After a second the fans screamed.' Mahmoud Karkar, Al-Ittihad's goalkeeper, inspected the net from outside to see whether it was ripped, because he couldn't fathom how the ball had gone in. Most of the fans were for the home team. 'They shouted some bad words about my sister,' laughed Firas.

That was a long time ago now. Firas feels he has three or four years in him at the top level, but it doesn't seem likely he will find a club, and he's thinking more about the next generation. His academy kids won a tournament outside the camp recently, against Turkish teams with older players. In the camp they train every day, and they are fiercely committed to Firas's training programme. 'I forgot everything and all the suffering I had for a moment when we won this competition.'

But, ultimately, Firas is focusing on his own children's future. While on the one hand he is struggling to help build up grass-roots football in Turkey, he is also looking for any opportunity he can get to leave Turkey and earn some money, while keeping his family together. Firas graduated from sports university, so he is hoping to become a coach or an agent when he retires.

While he wants to leave Turkey, he's adamant that he would never risk his children's lives by leaving via a smuggler's boat, nor would he take the risk alone, even if he could afford it. 'Maybe I could leave my wife for a year or two, but not my children. Do you have children? You would know the feeling.'

I wondered if Firas ever regretted the revolution. He had a comfortable life in Syria, a great career and adulation. 'Sometimes,' he replied, and he continued:

> The revolution had so many positive things and some negative things, and the positive outweighs the negative. We know so many things we didn't know before and that we couldn't talk about – now we can talk. So many things are clear now for us and we know what we want. We didn't have our rights and there was no justice – other Syrians took more than they deserved. Now you can talk loud – no one will stop you, no one will hear you and take you and make you disappear for 30 years. The rocket that falls on your house is easier to deal with than someone sending a report to the police to take you because you spoke.

Sitting near to the border, close but cut off from his lost home, Firas spoke about his son. 'He doesn't ask to go back to Syria or to go back to his village or anything because he was only a year old when he left. The camp is all he's known – it's his home.'

9

Dreaming at the Edge of Europe

In the summer of 2016, Manchester United broke the world record transfer fee to re-sign Paul Pogba, shelling out almost £90 million to Juventus. Pogba would reportedly earn at least £220,000 per week.[1] The summer transfer window is exciting for fans of big clubs, as huge stars move for scarcely comprehensible sums of money. But, as the days and minutes of the window close down towards the deadline, it is a fraught time for many players at the less glamorous end of the scale – especially for the many African players in Turkey trying to make it big or, more often, trying just to make ends meet.

'I think I started playing football as soon as I could walk,' said Nazir Mohammed, a smart, chirpy 22-year-old from Accra, Ghana. His father died when he was young, leaving his mum to bring up several kids. She couldn't find work and his wider family struggled to support them. 'Where I come from it's either football, boxing, or the police or military.'[2] Nazir made a decision at a young age to focus on football and forget school.

Nazir played as a forward for the Ghanaian third-tier side Polo Academy, but the pay was practically nothing – he repaired mobile phones on the side to survive. The conditions for football were poor: 'I think it's the lowest you have ever seen. You are playing in the dirt, full of stones, under the sun.' When Nazir's boots wore out he would patch them up himself or take them to a cobbler. 'Even for those playing in the premier league, it's not easy,' says Nazir. 'They are not getting paid. We do it cos we love it. I'm not a mechanic; I'm not an engineer; I'm not a doctor. All I know is football. It's my trade. So you ain't getting paid but [you think] hopefully some day it will bear fruit.'

African footballers have come to Turkey in ever greater numbers over the past decade – particularly from countries such as Ghana, Nigeria, Cameroon and Sierra Leone. Many are escaping economic crises, and football is seen as a feasible way out of poverty. It is relatively easy to get a visa for Turkey, there are scores of clubs, and it is regarded as a stepping stone to Europe. After Nazir turned 21, the pressure was growing, his family needed money, and he couldn't see a future in Ghanaian football. He decided to strike out for Turkey – he got a visa to attend a religious conference in Istanbul. 'Travelling from Ghana to any country is not easy cos they know when you go you are not coming back.'

He arrived in May 2015 with just $100 in his pocket, not even enough for a month's rent. Before Nazir could think about football, he had to make some money. He found a Ghanaian connection who gave him somewhere to crash and found him a job. He was working 13 or 14 hours a day, six days a week – it left no time for football, and he was working for a pittance – perhaps 250 TL per week, if he even got paid at all. He worked at a textile company, in a factory making bicycle parts, and assembling lamps: 'I had to do hook and crook, man.'

Bit by bit he scraped together some money. First he had to pay for his residence permit, which he needed in order to sign for a team. Then he had to save some money to quit work and start training full-time for Turkey's 'African Nations Cup', a tournament held in Istanbul every May, so he could impress the scouts and agents that come to watch.

Nazir's friend Jonas Suka, 20, is also from Ghana. As a striker for Asante Kotoko, he won the Ghanaian Premier League two years in a row. Even at that level, Jonas was barely paid and he wanted to make it big in Europe. He came to Turkey at a similar time as Nazir and fell into odd jobs to survive. 'It was like spiritual suicide. My spirit didn't like what I was doing,' he said.[3] 'I want to play football but look at me – washing plates.' Jonas also struggled to get paid: 'You have to say, "I don't have anywhere to sleep, I don't have anything to eat" and this and that, before they give you some – not all, just some.' They complained about racism in Turkey. 'You doing all the donkey stuff,' said Nazir. 'You doing all the dirty stuff, all the shitty jobs.'

Nazir lives in a tough neighbourhood, not far from Taksim Square, where rents are low. He'd had to fight off muggers before. Despite the racism they face, they are perhaps the only people in Turkey I have met who have anything positive to say about the police. 'They don't hassle you, they don't do nothing; all they want to do is take your picture and ask where you're from – "What's up with you?"' laughed Nazir. 'The police are very cool – they like black people, I don't know why.'

'Because blacks don't give them problems,' said Jonas. 'Because for blacks, all we have is to work and get paid.'

They felt better once they were playing football again. All the hardship they have endured is geared around playing in the African Nations Cup before the transfer window opens in June. 'So you take it seriously – it's a do-or-die situation, all or nothing,' said Nazir.

Both were playing for the Angola team, because the Ghanaian team was full. 'Angola' did not actually have any Angolan players. They were mostly from Cameroon, with a couple from Ghana and Nigeria. Jonas was excelling in the tournament, but Nazir had suffered a cruel blow – he had missed the first game through a knee injury, but was staying upbeat and hoping to feature later in the tournament.

For players like Nazir and Jonas the stakes are high. Neither has a plan B if football doesn't work out. 'Everybody's eyes are on you,' says Jonas. 'Your family, your friends, everyone knows that you are [supposed] to be playing for a team here and earning lots of money.' Going home empty-handed is not an option. 'All my family's hope is on me. A lot of pressure.'

Istanbul's African Nations Cup

Angola lost their first group game of the tournament. Their second against Kenya was a must-win. Shabby apartment blocks overlooked the rubber-mottled synthetic green of Fatih's municipality pitch. A breeze blew plastic bags and seed husks over dusty plastic seats in the stadium's single stand.

It was a hearty contest, with tackles booming in. Jonas was playing out of position, but was bossing central midfield for Angola. Nazir was on the bench, still not 100 per cent fit. Kenya took an early lead, but Angola pulled back an equaliser. The stress of the occasion seemingly got to Angola's centre back, who earned a second yellow card for slapping a Kenyan player and gave the crowd the middle finger as he trudged off.

But going down to ten men galvanised Angola – they took the lead in the second half, prompting some of the wildest celebrations I've ever seen on a football pitch. At least two people flung their bodies into multiple somersaults – a third, inspired by his teammate's acrobatics, attempted a backflip, just about landed on his feet, and stumbled backwards on his heels until his momentum was checked by some teammates. It was a bodily demonstration of what this cup means to the players – and perhaps well-executed acrobatics can also catch the eyes of the scouts and agents in the stands.

When Angola added a third goal, Jonas screamed in elation, while Nazir leapt out of the dugout and did a victorious jig. Angola closed out the 3–1 victory. Nazir didn't make it onto the pitch – he had been set to come on until his teammate's sending off prompted a rethink.

At 23 years old, Angola's captain, Henry Chindo, is already a veteran journeyman. Henry, from Enugu State, eastern Nigeria, arrived in Turkey two years ago – before that he was playing in the Bangladeshi football league. In his first year in Turkey he had struggled to find a club; then he began training with Angola and played in the African Nations Cup, where he was spotted by a scout and signed for Karacabeyspor in the amateur league. He got $8,000 for an eight-month contract – but had to pay around $2,000 for his licence.[4] It's the kind of money that Wayne Rooney earns in five seconds of scratching his arse and thinking about what's for dinner, but it's better than anything Henry could earn in Nigeria.

Henry says African players have to perform to a higher standard than Turks because they are more easily disposed of and easy to blame. Last season he scored 12 goals. Karacabeyspor gained promotion and wanted to re-sign him. But Henry was holding out for something better – his wife recently arrived in Turkey and she had news: 'I have a baby on the way!' So Henry was back in the African Nations Cup, trying to impress again. 'And if it doesn't work out [in Turkey] I can always move to the next country. This is my job.'[5]

When African players do get contracts at Turkish clubs, it is not always straightforward. Often they are signed by clubs in small Anatolian cities where few speak English or French, and where there are seldom other Africans. It can be quite a culture shock. Many clubs take great care of their African players – taking an intense, almost paternalistic interest in helping them settle in. But many clubs have financial problems, and players are often paid late or less than is stated in their contracts.

When the African Nations tournament was set up just over a decade ago, it was partly for fun and friendship in the African community, but it became increasingly geared towards helping players find clubs as increased numbers of Africans started turning up, many lured to Turkey under false pretences.

In the last 15 years there has been a proliferation of dodgy agents – Turkish, European and African – who dupe or manipulate young African footballers and their families into paying thousands of dollars with tantalising trials and contracts, only for those promises not to materialise.[6] Some of the agents are fake; others are registered but unscrupulous. 'In Africa, everybody tries to dream,' says Bertrand Joseph Ndong, a coach, agent and football consultant who also works for the African Football Association in

Turkey. '[But often] when they come here it is not a dream they have been offered but a very big deception.'[7]

The tournament has grown from four teams to 16. 'In other parts of the world we don't get these opportunities,' said Ndong, who praised Fatih municipality for sponsoring the cup and providing the stadium, Turkish Football Federation-approved referees, water and some equipment.

Njayedi Francois Viete is the Angola coach and runs a training academy alongside Ndong. They both agree that the families and the players also need to become more savvy and more realistic about their talents. 'They are dreaming because, how come I'm not playing in the top league in my country and then someone proposes to bring me to Fenerbahce and I accept!?' says Viete. Sometimes, mediocre players beg unwilling agents for the chance of a trial. 'For many guys it is better to come here and do nothing, rather than staying in Africa and playing football. That is the problem.'[8]

Ndong says that, although they won't be playing for Fenerbahce or Galatasaray as often promised, the vast majority of players in the cup will find paying clubs, at some level – but very, very few make it to the top two tiers of Turkish football. It's hard for African players to make the jump between semi-professional divisions and the top two tiers of Turkish football because of the ban on foreign players in the third and fourth tiers.

Ghana's coach Julius Kugor, 31, is an ex-footballer who played in Bulgaria, Egypt, Tunisia and Turkey during his career. He says that 90 per cent of the players have had bad experiences with agents. They often come to him for help, and he asks them whether they want help to go home or to stay. 'I can tell you that 99 per cent don't want to go back because they are here to play football and some of them have nothing back home.'[9] Julius runs a training programme and helps talented players get trials or find other work.

Yusif Rakibu and Abdul-Karim Issaka are both 19, both wingers, both from Ghana and played in the second tier, and both feel exploited by their agent, who brought them to Turkey as part of a group of 17 players – each paid the agent $1,800, a fortune for their families. The agent promised them trials and guaranteed they would get contracts. They were put up in a hotel in Antalya, played a couple of matches, mostly among themselves. Only Yusif was offered a trial by a club, while the rest were advised that they weren't good enough and told to go home and return later in the year. It was a laughable prospect: most players had sold all their possessions or had got their families into significant debt to afford the one-way journey.

The agent disappeared and didn't tell them they needed to get residence permits within 90 days in order to stay in Turkey and sign for a club. Yusif and Abdul-Karim were now playing for Ghana in the African Nations Cup, but their visas had expired, and they were trapped – unable to play for any teams that wanted to sign them, and unwilling to go home to Ghana where everyone was depending on them.

They had tried to get help from the Ghanaian embassy, with no luck. It seemed like they would have to leave the country – but, even if they got the money together to leave for Ghana, since they have already visited Turkey, they probably wouldn't get a second visa to return. It would be hard for them to get visas for neighbouring countries, especially in Europe. Two players in their group had paid smugglers to go by boat to Greece to claim asylum. Yusif and Abdul-Karim wouldn't countenance that – they just wanted to play football. 'Because football is my talent, God gave me that talent so I don't want to joke with it,' said Yusif. 'So if I can go [anywhere], get a team and get a small amount of money that I can feed my family with, I will be happy.'[10]

They were playing well in the African Nations Cup, hoping against reality that something would turn up. They held out a forlorn hope that they could impress in the tournament and convince a Turkish club to pay for them to travel to Ghana to apply for new visas to return to Turkey. The chances of that seemed vanishingly small. At least things were going well for them on the pitch. Ghana were the reigning champions and fancied themselves to retain the trophy. After a stuttering start, they had begun to heat up – beating Senegal to get out of their group, then defeating Somalia to reach the semi-finals.

Following their 'must-win' win, Angola crashed out of the cup in the group stages, losing their final match 4–2 to Gabon. Nazir was frustrated: 'We had to win that match and we went all out for the win, but we forgot to defend. We were winning in that match actually but then it all fell apart.' He hadn't appeared in that game either.

On an overcast June afternoon in Fatih, Prince Amoakohene, 19, was watching the semi-finals from the stands. Normally, Prince plays for Ghana, but around a month ago he felt something go in his groin – it was like a rope snapping. He will miss the whole tournament. Prince has a mantra: 'It's not easy, it's not easy.' He's putting it mildly.

Prince is a defensive midfielder from Ghana; his hero is his compatriot Michael Essien, who starred for Chelsea, Real Madrid and AC Milan. Prince's agent had found him a club in Northern Cyprus, but the club didn't pay him for several months and forced him to live in a tiny store-room in the car park underneath the stadium. They wouldn't give him a heater during the winter. They kept his passport, so when he finally had enough and wanted to leave, the club handed his passport to the police. He managed to get the passport back and his agent helped him get a visa for Turkey in 2015.

Prince played every minute of every game in Ghana's victorious 2015 campaign, but his residency permit was delayed, and by the time it was ready the summer transfer window had almost closed. He failed to get a club. He began doing odd jobs – painting and decorating, paying 40 TL per day. He fell behind on his rent. One day he came home to find he had been evicted, his belongings piled on the street.

Destitute and homeless, Prince turned to Julius and his cousin, who works at a football club in Ferikoy. They found a room for him in the clubhouse but he has to find the money for his own food and travel. While he was training regularly and playing football, sometimes he couldn't get enough to eat. But he hadn't much felt like eating recently – a couple of weeks earlier he had got a call from his family, who told him his father was ill. He spoke to his father, but no one seemed to know what the problem was. He didn't hear from him again. A few days later his family rang and told him his father had died. 'I'm OK, I'm OK, I'm OK,' said Prince and he went silent and looked down, his mouth tugged into a grimace, shutting down the topic. He had been close to his father. 'But God knows the best. We have to give thanks to God.'[11]

Prince doesn't know where his mother is: she left when he was young. His father remarried but his stepmother had thrown him out of the house when he was 16. With several full and half siblings, she saw Prince as a burden. Now she was calling him, asking for money for the funeral and other support – she didn't believe him when he told her he had nothing. As far as she was concerned, Prince was playing football in Turkey and must be earning good money. He stopped taking her calls. 'When I get a contract I will call and send them money,' he said.

But his injury was a major setback and he had to forgo physiotherapy and other treatment that could hasten his recovery. All he could afford was some ice to hold to his groin. 'Sometimes I just keep quiet, I don't even talk,' Prince told me. 'I keep asking myself, why me? Always me – why? Today this, tomorrow that. Why?' His only consolation was that he had begun training again.

Ghana played a hectic semi-final against Liberia. They were two goals up at half-time and Liberia were down to ten men. Both Yusif and Abdul-Karim were playing. Abdul-Karim had won the penalty for the first goal, and nodded in a cross at the far post for a second. Ghana became complacent. Liberia got one goal back, then equalised, then, with Ghana in disarray and Julius berating his players, his lower lip jutting out in a pout, Liberia took a 3–2 lead through a penalty. Ghana finally woke up, equalised and took the game to extra time. They scored again to win 4–3. One Ghana player celebrated the goal by stuffing the ball under his shirt, facing the crowd, and jiggling it like a pregnant stomach, while holding his finger to his lips and laughing.

Ghana faced Sierra Leone in the final just over a week later. A sound system blared out Ghanaian pop, including a love song about G spots that was played on repeat. The stands were full of excitable Ghanaians waving flags, and a smaller contingent of Sierra Leone supporters. The players lined up, the Turkish national anthem was played, and then the players and crowd sang an impromptu Ghanaian national anthem, hands over hearts. Music soundtracked the match, periodically interrupted by the marimba of an iPhone call, and by the MC who kept up a steady patter – 'This the place to be! Fatih!' – alongside shout-outs to the dignitaries from Ghana and Cameroon in attendance: 'Highly welcome sir!'

The heat, even in the shade of the stands, was sweltering, and the players were at full pelt. It was a typical, tense, tight, fractious final, with few chances: goalless at half-time. In the second half, Sierra Leone had a player sent off and scuffles broke out. 'No fighting! No fighting! This is about fun!' pleaded the MC. The teams couldn't be separated, even with the sending-off – not after full time and not after extra time. The regulations stated that 'if equality persists' it should go to penalties. 'It's hard,' lamented the MC several times.

Sierra Leone stepped up first – the volume on the sound system fell a notch – they scored: 1–0.

Ghana made it 1–1.

For about the eighth time today the Shakira World Cup 2010 song came over the sound system: 2–1 to Sierra Leone.

Then Emike, Ghana's only Nigerian player, stepped up, kissed the ball, took a staccato run-up, haltingly, scored – top right – 2–2.

'It's not easy, especially after more than 90 minutes,' said the MC.
Sierra Leone... a weak shot to the left, saved!

It went 3–2 to Ghana, then 3–3, 4–3, 4–4.

The final kick, sudden death. Ghana's chance to win the cup: they score!
There was pandemonium in the stands and on the pitch, fans burst through
the gates and onto the field, Julius was lifted up and paraded, flags shaken,
fisticuffs broke out between the two teams, there was some stupendous
dancing, shirts whipped off, flailed around heads. The medals handed out.
Ghana had defended their title, was it ever in doubt?

The summer window

Nazir had endured a disappointing African Nations Cup and was missing
his family back home, and he was missing Ghanaian food. 'You can't eat
so much bread,' he complained, referring to Turkish cuisine. 'You get
constipated.'

Jonas missed his siblings and his girlfriend. She was back in Ghana. A
long-distance relationship was tough, but he planned to bring her out to
Turkey once he started earning good money. Nazir had broken up with his
girlfriend from home. 'I sacrificed my relationship for football.'

What if you don't get signed this summer? 'You go back to working hard
at your jobs,' said Nazir, looking downcast, while Jonas hissed through his
teeth at the thought. 'And do the whole cycle again.'

Those who don't find clubs by the time the summer transfer window
closes face tough choices. They can save up pittance pay at odd jobs, so
that they can train before January's transfer window opens again, or play in
the African Nations Cup again the following May. Or they can give up on
football and try to find an alternative livelihood in Turkey. Or they can leave
Turkey, perhaps illegally, to try their luck elsewhere. When their family and
friends are relying on them to be successful, going home empty-handed is
rarely an option.

Throughout the summer they tried to stay upbeat. They posted defiant
slogans of grit and struggle online. 'It is about determination and faith,'
Jonas told me. 'This world itself is a mean and nasty place, it will beat you
to your knees if you let it.'

By mid-August Henry Chindo had put pen to paper for Nilufer
Erdemlispor in Bursa, a club playing in Turkish football's fifth tier. He had

secured a better deal than last season and was happy to be in Bursa. 'Too many people in Istanbul,' he noted. His wife gave birth to a son.

Yusif and Abdul-Karim were still stuck. Their agent had stopped taking their calls and Yusif said the situation was making him ill.

Jonas was training with Cine Madranspor, also in the fifth tier, down in the city of Aydin – in Turkey's Aegean region. His agent had found him the club, although it wasn't quite the Super League or the second tier as he'd been promised.

Prince was surviving on handouts. He had begun training with a club but, heading into the final weeks of the transfer window, it was not clear yet whether they would sign him. Nazir was in the same position.

The transfer deadline loomed. Jonas signed for Cine Madranspor. After he'd paid for his licence he wasn't left with much, but it was enough to survive on until next year's African Nations Cup and the summer transfer window, and next season was bound to be better. He had already become popular with the fans – scoring in several preseason friendlies, and in their first league match of the season: a 2–2 draw. Jonas has a thing for Bursaspor – he was getting his head down, working hard and dreaming of joining them in a year.

The transfer deadline passed.

Yusif and Abdul-Karim were planning to save money, return to Ghana, and then try to get a visa for Turkey again by next year. It seemed like a tall order. Yusif needed $600 just to pay his fine for overstaying his visa and to get home. An agent in Ghana was asking him for $1,200 to ensure a tricky second Turkish visa. It sounded like another scam. He didn't even have a job. Abdul-Karim was working ten hours a day, assembling pipes and shower products: 'We work fast like machines.'

Nazir's amateur club had wanted to sign him but they couldn't afford to pay for his licence. He was still training with them three nights a week while they tried to figure out a way to raise the money. He'd found a job assembling light fixtures, chandeliers and lamps, earning 250 TL a week. It's more than he could earn in Ghana. 'It's enough – it pays the bills and I can still send a bit home to my mum.' Now at least he was training regularly with his first Turkish team, and he'd met an agent. He thought the January window could be an option. Nazir looked tired; he fitted the training in around long hours at work, but was upbeat as ever. 'I'm still here. It will happen,' he smiled.

When I met up with Prince again at the end of the transfer window, his features looked blunter, the skin less strained against his cheekbones. He'd spent two months training with a team down in Hatay, arranged by an older Ghanaian friend who speaks Turkish after several years in the country. The club offered him just 3,000 TL for the eight-month season, and his friend would have taken a cut. Prince turned it down and had come back to Istanbul the week before. He didn't have anything else set up – his agent was meant to come to Turkey during the transfer window, but was in Cyprus instead. He phoned Prince now and again to see if his 'client' had found himself a club; they'd signed a contract guaranteeing him a commission. 'All he wants is his percentage,' said Prince. 'He doesn't know where I sleep, what I wear, what I eat. But he still says I'm his player.'[12]

Prince was looking for a job to work for a month or two, as he needed to save for his residence permit renewal and to start training again for trials in the brief January transfer window. He was sharing a room with three others, four people spread across two beds. The rent was only 100 TL a month, but he was still in arrears to his flatmates. His diet was rudimentary: he survived on rice and a few vegetables. A couple of jobs had fallen through. No other African players could help him find work, and nor could the African Football Association. 'For now they are just telling me to hold on.'

10

'I fell in love with football'

Malatya is the world capital of apricots. Orchards full of stout apricot trees surround the city. On some downtown streets you can smell apricots on the breeze. There are bazaars dedicated to apricots, giant statues of apricots crown major intersections, there are apricot telephone booths, ATMs as apricots. At dusk the fading pink and gold light casts an apricot glow over the bare mountains beyond the city.

Malatya is in the largely poor, conservative eastern interior of Anatolia, and apricots define many of the poorer lives here – particularly of young women, who often drop out of school at 14 or 15, work in apricot processing and packing factories until they have enough for a dowry, and get married young – often at 15, 16 or 17.[1] They start having kids: families of nine or ten are not uncommon, and before long the lives of their daughters resemble theirs. Domestic violence is common, as is drug abuse. But some girls in Malatya have found a way to break this cycle – through football.

Ikranur Sarigul, 17, grew up with her nine siblings in a two-bedroomed house in Kiltepe, a low-income, conservative neighbourhood on the edge of Malatya. Her parents slept in one room, and all the siblings shared two beds in the other. Breakfast was often just a few olives, and she usually had no money for food during the day, while dinner might be some roasted onions. The family often couldn't afford pencils and notebooks for school, or new shoes. When Ikranur was young, her eldest brother was studying at a sports academy and much of the family's resources went on supporting him: 'In the eyes of the family, boys are always much more important,' she said, 'so they forgot [the girls].'[2] None of Ikranur's five sisters had graduated from high school, although one managed to graduate from middle school, leaving at 15. Her elder sisters were married by 16 or 17, and at least one suffered from domestic abuse – beaten by her mother-in-law. Ikranur doesn't blame her parents for marrying them off: the family was poor and they struggled to cope.

Ikranur's parents worried about her; they were strict. She was barely allowed to go to the shop to buy bread, and she was strictly forbidden to talk to boys. At ten she used to watch kids playing football in the street and it captivated her, but her family told her that football is for boys. Girls playing football was something strange and shameful, and they feared that neighbours would gossip about their daughter. But by 11 Ikranur was taking any opportunity to sneak off and play football – if her mum went to a neighbour's house, or if she was sent to the shop, she would join a game. When her family found out she'd been playing football they would yell at her and confiscate her shoes. Ikranur would go to school in her slippers, feeling humiliated.

They did this out of love and ignorance, says Ikranur. Her childhood was happy, despite the many strictures. Her parents were often making jokes, and there was a sense of togetherness. But it could be frustrating. 'I wanted to do what I love, and I fell in love with football.'

As Ikranur approached her teens, her horizon was shortening and it wouldn't be long before she would likely drop out of school, take a menial job and get married. Perhaps she would start drinking like some of the girls in her neighbourhood, or even inhaling opium by the railway tracks in a part of town where the police don't dare venture. Maybe she would be tempted to sell drugs.

But she was still playing football where possible, including at school. Dogan Deniz Celebi, her PE teacher in Kiltepe, spotted her and invited her to join the school's team. She didn't tell him that her parents had forbidden her to play.

I met Celebi, 41, in the centre of Malatya one day in early summer and we drove out of the city on a radial, passing through an industrial area, appropriately called Sanayi – 'industry': street after street of car repair workshops, garages crammed full of tyres, others stocked to bursting with hubcaps. Cars in various states of ill health were held in the air by mechanical arms. Many working-class men from Kiltepe end up in this district when their eight years of compulsory education is over.

Kiltepe – 'Clay Hill' – was just beyond Sanayi. The streets were largely empty as many residents were in the orchards picking apricots. Fences put together with lopsided panels looked like rows of crooked teeth. Many of the buildings were small, single-storey bungalows with metal grilles covering the windows, and cross-hatched roofs made of weak, thin-looking wood, warped in places, some with holes stuffed with cardboard. There was little in the way of shops. A single railway line cut through the area, dividing it from a more salubrious part of town, in which there was a factory and modern apartment blocks. In some streets apricots were laid out on tarpaulins held down by plastic crates, drying out under the sun. Kiltepe's ramshackle buildings quickly gave way to fields and orchards.

We pulled into the entrance of a neat and tidy school, whose small car park doubled as an asphalt football pitch, with two metal goalposts on coasters. 'This is where we raised the fourth-best team in Turkey,' said Celebi, with a smile.[3] He started a girl's school team around 2008, with the aim of keeping the girls in education and out of trouble and an early marriage. The school team thrived and became champions in the region, and one of the best in the country. A cabinet inside the school's entrance was overflowing with trophies.

Ikranur had to tell Celebi that her family did not consent to her playing football. Celebi began paying regular visits to the family home, reassuring them and explaining the benefits. Their attitude softened but they were inconsistent – sometimes they let her play, sometimes they said no.

Celebi set up Malatya Bayanlar Spor Kulubu – Malatya Women's Sports Club – in 2012 to expand the project beyond the school. 'I'm president, kit man, medic, bus driver and ball boy!' said Celebi. He convinced his family and colleagues to become members and to donate money. Much of his modest teacher's salary was being spent on the club. 'They became my daughters,' he said.

Like the school's team, the club aimed to keep the girls in education, but also to find them university places to become teachers or sports coaches. A Turkish Football Federation licence automatically gains credits that give a huge boost in university exams. When the girls get places at universities, Celebi asks local businesses to pay the girls' scholarships. 'The main point was not only football – but to save the lives of the girls,' says Celebi. 'Football was a tool.'

In the 2015/16 season, Malatya won their regional division in the third tier of women's football and lost on penalties in the first play-off round for promotion to the next division. He had around 40 girls in the squad. Ikranur joined the team from its inception and she began to see a career path: she passed exams to get into a sports high school and aims to become a teacher. As her family saw the educational benefits more clearly, their attitudes shifted further. It took around two years of persuasion for them to reach full acceptance. 'Before, my family got angry with me when I went to training, but now my family criticise me if I don't go to training!' said Ikranur. Celebi gained UN funds to hold workshops with the girls and their families on gender equality, sport and health, nutrition, violence against women, communication skills and career opportunities. Prestigious thinkers visited and gave speeches. Ikranur understood her rights for the first time.

While Ikranur's family had changed, many of the boys in her neighbourhood gave her a hard time. 'They told me: "Football is a man's business." Well, they made a mistake. They stopped studying, they stopped playing football. Now they are workers in Sanayi, they dropped out of school, but we pursued our dreams.' Their comments hurt but they also motivated her to dedicate herself to football. At the sports high school Ikranur was improving dramatically, and she broke into Malatya's first 11. Ikranur plays as a kind of free-spirited defender/libero. She admires Real Madrid's Sergio Ramos, a similarly roaming, adventurous but tough defender: 'The ball may pass, but not the player!' she said, laughing.

The team offers precious opportunities to travel. 'It was maybe the first time they had stayed in a hotel, or ate in a restaurant in another city, or even seen another city. They could see there is a world beyond Malatya,' said Celebi. Football and travelling have given Ikranur huge self-confidence, particularly because her family trusts and believes in her. She now makes friends easily, and she is optimistic. She speaks in earnest, fluent torrents. Before joining the team she'd only left Malatya once – to visit her elder brother in Kayseri. Now she travels every couple of weeks. 'If you deduct football from my life, I am nothing.'

Football can't always save the girls: the week before we met, one talented player had dropped out of the team and got married after her family discovered that she had a secret boyfriend. She is just 17 years old. Her teammates were devastated.

Celebi has also had to take several of his players to get help with drug abuse. 'People may look conservative, and act conservative, but behind closed doors they can do everything,' he said.

When I met Celebi in the morning he looked youthful and fresh-faced; through the day he fielded call after call, juggling queries from the girls with business calls, turning increasingly drawn, lines etching at the sides of his eyes. 'They are making me old!' he joked. It is a constant, wearying battle to keep the project afloat, mainly because of parlous finances. 'In western

Turkey there is an established culture of women's football. People are aware of it and local municipalities support the clubs. Also, the players' families support their children,' he said. 'There they pay to come, here we pay them to come!' The biggest expense is transportation – renting minibuses and collecting the girls and dropping them home three times a week for training, and at weekend matches, often in other cities.[4]

Celebi tries to strike a balance between local talent and transfers. The football federation wrings its hands in desperation at teams with financial problems spending money on transfers, but Celebi insists it's necessary. 'We needed the transfers and success on the pitch to get the public attention.'

A lack of facilities is a major headache. Celebi complains about a complete lack of support from Malatya's AKP municipality, even though they support men's football, and claims they won't even grant him a meeting.[5] 'The municipality in Malatya pretends that women's football in Malatya doesn't exist. They don't want to acknowledge it. This is the reality of Turkey. What Turkey is, Malatya is the same – inequality between the genders.'

The World Economic Forum ranks Turkey 130th out of 145 countries for gender equality.[6] Just 33.6 per cent of Turkish women are employed, one of the lowest rates in Europe or the Middle East,[7] while 20 per cent of Turkish women are illiterate and men own 92 per cent of all property.[8]

In the Ottoman era, women were subject to strict rules regarding their behaviour and appearance in public. They were often veiled and restricted to the home. Ottoman women struggled for labour rights, for political representation and to end forced marriage and polygamy.[9]

Women won equality under law in the early years of the Turkish Republic, and they gained the vote in 1934 – before many European countries. With the abolishment of Islamic sharia law, the legal constraints on women playing competitive sports ended. But Turkish society remained highly patriarchal, and women were often marginalised, especially those who wore the headscarf, which was banned in public institutions. Kemalist governments were in power for most of Turkey's history, and the largely conservative nationalism they propagated held women in check. Violence against women was common and scarcely acknowledged, held as something normal.

Yet, while Turkey has always had a chequered record on gender equality, many say that it has become increasingly misogynistic and patriarchal under the socially conservative AKP. The AKP's gendered morals are defined by the traditional sanctity of faith and family; family honour is linked to women's controlled virtue,[10] and emphasis is placed on women's 'primary' roles as wives, mothers and care-givers – guardians of the heterosexual family.[11]

As might be expected under an Islamic government, the AKP lifted the headscarf ban in universities in 2010, in state institutions in 2013, and in high schools in 2014. Ravza Kavakci Kan – a female AKP member of parliament who wears a headscarf – says this is vitally important. 'One of the things I'm most proud of is that the discrimination that women faced in many areas has been lifted,' she said.[12] 'So before, women who wore the headscarf, when I was growing up in Turkey, weren't allowed in universities to get an education, they weren't allowed to work in state offices and they were definitely not allowed in the parliament.' Her sister Merve Kavakci was prevented from being sworn in as a member of parliament in 1999 as she wore a headscarf. 'So many women have lost their dreams, have lost their psychological balance because of [the headscarf ban] – but it was never seen as a problem for many years.'

Kavakci says she has found Erdogan to be a 'gentleman', especially around women. But Erdogan has stated that he doesn't believe in equality between men and women,[13] that abortion is murder, and that birth control is treason. 'What do they want to do?' asked Erdogan of the 'West' in a speech in 2008. 'They want to put an end to the Turkish nation. If you do not want our population to cease, a family must have three children.'[14]

Kavakci is keen to defend him: 'So I think there should be justice, in the sense that men and women are equal, but I think that's where President Erdogan is coming from, because I did hear him mention the concept of gender justice,' she said. 'When you say "equality" the justice part is left out. Yes, men and women are equal, but also there should be areas where women are given support for the things they want to do that men may not have to deal with.'

She says Erdogan is just worried about Turkey's ageing population. 'Of course, he has his opinions, he makes suggestions, and people may act as they wish.'

There is an epidemic of violence against women, which has soared under the AKP. Nearly 40 per cent of married women are exposed to physical or sexual violence.[15] Verbal harassment on the street is common. Honour killings still occur in conservative areas.[16] But domestic violence is not only a 'conservative' problem in Turkey, though it may be worse in some conservative communities: it is prevalent across society.

In the southern city of Mersin in 2015, a 20-year-old student called Ozgecan Aslan was beaten with an iron bar and stabbed to death by a minibus driver after she had resisted rape. Her body was dismembered and burned. The brutality of her death provoked outrage and punctured some of the denial and ignorance surrounding violence against women in Turkey. Erdogan stated that domestic violence was Turkey's 'bleeding wound'.[17] In the month before Ozgecan Aslan was killed, 27 women were murdered across Turkey – an increase of 20 per cent on the previous year.[18] Men who attack women often escape with little or no punishment, while men who murder women often have their sentences drastically reduced, because the victim was wearing 'provocative' leggings, for example.[19]

Some attribute it partly to the AKP's language and conservative attitudes towards women – that some men feel emboldened.[20]

Kavakci doesn't accept the statistics. 'I don't think it's been growing under this government – I think there are just more statistics being done. Before 2002 we had some statistics but there wasn't that much deep, detailed research done.'

But by their own statistics *since* they came to power, violence against women increased by 1,400 per cent between 2002 and 2009, when they stopped releasing the numbers.[21]

Celebi has no connection with any party – he doesn't like politics. 'I am just an ordinary Muslim and I believe in God, and thanks to my religious belief I want to do something to provide a future for my team's children.'

Despite the project's success, it is now teetering on the brink of collapse. Celebi has nearly exhausted his own resources. He says he has become a 'beggar' for the club. They have struggled to find sponsors: companies don't want to support women's football because it has no visibility in the media. Friends, colleagues and family members have supported for years, but they are becoming reluctant to pay more and have suggested that maybe it's time to stop.

Support from the Aydin Dogan Foundation saved the team from closure in 2015/16 and eight players got into university that year. It wasn't clear whether that support would be repeated in 2016/17. They would know whether the club will survive after the summer. When Celebi told the girls that the club might have to close, some of them wailed in anguish. 'They said, "Why are you leaving us in the lurch? This is our future."'

Female pioneers

'I am a dinosaur of football,' joked Hande Denziger, now 55.[22] When Hande was a child, the boys let her play football with them in the street but they teasingly called her 'Hamdi' – a macho boy's name. 'I was a bit upset but I didn't want to lose those friendships and I really wanted to play football, so I didn't complain.'

One day, when Hande was 12 or 13, some of her friends ran up to her: 'Hamdi, Hamdi! There is a girl's football team – you should join!' That's how she first heard about Dostlukspor[23] – the first women's team to be licensed by the Turkish Football Federation.[24]

In 1969 Haluk Hekimoglu set up a women's team on Kinaliada, one of the Princes' Islands close to Istanbul, but had been unable to get the club registered with the federation. He decided to set up Dostlukspor in Moda, on the Asian side of the city, in 1972, and it was registered with the football federation in 1973.

There were no other female football teams for Dostlukspor to play against, so they played exhibition matches against male teams across the country. They recall little abuse; they were treated more as a curiosity or an oddity. Dostlukspor became a trailblazing exhibition team, travelling the country, encouraging women and drumming up support for women's football – proving to a sceptical population that women could play the game. 'It took a long time to form a women's league because it took a long time to convince people that women can do what men do,' said Nedim Yazir, 63, who was the chief administrator of Dostlukspor from 1975 until 1980.[25]

The profile of women's football was slowly growing. By the late 1970s other women's teams had formed – Dostlukspor won their first match against a women's team in 1978, beating Feliz Spor of Izmir 14–0.

In 1980 Hande joined a new breakaway club formed out of Dostlukspor and called Atilim Spor. By the 1980s women's teams had formed in Ankara, Kocaeli, Samsun and elsewhere in Istanbul. The first football tournament between women's teams was held in 1984, involving Atilim Spor, Dostlukspor and Derya Spor. The football federation first considered creating a women's league in 1985; however, the idea was shelved when it became apparent that there were still not enough quality women's teams.

In most countries, the women's game has only become firmly established professionally in the past two decades. Women's football had been growing in popularity in the UK after World War I. A women's match at Goodison

Park in 1920 attracted a record attendance of 53,000 but the FA banned women's football from its grounds the following year, stating that 'football is quite unsuitable for females and ought not to be encouraged.'[26] The FA didn't lift its ban until 1971.

Turkey's first professional women's league wasn't established until 1993. Sixteen teams competed in the inaugural season, including Dostlukspor. Istanbul-based Dinarsu Spor became champions. The first Turkish women's national team was formed in 1995.

However, women's football was still struggling to take off. Dinarsu Spor won the league four times in a row, before dropping out in 1997, citing a lack of interest shown by the federation in developing the sport.[27] It was a harbinger of problems to come. The national team stopped playing matches in 2000. By 2003 there were just ten active club teams. A series of lurid reports appeared in the media, involving supposed lesbian relationships between players, sex between coaches and girls, allegations of match-fixing, nepotism, and fights between players. Some sections of the press dubbed it 'The Scandals League'.[28]

Many clubs were plagued by financial problems and several closed down. There remained widespread indifference to the sport, beyond salacious news reports. The football federation suspended the women's league in 2003. Dostlukspor's women's team folded for financial reasons in 2004.[29]

After a three-year hiatus, the Turkish women's football league was rebooted in 2006, starting from scratch with just seven teams. With money and pressure from UEFA, and more sustained attention from the football federation, women's football finally started gaining some momentum. The number of clubs and players steadily increased across the country. There is now a first division, a second tier, and eight regional third divisions.

For the past several seasons the top flight of women's football has been a duopoly, dominated by Konak Belediyespor – a team from Izmir who have won the league every year from 2013 to 2016 – and Atasehir Belediyespor, who won the league in 2011 and 2012 and have pushed Konak close. But 2015/16 saw a marked improvement in competitiveness, including the emergence of another strong contender for the title: Trabzon Idmanocagi. They won their first match of the season 19–0.

Trabzon were top of the league with just a few weeks to go, but then they had two bad weeks: first they had three players sent off and surrendered a two-goal lead to lose in one match, and then they were held 1–1 away at Kirecburnu. Trabzon found their rhythm and started winning again but it was too late. Konak clung on to a four-point lead to win the championship yet again. But the two sides were to meet in the final match of the season. After an eventful and bruising season it promised to be a grudge match – the liveliest of dead rubbers, that had assumed the status of a cup final, and exposed the progress and the problems in Turkish women's football.

The Trabzon president, 41-year-old Hasan Sahinkaya, was watching his team ping pinpoint passes to each other under a leaden sky during their final training session before the match. Hasan has the build and bearing of an East End boxer, bright-blue eyes, a shaved head – albeit a very warm and friendly pugilist. He is a PE teacher, ex-amateur player and a businessman – and he has transformed Trabzon since becoming the president a year before. The previous year they had very few supporters, and they were languishing in mid-table mediocrity, unable to compete with the front-running teams. They didn't even have enough kit or equipment.

Hasan put his own money into the club and did what Turkish teams do – he turned to the transfer market, spending money on Turkish players, German players of Turkish descent and African talent. They now have four Turkish internationals in the squad. He spent a club record 25,000 TL on one player – a huge sum of money in women's football.

Trabzon's biggest challenge was financial, and Hasan complained about poor facilities and a lack of support from the federation. When I asked why he spent so much on transfers, he replied – as everyone always does – that it was essential for success.

Beyond finances, culture was still an issue for the team. 'If [the players] don't act feminine, the families don't want to send their daughters here,' explained Hasan.[30] 'This is the biggest obstacle in improving and developing Turkish women's football, because the families all think that their daughters are going to turn lesbian.' What do you do when you have an LGBT player? 'I respect their choices and, as long as they keep it in their private lives and they don't display it publicly, it's fine with me,' replied Hasan.

Once training had finished I chatted with some of the players. 'There is some prejudice about girls playing football because they think that girls will start to act like men; they will have muscles like men, they will walk like men, and they will talk like men,' said Tugba Karatas, Trabzon's 24-year-old right back. 'On the pitch we can act like men, but off the pitch we are expected to act like women.'[31]

Nagehan Aksan, a 28-year-old central defender and the team captain, said she didn't pay any attention. 'We are adults, no one can tell us what to do – not even the president, not our families, cos we are old enough to do what we want. So we don't care what people say.'

Men are often very surprised when they find out they are footballers. 'They find it unbelievable,' says Arzu Karabulut, 25, who had arrived from Germany at the beginning of the season and was the division's top goalscorer on 23 goals. 'They say: "What – is it normal football?" And I say: "It's the football we play with our feet." Then they say: "Is it 90 minutes?", "Are the goals the same size?"'

During the season the girls mostly live together in two houses. They get paid a modest wage. Once the season ends they head back home, and typically work or study. Those playing and working in women's football tend to say the same thing: that Turkish women's football needs more sponsorship, that money could be raised through inclusion in the betting pools, that they need live games on TV and more positive exposure in the media. The players also complain that the season, at just over four months, is far too short. 'When we start a new season we feel like we're learning to play football all over again,' said Tugba.

The final match of 2015/16 was clouded by rancour and recriminations. Trabzon were bitter about their failure to win the league: they saw something fishy in the three red cards they had received against 1207 Antalyaspor and regarded Kirecburnu's 6–1 capitulation to Konak in a dim light. The Izmir side simply accused Trabzon of being sore losers and denied any wrongdoing. The players had been trading insults online.

'The match will be like *Braveheart*,' declared Trabzon's coach, Gurkan Cavdar. 'You know in the end? When he shouts "freeeeeedom"? This is war.' So Konak are the English and Trabzon are Scottish? Cavdar frowned. He didn't much like being compared to Scotland. 'It's more like Manchester United vs Manchester City,' he corrected. 'We just want to play football. But it will be spicy.'

Two days later and the teams had arrived at an artificial pitch next to Trabzonspor's Huseyin Avni Aker Stadium. Photos of past Trabzonspor stars adorned the outer walls of the stadium, so that those playing on the less salubrious pitch in its shadow could be inspired by some glory and nostalgia. There were two ragged stands – one tiny, shed-like one opposite the stadium, and a larger but equally decrepit one behind one of the goals. Hasan pulled up chairs from the concourse café to make a VIP area of sorts on the grotty, foot-blackened, sticky steps – he didn't fancy sitting on the scuzzy seats. In total there were maybe 200 spectators, nearly all men.

Trabzon made a lively start, dominating possession but creating few chances. It was set to be a tight match. Konak felt their way into the game, and began putting a tidy array of moves together. The crowd was quiet, and the shouts of the coaches and the players rang out clearly. A few robust challenges flew in.

Trabzon were causing Konak some problems through their pacy Cameroonian winger, Henriette Akaba, who was running at defenders and looking to put crosses into the box. But some of Trabzon's tackles were too robust – they were giving away free kicks in midfield and around their own box. After half an hour, Konak swung in a free kick, Trabzon failed to clear, the ball bobbled around a bit, and Konak poked it into the net to make it 1–0.

The rest of the match remained cagey, full of thumping tackles and rare, squandered opportunities – it ended 1–0 to Konak. The end of the match was a cue for the latent aggravation to break out. Two players grabbed at each other, people tried to separate the growing melee, and Hasan hurried off from the makeshift VIP area. The crowd on the far side began throwing objects at the officials and shouting abuse, while a coterie of police officers formed a protective cordon around the anxious-looking officials. I stayed in the stand, trying to keep track of all the mini-battles that were breaking out in tributaries of the main fight.

One very angry voice rose above all others – it was Hasan, striding onto the pitch and raging against the referee. The fighters had been separated, and Konak's players and coaches hurried into their dressing room as the police ushered everyone off the pitch and back behind a fence. Hasan could not be appeased, he kept shouting and pointing: 'I'm going to break his head!' The sound of ranting echoed out from the Trabzon dressing room. Hasan went in and gave a team talk – he told them they'd played well, that the result wasn't fair, and that he was proud of them. He emerged a bit calmer but was still waiting for the referee. The Trabzon players came out of the dressing room to applause; some were wiping their eyes, others were limping. The Konak players came out smiling and made their way to the bus. Some of the Konak and Trabzon players hugged and chatted.

While everyone started to drift off, Hasan paced in front of the fence and gradually became more amiable again. The officials either slipped out through a back door or were waiting it out until Hasan left. How unhappy is the one who says, 'I am a Turkish referee,' not least in Trabzon.

The drama made the newspapers. Yet Dostlukspor's old administrator Nedim Yazir had a different reading of the kerfuffle a few weeks later. He said it revealed progress: it showed how seriously women's football is taken now:

> Women's football changed 100 per cent – and in a good way. At the beginning of the 1970s supporters came and encouraged them – 'You can do it.' But now the supporters come and say, 'Why didn't you win the match?' They accepted that women can play professional football and can be successful.[32]

Eastern battles

Erden Or is the manager of the Turkish Football Federation's Development League, and has been responsible for women's football since 2008. No one else wanted the post – it just sat there vacant. Or saw the potential to build up the women's sport and volunteered for the role. It should be noted that Erden Or is a man: when he goes to UEFA committees on women's football, his counterparts from other countries are invariably women. 'I'd prefer to give my seat to a lady! But there is no demand. I offered myself as a donkey,' he told me.[33]

In 2008 Or's main focus was on culture – convincing families to let their daughters play football. Now the focus is more on ensuring the league runs smoothly, and on building it up, and getting more female coaches, spectators and administrators in both the men's and women's games.

Or defends the federation from accusations of being tight-fisted: he says he is happy with the amount of money earmarked for women's football and that more funds would simply get spent on more outlandish transfers, or might disappear into the pockets of some club officials, or could be diverted to men's teams. Or claimed it was not possible to implement a functioning auditing system to track money.

He wants clubs to be more proactive:

> In Turkey the biggest problem is that the clubs act like a baby bird in the nest – they wait for the [federation] to feed them all the time. It's not necessary. They need to find their own sponsors, they need to pay attention to marketing. But they say, 'We are waiting for your support.'

For Or, what is important is that Turkish football is going in the right direction, as shown by the spread of the sport throughout the poorer, more conservative south-east of the country.

Guzide Alcu, 19, watched boys playing football in the streets of Diyarbakir while growing up. She started thinking: 'What's the deal with only men playing football?' She wondered if it was something she was meant to do. Amedspor's women's team was formed in 2007 – Guzide plays on the right wing and captains the team – she has played for the team since she was 12. Making the jump from playing in the street to playing on a pitch as an adolescent bothers a lot of the families in this socially conservative, largely Kurdish city. Guzide's family's attitudes changed over time from initial hostility to enthusiasm. 'If you don't have any knowledge, you just judge everything. When you learn you get used to things and understand, so they got used to it. Of course there are still men who judge us but we don't care.'[34]

The club formed in 2007 with a social mission – to support education of the players, help them gain university places and scholarships, and provide opportunities for socialising and learning. It also veers into politics – the club sees itself as providing positive role models for Kurdish women. The players are all Kurdish and from the region. Said Adnan Zengin, an administrator of the club, explained:

> Our policy is that we see ourselves as a pro-Kurdish team. I cannot say that we are trying to raise all players in our club as 'Kurdish nationalist' people, but of course there is a Kurdish issue, a Kurdish problem in this region. So a good way to explain our issues and problems is via sport.[35]

The psychology of being a female footballer is more intense in this conservative and volatile region. We were sitting on the team bus on the way to training. The team was still a bit shaken up from a match the week before in Igdir, which had descended into violence. Amedspor came back with lurid tales. Amedspor's coach said that eight of Igdir's players were of indeterminate gender. 'I spoke with some of their players. They had low voices and stubble, they were big. I could see that they were not women.'[36]

He pulled out his phone and began scrolling through photographs, and then showed me an image. 'What do you think?' The player could have been male or female. It was impossible to say, because the photo was shot from a distance on a shaky camera phone, and zoomed in to become a pixelated blur. 'Two were certainly taking pills,' he added. I was confused – was he saying they were men posing as women, or transgender women, or women who had taken steroids or hormones, or what? 'I don't know. But the federation's rules are clear – they state that you have to be 100 per cent sure that your opponents are women.' An outraged voice piped up from a player further back on the bus: 'If they don't look like women, they shouldn't play!'

Amedspor lost the physical, bruising match against 76 Igdirspor 1–0. At the end of the game a fight broke out between the players, and a male Igdirspor spectator ran onto the pitch and kicked Amedspor's goalkeeper *in the crotch*. She had to go to hospital and was understandably feeling a bit shaken up a week later.

The football federation often receives complaints regarding the 'masculinity' of female players. For them, it is a straightforward matter: in Turkey identity cards are colour-coded – blue for male, pink for female. If players have pink cards, they are female – it's as simple as that, as far as the federation are concerned. They say they have never found a genuine case where a male player was found to be posing as female, or anything to do with hormones or steroids. They are certain that all Igdirspor's players are female.

During training, Amedspor's assistant coach Newroz Gon said that they didn't want to take any chances with their own team. 'We have two players with short, boyish haircuts,' she said, pointing out a couple of players, who just looked like young women with short hair. 'We had a word with them and asked them to grow their hair in order to avoid these kinds of issues. They both said, "OK".'[37]

The widespread preoccupation with 'feminine' appearances is shared by the football federation, as Erden Or explained:

In our national team we pay attention to how the girls look. Because it's very important for the potential families. This is a girls' team, it's better to look like a girl. In the past most of the families didn't want to send their girls into women's football because of this reason. But now they trust the [federation] and they trust clubs, and there are some clubs who have similar problems right now, but when you see our national team they are very good-looking girls and they put make-up on prior to the match.

I become frustrated – it's annoying that the federation reinforces these sexist and homophobic tropes about appearances. Or insists that culture has to be taken into account if they are going to develop women's football. The federation say they only encourage the girls to look a certain way, and they deny choosing players according to appearance over talent. 'It's not like choosing an apple in the market,' said Or.

The academic and ex-footballer Lale Orta laments the 'shallow' view taken of female sports in modern Turkey, and beyond, and says it negatively affects women. 'The general approach to sportswomen who have achieved significant success in their branch is mainly focused on their style, the beauty of their legs, make-up and hips and so on rather than their success.'[38]

Turkish men's football has evolved to some extent in terms of gender over the past two decades. There are now more female academics, journalists and commentators in the world of football, and much greater numbers of female spectators in the stands.

But when women enter traditionally male, macho domains in Turkey – whether the military, police, parliament or the football stadium – they are expected to downplay their femininity and sexuality, says Itir Erhart, an academic who researches gender and football fandom. 'When you go to the movies, you can just be who you are. But as a woman in the world of football – as players, fans, managers, writers, researchers – we always have to [think], "OK, shall I do this, wear this, say this?"' she says. 'You have to try harder to prove you're competent in this field.'[39]

Erhart has documented a group of fans called Ladies of Besiktas, who formed in 2006 to disrupt gender stereotypes and norms in the stadium.[40] They didn't want to be passive wallflowers, like some of those dragged along by boyfriends, and neither did they want to downplay their femininity or join in with misogynistic expressions of fandom. The group went to Besiktas games together wearing identical black-and-white scarves, supported the team volubly, and many also looked conventionally 'feminine' and wore make-up, and they blew whistles during sexist and homophobic chanting. Erhart says their stances were important, although the group is no longer active. '[They showed] you can be a genuine fan who doesn't approve of swearing – and you can put on make-up! I thought that was very important because many of us feel trapped.'

Ladies of Besiktas inspired similar fan groups to form – such as 'GFB Angels of Fenerbahce' and the 'Female Fans of Trabzonspor' – but they received a mixed response from other Besiktas fans. They were booed and harangued for bringing whistles into the stadium, to the extent that they stopped the practice. They were also criticised by the then leader of Carsi, Alen Markaryan, for creating a 'spectacle', and some fans accused them of being bourgeois, with their tailored jackets and trendy dress sense.[41]

Most female players come from poorer backgrounds and they often have to overcome conservative attitudes.[42] However, female football fans inside stadiums are, in general, more middle-class, especially at the big clubs where ticket prices are high. Part of the federation's attempt to gentrify Turkish football is to make stadiums more middle class and therefore theoretically more appealing to women, which they believe will also cut violence and swearing in a kind of virtuous loop. The federation has used female spectators to sanction misbehaving male spectators: instead of issuing stadium bans and playing behind closed doors, the federation began ordering matches to be played with women and children-only crowds (a total of 58 matches across three seasons starting in 2011/12[43]).

The policy rests on an understanding of supposedly natural differences between men and women: that men are tough, angry, aggressive, brave, determined and competitive; while women are supposedly meek, passive and fragile; that football is a natural male domain, while women are perhaps bamboozled by the complexities of the offside rule. The idea of playing matches attended only by women and children was to soften the atmosphere, and eliminate violence and swearing.

But numerous swearing chants were heard during the first women and children-only match, between Fenerbahce and Manisaspor, provoking consternation. The only explanation that the then Minister of Youth and Sports, Suat Kilic, could come up with was that men must have infiltrated the stadium dressed as women. 'It can't be women's doing,' he said. 'Turkish women do not sing ugly chants.'[44] The media ran reports and photographs of 'a male intruder', who later turned out to be a very offended woman in a hijab.

Subsequent women and children-only matches were also characterised by disturbances and swearing, much of which was sexist and homophobic – including Besiktas female fans inviting Fenerbahce to 'suck my balls'. Besiktas was fined by the federation after a loud chorus of 'Fener fags, you can't be champions' rang out in one women and children-only derby match.

The women-only practice received significant criticism: for essentialising gender, for infantilising women by lumping them in with children, for denying the proper fandom of women. The practice was abandoned after 2013/14.

On the way back from Amedspor's training, the coaches discussed the psychological sessions that each female player is obliged to attend. It is not deemed necessary to give Amedspor's male players the same psychological support. The main reason, says the head coach, is gender confusion brought on by playing football. 'They are confused because they react or think like men. And some things happen when women play football – we saw what happened with Igdirspor,' he said. 'We are worried about them becoming men or like men.'

The reason Amedspor give their players psychological help is that they care deeply about their well-being. They offer help with other issues – including those related to the conflict in the region, issues at home, relationship concerns and so on.

In a way, their concern for mental health is refreshing, but it is also revealing of prevailing, retrograde gender assumptions that persist even among those dedicated to women's football: that women can be 'confused' by football, that there should be a set way to look and act as a woman. And aren't the male players in need of psychological support too? Don't they have problems at home or suffer fallout from the violence in the region?

The national team have a mentoring programme, but it's more geared to helping with personal problems and anxieties, and it's not psychological therapy. 'We don't say, "Hey, why are you playing football, are you mentally ill?"' laughed Or.

The day after training, Amedspor played a league match against Gecit Belediyespor. A noisy bunch of lads bounced and sang in the far corner of the stand, chanting Kurdish nationalist songs: 'The colour of the team is the meaning of life!' Kader Ates, 19, sat in the opposite corner of the stand, as far from the boys as possible. She had kohl-lined eyes, a flowery headscarf, and fluorescent trainers poked out from underneath a long *abaya*. She was here to support her friends who play for the team:

Mostly the neighbourhood judges women players. They wonder how women can wear shorts and run around in front of all these people, all these men. Old people especially have this mentality – but if they get the chance to come to these matches and they actually watch the women, they change their minds.[45]

When I asked if she felt comfortable attending the matches, she replied:

We don't feel comfortable here at all! I feel nervous in this atmosphere, we don't know how to deal with it, but we come here anyway. There should be a limit on the words the male supporters use – they shouldn't be allowed to use sexual terms, especially about women. That's why women and families don't feel comfortable coming to matches here. There's also a problem with their behaviour – especially when there are supporters of other teams here – they are very aggressive.

A small group of middle-aged women wearing the hijab were sitting close to the noisy male supporters, looking at ease. Guler Gormez, 49, is the mother of Devran – Amedspor's 19-year-old midfielder. 'There are not many places for girls to go where we live. Everything is for men,' she said. 'But we raised Devran to be able to do everything she wants, and I was very happy when she started playing for this team. She got the chance to study at university as well.' Guler would have liked to have played football but she never got the chance. 'I was the eldest of seven children. My mother always told me I had to help her straight after school – she said I didn't have time for anything else!'[46]

Allowing your daughter to play football can affect your standing in the community – you have to be tough and assertive:

I hear so many things from my neighbours: 'How can you let your daughter play football in front of lots of men?', 'How is this normal?' I tell them women can do what they want and they need to be courageous. They also say: 'How can you let a girl out at night? She's not wearing a headscarf, she's not praying.' But my daughter prays, she wears what she wants, and she's still Muslim. Yet they are still complaining for religious reasons.'

On the pitch Amedspor ran out easy 6–1 winners: Guzide scored four goals. 'Please stop, have pity on Gecit,' sang Amedspor's fans gleefully.

In addition to the conservative attitudes encountered in their own society, the Amedspor players say they face discrimination when they play away from home. 'People target us wherever we go just because we are Kurds. They are always calling us "terrorists", trying to intimidate us. That's not only happening in the west – it happens in the south-east,' said Guzide, Amedspor's captain, after the match. 'But we are all the same. We all came from the land and we all go back to the land at the end.'

Some players face conflict, literally on their doorsteps. Aysegul Bitgin, 17, lives in Surici – a neighbourhood in the historic Sur district of Diyarbakir that has been behind Kurdish militant barricades and subject to attack by the security forces. Her neighbourhood had been under repeated curfews – she was trapped at her grandmother's house for several days and had to miss training. 'When I opened the window the house filled up with the smell of pepper gas. We saw police bombing, firing guns, it was a horrible experience.'[47]

Her neighbourhood has been emptying, with people fleeing the destruction, and she feels fearful and encircled by the police, but she tries to focus on football and has been inspired by recent events involving women:

> Before, we were talking about are we here or not. If we exist or not. But after Kobane[48] we see the Kurdish women there – how they are resisting, how they are changing the war. So we got more ambitious – we said, OK they are Kurdish women, and we are Kurdish women, and we will resist and we will get the revolution through sport, through football – in this way. Now we believe in ourselves so much. Kurdish women realised how powerful they are when they see the Kurdish women of Kobane.

Turkey has always had a very small proportion of female parliamentarians,[49] but women are much more prominent in the left-wing Kurdish nationalist movement. The pro-Kurdish HDP fields an even 50–50 gender split in candidates, and Figen Yuksekdag is the HDP's female co-chair alongside Selahattin Demirtas. After the June 2015 elections, the number of female parliamentarians reached 98 – a record high, constituting 18 per cent of parliament. However, these numbers fell considerably in the snap election of November 2015, as the Kurdish peace process broke down and the AKP's vote surged. The number of female parliamentarians fell to 82 – 14.8 per cent. Women made up only 10.7 per cent of the AKP's MPs.[50] After the election there was only one female minister – Fatma Betul Sayan Kaya, Minister of Family and Social Policy[51] – meaning there were then more men in the cabinet called Faruk than there were women.

Ravza Kavakci Kan – a female AKP politician who first became a member of parliament in 2015 – points out that, while female representation is not as high as she'd like, the trend is in the right direction. When the AKP came to power in 2002, the proportion of female parliamentarians was just 4.4 per cent.

Kavakci says that the headscarf ban held many women back, particularly conservative women. 'I was one of the few lucky ones who was able to go abroad and get an education and come back and wait and fight for discriminations to be lifted. So not all of us had that opportunity.'[52] She points to the AKP's record in encouraging the education of girls and offering financial support for women with children to stay in work:

> But still it's not at a level that we would like it to be. With better education, and with the lifting of discrimination, there isn't any institutional, legal discrimination. But the discrimination in people's minds, that also takes some time to break. That is something I think women all around the world have to struggle with.

Meanwhile, the Amedspor player Aysegul Bitgin is already thinking about her future after football, amid all its perils and uncertainties. She wants to be a coach and pass down her experience. 'If we live long enough, if something doesn't happen to me and I don't die, I will do this.'

I visited Amedspor women's team in November 2015 – within a couple of weeks, parts of Diyarbakir were back under curfew, this time for longer than before, with more violence, as the security forces battled Kurdish militants. Amedspor ploughed on. In January 2016, they took revenge on manly Igdirspor, beating them 3–1. Amedspor won their division, finishing level with Igdirspor on 55 points, but with a better head-to-head record. Amedspor progressed through the play-off rounds, defeating several teams to secure promotion to the second tier.

There is a sense that women's football is travelling vaguely in the right way, but that it should be travelling faster, and with more direction. The federation do not have any concrete targets for women's football.

Erdem Gokturk is the general secretary of Dudulluspor women's club and he is highly respected as a thinker and organiser of women's football. Dudulluspor is a girl's team with a social mission similar to Malatya's. Dudullu was a village that has been subsumed into Istanbul's suburbs on the Asian side of the city. It is largely a poor, conservative area, with many recent migrants from the east escaping poverty and conflict. Domestic violence, drug abuse and lack of education are prevalent.

Dudulluspor was set up in 2012. The team only selects girls from the local area, training four times a week and working closely with teachers and schools. 'If they fail in education then they can't stay with us,' said Gokturk, 'so they stick to the education system and that brings them to the end of high school.'[53] The club also helps the girls socialise, free from the restrictions of their parents but in a safe environment.[54]

Gokturk criticises clubs for being too dependent on the federation and not doing enough to help themselves. A legacy of dirigisme and authoritarianism can mean that some opt for passivity, waiting for the patrician benevolence of the state. But while Gokturk says that the federation has done well to expand women's football, he points out that clubs can only do so much by themselves, that they struggle to sell themselves in a league that is not visible, and criticises the federation for failing to have a better vision for the sport. Clubs like Malatya are doing exactly what the federation wants, desperately searching for sponsors and marketing the club, but to no avail.

Erden Or at the Turkish Football Federation is not free to focus solely on women's football – he is also responsible for futsal and beach football, which suggests that his superiors in the federation regard women's football as a similar kind of novelty sport (there are celebrity versions of these sports featuring former pros labouring and hauling their middle-aged frames around a lurid indoor court, generally increasing the *huzun*[55] count by making fans wistful for long-lost glories). Unlike futsal and beach football, women's football doesn't have TV rights. It is not included in the state's betting pools, unlike women's volleyball. 'But at the same time women's sports is a very sellable concept,' claims Gokturk. 'Nobody is pushing. The federation should have done a better job promoting the league to create funds for the clubs.'[56]

The emergence of Besiktas women's football team – who emphatically won the second division in 2015/16 and earned promotion to the top flight – could raise interest in the women's sport by virtue of 'Big Three' stardust. It is perhaps revealing of football's traditionally exalted role in Turkish masculinity that the big clubs have not invested much in women's football, although many run female branches in basketball and volleyball.[57]

Gokturk says that he doesn't know what the Turkish Football Federation's targets for women's football are. I tell him they don't have any. 'That's what I'm saying!' he exclaimed. 'That's why I think the targets the clubs should take should be less aspirational in sports and more social, because they are not going to get the support from the federation.'

At least the spread of football teams to almost every eastern city shows progress. 'I'm less worried about the cultural resistance part than I am about the lack of strategy from the football federation,' says Gokturk, who believes that women's football is here to stay in Turkey, that it has passed the point of no return. 'If we can maintain it at the local level it's not going to collapse.'

Autumn in Malatya

All football has a recursive quality. Turkish football goes round and round in the cycle of seasons, but the circles aren't static – sometimes they are wheeling towards an edge.

Malatya made it to the new season. I returned in mid-November 2016 for the first match of 2016/17. The apricot trees had burst into an autumnal flame, and the skeletons of the near-black branches were visible through the thinning, yellow foliage. Malatya women's team were kicking off their season with a home match taking place way out of the city, at the university's stadium. For the past two seasons they had played near the centre of Malatya, and two or three of the girls' families had come to watch, along with other spectators. Now, the Turkish Football Federation had shunted them back out to the margins of the city, where no one wanted to travel. When the club's president, Dogan Deniz Celebi, complained, he was told that the pitch in the city centre was being used by men.

Celebi had found a way to keep the team alive for the new season. He had let many of the transferred players go and was now focusing almost exclusively on the young, local players. Success had been necessary to gain attention, but the attention had not gained financial support, so he was going back to basics. So while Celebi has kept the team going, he has also said that he can only support it from his own pocket for this season and next season to see the current crop of players through. Then the team will end in 2018 unless it can find some hitherto untapped support. By that point the club will likely have helped almost 50 girls to go to university, and dozens of others to stay out of trouble, socialise and gain skills and confidence. The prospect of its demise had left Celebi despondent and exhausted. 'Women's football is like an orphan,' he said.

In the opening match of the season, Malatya were taking on their local rivals, Elazig Bordo Atletik Spor, who were facing many of the same problems. Their coach had sold his car to finance the team. In the past few years they had also helped around 20 girls to get into university but they were considering shutting down the team. They turned up to play against Malatya with only ten players.

Celebi had gone inside the stadium to check on the girls, and when he came striding out of the tunnel five minutes later his face looked like a jigsaw that had lost a few pieces. 'They sent us out here and there's not even any hot water,' he said.

Mountain ridges peered over the top of the stand. The stadium had such a bleached feel – the washed pink of the running track, the lost colours on the seats no longer spelling letters. The regulation quorum of police arrived with riot shields and batons, which they promptly set aside as they began to lay out a picnic. The stands clicked with the sound of threshing seeds. A few curious university students turned up, their occasional shouts and chants ricocheting off thousands of empty plastic seats. The synthetic pitch was as hard as bare winter earth – players went down injured regularly, and patches of skin were shaved off. There were no medics. A cold bottle of water was rolled down an injured shin by way of treatment. Malatya spent the match ensconced in Elazig's half. They missed countless chances but still ran out 4–0 winners.

'Did you see my goal?' asked Ikranur after the match. Early in the first half she had taken a short corner on the left, received the ball back again on the edge of the area, and fired a looping shot that dipped over the goalkeeper, into the far corner of the net. Sergio Ramos would have been proud.

Ikranur's proudest moment had been a match the previous season in Kayseri, where her elder brother works as a sports teacher. He came to watch her play. Her teammates kept giving her the ball, aware that her brother was in the stands, and Ikranur set up two goals (and boasted she had got another player sent off). Her brother used to oppose her playing football. 'At the end of the game my brother came and kissed and congratulated me and was very proud, so I was happy.'[58]

Ikranur escaped an almost predestined life. Others are not so lucky, and the future looks bleak for many young women. In November 2016, the government provoked fury and disbelief by proposing a bill that would overturn men's convictions for child sexual assault if they agree to marry their victims and if the act was committed without 'force, threat, or any other restriction on consent'.[59] The government insisted, in a piece of grotesquely absurd circular non-logic, that it was aimed at dealing with the widespread custom of child marriages. It's not clear how the custom of child marriage would be defeated by facilitating it via paedophilia. Following street protests, the bill was later withdrawn to be reconsidered.[60]

The liberal high hopes of the early AKP era encompassed women, and there has been progress in terms of gender equality, but women have also suffered as a result of the retrograde, militaristic, authoritarian tendencies of the government. It is estimated that more than half of the Gezi protesters were women.[61] Perhaps the most emblematic image of Gezi was of a woman in a red dress being pepper-sprayed in the face by riot police. There will be profound implications for women under an all-powerful Erdogan, who has embraced and evolved the traditions of a certain model of Turkishness which sidelines women. The visible pillars of 'New Turkey' under the AKP are the nation, the mosque and the family, all traditionally associated with patriarchy, but underpinned by economic and patronage networks of property, big business and the state, from which women are also largely excluded.

Amid all the current and projected strife, Turkey is still slowly changing for women, and there is progress, striving and flourishing amid the myriad of frustrations and setbacks.

Ikranur and a large group of female friends watch every home match of the local men's team, Yeni Malatyaspor, who won promotion to the Super League in 2017. In 2015/16 the girls had not been accepted by the ultras' group Derebeyleri, so they had stood apart in a group of 27 and cheered. The next season, a leading member of Derebeyleri invited them to join and they now stand in the middle of the ultras and are scolded if they don't sing up for the team. 'In the beginning they thought that girls didn't know anything about football and maybe they thought that their slang and swearing wouldn't be appropriate in front of us!' said Ikranur. 'We told them we play football, we know football.' When the men sing sexist chants they just keep quiet. 'It's not good, but no problem for us. They don't chant at us – they chant at the other team.'

Ikranur plans to gain a master's degree, to work in education, and to play for, and eventually coach, the national team. She would love the chance to play club football in Germany or Spain, where women's football is better supported.

Women's football has helped change but not transform her home neighbourhood of Kiltepe. Drug abuse and domestic violence are still common, and child marriage remains prevalent.[62] 'Sometimes men still think that women have no rights, that women have no right to talk,' said Ikranur. Any gains made by the football team are precarious. Ikranur talks urgently and passionately about the risk of the team folding:

> It is going to affect the area very badly because if the club is closed down then people, especially in Kiltepe, won't let their daughters play football. Because they trust in Dogan [Celebi]. They would never allow their daughters to go to other clubs to play football. So their future will be

totally devastated. For me, it's OK, my destiny is in my own hands, but others don't have that.

Earlier that day, Ikranur had gone into a shop to buy tights to wear under her football shorts. The shopkeeper asked if she played volleyball. He was shocked when Ikranur told him she played football. 'Should girls play football?' he asked.

'If men play football and volleyball, we can also play football or volleyball. We live in 2016 and maybe we will be a member of the European Union and you still criticise us for playing football?' Ikranur told him. 'He was silenced,' she said with a laugh. 'And then we left his shop without buying anything.'

EPILOGUE

'Football is faster than words'

Of course, it's also clear that the reporter always lags behind the event itself and therefore constantly has to edit his words. Football is faster than words.

ORHAN PAMUK[1]

[They] are taking a corner from a very dangerous position.

BULEND KARPAT, TURKISH TV COMMENTATOR[2]

The world turns around a spinning ball.

EDUARDO GALEANO[3]

Preseason: a time to rest and to take stock, to mourn or celebrate the past season and look forward in hope or dread, a time to build and to tear down, a time of cloying boredom and blank weekends, and of the mad-cow foam and blather of the transfer rumour mill, only eclipsed by the stupefying reality of the transfer market.

Turkish football was more competitive in 2017: tiny Basaksehir finished second, just behind Besiktas. Konyaspor won the cup. Basaksehir's 20-year-old star winger, Cengiz Under, was sold to Roma for €13.4 million and became the most expensive ever Turkish transfer to Europe: a source of pride amid Turkey's increasingly fraught relationship with the continent.

Preseason is a time of big talk, of puff pieces about Besiktas becoming the 'Turkish Chelsea',[4] of average attendances creeping back above 10,000, foreign broadcasting rights, growing revenues.

But it's also a time to ignore warnings and bad omens: that Turkish football's debt is at record levels; that Turkey is the only European country where club debts and liabilities are bigger than club assets. 'European clubs improved substantially overall while aggregated losses of Turkish clubs quintupled,' Andrea Traverso, UEFA's head of club licensing and Financial Fair Play (FFP), warned recently.[5]

The beef-witted, atomic sums of money at one end of the spectrum jar with the shrapnel of loose change at the other, where preseason is a time to improvise and hustle: like the African teams who scraped together the money to pay for their own African Nations Cup after Fatih municipality's funding ran out; or the reprisal of the alternative Syrian national team from the grassroots by the players and supporters themselves. Malatya's women's team struggled on with minimal support and will compete in 2017/18, though it still looks like being their final season. But it's a time of activism and new projects for those using the power of football to change society.

Preseason is a time to keep your head down if you're Deniz Naki, who has stayed safe and out of jail for now.

It encompasses the match-fixing scandal, which still casts a long shadow and fuels Trabzonspor's Sisyphean legal battle with Fenerbahce. A new case was lodged with FIFA on 3 July.

It's a time to rest, but not too much because the season starts ever earlier. Galatasaray – banned from European football the previous season under FFP rules, and still in huge debt – signed tens of millions' worth of mostly ageing players, and made their return to European football in July 2017 – only to be promptly dumped out of the Europa League in the very first preliminary round by Ostersunds, a tiny club from Sweden.

And, if you're Fatih Terim, preseason is a time to drive 200 miles to have a brawl at a kebab restaurant, owned by a Turkish Football Federation official, and then agree 'by mutual consent' to part ways with the national team.[6] A fourth stint at Galatasaray was immediately rumoured.

Ankaragucu finally won their division and hauled their way out of the third tier of Turkish football in 2017. It was announced that their creaking, ancient 19 Mayis Stadium – the site of so much glory, shenanigans and heartbreak – was finally to be demolished and a new stadium with a capacity of over 40,000 built in its place.[7]

This great club, with its raucous, working-class fan base, was finally heading in the right direction, but it is also re-entering Turkish football's higher echelons with all its opportunities and pitfalls. How would fans fare under the Passolig system? Would ticket prices soar? How would the TV revenues bonanza be spent? The club is still in debt, still owes money to former players, but began snapping up new signings.

Across the city, mayor-backed Osmanlispor also have a new stadium project in the pipeline. Ankara's new stadiums add to the mind-blowing frenzy of stadium construction in the country. They will all help as Turkey vies with Germany to host Euro 2024.

The venues were set to be also much-delayed, much-welcomed bits of prestige for the city's mayor – especially as they should conveniently be opened by 2019, when Melih Gokcek was expecting to face another election.[8] The mayor had been busy finding support for Ankaragucu in the wake of promotion, with three companies linked to the municipality announcing sponsorship, to the wariness of some fans. 'There's always free cheese in a mousetrap,' noted Ankaragucu fanatic 'Posh Kanka'.[9]

2019 is the year Turkey officially moves from being a parliamentary democracy to an executive presidency and holds local and national elections. 'That will be a beginning,' says AKP politician Ravza Kavakci Kan.[10]

She was elected in 2015 – since then the country has passed through huge turbulence. 'But we survived all of this – our economic growth continued, and also social change continued,' she said. 'So I see a Turkey in which economic development comes to a higher level, and I see more improvements in areas of democracy […] I think in our democratisation process we have come a long way but we have a long way to go. So I am hopeful for the future of Turkey.'

Many are much less sanguine. Huge numbers of Turkey's brightest are leaving the country amid a climate of fear, repression and uncertainty.[11] Football academic Daghan Irak says the government's authoritarianism is such that everything feels both very controlled and also very parlous: 'The whole thing is like *The Truman Show*: it's intriguing, it's interesting, it's unexpected, it's unpredictable – but it's kind of scripted. It's not very life-like.'[12]

The hope that he had in the late 1990s and early 2000s has gone. 'For the very first time in my life I have to admit I am pessimistic person,' he said. 'We never know what will happen tomorrow.'

Dawn, 16 July 2017, exactly a year since the failed coup plotters had bombed the parliament, Recep Tayyip Erdogan looked out over a sea of people in Ankara.

'Did my nation march against the scoundrels and traitors with weapons in their hands?' he asked the crowd. 'No, my nation march with their flag and their faith.'[13]

He gave another speech that day at the Bosphorus Bridge (renamed '15 July Martyrs Bridge' following the failed coup), which had been seized by rebel soldiers, and taken back by those resisting the coup. Both speeches were heavy with religious symbolism and anger at dissenters, opposition politicians, journalists, foreign powers – all part of the narrative that Turkey is facing a second 'War of Independence'. He threatened to 'chop the heads off' traitors.[14]

There are so many questions left unanswered from what has been called Turkey's longest night: to what extent were non-Gulenists involved? What was the exact timeline and sequence of events? When exactly did the government learn of the attempt? What are the lessons to be learned? But the only question Erdogan seems interested in is: are you with me or against me?

He is afraid. He has made so many enemies, and amassed such wealth and control, been accused of many crimes, that he probably can't afford to hand over power.

The singular role played by Erdogan in Turkey's travails is perhaps often overstated – many of Turkey's problems relate to enduring systemic and historical forces, as well as global and regional pressures. But Erdogan's rhetoric, personality and policies are the source of much of Turkey's current division and instability. Like Ataturk, Erdogan has tried to shape Turkey in his own image.

Erdogan may frequently draw on the power of football, but he does not see politics as a team sport and he does not tolerate competition. Erdogan is tying Turkey's fate to his own: the state is increasingly embodied by the refounding father of 'New Turkey'. But what happens when Erdogan is gone and a vacuum opens up at the heart of the political system shaped for him?

Paradoxically, while Turkey is becoming more authoritarian and conservative in some areas, it is also becoming more liberal in others. A huge number of people are opposed to Erdogan, some of his supporters are actually lukewarm towards him, and he often struggles – demonstrated by his difficulties in winning a dubious referendum, his terror of mass protests, and divisions that cut across his own party and all institutions of the state. For all the AKP's success, it has never won a majority of the popular vote in a general election. Imam Beckenbauer's game is waning: now more New York Cosmos era than Bayern Munich.

The signs for Turkey are ominous: ongoing war with the PKK, repression of all dissent, regional instability and a faltering economy – all taking place in a dangerous situation where the conditions of power are based on division and antagonism around Erdogan's cult of personality.[15] The outcome of any future struggle over power could well be bloody. Yet I also found many signs of hope – so much that brings people together in Turkey, and so many people living extraordinary lives.

As shown, many of Turkey's fears, volatility and struggles are reflected in football – its division, financial strife, corruption, violence, patriarchy, xenophobia and the desire for a strongman.

But football also reflects its beauty and its dreams – all that is so beguiling and enthralling about this country at the centre of the world: its passion, hospitality, colour, history, humour, energy, warmth and diversity; its love of life, its ambition and courage. Turkey is in rapid flux and football will continue to be an arena for these tensions to play out.

Turkish football is many things: a golden ticket; intoxication; a bankrupt money-spinner; re-enactment of history; a shortcut and a language; a stage; carnival and doldrums; crookedness and innocence; a monument; a gladiatorial arena; gentrification; a site of resurrection; respite; dissent; a plaything; a lifesaver; an insatiable mouth; a blueprint; a tool; love and dread; a livelihood; an orphan; a family, a religion; a nation – a fixture at the heart of Turkish life.

ACKNOWLEDGEMENTS

I would like to thank the countless people who went well out of their way to help me with this project, everyone who spoke to me for this book, and the many translators and fixers who worked with me.

It was a huge privilege to travel around this amazing country, meeting all kinds of people who were unbelievably warm and welcoming – I was treated to a staggering amount of food, tea and beer. There are far too many of them to thank by name.

I would like to say a huge thanks to Akin Aytekin, Colleen Carroll, Kaya Genc, April Key, Agnese Lace, Lily Leach, David Hardy, James Hardy, Virginia Jordan, Owen Powell, Firat Tasvur, Lorenzo Woodford and Orcan Yigit for their support.

I am very grateful to Tomasz Hoskins at I.B.Tauris for his fantastic editing, and to David Inglesfield for his sharp-eyed copy-editing.

I would like to send love and thanks to Mum (aka Maureen Keddie), Shonagh Keddie and Kate Keddie.

Above all I send my endless love and gratitude to Eylul Ertas.

NOTES

Introduction

1 'Facial hair in Turkish politics: a tale of mustaches and men', *Hurriyet Daily News*, 6 August 2010. http://www.hurriyetdailynews.com/default.aspx?pageid=438&n=facial-hair-in-turkish-politics-a-tale-of-moustaches-and-men-2010-08-06.

2 Karl Vick, 'Secular democrat or Zealot?', *Washington Post*, 10 November 2002. https://www.washingtonpost.com/archive/politics/2002/11/10/secular-democrat-or-zealot/895c46b0-eee2-44f4-9081-a47161a852a0.

3 Actually, like Putin, Erdogan has also been known to ride a horse – although fully clothed. It's arguable that Erdogan is tougher than Putin, because Erdogan once fell off a horse, the horse *stood on his testicles*, and Erdogan got up straight away, apparently fine.

4 'Turkish PM Erdogan scores a hat-trick', *Daily Sabah*, 28 July 2014. http://www.dailysabah.com/football/2014/07/28/turkish-pm-erdogan-scores-a-hattrick.

5 'Protesters at new stadium "ungrateful", Turkish PM says', *Hurriyet Daily News*, 16 January 2011. http://www.hurriyetdailynews.com/default.aspx?pageid=438&n=erdogan-says-protests-at-galatasaray-stadium-unfair-2011-01-16.

Prologue: Ultra

1 Joe Parkinson and Emre Peker, 'Turkish court tries alleged coup plotters', *Wall Street Journal*, 16 December 2014. http://www.wsj.com/articles/turkish-fans-of-besiktas-soccer-club-face-coup-charges-1418730926.

2 Ex-Reading coach.

3 Elif Batuman, 'The view from the stands', *New Yorker*, 7 March 2011. http://www.newyorker.com/magazine/2011/03/07/the-view-from-the-stands.

4 Arda Alan Isik, 'Why I am critical of the Turkish national team and why everyone should be', *Daily Sabah*, 10 September 2016. http://www.dailysabah.com/football/2016/09/10/why-i-am-critical-of-the-turkish-national-team-and-why-everyone-should-be.

5 Yagmur Nuhrat, 'Fair enough? Negotiating ethics in Turkish football', PhD thesis, Brown University, May 2013. https://repository.library.brown.edu/studio/item/bdr:320642/PDF/?embed=true.

6 They generally preferred gymnastics, wrestling or swimming – sports deemed more useful for the 'defence of the state'.

7 Characterised by privatisation, scrapping of protectionism, lower tax rates, the promotion of financial service industries and the weakening of labour and trade regulations.

8 Cem Emrence, 'Playing with global city: the rise and fall of a Turkish soccer team', *Journal of Popular Culture*, 40:4 (August 2007), pp. 630–42.

9 Daghan Irak, 'The transformation of football fandom', MA thesis, Bogazici University, January 2010, p. 163. http://www.daghanirak.com/tezprefinal.pdf.

10 Interview with the author, 20 April 2016.

1   Fathers and Sons

1 Interview with the author, 30 January 2015.

2 'Dinamo Mesken' by Ege Berensel was exhibited at SALT Ulus gallery, Ankara, from 27 January to 14 March 2015. Berensel has chronicled Dinamo Mesken's story through documentary films, found footage and memorabilia.

3 Interview with the author, 15 February 2015.

4 Berensel has also documented at least three other amateur football clubs in Bursa, and others in Ankara, that were forced to close following the coup. Berensel says that the closure of the football club was part of a wider attempt to subdue and control Mesken. The authorities tried to alter the neighbourhood's political demographics by arresting people or forcing them out of the area, and by building a police settlement in their midst.

5 Yagmur Nuhrat, 'Fair enough? Negotiating ethics in Turkish football', MA thesis, Brown University, 2008, p. 26. https://repository.library.brown.edu/studio/item/bdr:320642/PDF/?embed=true.

6 Fuat Husnu played for other teams, such as the British–Greek team Cadi-Key, under the pseudonym 'Bobby'. He went on to play for Galatasaray and later coached their arch-rivals Fenerbahce.

7 Clipping courtesy of Mehmet Yuce.

8 Daghan Irak, 'The transformation of football fandom', MA thesis, Bogazici University, January 2010, p. 85. http://www.daghanirak.com/tezprefinal.pdf.

9 Galatasaray gained a reputation for elitism as, initially, only Galatasaray High School students were permitted to play. Fenerbahce also had links to a prestigious school, Robert College in Kadikoy; however, unlike Galatasaray, the team was open to others among the elites beyond the school, and gained a reputation as a less aristocratic team. See Irak, 'The transformation of football fandom', pp. 27–30.

10 While Besiktas Gymnastics Club was formed in 1903, the football branch wasn't established until 1911.

11 Both teams, however, had several non-Muslim, non-Turkish players.

12 On the eve of the Great War, the Ottoman Empire was losing much of its remaining European territory in the Balkan Wars. Mustafa Kemal's mother arrived in Istanbul as a refugee, after his birthplace of Salonika fell to the Greeks in 1912. Both Greece and Russia coveted Istanbul.

13 Irak, 'The transformation of football fandom', p. 34.

14 Arab lands were given to the British and French as mandates. A swathe of eastern Anatolia, including Trabzon, would form an Armenian state. A Kurdish state in southern Anatolia was also mooted. France, Italy and Greece had designs on other regions. Sèvres planned for the international administration of the Bosphorus and the Sea of Marmara. The fate of Istanbul was not clear but Greece still coveted the city.

15 Hay Eytan Cohen Yanarocak, 'The last stronghold: the Fenerbahce sports club and Turkish politics', Tel Aviv Notes, 6:10 (28 May 2012). https://www.academia.edu/1597564/The_Last_Stronghold_The_Fenerbahce_Sports_Club_and_Turkish_Politics.

16 Hasan Kamil was the first player to score in a Fenerbahce vs Galatasaray derby.

17 Paul Sarahs, 'War, English influence and a triumphant fight for freedom in Turkey: the Harrington Cup', FourFourTwo, 9 December 2014. http://www.fourfourtwo.com/features/war-english-influence-and-triumphant-fight-freedom-turkey-harrington-cup#:MkdTbGIvrkBTIA.

18 Many religious minorities had emigrated, or been forced out or killed, and there were millions of recent Muslim immigrants from Greece, Macedonia, Bulgaria and Crimea – many of whom didn't even speak Turkish; as well as Alevis, Circassians, Laz, Kurds, Zazas and remaining Arabs, Armenians, Assyrians, Greeks and Jews who, until recently, had largely considered themselves Ottoman.

19 This included a cultural emphasis on Sunni Islam.

20 The word is derived from the French word *laïcité*.

21 Kemalism is broadly defined as consisting of six core principles: republicanism, nationalism, populism, statism, laicism (secularism) and revolutionism.

22 Enes Calli, 'The tragic life of Zeki Riza Sporel', The Kebab and Camel (n.d.). http://thekebabandcamel.com/the-tragic-life-of-zeki-riza-sporel/.

23 Alaa Al Aswany, 'Egypt's enduring passion for soccer', *New York Times*, 16 April 2014. https://www.nytimes.com/2014/04/17/opinion/egypts-enduring-passion-for-soccer.html. In his visits to Egypt around 450 BC, Herodotus noted young men playing with balls made of goatskin and straw.

24 'Who invented football?', Football Bible, 19 June 2014. https://www.football-bible.com/soccer-info/who-invented-football.html. Cuju emerged in ancient China and translates roughly as 'kick the ball with foot'. A form of football was played in Ancient Rome and at the first Olympics. Balls made of linen were found in Egyptian tombs dating to 2500 BC. Drawings suggest that ancient Egyptians played ball games during fertility feasts.

25 Irak, 'The transformation of football fandom', p. 18.

26 'Turkish President Recep Tayyip Erdogan attempts to re-brand himself as a nationalist by renaming football stadiums', thisisfootballislife, 4 June 2017. https://thisisfootballislife.wordpress.com/2017/06/04/turkish-president-recep-tayyip-erdogan-attempts-to-re-brand-himself-as-a-nationalist-by-renaming-football-stadiums/.

27 Interview with the author, 28 August 2016.

28 Irak, 'The transformation of football fandom', p. 43.

29 Ibid., p. 72.

30 Hakan Arslanbenzer, 'Adnan Menderes: May, the cruelest of months', *Daily Sabah*, 30 May 2014. http://www.dailysabah.com/life/2014/05/31/adnan-menderes-may-the-cruelest-of-months.

31 Calli, 'The tragic life of Zeki Riza Sporel'.

32 Charles King, *Midnight at the Pera Palace: The Birth of Modern Istanbul* (New York: Norton, 2014), p. 370.

33 Irak, 'The transformation of football fandom', p. 63. Fenerbahce were threatened with dissolution by some in the military after the 1960 coup – two of their presidents had been from the DP.

34 Interview with the author, 15 June 2016.

35 Emre Sarigul, 'Metin Oktay – "the uncrowned king" of Galatasaray & Turkish football', *Turkish Football*, 2 February 2017. http://turkish-football.com/metin-oktay-uncrowned-king-galatasaray-turkish-football/.

36 Ibid.

37 Emrah Guler, 'Love in between football matches', *Hurriyet Daily News*, 12 September 2016. http://www.hurriyetdailynews.com/love-in-between-football-matches.aspx?PageID=238&NID=103792&NewsCatID=381.

38 Interview with the author, 4 August 2016.

39 The 1954 squad was relatively cosmopolitan as it also featured a Jewish player, Rober Eryol, who played for Galatasaray.

40 'Lefter teybi kapattirdi ve "Bunlari yazma" dedi', *Milliyet*, 15 January 2012. http://www.milliyet.com.tr/lefter-teybi-kapattirdi-ve-bunlari-yazma-dedi/gundem/gundemyazardetay/15.01.2012/1489026/default.htm.

41 Although many Galatasaray fans live on that side, as many Fenerbahce fans live on the European side.

42 Interview with the author, 13 June 2016.

43 Souness had undergone heart surgery 18 months prior. See Joe Bernstein, 'Graeme Souness, Fenerbahce and the Galatasaray flag: remembering the Scot's most brazen act exactly 20 years on', *Mail Online*, 26 April 2016. http://www.dailymail.co.uk/sport/football/article-3559467/Graeme-Souness-Fenerbahce-Galatasaray-flag-Remembering-Scot-s-brazen-act-exactly-20-years-on.html.

44 Interview with the author, 6 June 2016.

45 Interview with the author, 10 September 2016.

46 This is quite an insulting slang term which literally means 'spade' but is quite derogatory, much like 'tool'.

47 Erbakan founded the 'Milli Gorus' – 'National Vision' – movement in 1969, which promoted political Islam and argued against secularism and 'Western' values. His many political parties largely espoused the views of this movement.

48 This sounds like a pretty turgid story. *Mas-Kom-Ya* stands for 'Mason-Communist-Jew'. Erdogan played a factory owner's son, who had left Turkey to study in Europe, where he struggled with his Islamic Turkish identity and values but rediscovered them on his return to Turkey, after finding that his father has been taken hostage by workers, whose leader was Jewish.

49 Nicolas Cheviron and Jean-François Pérouse, *Erdogan: nouveau père de la Turquie?* (Paris: François Bourin, 2016), p. 60.

50 Interview with the author, 6 June 2016.

51 Bursaspor won the Super League in 2010 and became the second Anatolian team, after Trabzonspor, to win the championship.

52 Interview with the author, 5 February 2016.

53 Interview with the author, 5 February 2016.

54 See Introduction.

55 Interview with the author, 6 June 2016.

56 Turkish sausage.

57 Interview with the author, 5 July 2017.

58 Interview with the author, 10 September 2016.

59 Tanil Bora, 'Football and its audience: staging spontaneous nationalism', in Stefanos Yerasimos, Gunter Seufert, and Karin Vorhoff (eds), *Civil Society in the Grip of Nationalism: Studies on Political Culture in Contemporary Turkey* (Würzburg: Ergon, 2000).

60 Interview with the author, 6 February 2016.

61 Interview with the author, 5 February 2016.

62 Interview with author, 6 February 2016.

63 Radikal members interviewed by the author on 6 February 2016.

64 Galatasaray play in red and yellow.

65 Interview with the author, 4 August 2016.

66 Turkish clubs can be very thoughtful towards their foreign opponents. When playing a Champions League match against Rangers in Glasgow, Bursaspor announced they would change their green and white strip, in order to avoid upsetting their hosts by reminding them of their Old Firm rivals, Celtic. See Anthony Haggerty, 'We won't wear hoops to avoid winding up Rangers supporters, insist Bursaspor stars', *Daily Record*, 29 September 2010. http://www.dailyrecord.co.uk/sport/football/we-wont-wear-hoops-to-avoid-winding-1071272.

67 Anfield is home to Liverpool – Manchester United's hated rivals.

68 Rob Smyth, 'Not so forgotten story: Manchester United v Galatasaray, 1993', *Guardian*, 19 September 2012. https://www.theguardian.com/sport/blog/2012/sep/19/forgotten-story-manchester-united-galatasaray.

69 Bora, 'Football and its audience'.

70 Smyth, 'Not so forgotten story'.

71 Bora, 'Football and its audience'.

72 Paul Stokes, 'Turk jailed for killing Leeds fans', *Telegraph*, 2 May 2002. http://www.telegraph.co.uk/news/worldnews/europe/turkey/1392950/Turk-jailed-for-killing-Leeds-fans.html.

73 I have been asked by several Turkish people to explain this behaviour and I struggle to come up with a satisfactory answer, beyond that it is some people's idea of obnoxious, drunken fun.

74 The Turkish government did everything possible to support Galatasaray in its cup run – postponing league matches before European games, and providing private planes and financial support. A third of Turkey's parliament went to Copenhagen to watch the final.

75 Cem Emrence, 'Playing with global city: the rise and fall of a Turkish soccer team', *Journal of Popular Culture*, 40:4 (August 2007), pp. 630–42.

76 Simon Waldman and Emre Caliskan, *The 'New Turkey' and Its Discontents* (London: Hurst & Co., 2016), p. 24.

77 Soner Cagaptay, *The Rise of Turkey* (Lincoln, NE: Potomac Books, 2014), p. 129. Since 2005 dozens more chapters have been added.

78 Bora, 'Football and its audience'.

79 Orwell held a lofty disdain for football – the full quote reads: 'Serious sport has nothing to do with fair play. It is bound up with hatred, jealousy, boastfulness, disregard of all rules and sadistic pleasure in witnessing violence: in other words it is war minus the shooting.' See George Orwell, 'The sporting spirit', *Tribune*, December 1945. Available online at http://www.orwell.ru/library/articles/spirit/english/e_spirit.

80 Gabriel Kuhn, *Soccer vs. the State* (Oakland, CA: PM Press, 2011), p. 51.

81 Bursa was the first capital of the Ottoman Empire. The tomb of Osman Gazi, the father and founder of the Ottoman dynasty, lies in the city. However, before becoming the Ottoman capital, Bursa had been under Byzantine rule for almost 1,000 years. Before that, the settlement had been Roman and Greek.

82 Interview with the author, 21 June 2016.

83 Interview with the author, 21 June 2016.

84 Ibid.

85 Martyrdom is equally venerated in Ottoman and Turkish republican traditions.

86 Interview with the author, 21 June 2016.

87 Interview with the author, 1 June 2016.

88 'Andrea Pirlo'dan Fatih Terim icin sok yorum!', *Goal*, 19 June 2016. http://www.goal.com/tr/news/454/turkiye-haberleri/2016/06/19/24791172/andrea-pirlodan-fatih-terim-icin-sok-yorum.

89 Pinar Tremblay, 'Why some Turks no longer rally behind their national soccer team', *Al-Monitor*, 16 October 2016. http://www.al-monitor.com/pulse/originals/2016/10/turkey-violence-corruption-spread-to-soccer.html.

90 'Turkish football Best Mover of the Year', *Daily Sabah*, 3 December 2015. http://
www.dailysabah.com/football/2015/12/04/turkish-football-best-mover-of-the-year.
Turkey became FIFA's best 'mover' in 2015, rising from 37th to 21st in the world
rankings.

91 Hakan Bas, 'Turkish coach improves his world record', *Daily Sabah*, 24 December
2016. http://www.dailysabah.com/football/2015/12/25/turkish-coach-improves-
his-world-record.

92 Interview with the author, 8 June 2016.

93 Earlier in 2016/17 he was sacked just six days into his coaching job at Genclerbirligi
– although it was widely acknowledged that Genclerbirligi's octogenarian president Ilhan
Cavcav's eccentricities were probably to blame. Cavcav sacked more than 50 coaches
during his 30-year presidency, including six in 2015/16.

94 'Antalyaspor wins at last', *Hurriyet Daily News*, 18 September 2006. http://www.
hurriyetdailynews.com/antalyaspor-wins-at-last.aspx?pageID=438&n=antalyaspor-
wins-at-last-2006-09-18.

95 Interview with the author, 8 June 2016.

96 There is a common saying in Turkey, 'The Turk has no friend but the Turk,' and
Ataturk's proverb 'How happy is the one who says "I am a Turk"' is sometimes turned
into a football chant.

97 Halil Karaveli, 'Turkey the sentinel – with a license for authoritarian rule', *Turkey
Analyst*, 7 December 2015. http://turkeyanalyst.org/publications/turkey-analyst-
articles/item/486-turkey-the-sentinel-with-a-license-for-authoritarian-rule.html.

98 The AKP emblem does not feature the Turkish flag or colours; rather it is a light bulb,
evoking energy, industry and a religious connotation of light.

99 The AKP is certainly Islamic, but not always Islamist. While the majority of Turks
practise religion, the vast majority are opposed to sharia law, and Erdogan's moves are
broadly in line with this mainstream thinking. Who is a Kemalist and who is an Islamist is
often not clear-cut: one survey found that 40 per cent of young AKP supporters defined
themselves as Kemalist, while a substantial number of CHP supporters put their Muslim
identity first, over Turkish identity. See Jenny White, *Muslim Nationalism and the New
Turks* (Princeton: Princeton University Press, 2014), p. 65.

100 Interview with the author, 10 September 2016.

101 'God / In the name of God / God is great'.

102 'Turkish fans boo moment of silence for victims of Paris attacks', *Hurriyet Daily News*,
18 November 2015. http://www.hurriyetdailynews.com/turkish-fans-boo-moment-of-
silence-for-victims-of-paris-attacks.aspx?pageID=238&nID=91320&NewsCatID=341.
'We're staging a moment of silence for people that have died. Can't we be patient for
one minute? When we go abroad, we're not able to explain this,' said Fatih Terim after
the match. 'It doesn't reflect well on us at all.'

103 Many of the fans in Basaksehir are conservative and nationalist. The club gives out
cheap and free tickets to some of these fans and is linked directly with the AKP.

104 Tom Sheen, 'Turkish fans boo minute's silence for Paris attack victims – but it wasn't
a mark of disrespect, claim social media commentators', *Independent*, 18 November
2015. http://www.independent.co.uk/news/world/europe/turkey-fans-boo-minutes-
silence-for-paris-victims-but-it-was-not-a-mark-of-disrespect-claim-a6738741.html.

105 Conversation with the author, 13 April 2016.

106 Raziye Akkoc, 'Turkey's most powerful president since Ataturk: a profile of
Recep Tayyip Erdogan', *Telegraph*, 20 April 2015. http://www.telegraph.co.uk/news/

worldnews/europe/turkey/11548369/Turkeys-most-powerful-president-since-Ataturk-A-profile-of-Recep-Tayyip-Erdogan.html.

107 It wasn't until the constitution could be amended in 2003, to allow convicts to run for office, that Erdogan became prime minister. He has not acknowledged the irony in the prosecution of numerous artists and writers under his rule..

108 Waldman and Caliskan, *The 'New Turkey' and Its Discontents.*

109 Esra Ozyurek, *Nostalgia for the Modern: State Secularism and Everyday Politics in Turkey* (Durham, NC: Duke University Press, 2006).

110 Interview with the author, 6 June 2016.

111 Isaac Chotiner, 'How Turkey came to this', *Slate,* 15 July 2016. http://www.slate.com/articles/news_and_politics/interrogation/2016/07/why_turkey_s_latest_attempted_coup_was_different.html. If secularism is understood as the separation of religion and state, then Turkey has never been secular. Kemalist *laiklik* reforms asserted state control over religion through the creation of the Diyanet – the Religious Affairs Directorate – and prioritised Sunni Islam identity and heritage as part of its Turkish nationalism, while restricting public expressions of its beliefs and practices. Under Erdogan, the powers of the Diyanet expanded hugely and expressions of religion became ever more public.

112 Interview with the author, 6 June 2016.

113 The movement has no official name – it is often referred to as the Gulen movement and its followers as Gulenists, or as the *Cemaat,* or as the *Cemia,* or – as Gulen himself refers to it – as the *Hizmet* – 'Service'.

114 Gulen is a globalist but also espouses a form of Turkish nationalism that is seen as able to lead the Muslim world.

115 Halil Karaveli, 'Turkey's journey from secularism to Islamization: a capitalist story', *Turkey Analyst,* 13 May 2016. https://www.turkeyanalyst.org/publications/turkey-analyst-articles/item/542-turkey%E2%80%99s-journey-from-secularism-to-islamization-a-capitalist-story.html.

116 Claire Berlinski, 'Who is Fethullah Gulen?', *City Journal,* Autumn 2012. http://www.city-journal.org/html/who-fethullah-gulen-13504.html.

117 This is a supposed network within the military, intelligence services, judiciary and organised crime.

118 James M. Dorsey, *The Turbulent World of Middle East Soccer* (London: Hurst & Company, 2016), p. 145.

119 Interview with the author, 6 June 2016.

120 Gulen opposed Erdogan's peace negotiations with the PKK, and did not share Erdogan's tough stance towards Israel following the attack on the Mavi Marmara, or Erdogan's eventual antipathy towards Syrian dictator Bashar al-Assad.

121 Berivan Orucoglu, 'Why Turkey's mother of all corruption scandals refuses to go away', *Foreign Policy,* 6 January 2015. http://foreignpolicy.com/2015/01/06/why-turkeys-mother-of-all-corruption-scandals-refuses-to-go-away/.

122 'Ex-footballer Hakan Sukur resigns from ruling AKP', *Hurriyet Daily News,* 16 December 2013. http://www.hurriyetdailynews.com/hakan-sukur-resigns-from-ruling-akp.aspx?pageID=238&nID=59696&NewsCatID=338. 'I have known and loved the *Hizmet* [Gulenist] movement and *Hocaefendi* [Gulen] for more than 20 years. Treating these sincere people, who supported the government on every issue that they thought was for the good of the people [...] as if they are enemies, is nothing but unfaithfulness,' read Sukur's statement.

123 'A humbling few days for former Turkish soccer great Hakan Sukur may portend further moves by the Turkish government', thisisfootballislife, 15 April 2014. https://thisisfootballislife.wordpress.com/2014/04/15/a-humbling-few-days-for-former-turkish-soccer-great-hakan-sukur-may-portend-further-moves-by-the-turkish-government/.

124 John Konuk Blasing, 'Turkish PM fires another salvo at Hakan Sukur on the campaign trail', thisisfootballislife, 22 July 2014. https://thisisfootballislife.wordpress.com/2014/07/22/turkish-pm-fires-another-salvo-at-hakan-sukur-on-the-campaign-trail/.

125 Ibid.

126 'Former Turkish football star charged with insulting President Erdogan', *Guardian*, 24 February 2016. https://www.theguardian.com/world/2016/feb/24/turkish-football-charged-insulting-president-erdogan-hakan-sukur.

127 By March 2016 there had reportedly been nearly 2,000 cases of 'insulting the president' prosecuted by the Justice Ministry since Erdogan assumed office in 2014. See Kareem Shaheen, 'Turkish journalists accuse Erdogan of media witch-hunt', *Guardian*, 2 May, 2016. https://www.theguardian.com/world/2016/may/02/turkish-journalists-accuse-erdogan-of-media-witch-hunt. Onur Erem, a journalist at the leftist newspaper *Birgun*, was worried because he hadn't been sued by Erdogan. Then he wrote a piece about search engines, in which Erdogan's name was accompanied by autosuggest terms such as 'thief' and 'murderer'; it brought a charge and a weird sort of relief. 'As a journalist, if you don't get accused of insulting Erdogan, you are not doing your job!' he told me. Erem was soon charged again, this time for an interview with the academic Tariq Ali. Erem faces five years in jail if convicted.

128 Pinar Tremblay, 'How Erdogan used the power of the mosques against coup attempt', *Al-Monitor*, 25 July 2016. http://www.al-monitor.com/pulse/originals/2016/07/turkey-coup-attempt-erdogan-mosques.html. The government sent messages to imams to broadcast the sala prayer, traditionally recited for funerals, but also recited under the Ottoman Empire during times of war.

129 Text messages from the president encouraged people to keep taking to the streets to defend 'democracy'.

130 Metin Gurcan, 'What went wrong with Turkey's WhatsApp coup', *Al-Monitor*, 19 July 2016. http://www.al-monitor.com/pulse/originals/2016/07/turkey-coup-attempt-basic-cause-was-premature-birth.html. The planned coup may have been hastily implemented: brought forward before an expected reshuffle of military personnel in August which would finally deal with many Gulen partisans, and then brought forward again several hours on Friday, 15 July after suspicious movements of military units were detected.

131 There are still questions regarding the extent of Gulenist and Kemalist involvement in the uprising, and to what extent Gulen is really in charge of his 'movement'.

132 Andrew Finkel, 'Turkey was already undergoing a slow-motion coup – by Erdogan, not the army', *Guardian*, 16 July, 2016. https://www.theguardian.com/commentisfree/2016/jul/16/turkey-coup-army-erdogan.

133 Mark Lowen, 'Turkey torture claims in wake of failed coup', BBC, 28 November 2016. http://www.bbc.com/news/world-europe-38123926.

134 Alison Flood, 'Free speech groups condemn Turkey's closure of 29 publishers after failed coup', *Guardian*, 3 August 2016. https://www.theguardian.com/books/2016/aug/03/free-speech-groups-condemn-turkeys-closure-of-29-publishers-after-failed-coup. Alongside newspapers, magazines, television channels and news agencies, the government closed at least 29 publishing outlets under the state-of-emergency law.

135 'The purge continues: Amnesty responds to closure of Turkish NGOs', Amnesty International, 22 November 2016. https://humanrightsturkey.org/2016/11/22/the-purge-continues-amnesty-responds-to-closure-of-turkish-ngos/.

136 Conversation with the author, 2 October 2016.

137 Interview with the author, 5 July 2017.

138 More than 120 media workers are in Turkish jails in connection with their work – a third of all jailed journalists worldwide – and 156 media outlets have been closed since the failed coup. See 'Turkey: journalism is not a crime', Amnesty International, 3 May 2017. https://www.amnesty.org/en/latest/campaigns/2017/02/free-turkey-media/.

139 Interview with the author, 28 August 2016.

140 Less than a month previously, Amnesty International's Turkey chair Taner Kilic had also been arrested and remanded in prison. See 'Director of Amnesty International Turkey must be released from incommunicado detention', Amnesty International, 6 July 2017. https://www.amnesty.org/en/press-releases/2017/07/director-of-amnesty-international-turkey-must-be-released-from-incommunicado-detention/.

141 Christopher de Bellaigue, 'Turkey chooses Erdogan', *New York Review of Books*, 6 August 2016. http://www.nybooks.com/daily/2016/08/06/turkey-chooses-erdogan/. 'The combination of nationalism and religiosity is like nothing I have seen in twenty years of following Turkish politics,' wrote Christopher de Bellaigue.

142 There are significant misgivings among MHP supporters and politicians about this approach. The government helped Bahceli shut down a conference held by leadership dissenters in the party, and a popular challenger to Bahceli's rule, Meral Aksener, was subsequently expelled from the MHP.

143 Kaya Genc, 'Mark Rothko, the flag and Turkey's red future', *National*, 9 August 2016. http://www.thenational.ae/opinion/comment/mark-rothko-the-flag-and-turkeys-red-future.

144 'CHP needs to be careful regarding statements on coup attempt: Turkish PM', *Hurriyet Daily News*, 11 October 2016. http://www.hurriyetdailynews.com/chp-needs-to-be-careful-regarding-statements-on-coup-attempt-turkish-pm-.aspx?pageID=238&nid=104849.

145 Interview with the author, 2 September 2016.

146 See Chapter 2 for more on Gokcek and his attempts to use football clubs in Ankara as a political tool.

147 'Ankara mayor suggests Gulen uses genies to "enslave people"', *Hurriyet Daily News*, 24 July 2016. http://www.hurriyetdailynews.com/ankara-mayor-suggests-gulen-uses-genies-to-enslave-people.aspx?PageID=238&NID=102005&NewsCatID=341.

148 'Turkish mayor suggests Gulen plotting earthquake to harm economy', Reuters, 7 February 2017. http://af.reuters.com/article/worldNews/idAFKBN15M1K6?sp=true.

149 James M. Dorsey, 'Erdogan vs Gulen: power struggle comes full circle in Turkish soccer', The Turbulent World of Middle East Soccer, 3 August 2016. https://mideastsoccer.blogspot.com.tr/2016/08/erdogan-vs-gulen-power-struggle-comes.html.

150 'Galatasaray expels ex-players Hakan Sukur, Arif Erdem after government warning', *Hurriyet Daily News*, 26 March 2017. http://www.hurriyetdailynews.com/galatasaray-expels-ex-players-hakan-sukur-arif-erdem-after-government-warning.aspx?PageID=238&NID=111252&NewsCatID=361.

151 'Fenerbahce chairman fires Gulen-link salvos at rival Galatasaray, football authority', *Hurriyet Daily News*, 25 August 2016. http://www.hurriyetdailynews.com/fenerbahce-chairman-fires-gulen-link-salvos-at-rival-galatasaray-football-authority.aspx?pageID=238&nID=103218&NewsCatID=509.

152 William Armstrong, 'Turkey's brain drain: purges and fear are driving Turkish scholars out of the country', War on the Rocks, 22 September 2016. http://warontherocks. com/2016/09/turkeys-brain-drain-purges-and-fear-are-driving-turkish-scholars-out-of-the-country/.

153 Waldman and Caliskan, The 'New Turkey' and Its Discontents, p. 4.

154 https://twitter.com/MtnOzd/status/807684351798419456.

155 Simon Waldman, 'A sombre mood envelops Turkey after football stadium bombing', National, 13 December 2016. https://www.thenational.ae/opinion/a-sombre-mood-envelops-turkey-after-football-stadium-bombing-1.204247.

156 At home, Erdogan's father tells him: 'A man was murdered today, Tayyip. A man who would have died for his country.'

157 James M. Dorsey, 'Mixing politics and sports: Turkish soccer campaigns for President Erdogan', Huffington Post, 28 March 2017. http://www.huffingtonpost.com/entry/mixing-politics-and-sports-turkish-soccer-campaigns_us_58da140fe4b0e6062d9230af.

158 Ibid.

159 'Football: Turkey's Erdogan wins Arda Turan backing for campaign', World Soccer Talk, 25 January 2017. https://worldsoccertalk.com/2017/01/25/football-turkeys-erdogan-wins-arda-turan-backing-for-campaign/.

160 'Turkey takes Erdogan referendum battle to social media', Deutsche Welle, 28 January 2017. http://www.dw.com/en/turkey-takes-erdogan-referendum-battle-to-social-media/a-37316905.

161 'Turkey's Erdogan could govern until 2029 under plans to change constitution', Reuters, 16 November 2016. http://www.reuters.com/article/us-turkey-politics-idUSKBN13B1BK.

162 'In winning referendum, Erdogan loses cities', EurasiaNet, 26 April 2017. http://www.eurasianet.org/node/83361.

163 William Armstrong, 'What a new film reveals about Turkey and its brawl with Europe', War on the Rocks, 14 March 2017. https://warontherocks.com/2017/03/what-a-new-film-reveals-about-turkey-and-its-brawl-with-europe/.

164 'Ryan Gingeras on Turkey's "deep state of crisis"', Turkey Book Talk, 19 May 2017. https://armstrongwilliam.wordpress.com/2017/05/19/ryan-gingeras-on-turkeys-deep-state-of-crisis/.

165 'In film and life, "Chief" Erdogan looms large ahead of Turkish referendum', Reuters, 2 March 2017. http://www.reuters.com/article/us-turkey-referendum-erdogan-film-idUSKBN1692B3.

166 'Ryan Gingeras on Turkey's "deep state of crisis"'.

167 Ibid.

168 Dorsey, The Turbulent World of Middle East Soccer, p. 5.

169 Interview with the author, 15 February 2015.

170 Interview with the author, 15 February 2015.

171 Interview with the author, 15 February 2015.

2   The Battle for Ankara

1 Not his real name. Conversation with the author, 20 September 2015.

2 Chalmers is otherwise known as Eski Kanka – a key contributor to 'The Round Ball in Ankara' blog. 'Eski' means old in Turkish, while 'Kanka' means 'blood brother'. A community of expats and locals has grown around the blog and they attend matches

together. They include: 'Cider Kanka', 'Maniac Kanka', 'Oz Kanka', 'Posh Kanka', 'Battle Damaged Kanka' and 'Scouse Kanka', among others.

3 Conversation with the author, 19 September 2015.

4 Daghan Irak, 'The transformation of football fandom since the 1970s', MA thesis, Bogazici University, 2010. http://www.daghanirak.com/tezprefinal.pdf.

5 'No love lost as Ankaragucu's young guns fall short', Hurriyet Daily News, 29 February 2012. http://www.hurriyetdailynews.com/no-love-lost-as-ankaragucus-young-guns-fall-short-.aspx?pageID=238&nID=14869&NewsCatID=444.

6 It's now also the name of a stand in their stadium where they congregate.

7 Melih Gokcek might be gobby when on Twitter and friendly media, but he clams up when given the chance to talk to someone he can't control. He declined to be interviewed.

8 The park has reputedly cost the municipality at least 8.6 million TL. Emiko Jozuka, 'Giant robot and dinosaur statues are taking over Turkey's capital', Vice, 8 May 2015. http://motherboard.vice.com/read/giant-robot-and-dinosaur-statues-are-taking-over-turkeys-capital.

9 The choice of robots remains inexplicable. Turkey does not have any robot-manufacturing industries.

10 'Gokcek robotu savundu', Hurriyet, 9 April 2015. http://www.hurriyet.com.tr/gokcek-robotu-savundu-28682272.

11 'Gokcek dynasty completes Ankaragucu takeover', Hurriyet Daily News, 30 August 2009. http://www.hurriyetdailynews.com/gokcek-dynasty-completes-ankaragucu-takeover.aspx?pageID=438&n=0830135819216-2009-08-30.

12 'Food and fuel trump graft for Turkey's local elections', Reuters, 21 March 2016. http://www.reuters.com/article/us-turkey-elections-ankara-idUSBREA2K07V20140321.

13 By 2001, 22 per cent of professional teams had municipal mayors in top administrative positions. See Cem Emrence, 'From elite circles to power networks: Turkish soccer clubs in a global age', Soccer and Society, 11:3 (November 2015), pp. 242–52.

14 Interview with the author, 10 February 2015.

15 See Chapter 3 for more on the toxic indebtedness that is crippling Turkish football.

16 Interview with the author, 21 September 2015.

17 'Gokcek dynasty completes Ankaragucu takeover'.

18 Ibid.

19 Interview with the author, 30 April 2016.

20 At the end of October 2017, one Turkish lira was worth $0.26.

21 'Ankaragucu nasil bu hale geldi?', SoL, 16 January 2012. http://haber.sol.org.tr/spor/ankaragucu-nasil-bu-hale-geldi-haberi-50542.

22 https://www.youtube.com/watch?v=Qgkchk_-HJs.

23 Benji Lanyado 'Darius Vassell: the blogging footballer', Guardian, 6 January 2010. https://www.theguardian.com/football/2010/jan/06/footballer-darius-vassell-turkey-blog.

24 Interview with the author, 30 April 2016.

25 Conversation with the author, 20 September 2015.

26 Interview with the author, 16 November 2015.

27 Timur was a Turco-Mongol conqueror.

28 'Timur's elephants', The Round Ball in Ankara, 10 August 2015. http://ankarafootball.blogspot.com.tr/2015/08/timurs-elephants.html.

29 'Abbas welcomed at Turkish presidential palace by Erdogan – and 16 warriors', Guardian, 12 January 2015. https://www.theguardian.com/world/2015/jan/12/abbas-erdogan-16-warriors-turkish-presidential-palace.

30 I know this because, although I have yet to use the palace's facilities, Erdogan will sue anyone who claims it has gold toilet seats.

31 None of Osmanlispor's fan groups would talk to me – they seemed nervous of repercussions.

32 Interview with the author, 30 April 2016.

33 John Konuk Blasing, 'The games behind the game: the process of democratic deepening and identity formation in Turkey as seen through football clubs', MA thesis, University of Texas at Austin, 2011. https://repositories.lib.utexas.edu/handle/2152/ETD-UT-2011-05-3490.

34 Conversation with the author, 19 September 2015.

35 'Ahmet Gokcek pays 22 million tax bill!', The Round Ball in Ankara, 28 December 2014. http://ankarafootball.blogspot.qa/2014/12/ahmet-gokcek-pays-22-million-tax-bill.html.

36 Interview with the author, 25 April 2016.

37 'From football to industrial football to political football: the slow death of Ankara's Sekerspor', thisisfootballislife, 14 July 2015. https://thisisfootballislife.wordpress.com/2015/07/14/from-football-to-industrial-football-to-political-football-the-slow-death-of-ankaras-sekerspor/.

38 'Ankaragucu 0–1 Tepecikspor', The Round Ball in Ankara, 7 February 2016. http://ankarafootball.blogspot.com.tr/2016/02/ankaragucu-0-1-tepecikspor.html?spref=fb.

39 Conversations with the author, 24 April 2016.

40 Conversation with the author, 24 April 2016.

41 Interview with the author, 25 April 2016.

42 Interview with the author, 26 April 2016.

43 'Ankara'ya yeni stat mujdesi', Haberturk, 2 May 2016. http://www.haberturk.com/spor/futbol/haber/1233914-ankaraya-yeni-stat-mujdesi.

44 In 2017 the 19 Mayis Stadium was scheduled for demolition and a new stadium for Ankaragucu and Genclerbirligi was promised.

45 Conversation with the author, 20 September 2015.

3   'We are watching a puppet show'

1 'CAS 2013/A/3256 Fenerbahce Spor Kulubu v. UEFA', Court of Arbitration for Sport (CAS), 11 April 2014, p. 77, paragraph 334. CAS concluded that the term 'plowing the fields' was 'intended cryptically and referred to illegal conduct' (p. 77, paragraph 337). CAS concluded that – through the actions of at least one of its officials – Fenerbahce attempted to fix their match on 7 March 2011 with Genclerbirligi. http://www.tas-cas.org/fileadmin/user_upload/Award_3256_FINAL_internet.pdf.

2 'Amigo' is a name given to supporters who lead chants.

3 Interview with the author, 19 April 2016.

4 Interview with the author, 28 October 2016.

5 Ender Kuyumcu, 'Believe nothing in Turkish football – it is rotten to the core and nobody will act', Sporting Intelligence, 18 March 2014. http://www.sportingintelligence.com/2014/03/18/believe-nothing-in-turkish-football-it-is-rotten-to-the-core-and-nobody-will-act-170301/.

6 Now known as Istanbul Basaksehir FK.

7 Jamie Rainbow, 'Background to the match-rigging scandal that has rocked Turkey', World Soccer, 19 August 2011. http://www.worldsoccer.com/blogs/turkey-match-fixing-scandal-revealed-330963.

8 Yagmur Nuhrat, 'Fair enough? Negotiating ethics in Turkish football', MA thesis, Brown University, 2013. https://repository.library.brown.edu/studio/item/bdr:320642/PDF/.

9 Ibid.

10 Interview with the author, 28 October 2016.

11 In George Orwell's *Nineteen Eighty-Four*, Winston Smith is tortured into accepting that 2 + 2 = 5, or whatever the Party wants it to be. In Turkey, it's achieved by bewilderment.

12 When he became president, Fenerbahce had won more titles than Galatasaray – now they have won fewer. He gained some respect for rebuilding the stadium and for his success in basketball and volleyball. But it has hardly been a golden era for the football team.

13 Elections mask a democratic deficit, as elites within clubs jealously prevent too many fans from becoming members – demanding high entrance fees and requiring approval from the board.

14 'CAS 2013/A/3256 Fenerbahce Spor Kulubu v. UEFA', Court of Arbitration for Sport (CAS), 11 April 2014, pp. 103–4, paragraph 469. CAS ruled that it was 'comfortably satisfied' that the conversation above referred to four Ankaragucu players and that the reference to 'wheat' was coded language. CAS concluded that Fenerbahce officials attempted to fix the match between Fenerbahce and Ankaragucu that took place on 15 May 2011. http://www.tas-cas.org/fileadmin/user_upload/Award_3256_FINAL_internet.pdf.

15 This investigation likely began after a German betting and match-fixing probe in 2009 implicated some Turkish figures.

16 It was prohibited under Turkish Football Federation sporting regulations. Law '6222' against violence in sports was many years in the making, but match-fixing offences were only added relatively late to the legislation as it was going through parliament, with severe punishments for those found guilty.

17 Gulen has been quoted as saying in a phone call to Yildirim: 'There is nothing bad in my heart against you. I am not involved in this. There might be people who did wrong against you but I am not aware of this if it was my people.' James M. Dorsey, *The Turbulent World of Middle East Soccer* (London: Hurst & Company, 2016), p. 146.

18 Of the 93 people tried, 48 were convicted, including several Fenerbahce officials, and officials from Besiktas, Eskisehirspor, Sivasspor, Giresunspor and Diyarbakirspor. 'Turkish football guilty of match-fixing, court rules', *Hurriyet Daily News*, 3 July 2012. http://www.hurriyetdailynews.com/turkish-football-guilty-of-match-fixing-courtrules.aspx?pageID=238&nID=24597&NewsCatID=362.

19 'Turkish PM pays remarkable visit to Trabzonspor', *Hurriyet Daily News*, 28 August 2013. http://www.hurriyetdailynews.com/Default.aspx?pageID=238&nID=53356&NewsCatID=362.

20 Aydinlar had links to Fenerbahce, while Gumusdag was president of Istanbul Buyuksehir Belediyespor, who had also been implicated in the scandal.

21 However, their statements have been confused, as if their limbs were being pulled in different directions. They stated that 'although there were efforts to manipulate games, this was not reflected on the pitch.' (See 'Turkish PM pays remarkable visit to Trabzonspor'.) This meant that, while the federation found that some officials had attempted to fix matches, it ruled that board members were unaware of these attempts – making the club as an entity not guilty.

22 Berivan Orucoglu, 'Why Turkey's mother of all corruption scandals refuses to go away', *Foreign Policy*, 6 January 2015. http://foreignpolicy.com/2015/01/06/why-turkeys-mother-of-all-corruption-scandals-refuses-to-go-away/.

23 Saracoglu, an ex-CHP prime minister, was Fenerbahce president from 1934 to 1950.

24 'CAS 2013/A/3256 Fenerbahce Spor Kulubu v. UEFA', Court of Arbitration for Sport (CAS), 11 April 2014. http://www.tas-cas.org/fileadmin/user_upload/Award_3256_FINAL_internet.pdf.

25 'CAS 2015/A/4345 Trabzonspor Sportif Yatirim A.S. v. UEFA' and 'CAS 2015/A/4347 Fenerbahce SK v. Trabzonspor A.S. and UEFA', Court of Arbitration for Sport (CAS), 13 April 2017. https://www.uefa.org/MultimediaFiles/Download/uefaorg/CASdecisions/02/47/24/42/2472442_DOWNLOAD.pdf.

26 'Fenerbahce'ye yeniden yargilama karari cikti!', *Milliyet*, 23 June 2014. http://www.milliyet.com.tr/fenerbahce-ye-yeniden-yargilama-fenerbahce-1901547-skorerhaber/. The new procedural amendments had been made under law no. 6526.

27 It is difficult to understand the legal reasoning behind this decision. Turkey's legal system is notoriously opaque. I spoke to several lawyers, but none of them could explain it in legal terms, and they said it was legally unprecedented.

28 'Yildirim'i duyan dilekce verdi', Al Jazeera Turk, 2 July 2014. http://www.aljazeera.com.tr/al-jazeera-ozel/yildirimi-duyan-dilekce-verdi. The retroactive use of the procedural law change in the match-fixing trial seems to have been a one-off. Several lawyers tried – unsuccessfully – to use the same procedural amendment to help their clients.

29 Interview with the author, 28 October 2016.

30 Interview with the author, 26 October 2016.

31 'CAS 2013/A/3256 Fenerbahce Spor Kulubu v. UEFA', Court of Arbitration for Sport (CAS), 11 April 2014, p. 114, paragraph 501. http://www.tas-cas.org/fileadmin/user_upload/Award_3256_FINAL_internet.pdf. They are talking ahead of Fenerbahce's final match of the season against Sivasspor on 22 May 2011 – CAS ruled that it was 'comfortably satisfied' that Fenerbahce officials tried to fix the match.

32 'Turkey: 38 arrested for "framing" Fenerbahce officials', Associated Press, 19 April 2016. http://bigstory.ap.org/article/f323f4db084a46089308d2f840902421/turkey-38-arrested-framing-fenerbahce-scandal.

33 Claire Berlinski, 'Who is Fethullah Gulen?', *City Journal*, Autumn 2012. http://www.city-journal.org/html/who-fethullah-gülen-13504.html.

34 Interview with the author, 10 September 2016.

35 Interview with the author, 2 September 2016.

36 Interview with the author, 18 October 2016.

37 Interview with the author, 9 August 2016.

38 Declan Hill, *The Insider's Guide to Match-Fixing* (Toronto: Anne McDermid & Associates, 2013).

39 'Match-fixing trial begins', *Hurriyet Daily News*, 20 July 2002. http://www.hurriyetdailynews.com/match-fixing-trial-begins.aspx?pageID=438&n=match-fixing-trial-begins-2002-07-20.

40 Irfan Demir and Kutluer Karademir, 'Catching sports cheaters: an example of successful police operations', in M. R. Haberfeld and Dale Sheehan, *Match-Fixing in International Sports* (Basel: Springer International Publishing, 2013), p. 338.

41 'Government to join match-fixing probe', *Hurriyet Daily News*, 25 July 2006. http://www.hurriyetdailynews.com/government-to-join-match-fixing-probe.aspx?pageID=438&n=government-to-join-match-fixing-probe-2006-07-25.

42 'Police to probe match-fixing allegations during Ulusoy era', *Hurriyet Daily News*, 20 March 2008. http://www.hurriyetdailynews.com/police-to-probe-match-fixing-

allegations-during-ulusoy-era.aspx?pageID=438&n=police-to-probe-match-fixing-allegations-during-ulusoy-era-2008-03-20.
43 'Match-fixing inquiry probes 200 European football games', BBC, 20 November 2009. http://news.bbc.co.uk/1/hi/world/europe/8370748.stm.
44 'Turkish stars held in Turkish match-fixing probe', CNN, 25 March 2010. http://edition.cnn.com/2010/SPORT/football/03/25/football.turkey.match.fixing/index.html.
45 Demir and Karademir, 'Catching sports cheaters', p. 334.
46 Hill, *The Insider's Guide to Match-Fixing*.
47 'Probe launched into mafia leader's "bloodbath" threats against academics', *Hurriyet Daily News*, 14 January 2016. http://www.hurriyetdailynews.com/probe-launched-into-mafia-leaders-bloodbath-threats-against-academics-.aspx?pageID=238&nID=93884&NewsCatID=509. In January 2016, Peker – now out of prison – threatened academics who had signed a petition calling for peace with the PKK: 'We will spill your blood in streams and we will shower in your blood.'
48 Demir and Karademir, 'Catching sports cheaters', p. 338.
49 'Sedat Peker yeniden yargilaniyor', *Sabah*, 22 September 2008. http://arsiv.sabah.com.tr/2008/09/22//haber,DE738449464A4A30B0CA36A85B5EE9BF.html.
50 'Match fix indictment alleges mafia was a player in football', *Hurriyet Daily News*, 10 December 2011. http://www.hurriyetdailynews.com/match-fix-indictment-alleges-mafia-was-a-player-in-football.aspx?pageID=238&nID=8874&NewsCatID=362.
51 Demir and Karademir, 'Catching sports cheaters', p. 338.
52 A Trabzonspor player, Gokdeniz Karadeniz, was found guilty of fixing matches in 2005. See 'Gokdeniz ban after betting scandal', UEFA, 30 September 2005. http://www.uefa.com/memberassociations/news/newsid=347884.html.
53 Ryan Gingeras, *Heroin, Organized Crime, and the Making of Modern Turkey* (Oxford: Oxford University Press), p. 253.
54 Trabzonspor's president, Ibrahim Haciosmanoglu, is a classic example: he totally disbelieves the evidence in the December 2013 corruption allegations against the government, but totally believes in the 2011 match-fixing evidence.
55 Interview with the author, 12 October 2016.
56 Interview with the author, 23 September 2016.
57 Journalist and commentator Ugur Turker says that controlling Galatasaray through Gulenist players is not plausible. 'If you can control Manchester United with Wayne Rooney, yes it's possible to control Galatasaray with Hakan Sukur,' he said dryly. To control a club, you would have to control the president and key members. Galatasaray remain staunch secularists. But he says it seems likely that players like Sukur could have been useful to the movement, influencing teammates and raising donations.
58 Interview with the author, 28 October 2016.
59 'CAS 2015/A/4343 Trabzonspor v TFF, UEFA and Fenerbahce', Court of Arbitration for Sport (CAS), 27 March 2017, p. 22, paragraph 109.
60 Hakan Bas, 'Aziz Yildirim: Fenerbahce lost $500M due to FETO plot', *Daily Sabah*, 25 August 2016. https://www.dailysabah.com/football/2016/08/26/aziz-yildirim-fenerbahce-lost-500m-due-to-feto-plot.
61 Conversation with the author, 3 July 2016.
62 Conversation with the author, 3 July 2016.
63 Conversation with the author, 3 July 2016.
64 Burcin was wearing a T-shirt with an image of Trabzonspor player Salih Dursun brandishing a red card at a referee. Dursun became a hero in Trabzon after a match in

February 2016 against Galatasaray, in which three of his teammates had been sent off. Dursun picked up the red card, dropped by the referee, and held it up to the official, and subsequently became the fourth Trabzonspor player to be sent off in that match.

65 Interview with the author, 9 June 2016.

66 Interview with the author, 21 June 2016.

67 These include matches between Besiktas and Bursaspor, and between Ankaragucu and Besiktas.

68 These numbers were dragged up by the high attendances of Fenerbahce and Galatasaray – when their attendances are removed, the 2011/12 average attendance was around 8,000. See 'Alarm bells ringing as football stadia attendance hit new low', *Hurriyet Daily News*, 27 December 2011. http://www.hurriyetdailynews.com/alarm-bells-ringing-as-football-stadia-attendance-hit-new-low.aspx?pageID=238&nID=10075&NewsCatID=362.

69 Interview with the author, 28 October 2016.

70 Interview with the author, 9 August 2016.

71 Interview with the author, 25 January 2015.

72 Conversation with the author, 2 November 2016.

73 'Super Lig'in rekorlari ve ilkleri', *Milliyet*, 28 August 2014. http://www.milliyet.com.tr/super-lig-in-rekorlari-ve-ilkleri---1932141-skorerhaber/.

74 Interview with the author, 4 December 2015.

75 'Cocuklarimin rizkini bile kulube veriyorum', *Milliyet*, 8 September 2013. http://www.milliyet.com.tr/-cocuklarimin-rizkini-bile-kulube/pazar/haberdetay/08.09.2013/1760390/default.htm.

76 While the 'Big Three' have bigger debts, Trabzonspor's debt-to-income ratio is much wider.

77 'Turkey's Trabzonspor lands blockbuster signing Oscar Cardozo', *Hurriyet Daily News*, 6 August 2014. http://www.hurriyetdailynews.com/turkeys-trabzonspor-lands-blockbuster-signing-oscar-cardozo-.aspx?pageID=238&nID=70046.

78 'Turkish giants pay high fees despite heavy debts', *Daily Sabah*, 25 August 2015. http://www.dailysabah.com/football/2014/08/25/turkish-giants-pay-high-fees-despite-heavy-debts.

79 According to financial figures provided by the club.

80 'Akbank named most valuable brand of Turkey', *Hurriyet Daily News*, 15 June 2015. http://www.hurriyetdailynews.com/akbank-named-most-valuable-brand-of-turkey-.aspx?pageID=238&nID=84005&NewsCatID=345.

81 Interview with the author, 6 December 2015. Attendances fell even further following the introduction of the controversial Passolig e-ticket system in April 2014.

82 John Konuk Blasing, 'Turkey's social malaise comes out on the pitch in Trabzon', thisisfootballislife, 13 March 2014. https://thisisfootballislife.wordpress.com/2014/03/13/turkeys-social-malaise-comes-out-on-the-pitch-in-trabzon/.

83 The season was suspended for a week. No one has yet been charged in connection with the incident. See John Konuk Blasing, 'Attack on Fenerbahce's team bus raises many questions: what is happening in Turkey?', thisisfootballislife, 7 April 2015. https://thisisfootballislife.wordpress.com/2015/04/07/attack-on-fenerbahces-team-bus-raises-many-questions-what-is-happening-in-turkey/.

84 'Complex hosting Turkish football club's new ground to be named after Erdogan', *Hurriyet Daily News*, 9 September 2014. http://www.hurriyetdailynews.com/complex-hosting-turkish-football-clubs-new-ground-to-be-named-after-erdogan.aspx?pageID=238&nID=71496&NewsCatID=362.

85 Maximilian Popp, 'America's dark view of Turkish premier Erdogan', *Spiegel Online*, 30 November 2010. http://www.spiegel.de/international/world/the-tribune-of-anatolia-america-s-dark-view-of-turkish-premier-erdogan-a-732084.html.

86 Conversation with the author, 5 December 2015.

87 John Konuk Blasing, 'Turkish Football Federation elections: Gaziantepspor vote to re-elect Yildirim Demiroren but might lose their youth team facilities to the government', thisisfootballislife, 29 June 2015. https://thisisfootballislife.wordpress.com/2015/06/29/turkish-football-federation-elections-gaziantepspor-vote-to-re-elect-yildirim-demiroren-but-might-lose-their-youth-team-facilities-to-the-government/.

88 'Turkey president intervenes after football boss takes referees hostage', *Guardian*, 30 October 2015. https://www.theguardian.com/world/2015/oct/30/turkey-president-erdogan-intervenes-football-boss-referees-hostage.

89 '"Sexist" Trabzonspor chairman suspended for "full-term pregnancy" after hostage scandal', *Hurriyet Daily News*, 4 November 2015. http://www.hurriyetdailynews.com/sexist-trabzonspor-chairman-suspended-for-full-term-pregnancy-after-hostage-scandal.aspx?pageID=238&nID=90715&NewsCatID=361.

90 Membership of at least two years is necessary to vote under the club's regulations.

91 'Medical Park'in sahibi Erdogan mi?', Haber 3, 27 March 2013. http://www.haber3.com/medical-parkin-sahibi-erdogan-mi-1867511h.htm.

92 Interview with the author, 6 December 2015.

93 Interview with the author, 3 December 2015.

94 'Haciosmanoglu'ndan yilda 167 milyon TL kazandiracak dev projeler', *Hurriyet*, 4 December 2015. http://www.hurriyet.com.tr/haciosmanoglundan-yilda-167-milyon-tl-kazandiracak-dev-projeler-40022731.

95 Figures provided by Futbol Ekonomi. http://www.futbolekonomi.com/.

96 Hakan Bas, 'Turkish football grows by 5 times in last 10 years', *Daily Sabah*, 14 October 2016. http://www.dailysabah.com/football/2016/10/15/turkish-football-grows-by-5-times-in-last-10-years.

97 Half of the most indebted clubs in the Stoxx European Football index are Turkish. 'Van Persie heightens stakes in Turkey's Champions League of debt', *Bloomberg*, 22 July 2015. http://www.bloomberg.com/news/articles/2015-07-21/van-persie-heightens-stakes-in-turkey-s-champions-league-of-debt.

98 Interview with the author, 23 January 2015.

99 'Turkish giants pay high fees despite heavy debts'.

100 Emerging, inflated football markets like China and Qatar may be a godsend to Turkey – new lucrative destinations to offload rickety stars.

101 Hakan Bas, 'Super League players oldest in Europe', *Daily Sabah*, 8 January 2016. http://www.dailysabah.com/football/2016/01/09/super-league-players-oldest-in-europe.

102 In 2016, the 18 Super Lig teams were $1.4bn in debt, with around half of this debt owed to banks. 'Debt-laden Turkish soccer clubs pay the price of ambition', Reuters, 3 February 2016. http://www.reuters.com/article/soccer-turkey-idUSL8N15H4SO.

103 Interview with the author, 10 February 2015.

104 'Lack of transparency drives Turkish football into the wall', *Hurriyet Daily News*, 28 January 2013. http://www.hurriyetdailynews.com/lack-of-transparency-drives-turkish-football-into-the-wall.aspx?pageID=238&nid=39934. See also Michael Long, 'Digiturk retains domestic rights to Turkey's Super Lig', *SportsPro*, 11 November 2014. http://www.sportspromedia.com/news/digiturk_retains_domestic_rights_to_turkeys_super_lig.

105 'Digiturk retains Turkish Super League TV rights with annual fee of $600M',

Daily Sabah, 21 November 2016. http://www.dailysabah.com/football/2016/11/21/digiturk-retains-turkish-super-league-tv-rights-with-annual-fee-of-600m (accessed 18 September 2017).

106 'Debt-laden Turkish soccer clubs pay the price of ambition'. See also Hakan Bas, 'Galatasaray's jaw-dropping spending spree', *Daily Sabah*, 26 January 2016. http://www.dailysabah.com/football/2016/01/27/galatasarays-jaw-dropping-spending-spree. Galatasaray's revenue is huge: they appeared in Deloitte's Money League of the top 20 earning European clubs three years in a row – the only club outside Europe's Big Five leagues to do so. But over the past three years they posted losses of €164 million. In the previous six seasons they had spent €150 million on 67 transfers – signing contracts worth €380 million – and sold just six players for €40 million over the same period.

107 See Chapter 4 for more detail – and how this relates to stadiums.

108 Interview with the author, 29 April 2016.

109 Interview with the author, 3 May 2016.

110 Interview with the author, 10 September 2016.

111 A few clubs are purely football clubs with no other sports branches, and a few are now private companies.

112 For example, in addition to football, Galatasaray Sports Club includes branches in basketball, wheelchair basketball, volleyball, handball, swimming, athletics, judo, waterpolo, equestrianism, motor sports, chess and bridge. Imagine Tottenham and Arsenal's rivalry also being fought out across cricket, rugby, sailing, croquet and poker, and you get some sense of the multiplier effect of rivalry in Turkish sport.

113 The 'Big Four' are among Turkey's top 100 most valuable brands. See 'Akbank named most valuable brand of Turkey'.

114 Interview with the author, 8 September 2016.

115 There are at least three other clubs in the top two tiers with this ownership model alongside Istanbul Basaksehir: Altinordu, Goztepe and Kasimpasaspor.

116 The Turkish Football Federation also believes the teams have to be transformed into firms – private or otherwise – but says that it needs the government to pass the necessary legislation.

117 By this the government seems to mean fourth-largest revenue. See 'Debt-laden Turkish soccer clubs pay the price of ambition'.

118 The combined debt of Besiktas, Fenerbahce, Galatasaray and Trabzonspor in February 2017 was 3.8bn TL, while their combined revenue was 1.1bn TL. 'Turkey's four big football teams' debt reaches peak record in nine months', *Hurriyet Daily News*, 11 June 2017. http://www.hurriyetdailynews.com/turkeys-four-big-football-teams-debts-reaches-peak-record-in-nine-months-.aspx?pageID=238&nID=114200&NewsCatID=361.

119 Interview with the author, 2 September 2016.

120 Some big, historic teams, such as Kocaelispor and Malatyaspor, have gone bankrupt and fallen down to the lower leagues.

121 Interview with the author, 23 January 2015.

122 Interview with the author, 10 February 2015.

123 Interview with the author, 9 August 2016.

4   Stadium Sagas

1 'Goodbye Izmir Alsancak Stadium: the past and present of a country as seen through the eyes of a football stadium', thisisfootballislife, 9 August 2015. https://thisisfootballislife.

com/2015/08/09/goodbye-izmir-alsancak-stadium-the-past-and-present-of-a-country-as-seen-through-the-eyes-of-a-football-stadium/.

2 Ryan Gingeras, *Mustafa Kemal Ataturk: Heir to an Empire* (Oxford: Oxford University Press, 2016), p. 108.

3 '"My Brother, My Enemy": Karsiyaka and Goztepe apply to come together in Izmir Derby', *Daily Sabah*, 29 October 2015. https://www.dailysabah.com/football/2015/10/29/my-brother-my-enemy-karsiyaka-and-goztepe-apply-to-come-together-in-izmir-derby.

4 It was owned by Altay and rented to Altinordu, Goztepe and Karsiyaka for their home matches. Other Izmir teams such as Bucaspor and Izmirspor have also used the stadium over the years in big games.

5 'Goodbye Izmir Alsancak Stadium'.

6 While Taraftar Haklari emerged in the battle to save Alsancak Stadium, their work broadened to encompass other fights for supporters' rights. They now have over 50 active members, including around ten women, and some members come from other cities.

7 Interview with the author, 17 October 2015.

8 'Requiem for a theater of dreams: Izmir Alsancak Stadium', thisisfootballislife, 22 September 2014. https://thisisfootballislife.wordpress.com/2014/09/22/requiem-for-a-theater-of-dreams-izmir-alsancak-stadium/.

9 The AKP has a wider urban-renewal project, ostensibly to make cities safer from earthquakes, which have historically been a major source of destruction in Turkish cities. The project has been dogged by allegations that much of the renewal is a cover for gentrification.

10 'There is nothing less empty than an empty stadium. There is nothing less mute than stands bereft of spectators,' wrote Eduardo Galeano. *Soccer in Sun and Shadow* (New York: Nation Books, 2013), p. 20.

11 Interview with the author, 17 October 2015.

12 'Goodbye Izmir Alsancak Stadium'.

13 Ibid.

14 Interview with the author, 17 October 2015.

15 It is not for nothing that the 'AKP' stands for the Justice and *Development* Party, whereas *ak* – as in the AK Parti – also means 'white', with religious connotations of purity and light.

16 'Turk sporunun cehresi degisiyor!', NTV Spor, 25 January 2015. http://www.ntvspor.net/futbol/turk-sporunun-cehresi-degisiyor-579e074ac873cc40a468c2ef?_ref=infinity.

17 Some fans saw his speech as disrespectful to a popular and recently deceased ex-president of Galatasaray who Bayraktar said had 'begged' and 'cried' for a new stadium.

18 TOKI has a role in the construction of at least 17 recent stadiums. 'Political shadow over the football industry', *Hurriyet Daily News*, 18 April 2016. http://www.hurriyetdailynews.com/political-shadow-over-the-football-industry.aspx?PageID=238&NID=97933&NewsCatID=361.

19 Such as a cheap loan from the state fund Ilbank.

20 This puts West Ham's 'great' £2.5 million annual deal to rent the Olympic Stadium into perspective.

21 Construction and related industries account for around 20 per cent of the economy. 'Gentrification tears at Istanbul's historically diverse fabric', Reuters, 29 October 2014. http://www.reuters.com/article/turkey-gentrification-idUSL5N0SM3DF20141029.

22 Interview with the author, 17 August 2016. Many of the stadiums in Turkey are part of wider sporting, business and leisure complexes, with conference centres, hotels, other sports facilities and shopping.

23 'Gentrification tears at Istanbul's historically diverse fabric'.

24 Erdinc Celikkan, 'Erdogan's giant Istanbul canal back on agenda with a new look', *Hurriyet Daily News*, 24 February 2015. http://www.hurriyetdailynews.com/erdogans-giant-istanbul-canal-back-on-agenda-with-a-new-look.aspx?pageID=238&nID=78745&NewsCatID=340.

25 Turkey has come second only to China nine years in a row in terms of volume of construction projects undertaken abroad. 'Turkish contractors rank second in world for ninth straight year', *Hurriyet Daily News*, 26 August 2016. http://www.hurriyetdailynews.com/turkish-contractors-rank-second-in-world-for-ninth-straight-year.aspx?pageID=238&nID=103260&NewsCatID=345.

26 Huge Kemalist companies like Koc or Sabanci stick carefully to their own sectors of expertise, otherwise the government could then look into their taxes and find excuses to fine them or hinder their work.

27 Interview with the author, 17 August 2016.

28 See Chapter 1.

29 'Besiktas' new stadium opens as a political event: what's in a name?', thisisfootballislife, 12 April 2016. https://thisisfootballislife.wordpress.com/2016/04/12/besiktas-new-stadium-opens-as-a-political-event-whats-in-a-name/.

30 'Interview: Esra Gurakar on cronyism in public procurement in Turkey', *Hurriyet Daily News*, 8 July 2017. http://www.hurriyetdailynews.com/interview-esra-gurakar-on-cronyism-in-public-procurement-in-turkey.aspx?pageID=238&nID=115236&NewsCatID=386.

31 Interview with the author, 17 August 2016.

32 It is no accident that one precursor of the AKP was called the 'Welfare Party'.

33 Some have referred to this as a kind of 'neoliberal populism'.

34 David Lepeska, 'Whistleblower in Istanbul fired from urban planning job, but not before being forced to count cats', *National*, 27 March 2014. http://www.thenational.ae/arts-culture/whistleblower-in-istanbul-fired-from-urban-planning-job-but-not-before-being-forced-to-count-cats#full.

35 Halil Karaveli, 'Walking for justice: the path forward for Turkey's opposition', *Turkey Analyst*, 22 June 2017. http://turkeyanalyst.org/publications/turkey-analyst-articles/item/584-walking-for-justice-the-path-forward-for-turkeys-opposition.html?mc_cid=10ba121fa0&mc_eid=b68dbae1d3.

36 'Turkey's state property developer building for votes', *Hurriyet Daily News*, 8 June 2011. http://www.hurriyetdailynews.com/default.aspx?pageid=438&n=turkey8217s-state-property-developer-building-for-votes-2011-06-08.

37 This followed a general pattern of stalling or stonewalling I encountered when trying to engage the gatekeepers of Turkish football – including government ministries, senior football federation figures and major companies involved in the sport.

38 Someone who has completed the Haj to Mecca.

39 Interview with the author, 20 February 2016.

40 'Kombine satislari belli oldu... Besiktas satislarda da sampiyon', *Cumhuriyet*, 15 August 2016. http://www.cumhuriyet.com.tr/haber/futbol/584878/Kombine_satislari_belli_oldu..._Besiktas_satislarda_da_sampiyon.html.

41 Rumi's mystical Sufism is far from conservative Sunni Islam: some of his poetry is about drinking wine and is infused with homoeroticism, so it is debatable how well he and Erdogan would have rubbed along.

42 Currently, the city's stadium is not fit for Super League matches – they are forced to play in Manisa, 50 kilometres away.

43 Onsel Gurel Bayrali, 'The relationship between state and capital: the reconstruction of soccer stadiums as an urban transformation project', MA thesis, Bogazici University, 2016.

44 Interview with the author, 17 August 2016.

45 Interview with the author, 8 September 2016.

46 Unusually, they didn't work with TOKI, but instead worked with Istanbul's AKP municipality, who sourced the land, and with Istanbul's housing administration.

47 'Kalyon Group', Media Ownership Monitor Turkey. http://turkey.mom-rsf.org/en/owners/companies/detail/company/kalyon-group/.

48 Interview with the author, 20 November 2016.

49 The club still retains some indirect links to the municipality – for example, the municipality provides stadium staff. Many argue that municipalities should be supporting amateur and youth sports, not professional football teams.

50 'Half built stadiums and promises left unkept: Turkey's political landscape seen through stadiums', thisisfootballislife, 12 June 2015. https://thisisfootballislife.wordpress.com/2015/06/12/half-built-stadiums-and-promises-left-unkept-turkeys-political-landscape-seen-through-stadiums/.

51 'New stadium: controversial opening of Crocodile Arena', StadiumDB, 21 December 2015. http://stadiumdb.com/news/2015/12/new_stadium_controversial_opening_of_crocodile_arena.

52 Interview with the author, 2 April 2016.

53 Hakan Bas, 'Turkish football grows by 5 times in last 10 years', *Daily Sabah*, 14 October 2016. https://www.dailysabah.com/football/2016/10/15/turkish-football-grows-by-5-times-in-last-10-years.

54 In Diyarbakir the largest attendances tend to be 1,000–1,500 at most for Amedspor, but a new 33,000-capacity stadium is under construction in the city. Mersin's new stadium, completed in 2013 but plagued with a grass problem, has a capacity of over 25,000. Their average attendance in 2015/16 was just over 5,000.

55 The word 'formality' was omitted from the subsequent English translation. 'Cumhurbaskani Erdogan Vodafone Arena'nin acilis toreninde konustu', A Haber, 10 April 2014. http://www.ahaber.com.tr/spor/2016/04/10/cumhurbaskani-erdogan-vodafone-arenanin-acilis-toreninde-konustu.

56 Interview with the author, 17 October 2015.

57 They claimed that, while Izmir is the third-biggest city in Turkey, little of their tax receipts returned by way of investment. When I pointed out that Izmir had a recently installed metro system, they replied that it has taken more than ten years to build. When I mentioned new investments – such as a marina under construction – they said that investments like this tended to benefit big corporations.

58 John Konuk Blasing, 'The games behind the game: the process of democratic deepening and identity formation in Turkey as seen through football clubs', MA thesis, University of Texas at Austin, 2011, p. 68. https://repositories.lib.utexas.edu/handle/2152/ETD-UT-2011-05-3490. Bucaspor only spent a year in the Super League but they remain a mid-table, second-tier side. Seboy was removed from the AKP's mayoral list in 2009 following allegations of corruption. Bucaspor's academy faltered as many staff members went to Izmir rival Altinordu.

59 In many Anatolian cities, major teams were formed in the 1960s through mergers in order to pool resources, build a large stadium, get the city behind one team, foster a greater sense of belonging to newly expanded cities and pose a greater challenge to the big Istanbul clubs. This did not happen in Ankara or Izmir due to the large size of the cities and the long-established football culture.

60 When Goztepe were relegated four times and ended up playing in the amateur league in 2007, their attendances were still much higher than most Super League clubs.

61 Other famous Greek teams have Ottoman origins: the 'K' in AEK Athens and PAOK relates to 'Konstantinoupoleos', revealing their roots in 'Constantinople'. Both teams were formed from players of Hermes Sports club, which later changed its name to Pera.

62 Fenerbahce's first match had previously been thought to have been against Moda in September 1908.

63 Interview with the author, 13 April 2016.

64 Eugene Rogan, *The Fall of the Ottomans: The Great War in the Middle East, 1914–1920* (London: Penguin Random House, 2015), pp. 183–4.

65 Ibid.

66 Charles King, *Midnight at the Pera Palace: The Birth of Modern Istanbul* (New York: Norton, 2014), p. 129.

67 'Gentrification tears at Istanbul's historically diverse fabric'.

68 Greeks of Ottoman descent have been returning to Istanbul in increasing numbers in recent years, especially following the Greek economic crises.

69 Adam Taylor, 'Is "Armenian" an insult? Turkey's prime minister seems to think so', *Washington Post*, 6 August 2014. https://www.washingtonpost.com/news/worldviews/wp/2014/08/06/is-armenian-an-insult-turkeys-prime-minister-seems-to-think-so/.

70 Ece Temelkuran, *Turkey: The Insane and the Melancholy* (London: Zed Books, 2016), pp. 16, 151, 153.

71 'Today you can build a mall in the place of the Alsancak Stadium because you once made the Alsancak Stadium in the place of the Panionios Stadium. Just like Istiklal Street's Circle D'orient and Saray Cinema can become malls because you chased away their real owners in 1955 with sticks, reformatting everyone's minds,' writes Irak. Translated and quoted by John Konuk Blasing in 'Goodbye Izmir Alsancak Stadium'.

5 'Everywhere is Taksim, everywhere is resistance'

1 Emre Zeytinoglu, 'Stadium', in Pelin Dervis, Bulent Tanju, Ugur Tanyeli (eds), *Becoming Istanbul – An Encyclopedia* (Istanbul: Garanti Galeri, 2008), p. 328. http://saltonline.org/media/files/becomingistanbul_scrd-4.pdf.

2 Ibid., p. 326.

3 Besiktas's logo.

4 Interview with the author, 22 January 2015.

5 Yagmur Nuhrat, 'Fair enough? Negotiating ethics in Turkish football', MA thesis, Brown University, 2013, p. 218. https://repository.library.brown.edu/studio/item/bdr:320642/PDF/?embed=true.

6 Ozlem Gezer and Maximilian Popp, 'Football fans challenge Erdogan', *Spiegel Online*, 5 July 2013. http://www.spiegel.de/international/world/football-fans-were-instrumental-in-fanning-protests-against-erdogan-a-909357.html.

7 Elif Batuman, 'The view from the stands', *New Yorker*, 7 March 2011. http://www.newyorker.com/magazine/2011/03/07/the-view-from-the-stands.

8 Elif Batuman, 'Occupy Gezi: police against protesters in Istanbul', *New Yorker*, 1 June 2013. http://www.newyorker.com/news/news-desk/occupy-gezi-police-against-protesters-in-istanbul.

9 Galatasaray's nickname.

10 Erdogan has suggested that environmentalists go and live in a forest, but this is becoming increasingly difficult as the AKP is busy razing woodland for construction projects.

11 Reporters Without Borders ranks Turkey 151st out of 180 countries on its 2016 press freedom index, down from 98th in 2005. https://rsf.org/en/ranking.

12 Jenny White, *Muslim Nationalism and the New Turks* (Princeton: Princeton University Press, 2014), p. 133.

13 Like other Turkish football fans, many Besiktas supporters revere Ataturk, and they also revere drinking, which they combine in a wry chant: 'In our father's footsteps / we'll die of cirrhosis.' See 'The view from the stands'.

14 A large number of ultrAslan members attended the Gezi protests as individuals, although their leadership later disavowed the protests under pressure from the government.

15 Interview with the author, 13 June 2016.

16 Interview with the author, 23 January 2015.

17 A reference to the year the Ottomans captured Constantinople. 1453 Eagles declined to talk. Carsi and 1453 Eagles blamed each other for a pitch invasion that halted a match between Besiktas and Galatasaray in September 2013.

18 'Turkey: football fans on trial for "coup"', Human Rights Watch, 15 December 2014. https://www.hrw.org/news/2014/12/15/turkey-football-fans-trial-coup.

19 '3 arrested in soccer fan round up case', *Bianet*, 1 October 2013. http://bianet.org/english/youth/150320-3-arrested-in-soccer-fan-round-up-case.

20 As well as buying individual and season tickets, users can also use it as a debit and credit card for shopping and withdrawing money, as a store discount card, and to enter sweepstakes – to meet players, for example – and win 'special gifts'. See https://www.passo.com.tr/en/common/test/faq.aspx.

21 He is now Minister of Energy and Natural Resources and seen as a potential future prime minister. 'Davutoglu's departure thrusts Erdogan son-in-law into limelight', *Financial Times*, 6 May 2016. https://www.ft.com/content/2cdd0178-1395-11e6-839f-2922947098f0 (access requires subscription).

22 Interview with the author, 22 January 2015.

23 Figures from NTVSpor. If you exclude the 'Big Four' and Konyaspor's whopping attendances, the average of the remainder was just over 4,000.

24 Sevecen Tunc, 'Putting the city on the map: a social history of football in Trabzon to 1967', MA thesis, Bogazici University, 2009, p. 98.

25 Ibid., p. 99.

26 A carnivalesque rivalry grew up between the Trabzon clubs Idmanocagi and Idmangucu. There was a political dimension to the rivalry – Idmanocagi were associated with the CHP and Idmangucu with the Democratic Party. The matches would often end in fights. Sometimes a donkey would be dressed in the colours of the defeated team and paraded through the city, or a coffin symbolising the losing side would be thrown into the river. The creation of Trabzonspor in 1967, by merging teams in the city, put an end to this rivalry, and the city began looking beyond Trabzon for its enemies – chiefly to Istanbul.

27 Yigit Akin, 'Not just a game: the Kayseri vs. Sivas football disaster', *Soccer and Society*, 5:2 (Summer 2004), pp. 219–32.

28 Ibid.

29 Ibid. Outside the stadium the clashes continued – Sivasspor fans went on a rampage in the city. In Sivas people looted and burned shops belonging to people of Kayseri origin. The violence was eventually brought under control by the police and the military, who blocked the road between the two cities.

30 Batuman, 'The view from the stands'.

31 Interview with the author, 17 October 2015.

32 Interview with the author, 13 April 2016.

33 Interview with the author, 13 June 2016.

34 Nuhrat, 'Fair enough?'.

35 Interview with the author, 2 September 2016.

36 Interview with the author, 13 October 2015.

37 Interview with the author, 25 January 2015. It is hard to analyse empirically the level of violence in Turkish society but, anecdotally, violence isn't that hard to find. While Istanbul often feels much safer than London, and the drunken violence that is common in British town centres late at night is all but absent in Turkey, it is not uncommon to see physical confrontations. The papers are full of anecdotal violent rages: people shooting up teahouses because they were angry with the price, or people shooting friends when they wouldn't let them pay for the bill. In the summer of 2015, some Adana residents became so enraged with the heat of the sun that they began firing their guns at it, and the local municipality was forced to issue a plea to ask them to stop.

38 Emre Sarigul, 'How a love story and a firearm incident tore the Turkey team apart', *Guardian*, 16 November 2014. https://www.theguardian.com/football/blog/2014/nov/16/turkey-gokhan-tore-omer-toprak-hakan-calhanoglu.

39 'Galatasaray and Besiktas brawl during wheelchair basketball match', *Guardian*, 9 May 2016. https://www.theguardian.com/sport/2016/may/09/galatasaray-besiktas-fans-brawl-wheelchair-basketball-iwbf-eurocup. This was by no means the first time there has been violence at wheelchair basketball matches between these teams – the police fired tear gas inside a basketball arena during a match between these teams in Istanbul in 2012 to separate the fans of both sides. Video footage emerged of players crawling from damaged wheelchairs amid the mayhem. See also John Konuk Blasing, 'Turkey's social malaise comes out on the pitch in Trabzon', thisisfootballislife, 13 March 2014. https://thisisfootballislife.com/2014/03/13/turkeys-social-malaise-comes-out-on-the-pitch-in-trabzon/.

40 Interview with the author, 27 November 2016.

41 Interview with the author, 23 January 2015.

42 Interview with the author, 27 November 2016.

43 Interview with the author, 20 September 2016.

44 Cavcav died in January 2017 at the age of 81. He had been club president for nearly 40 years and was renowned for sacking coaches – he went through more than 50 in his tenure.

45 The term originally referred to a Jewish sect in the Ottoman Empire which mostly converted to Islam in the seventeenth century but which was subsequently regarded with long-standing suspicion.

46 The boycotts boosted attendances in other sports, as football fans went to watch basketball, handball or volleyball instead.

47 'Large Turkish football sponsor quits backing game', *Hurriyet Daily News*, 14 January 2015. http://www.hurriyetdailynews.com/Default.aspx?pageID=238&nID=76929&NewsCatID=362.

48 Interview with the author, 16 November 2015.

49 When I asked Genclerbirligi fans if they could remember any violence among their fans, all they could think of was how in the 1990s they used to gently slap the hands of other fans who were doing the wolf hand signal during the national anthem, which is typically an expression of Turkish ultranationalism.

50 Interview with the author, 20 September 2015.

51 Not his real name.

52 Indeed, in October 2015, three Alkaralar fans were detained and fined for displaying banners at a football match in Ankara. They were calling for peace and protesting in the aftermath of a huge bomb in the city that had killed more than 100 people in Turkey's deadliest terrorist atrocity. See 'Three football fans detained over protesting Ankara bombings', Hurriyet Daily News, 25 October 2015. http://www. hurriyetdailynews.com/three-football-fans-detained-over-protesting-ankara-bombings. aspx?PageID=238&NID=90294&NewsCatID=341.

53 Interview with the author, 21 September 2015.

54 Interview with the author, 25 April 2016.

55 Interview with the author, 5 February 2016.

56 Conversation with the author, 23 May 2016.

57 Interview with the author, 18 October 2016.

58 Incidentally, there are many technical difficulties with the system. I was given the wrong type of card three times, including a card for under-18s that I was assured, wrongly as it turns out, 'works for foreigners and children'. Although it was Passolig's mistake, I had to pay for all of the cards. When I finally got the correct card I was unable to top up online, or at ATMs, or stadiums, or other outlets – Turkish friends and I rang the helpline more than 20 times; I spent hours waiting in Passolig ticket offices while they fired emails into oblivion to get help resolving the problem. The staff at one office told me: 'There are so many problems with Passolig but we haven't seen this before.' It was never resolved – I eventually discovered that the only way to top up my card was by physically going to the post office, queuing at times for more than an hour, and topping up there.

59 'As half [of the card's fees] go to Konyaspor we don't have a problem,' said Ibrahim Apali, the leader of Nalcacililar, the team's biggest fan group. 'Now they give us our share and they have their business, so we don't have a problem.'

60 'Turkish football club fans set own stadium on fire after losing game', Daily Sabah, 15 May 2016. http://www.dailysabah.com/football/2016/05/15/turkish-football-club-fans-set-own-stadium-on-fire-after-losing-game.

61 Interview with the author, 21 September 2015.

62 The price of football tickets varies wildly – for small teams in the Super League that do not get high attendances, the cheapest tickets can cost around 10–15 TL per match. But at the big clubs it is more typically five to ten times that much for the cheapest seats, depending on the match.

63 Interview with the author, 18 May 2016.

64 Interview with the author, 5 February 2016.

65 Interview with the author, 22 January 2015.

66 Interview with the author, 2 February 2016.

67 The term likely comes from a group of 20 Besiktas fans in the 1960s who called themselves the 'amigos', who turned up at Birol Peker's house in 1963 to try, unsuccessfully, to convince him not to transfer to Fenerbahce. 'Amigos' subsequently became the word for Turkey's first ultra leaders later that decade. See Daghan Irak, 'The transformation of football fandom in Turkey since the 1970s', MA thesis, Bogazici University, 2010, p. 177.

68 Batuman, 'The view from the stands'.

69 Interview with the author, 3 February 2016.

70 Interview with the author, 20 April 2016.

71 Interview with the author, 13 April 2016.

72 'Black! White! Champions! Besiktas!'

73 Interview with the author, 17 October 2015.

74 'Erdogan vows to "rebuild" Ottoman military barracks in Istanbul's Gezi Park', *Hurriyet Daily News*, 18 June 2016. http://www.hurriyetdailynews. com/erdogan-vows-to-reconstruct-military-barracks-in-istanbuls-gezi-park. aspx?pageID=238&nID=100645&NewsCatID=338.

75 Interview with the author, 13 June 2016.

76 Interview with the author, 18 May 2016.

77 Interview with the author, 5 February 2016.

78 Interview with the author, 17 October 2015.

79 Interview with the author, 27 November 2016.

80 Interview with the author, 2 February 2016.

6 Kurdish Cup Specialists

1 Conversation with the author, 28 January 2016.

2 The security rationale is groundless – once you take a paper ticket, you can hand it to anyone. The Turkish Football Federation later confirmed to me that this is not a sanctioned procedure, that they hadn't known it had taken place, and that they did not condone it.

3 Cizrespor went on an impressive cup run in 2014/15, but was forced to abandon the 2015/16 season due to the conflict.

4 Since December 2015 they have been known as Civil Protection Units (YPS).

5 Christopher de Bellaigue, *Rebel Land* (London: Bloomsbury Publishing, 2010; electronic edition), p. 169.

6 Interview with the author, 2 December 2015.

7 Tom Stevenson, 'Why Turkey's president fears a Kurdish rebellion from the east', *New Statesman*, 8 April 2016. http://www.newstatesman.com/culture/2016/04/why-turkeys-president-fears-kurdish-rebellion-east.

8 This is purely coincidental – the club has no particular Kurdish affiliations – but because of Ocalan's support, Galatasaray now has a large Kurdish following.

9 The OHAL was dismantled in 2002, but the quarantine and shock therapy of OHAL left a mark in the territory and in the political terrain. See Aysegul Aydin and Cem Emrence, *Zones of Rebellion: Kurdish Insurgents and the Turkish State* (Ithaca, NY: Cornell University Press, 2015), p. 10.

10 Ibid., p. 11.

11 Jenny White, *Muslim Nationalism and the New Turks* (Princeton, NJ: Princeton University Press, 2014), p. 102.

12 Interview with the author, 2 December 2015.

13 Alexander Christie-Miller, '"War is easy, peace is hard": the collapse of Turkey's Kurdish peace process', *White Review*, October 2015. http://www.thewhitereview.org/features/war-is-easy-peace-is-hard-the-collapse-of-turkeys-kurdish-peace-process/.

14 The YDG-H mostly comprises the children of those who were displaced in the 1990s by the state's scorched-earth policy of destroying villages thought to be supportive of the PKK.

15 Gareth H. Jenkins, 'Dreams and nightmares: Turkey's unspoken drift towards civil war', *Turkey Analyst*, 1 February 2016. http://www.turkeyanalyst.org/publications/turkey-analyst-articles/item/503-dreams-and-nightmares-turkey's-unspoken-drift-towards-civil-war.html.

16 As 'Amedspor' is used in conversation by the club, their fans and also many of their enemies and detractors, and even by the football federation in casual conversation, I will use this name throughout.

17 James Dorsey, 'Turkish soccer supports Erdogan's war against the Kurds', *Huffington Post*, 28 August 2016. http://www.huffingtonpost.com/james-dorsey/turkish-soccer-supports-e_b_8052456.html.

18 The HDP has appeared at rallies where there have been PKK symbols on display, and its leaders have attended some funerals of PKK figures. See Nate Schenkkan, 'What happens in Turkey doesn't stay in Turkey', *Foreign Policy*, 7 November 2016. http://foreignpolicy.com/2016/11/07/what-happens-in-turkey-doesnt-stay-in-turkey/.

19 The Turkish authorities feared the rising power of the Syrian Kurdish groups – some of which have direct links to the PKK – as they have carved out autonomous strips of land during the war in northern Syria, along the Turkish border.

20 Some kind of constitutional reform could greatly benefit the Kurds and other minorities. The current constitution was drafted by the military following the 1980 military coup and is widely recognised as authoritarian, illiberal and neglectful of minority rights.

21 Christie-Miller, '"War is easy, peace is hard".'

22 There had been violence even before the election – six people were injured in bombings at HDP offices in Adana and Mersin in May. At least three people were killed by explosions at an HDP rally in Diyarbakir two days before the election. See 'Death toll in HDP Diyarbakir rally rises to three', *Hurriyet Daily News*, 9 June 2015. http://www.hurriyetdailynews.com/death-toll-in-hdp-diyarbakir-rally-rises-to-three.aspx?pageID=238&nID=83722&NewsCatID=341.

23 'Suruc massacre: "Turkish student" was suicide bomber', BBC, 22 July 2015. http://www.bbc.com/news/world-europe-33619043.

24 Jenkins, 'Dreams and nightmares'.

25 Prohibitions on all movement.

26 'Human rights violations throughout the Cizre curfew: observation report', Human Rights Association (IHD), 15 September 2015. http://en.ihd.org.tr/wp-content/uploads/2015/10/Cizre-Observation-Report.pdf.

27 Benjamin Harvey, 'The Ankara bomber owned one of Turkey's most well-known ISIS hangouts', *Bloomberg*, 15 October 2015. http://www.bloomberg.com/news/articles/2015-10-15/ankara-bomber-traveled-public-path-to-turkey-s-deadliest-attack.

28 Max Hoffman and Michael Werz, 'Turkey's right rises again', Centre for American Progress, 3 November 2013. https://www.americanprogress.org/issues/security/news/2015/11/03/124968/turkeys-right-rises-again/?utm_source=Sailthru&utm_medium=email&utm_campaign=New%20Campaign&utm_term=%2AMideast%20Brief. During the campaign it emerged that the state broadcaster had devoted 59 hours of coverage to Erdogan and the AKP; 5 hours to the main opposition CHP; 70 minutes to the far-right MHP; and 18 minutes to the pro-Kurdish HDP.

29 Interview with the author, 23 November 2015.

30 Mahmut Bozarsian, 'Turkish Kurds flee "self rule" neighborhoods', *Al-Monitor*, 14 December 2015. http://www.al-monitor.com/pulse/originals/2015/12/turkey-clashes-pkk-kurds-flee-self-rule-neighborhoods.html.

31 Conversation with the author, 21 November 2015.

32 Some speculated that more seasoned fighters from the PKK had joined their ranks after a significant rise in security forces fatalities between December and January.

33 Dorian Jones, 'Turkey's crackdown on Kurdish rebels includes local mayors', *Voice of America*, 16 August 2016. http://www.voanews.com/a/turkey-crackdown-kurdish-rebels-local-mayors/3153877.html?utm_source=Sailthru&utm_medium=email&utm_campaign=New%20Campaign&utm_term=*Mideast%20Brief.

34 'Turkey: academics jailed for signing petition', Human Rights Watch, 16 March 2016. https://www.hrw.org/news/2016/03/16/turkey-academics-jailed-signing-petition.

35 'Turkey: state blocks probes of southeast killings', Human Rights Watch, 11 July 2016. https://www.hrw.org/news/2016/07/11/turkey-state-blocks-probes-southeast-killings.

36 Jesse Rosenfeld, 'Turkey is fighting a dirty war against its own population', *Nation*, 9 March 2016. https://www.thenation.com/article/turkey-is-fighting-a-dirty-war-against-its-own-kurdish-population/.

37 The Turkish sportswriter Ozgun Kelesoglu suggested that Senturk's actions demeaned the salute, which is meant to show respect to soldiers who have served their country, not to be used on a football pitch to rile up rival fans. Amedspor pointed out in a tweet after the match that Senturk had paid to avoid his military service. See John Konuk Blasing, 'Military salutes in Turkish football reflect wider societal malaise', thisisfootballislife, 31 January 2016. https://thisisfootballislife.wordpress.com/2016/01/31/military-salutes-in-turkish-football-reflect-wider-societal-malaise/.

38 Interview with the author, 20 November 2016.

39 'Soccer – Kurdish conflict in Turkey spills into sport as club, player punished', Reuters, 5 February 2016. http://news.trust.org/item/20160205124232-4mnyd/?source=shtw.

40 Ozgur Korkmaz, 'Amedspor wins to face pressure off field', *Hurriyet Daily News*, 4 February 2016. http://www.hurriyetdailynews.com/amedspor-wins-to-face-pressure-off-field.aspx?pageID=449&nID=94723&NewsCatID=497.

41 Galatasaray's Engin Baytar was banned for fewer matches (11) when he physically attacked a referee in 2012. 'Controversy prevails early in new Super League campaign', *Hurriyet Daily News*, 23 August 2012. http://www.hurriyetdailynews.com/Default.aspx?pageID=238&nID=28374&NewsCatID=444.

42 Interview with the author, 5 February 2016.

43 Interview with the author, 9 February 2016.

44 Interview with the author, 9 February 2016.

45 Interview with the author, 27 February 2016.

46 'Purple Barricade'.

47 Interview with the author, 27 February 2016.

48 'Amedspor'dan Sivas iddiasi', CNN Turk, 15 March 2016. http://www.cnnturk.com/spor/futbol/amedspor-kafilesine-sivasta-otel-verilmedi.

49 Elci had been arrested and received threats after saying that the PKK should no longer be considered a terrorist organisation.

50 David Sim, 'Turkey: families return to shattered Kurdish town of Cizre – "a second Kobani"', *International Business Times*, 2 March 2016. http://www.ibtimes.co.uk/turkey-families-return-shattered-kurdish-town-cizre-second-kobani-1547103.

51 As in the case of the three-month-old baby, Miray Ince, and her 82-year-old great-grandfather, Ramazan Ince, who were killed in Cizre. See 'Turkey: state blocks probes of southeast killings'.

52 Ibid. The government denies this, but evidence of abuses has been documented by a range of independent groups – such as Human Rights Watch, Amnesty International and the International Crisis Group – which also criticise the PKK's violence and its role in the destruction.

53 Interview with the author, 25 May 2016.

54 Claims of complete independence are pretty far-fetched – the PKK has never tolerated a rival Kurdish nationalist group. See Frederike Geerdink, 'Ankara bombing: PKK, TAK ties come under scrutiny again', *Middle East Eye*, 4 March 2016. http://www.middleeasteye.net/columns/after-ankara-bomning-questions-over-pkk-tak-ties-resurface-1097219220.

55 'Kurdish footballer faces jail for social media posts', *Green Left Weekly*, 10 October 2016. https://www.greenleft.org.au/content/kurdish-footballer-faces-jail-social-media-posts.

56 Ibid.

57 'Turkish-German footballer given suspended term for "terror propaganda"', *Hurriyet Daily News*, 6 April 2017. http://www.hurriyetdailynews.com/turkish-german-footballer-given-suspended-term-for-terror-propaganda-.aspx?pageID=238&nID=111695&NewsCatID=509.

7 The Rebel Referee

1 Interview with the author, 11 October 2015.

2 The word *'ibne'* is derived from the Arabic for son, and usually denotes a 'passive' homosexual man.

3 Emre Azizlerli, 'Proving you're gay to the Turkish army', BBC, 26 March 2012. http://www.bbc.co.uk/news/magazine-17474967.

4 'The case of Halil Ibrahim Dincdag: discrimination in employment', LGBTI News Turkey, 29 November 2013. https://lgbtinewsturkey.com/2013/11/29/case-of-halil-ibrahim-dincdag-discrimination-in-employment/.

5 Nicholas Birch, 'Turkey: football referee, barred for being homosexual, fights for rights', *EurasiaNet*, 25 June 2009. http://www.eurasianet.org/departments/insightb/articles/eav062609.shtml.

6 Ibid.

7 Interview with the author, 16 September 2015.

8 In the early part of that decade, Turkish civil society had been under extreme repression following the 1980 military coup. Towards the end of the decade new social movements emerged in support of human rights, environmentalism, feminism and LGBT rights.

9 Interview with the author, 29 September 2015.

10 Yagmur Nuhrat, 'Fair enough? Negotiating ethics in Turkish football', MA thesis, Brown University, 2013, pp. 161–2. https://repository.library.brown.edu/studio/item/bdr:320642/PDF/?embed=true.

11 Ibid., pp. 181–2. Besiktas's symbol is an eagle, while Fenerbahce's is a canary, and Galatasaray's is a big manly lion. Fenerbahce have their own homophobic slurs for their opponents.

12 Ibid., p. 181. The implication is of 'shaking your hips' like a belly dancer.

13 Birch, 'Turkey: football referee, barred for being homosexual, fights for rights'.
14 Nuhrat, 'Fair enough?', p. 92.
15 Interview with the author, 15 January 2016.
16 Interview with the author, 11 October 2016.
17 Homophobia is not limited to football. 'I think [all] sports in Turkey are homophobic but we talk about [homophobia] in football because we talk about football all the time!' says Burcu Karakas. Angel McCoughtry, an American basketball player, found herself in controversy whilst playing for Fenerbahce's basketball team because of an interview with a Turkish newspaper in which she spoke about her engagement to her girlfriend. McCoughtry claims that Fenerbahce tried to make her publicly recant her comments. She went from being a star player to falling out of favour, and later returned to the US.
18 Interview with the author, 12 October 2016.
19 'The silence over gay footballers', BBC, 27 January 2012. http://www.bbc.com/news/magazine-16722196.
20 Amal Fashanu, 'The Sports Charter shines a welcome light on homophobia in football', Guardian, 4 February 2012. https://www.theguardian.com/commentisfree/2012/feb/04/sports-charter-homophobia-football.
21 Adam Serrano, 'Robbie Rogers speaks with Howler Magazine's podcast', LA Galaxy, 26 July 2016. http://www.lagalaxy.com/post/2016/07/26/robbie-rogers-speaks-howler-magazines-podcast-insider.
22 'The Secret Footballer: fans stop gay footballers from coming out', Guardian, 12 March 2011. https://www.theguardian.com/football/blog/2011/mar/12/the-secret-footballer-gay-players.
23 Sam Jones, 'Gay referee in Spain receives death threats after return to football', Guardian, 13 September 2016. https://www.theguardian.com/world/2016/sep/13/gay-referee-in-spain-receives-death-threats-after-return-to-football.
24 Interview with the author, 16 September 2015.
25 'The AKP's LGBTI history from 2001–2015', LGBTI News Turkey, 26 September 2015. https://lgbtinewsturkey.com/2015/09/26/the-akps-lgbti-history-from-2001-2015/.
26 Interview with the author, 15 January 2016.
27 'The AKP's LGBTI History from 2001–2015'.
28 Ibid.
29 Ibid.
30 The number of women murdered per year rose by 1,400 per cent between 2002 and 2009, when the government stopped recording such data. See Erin Zaleski, 'Violence against women in Turkey runs deeper than Ozgecan Aslan's brutal murder', Bustle, 23 February 2015. https://www.bustle.com/articles/65418-violence-against-women-in-turkey-runs-deeper-than-ozgecan-aslans-brutal-murder.
31 'UN concerned over LGBT rights in Turkey, calls gov't to take action', Hurriyet Daily News, 15 July 2015. http://www.hurriyetdailynews.com/un-concerned-over-lgbt-rights-in-turkey-calls-govt-to-take-action-.aspx?pageID=238&nid=85465.
32 'Missing gay Syrian refugee found beheaded in Istanbul', Guardian, 4 August 2016. https://www.theguardian.com/world/2016/aug/04/body-missing-gay-syrian-refugee-muhammed-wisam-sankari-found-beheaded-istanbul.
33 'Trans Murder Monitoring results: TMM IDAHOT 2016 Update', Transrespect versus Transphobia Worldwide research project, Transgender Europe, 2016. http://transrespect.org/wp-content/uploads/2016/05/TvT_TMM_IDAHOT2016_Tables_EN.pdf.

34 'Hande Kader: outcry in Turkey over transgender woman's murder', BBC, 21 August 2016. http://www.bbc.com/news/world-europe-37143879.

35 'Police break up the 13th Istanbul LGBTI Pride Parade', Kaos GL, 29 June 2015. http://www.kaosgl.com/page.php?id=19716.

36 'Erdogan dined with Turkish transgender star after clashes at LGBT rally', *Guardian*, 20 June 2016. https://www.theguardian.com/world/2016/jun/20/erdogan-dinner-turkish-transgender-actor-bulent-ersoy-istanbul-lgbt-rally?CMP=twt_gu.

37 The number of conscientious objectors and draft evaders is growing.

38 Interview with the author, 29 September 2015.

39 Interview with the author, 18 October 2016.

40 Interview with the author, 25 October 2015.

41 Interview with the author, 24 October 2015.

42 Interview with the author, 25 October 2015.

43 Nuhrat, 'Fair enough?'

44 Interview with the author, 11 October 2015.

45 Gay pride parades are not held deliberately during Ramadan – many Gay Pride events across the world are held to commemorate the Stonewall riots in New York that began on 28 June 1969. In some years this coincides with Ramadan.

46 'Gay referee wins court battle against Turkish Football Federation', Deutsche Welle, 30 December 2015. http://www.dw.com/en/gay-referee-wins-court-battle-against-turkish-football-federation/a-18950595.

47 Interview with the author, 17 June 2016.

8   Free Syrian Football

1 Interview with the author, 2 April 2016.

2 I was unable to gain permission to visit the camp.

3 'Football in Syria: in the shadow of civil war', *World Soccer*, 31 August 2015. http://www.worldsoccer.com/features/football-in-syria-in-the-shadow-of-civil-war-364143.

4 However, both players returned to Syria's national team in 2017.

5 Patrick Johnston, 'In Singapore, defiant Syria football coach sports Assad T-shirt', Reuters, 16 November 2015. http://uk.reuters.com/article/uk-soccer-world-asia-syria-idUKKCN0T50TX20151116.

6 'Jose Mourinho rejects Syria coaching job – agent Jorge Mendes', BBC, 9 April 2016. http://www.bbc.com/sport/football/36006158.

7 A report by opposition newspaper *Cumhuriyet* alleged that Turkey's intelligence agency was supplying arms to jihadist groups, possibly including ISIS, which the government denies. The paper's reporters were charged with espionage following the report. See 'Turkish president: country not sending arms to terrorists in Syria', CNN, 2 June 2015. http://edition.cnn.com/2015/06/02/middleeast/turkey-syria-weapons/; and 'Turkish journalists charged over claim that secret services armed Syrian rebels', *Guardian*, 27 November 2015. https://www.theguardian.com/world/2015/nov/27/turkish-journalists-charged-over-claim-that-secret-services-armed-syrian-rebels.

8 'About us', Confederation of Independent Football Associations (CONIFA). http://www.conifa.org/en/about-us/ (accessed 8 November 2016).

9 See Chapter 6.

10 Interview with the author, 1 April 2016.

11 The licence costs around $2,000.

12 'Syria regional refugee response', United Nations High Commissioner for Refugees (UNHCR). http://data.unhcr.org/syrianrefugees/country.php?id=224.

13 Although Turkey was an original signatory to the UN's 1951 Refugee Convention, it maintains a 'geographical limitation', affording refugee status only to people coming from countries in the Council of Europe.

14 In July 2016, Erdogan announced that the government is working on plans to grant citizenship to skilled Syrians. See Lauren Zanolli, 'Syrian refugees: struggles in Turkey intensify', Al Jazeera English, 25 July 2016. http://www.aljazeera.com/indepth/features/2016/07/syrian-refugees-struggles-turkey-intensify-160717072943845.html.

15 'Why don't Syrian refugees stay in Turkey?', BBC, 15 July 2016. http://www.bbc.com/news/magazine-36808038. In Turkey only about 40 per cent of Syrian children are in education. Many Syrian children work instead of going to school.

16 'Turkey: no safe refuge: asylum-seekers and refugees denied effective protection in Turkey', Amnesty International, 3 June 2016. https://www.amnesty.org/en/documents/eur44/3825/2016/en/?utm_source=Sailthru&utm_medium=email&utm_campaign=New%20Campaign&utm_term=%2AMideast%20Brief.

17 Also known as Antakya.

18 There are also several projects being run by Turkish charities and groups, including tournaments in refugee camps and a so-called 'Free Syrian League', launched in Gaziantep. The girls have to play badminton. See '"Free Syrian Football League" organized in Turkey', *Yeni Safak*, 3 March 2016. http://www.yenisafak.com/en/sports/free-syrian-football-league-organized-in-turkey-2428276.

19 Many of the original moderate groups have been sidelined by radical Islamist groups. There have been numerous accounts of human rights abuses and alleged war crimes.

9   Dreaming at the Edge of Europe

1 Samuel Stevens, 'Paul Pogba to Manchester United: Juventus midfielder "agrees £220,000" salary as £100m deal draws nearer', *Independent*, 21 July 2016. http://www.independent.co.uk/sport/football/transfers/paul-pogba-to-manchester-united-juventus-midfielder-agrees-220000-salary-as-100m-deal-draws-closer-a7147906.html.

2 Interview with the author, 19 May 2016.

3 Interview with the author, 19 May 2016.

4 This is more than ten times what a Turkish citizen typically pays for a football licence.

5 Interview with the author, 22 May 2016.

6 This is a problem in many European countries, but is perhaps most acute in Turkey with its relatively relaxed visa regulations and vast footballing apparatus. No one seems to be getting to grips with the problem of agents and trafficked African footballers: not UEFA, not the Turkish Football Federation, nor African football associations. Most people I spoke to agreed the problem was at least as bad as it's ever been, or perhaps getting worse over time as ever higher numbers of African players end up in Turkey.

7 Interview with the author, 22 May 2016.

8 Interview with the author, 22 May 2016.

9 Interview with the author, 24 May 2016.

10 Interview with the author, 24 May 2016.

11 Interview with the author, 22 June 2016.

12 Interview with the author, 14 October 2016.

10 'I fell in love with football'

1 The minimum age for marriage was raised to 17 in 2002; however, the civil code allows for marriage at the age of 16 in 'exceptional circumstances'. Turkey has one of the highest rates of child marriage in Europe. UNICEF's figures for 2016 show that 15 per cent of Turkish girls marry before the age of 18. The real number is likely to be much higher, and many marry at younger than 16, as most child marriages are unregistered, unofficial religious marriages. See 'Turkey', Girls Not Brides. http://www.girlsnotbrides. org/child-marriage/turkey/.

2 Interview with the author, 13 November 2016.

3 Interview with the author, 11 July 2016.

4 The Turkish Football Federation only offers financial support when the round trip is longer than 400 km. Journeys to cities like Elazig, 100 km away, are paid for by the club, i.e. from Celebi's pocket.

5 Kadir Celik, the head of Malatya municipality's press office, declined to answer my questions on their support for Malatya women's team and women's football more broadly. He instead suggested questions I should have asked, which had alternative wording but were also about the municipality's support for women's football. When I invited him to answer his own questions, he declined to respond.

6 Gender Gap Index 2015, World Economic Forum. http://reports.weforum.org/ global-gender-gap-report-2015/economies/#economy=TUR.

7 Lauren Bohn, 'Turkey's kingdom of men', Lenny, 27 July 2016. http://www. lennyletter.com/politics/a487/turkeys-kingdom-of-men/?mc_cid=6ddf957f27&mc_ eid=ed45595994.

8 Itir Erhart, 'Ladies of Besiktas: a dismantling of male hegemony at Inonu Stadium', International Review for the Sociology of Sport, 48:1 (February 2013), pp. 83–98.

9 Semanur Karaman, 'Turkey elections mark the start of a revolution for women', Guardian, 19 June 2015. https://www.theguardian.com/global-development/2015/ jun/19/turkey-elections-revolution-hdp-women-female-mps.

10 In July 2014, deputy prime minister Bulent Arinc said that women should refrain from laughing in public because it is immodest. See Meira Svirsky, 'Turkish deputy PM: women shouldn't laugh in public', Clarion Project, 29 July 2014. http://www. clarionproject.org/news/turkish-deputy-pm-women-shouldnt-laugh-public.

11 Itir Erhart, 'Women and children only soccer in Erdogan's Turkey: empowerment or discrimination?', in Alberto Testa and Mahfoud Amara (eds), Sport in Islam and in Muslim Communities (London: Routledge, 2015).

12 Interview with the author, 5 July 2017.

13 David Harris, 'Domestic violence in Turkey at 40% says new gov't report', Clarion Project, 12 February 2015. http://www.clarionproject.org/news/domestic-violence-turkey-40-says-new-gov-report.

14 Erhart, 'Women and children only soccer in Erdogan's Turkey'.

15 Harris, 'Domestic violence in Turkey at 40%'. The number rises to 75 per cent of divorced or separated women.

16 Dan Bilefsky, 'How to avoid honor killing in Turkey? Honor suicide', New York Times, 16 July 2006. http://www.nytimes.com/2006/07/16/world/europe/16turkey. html?pagewanted=all.

17 In 2009, after 17-year-old Munevver Karabulut was murdered by her boyfriend and her dismembered body was found stuffed into a bin, Erdogan chose to say something

altogether different, reaching for a Turkish proverb which insinuated that blame lay with the victim and her family: 'If a girl is left unattended by her family, she will run away either to a drummer or a trumpeter.' See Christina Asquith, 'Turkish men get away with murder', *New York Times*, 23 February 2015. https://www.nytimes.com/2015/02/24/opinion/ozgecan-aslan-and-violence-against-women-in-turkey.html?_r=0.

18 Ibid. In 2014 nearly 300 women were murdered in Turkey.

19 Ibid. In 2014 a 62-year-old man appeared on a TV dating show and bragged about how he had killed two women: his wife and, later on, a lover (both allegedly in self-defence, the second 'accidentally' with an axe). For the two murders he served a total of 14 years in prison.

20 See Chapter 7 for more details.

21 Erin Zaleski, 'Violence against women in Turkey runs deeper than Ozgecan Aslan's brutal murder', *Bustle*, 23 February 2015. https://www.bustle.com/articles/65418-violence-against-women-in-turkey-runs-deeper-than-ozgecan-aslans-brutal-murder.

22 Interview with the author, 5 May 2016.

23 *Dostluk* means 'friendship' in Turkish.

24 Lale Orta also played for Dostlukspor – she eventually became Turkey's first female referee, and is now a sports academic. According to her research, the earliest record of women playing football in Turkey was a mixed-gender match in Izmir in May 1954. The first recorded all women's match was between teams from Istanbul and Izmir, played in Istanbul's Mithatpasa Stadium (later renamed 'Inonu Stadium') in July 1954. Another women's match was held during a sports festival in Mithatpasa Stadium in July 1955, but Orta couldn't find any subsequent records of Turkish women playing football until August 1969, when the Italian women's team played a mixed European team, which featured a Turkish player who scored in a 1–1 draw.

25 Interview with the author, 5 May 2016.

26 Gabriel Kuhn, *Soccer vs. the State* (Oakland, CA: PM Press, 2011).

27 Lale Orta, 'Women and football in Turkey', *International Journal of Humanities and Social Science*, 4:7 (May 2014). http://www.ijhssnet.com/journals/Vol_4_No_7_1_May_2014/12.pdf.

28 Ibid.

29 Dostlukspor branched into amateur sports for men and women, including aquatics, basketball, tennis and volleyball. An unrelated Dostlukspor team was set up in recent years for male African players hoping to gain contracts with Turkish clubs.

30 Interview with the author, 25 March 2016.

31 Trabzon players interviewed by the author on 25 March 2016.

32 Interview with the author, 5 May 2016.

33 Interview with the author, 12 April 2016.

34 Interview with the author, 22 November 2015.

35 Interview with the author, 22 November 2015.

36 Interview with the author, 21 November 2015. He did not want to give his name as he is working for the state as a schoolteacher.

37 Interview with the author, 21 November 2015.

38 Email correspondence with the author, 24 December 2015.

39 Interview with the author, 11 October 2016.

40 Erhart, 'Ladies of Besiktas', pp. 83–98.

41 Ibid.

42 Many middle-class parents often prefer their daughters to do more 'refined' sporting activities such as ballet or gymnastics.

43 Erhart, 'Women and children only soccer in Erdogan's Turkey'.

44 Ibid.

45 Conversation with the author, 22 November 2015.

46 Conversation with the author, 22 November 2015.

47 Interview with the author, 22 November 2015.

48 A city in Syria close to the Turkish border that was the site of a devastating battle of huge significance in 2015, in which Kurdish militias – including some linked to the PKK – defeated the so-called Islamic State.

49 Although Tansu Ciller was Turkey's first and only female prime minister between 1993 and 1996.

50 Pinar Tremblay, 'Women were big losers in Turkey's elections', Al-Monitor, 23 November 2015. http://www.al-monitor.com/pulse/originals/2015/11/turkey-women-are-losers-turkish-elections-akp.html.

51 It was called the 'Ministry for Women' until 2011.

52 Interview with the author, 5 July 2017.

53 Interview with the author, 5 May 2016.

54 Despite their meagre resources and very young team, Dudulluspor have enjoyed success in their brief history, finishing third and narrowly missing out on a play-off place in their third-tier division in 2015/16. Their under-17 side reached the national semi-finals. In 2016/17 they secured promotion to the second tier of Turkish football.

55 'Huzun' is a particularly Turkish kind of collective melancholy, often based on a sense of loss and decline.

56 The Turkish Football Federation calls on the government to do the same. 'If some matches were broadcast, it would be a great opportunity to showcase women's football. But there is no interest in the media,' says Or. 'If there is a fight in a woman's game you are in the newspaper – but there is no score, no interview, no interest.'

57 Galatasaray has formed a youth women's team which is competing in the under-15 leagues and will soon graduate to the professional divisions. Fenerbahce does not have any girls' football teams at present.

58 Conversation with the author, 13 November 2016.

59 'Fury at Turkish bill to clear men of child sex assault if they marry victims', Guardian, 22 November 2016. https://www.theguardian.com/world/2016/nov/18/turkish-bill-to-clear-men-of-child-sex-assault-if-the-marry-their-victims.

60 'Turkey withdraws child rape bill after street protests', BBC, 22 November 2016. http://www.bbc.com/news/world-europe-38061785.

61 Suzy Hansen, 'Turkey's women strike back', New York Review of Books, 19 August 2013. http://www.nybooks.com/daily/2013/08/19/turkeys-women-strike-back/.

62 The influx of Syrian refugees has also led to a rise in the number of child marriages. See 'Turkey', Girls Not Brides. http://www.girlsnotbrides.org/child-marriage/turkey/.

Epilogue: 'Football is faster than words'

1 'Interview with Orhan Pamuk: "Football is faster than words"', Der Spiegel, 4 June 2008. http://www.spiegel.de/international/europe/spiegel-interview-with-orhan-pamuk-football-is-faster-than-words-a-557614.html.

304 NOTES TO PAGES 263–7

2 Eksi Sozluk, 20 May 2003. https://eksisozluk.com/entry/2835792.
3 Eduardo Galeano, *Soccer in Sun and Shadow* (New York: Nation Books, 2013), p. 242.
4 Emre Sarigul, 'Going global: how Besiktas are aiming to become the Turkish Chelsea', *Guardian*, 20 July 2017. https://www.theguardian.com/football/2017/jul/20/besiktas-going-global-turkish-chelsea.
5 Ahmet Sait Akcay, 'Football: Turkish clubs lag behind financially', Anadolu Agency, 20 March 2017. http://aa.com.tr/en/sports/football-turkish-clubs-lag-behind-financially/775876. The financial debts of Turkish clubs increased from €40 million ($43 million) to €200 million ($215 million) over the past five years.
6 Marissa Payne, 'Following kebab shop brawl, Turkey's national soccer team coach is out of a job', *Washington Post*, 27 July 2017. https://www.washingtonpost.com/news/early-lead/wp/2017/07/27/following-kebab-shop-brawl-turkeys-national-soccer-team-coach-is-out-of-a-job/.
7 '19 Mayis Stadyumu yikiliyor', *Hurriyet*, 8 June 2017. http://www.hurriyet.com.tr/sporarena/19-mayis-stadyumu-yikiliyor-40483427.
8 The mayor resigned on 28 October 2017 – forced to step down by President Erdogan as part of his efforts to refresh the AKP ahead of 2019's elections.
9 Conversation with the author online, 16 July 2017.
10 Interview with the author, 5 July 2017.
11 William Armstrong, 'Turkey's brain drain: purges and fear are driving Turkish scholars out of the country', War on the Rocks, 22 September 2016. https://warontherocks.com/2016/09/turkeys-brain-drain-purges-and-fear-are-driving-turkish-scholars-out-of-the-country/.
12 Interview with the author, 28 August 2017.
13 Kareem Shaheen, 'Erdogan to continue crackdown as Turkey marks failed coup', *Guardian*, 16 July 2017. https://www.theguardian.com/world/2017/jul/15/erdogan-repeats-support-death-penalty-on-anniversary-of-turkey-coup-attempt.
14 Ibid.
15 Halil Gurhanli, 'The Turkish referendum that was not', *Turkey Analyst*, 28 April 2017. https://www.turkeyanalyst.org/publications/turkey-analyst-articles/item/581-the-turkish-referendum-that-was-not.html?mc_cid=6fa4bff5f6&mc_eid=b68dbae1d3.

INDEX